LIFE AND THOUGHT IN THE
GREEK AND ROMAN WORLD

SERIES IUNCTURAQUE POLLET—*Horace*

It is *continuity* and *connexion* that count

Life and Thought
in the
Greek and Roman World

BY

M. CARY
Professor of Ancient History, University of London

AND

T. J. HAARHOFF
Professor of Classics, University of the Witwatersrand

12 plates and 4 maps in the text

METHUEN & CO. LTD., LONDON
36 Essex Street, Strand W.C.2

This book was first published September 26th 1940
It has been reprinted six times
Reprinted 1959 and 1963

5.4
CATALOGUE NO. 2/7170/6

PRINTED IN GREAT BRITAIN
BY JARROLD AND SONS LTD, NORWICH

PREFACE

IN THIS book an attempt has been made to present a comprehensive survey of Greek and Roman life in a short space. Many books have already been written on this subject by competent scholars, but these seldom, if ever, cover the whole field. It has been the general practice of authors to confine their attention to the Greeks or to the Romans, and as a rule they have dealt only with certain selected aspects of Greek or of Roman civilization.

Our endeavour to treat Greek and Roman life as a single subject may call forth some criticism and will probably be condemned in some quarters as unscientific. In this age of specialization to the bitter end the prevailing tendency is to segregate the Greek and the Roman cultures, and to contrast rather than to compare them. For the advanced scholar this insistence on the difference between the two peoples no doubt has its advantages, but it is not the best method of approach to the study of the ancient classical civilizations. On a broad view of these civilizations it is the resemblances rather than the disparities that strike the eye.

The Greeks and Romans had their homes in contiguous countries possessing a similar climate and physical structure, and the 'geographical control' imposed upon them a fundamentally like manner of living. They came into contact at an early stage of their histories; for several centuries the Greek world remained incorporated in the Roman Empire, and eventually all citizens of Greek towns became citizens of Rome. The initial conquest of the Greek lands by the Romans brought with it the forcible transplantation of many Greek prisoners of war to Italy, and the subsequent era of the Roman Peace was an age of free travel and of a constant exchange of ideas between the Greek and the Roman worlds.

Broadly speaking, we may say that the Romans were the only people in the Mediterranean world who proved capable of accepting more than the outer show of Greek civilization. Fortunately for Europe, a harmonization of the two languages and cultures was reached by the first century B.C., and each people made its distinctive contribution to a richer whole without losing its individuality. For the natural gifts of the Greeks and of the Romans supplemented each other. Greek weakness on the political side was strengthened by Roman sagacity and power of organization; Roman heaviness in the artistic and philosophical sphere was quickened by Greek brilliance. And the complete Roman came into being only through a co-operation of the two elements.

The receptivity of the Romans for Greek civilization has been vital for our cultural tradition. What would have happened if the Romans had proved impervious to Greek influence? The Greek heritage would never have been handed down to us, and the whole fabric of our civilization would have been infinitely poorer. The conception of 'humanitas,' which constitutes to a large extent our claim to civilization, and which will have to be recovered if we are to avert an age of barbarism, would never have conveyed its message. It is only when we regard Greek and Roman civilization as a whole that we can understand that message.

For the general student of the ancient classics, and for the intelligent layman who wishes to know where his own culture has its roots, it is the joint product of Greek and Roman culture, rather than the separate elements out of which it was compounded, that should be the centre of interest. In this book, accordingly, we have noted occasional differences between Greek and Roman ways of life that seemed to us of more than passing significance, but we have endeavoured, as far as possible, to treat Greek and Roman civilization as an integral unit.

In a work of such large scope and small compass as the present one it has been impossible to confirm the statements of the text with a mass of corroborative detail, or to guard them against all possible misunderstandings by hedging them in with qualifying epithets and deprecatory parentheses. Our readers will understand that our generalizations about Greek and Roman life do not cover every particular case, and that exceptions may be found to every rule that we have set up.

We desire to express our obligations to Mr. C. R. Bailey, to

CONTENTS

Professor H. M. Last, and to Dr. H. H. Scullard, for valuable criticisms and suggestions; and to Miss M. V. Williams, M.A., of the University of the Witwatersrand, for reading over the section on Philosophy and Science, and for help in correcting the proofs.

MAPS

PLATES

All together preceding Index

I

The Geographical Background

1. THE MEDITERRANEAN REGION

THE CIVILIZATION of the Greeks and Romans was a product of the special conditions of life which the Mediterranean region imposes upon its inhabitants. This region constitutes a world of its own in a geographical sense. It possesses a distinctive climate and a special type of vegetation; and it is to a large extent isolated by natural barriers from the adjacent continents.

The Mediterranean area is cut off from its hinterlands by an almost continuous fringe of mountain ranges and deserts. Its European seaboard is separated from the mainland by a series of transverse mountain ranges—the Pyrenees, the Alps, the Dalmatian highlands and the main Balkan range. Asia Minor is similarly confined by the Armenian highlands, the Taurus and the anti-Taurus chains, and the Arabian desert. North Africa is hemmed in by the Sahara and Mount Atlas. The gaps in this ring are few and far between, and not all of them were in constant or even in frequent use in ancient times. In Africa the Nile valley lay open from very early days as far as the First Cataract, but it never served as a regular highway into the negro lands. In Asia the 'Gap of Aleppo' has given passage to an unbroken stream of traffic between Syria and Mesopotamia from prehistoric times to the present day. On the other hand, the seemingly broad and easy gateway into Europe by way of the Black Sea and the rivers that flow into it was not explored until the Middle Ages. The 'Gap of Nish' at the head of the Vardar valley provides a relatively easy passage from Salonika to Belgrade, and the low cols over the Julian and Carnic Alps give ready access from Italy to the Danube basin. These passes conveyed many a band of prehistoric migrants from the heart of Europe to its Mediterranean border, but they were not transformed into regular lines of communication until the days of the Roman Empire. The most commodious of all the trans-Continental routes, which

I

makes a gentle ascent of the Rhône basin and drops imperceptibly to the Atlantic by way of the Seine or the Rhine, was apparently neglected until the last centuries of the pre-Christian era, and the Romans were the only Mediterranean people to take full advantage of it.

The Mediterranean region may therefore be described as an island within the land-masses of the Old World. Within this island the Mediterranean Sea forms as it were an inland lake, providing a relatively easy passage from shore to shore. Considered as a lake, it is of immense size (with a length of 2300 miles), and its navigation may be attended with dangers comparable to those of open seas. It is swept by frequent winter gales. Its coast is rock-bound in long stretches (notably in Dalmatia and southern Asia Minor, and along the Moroccan Riff). Its river estuaries are a positive danger to shipping, by reason of the silt which, in the absence of a strong tidal scour, accumulates into mud-banks. These obstacles to navigation were sufficient to make winter communications across the Mediterranean uncertain and intermittent in ancient times (pp. 135–6).

Yet the Mediterranean Sea is one of the world's natural highways. In summer it is under the influence of regular trade-winds which provide a steady motive power for sailing vessels. Near the coast the land- and sea-breezes that spring up at nightfall and noon may be used to follow a course contrary to the prevalent open-sea winds. Should the weather freshen into a gale, shelter may readily be found in the numerous gulfs and bays which indent the European and Asiatic coasts, and under the lee of the islands with which the open waters are studded. Except in the neighbourhood of river bars, and in the bay of Tripoli, the coast is free from dangerous shoals and breakers. The approach to the shore is also rendered easy by the absence of high tides, for the Straits of Gibraltar intercept the ebb and flow of the Atlantic, and inside the Mediterranean the difference of level between high and low water rarely exceeds twenty inches. But for ancient seafarers, who lacked the mariner's compass, the chief advantage of navigation on the Mediterranean lay in the abundance of its landmarks. In the summer sky its coastal ranges and island peaks stand out clearly at distances of fifty to a hundred miles. North Africa is visible from Sicily; the mountains of Epirus show up plainly from the heel of Italy. Travellers proceeding westward from Greece may descry Mount Etna many hours before they reach Sicily; those bound from France to Africa need never lose sight of land, if they keep close to Corsica and Sardinia in mid-journey. The Mediterranean therefore has always acted as a link between the lands that environ it. These lands turn their back on the Continent, and their face to the sea.

The Mediterranean lands also form a region apart by reason of their climate, which differs from that of the three adjacent continents, and indeed is not reproduced elsewhere in the world, save in a few restricted coastal areas of similar latitude (South California, Central Chile, Cape Province, and South Australia).[1] The Mediterranean winter is boisterous and wet; yet it also enjoys long intervals of sunshine and is not continuously cold. Frequent westerly gales break in from the Atlantic, and are reinforced by local wind-eddies, due to an influx of air from the chilled mainlands to the warmer sea-basin. The prevalent weather is of a cyclonic type, with sharp squalls and sudden spurts of heavy rain. When the wind veers to north, it brings a spell of biting cold and buries the uplands in snow. On the other hand, if 'Zeus packs the clouds' with his driving gusts, by the same agency he dispels them. Between the periods of wild weather the sun shines strongly out of a clear sky, and raises the temperature to that of an English spring.

The Mediterranean summer is a season of set-fair weather. At this time of the year the furnaces of the Sahara and of the Arabian desert induce a persistent draught of air from the European mainland, and this current becomes progressively warmer and drier as it crosses the Mediterranean area. Under its influence clouds evaporate entirely, or are reduced to thin streaks of white scud; for weeks or months no rain falls save in an occasional thunderstorm, and the sun beats down with almost vertical rays. The intensity of the solar heat is mitigated by the dryness of the

[1] The general climate of the Mediterranean has not altered since prehistoric times. Local variations have taken place, mainly as a result of deforestation.

THE MEDITER

RANEAN AREA

atmosphere, and cool nights partly atone for sweltering afternoons. But dazzle and dust render the Mediterranean summer somewhat trying to persons not of robust health, and the insufficiency or complete absence of rainfall causes a recurrent dearth of water.

The landscape of the Mediterranean region is as distinctive as its climate. Its special charm is due in part to its lucid atmosphere, in which outline and colour of physical features are perceived truly and sharply, and in part to the pervasive contrast between land and sea, and between mountain and valley. The intimate interplay between land and water gives endless variety to the coast-line, and shows up the land-masses against a bright and richly coloured background. The mountains, whose ridges of hard limestone or granite have as yet been little worn down by the weather, stand out in sharp relief and frame the lowlands within a bold and clear-cut sky-line.

The vegetation of the Mediterranean lands is also of a peculiar type, being specially adapted to their climate and physical structure. Plant life is benefited by the mild winters, which foster the growth of many evergreen species, and allow cultivation to proceed uninterruptedly. On the other hand, it is restricted by the drought that regularly accompanies the hot weather. The scarcity of water, moreover, is aggravated by the low storage capacity of the Mediterranean mountains. Since these seldom exceed a height of 10,000 feet, they are stripped of their snow mantle before midsummer, and their impervious rock-formations hinder the percolation of rain into the subsoil. The rivers of the Mediterranean lands in consequence carry a very uneven volume of water. In winter they swell into torrents after every downpour; in summer they shrink into mere dribbles, or even disappear altogether.

The dearth of summer water determines more than anything else the character and the distribution of the Mediterranean flora. Three contrasted zones of vegetation succeed each other. On the mountain flanks, where the snow lies longest and currents of cooler air precipitate occasional rain throughout the hot season, pines and deciduous trees (principally oaks, beeches, and Spanish chestnuts) grow in copses, and the open ground is matted with summer pasture. At this level Mediterranean plant life most nearly resembles that of continental Europe. The intermediate upland zone wears a more peculiar aspect, for here the summer drought achieves its fullest effect. Between patches of bare rock or scree small pockets of soil sustain a sparse and stunted growth of evergreen bush (myrtles, oleanders, dwarf oaks) or scrub (broom, thyme, acanthus).

The lowland zone also suffers from lack of water, but not to the same extent as the hill-sides. The severity of the drought is alleviated by copious perennial springs, which are fed by rainwater permeating through occasional cracks in the upper limestone formations and collecting in underground reservoirs. In the plains the hand of man has further corrected the shortcomings of Nature by storing up the winter flood-water in irrigation canals. On the seaboard there is even danger of waterlogging, for the winter torrents, when left to their own devices, choke their estuaries with solid detritus, and so thrust out a fringe of fenland into the coast-line. In regions where the water-supply is adequate, the fertility of the lowlands is generally high. The soil for the most part consists of a light clay or loam which is rich in plant food and easy to cultivate. The strong and continuous sunshine of the summer season brings crops to rapid maturity and imparts a fine flavour to fruits and orchard produce.

The vegetation of the Mediterranean lands has been enriched since ancient times by the introduction of many new species. On the other hand, there is abundant evidence in Greek and Latin authors that the forests of deciduous timber were formerly more plentiful, and extended further down towards the lowlands. The shrinking of the wooded zone has been mainly detrimental, for the forest performed the function of securing a somewhat more equable distribution of rainfall, of maintaining a more constant level of water in the streams, and of retarding the erosion of soil in the uplands. In the long run the thinning down of the protective covering of trees has reduced rather than extended the cultivable area.

The reputation for high fertility which the Mediterranean region enjoys in more northerly countries is somewhat delusive, for it is based on the exceptional richness of certain favoured territories, rather than on its general level of productiveness. A large part of its area, consisting of mountain ranges or arid uplands, is of slight economic value, and the fruitfulness of its most prolific lands is in no small measure due to man's improvements upon Nature.

The Mediterranean Sea itself is an additional source of food-supply. It lacks the shallow banks that provide the best breeding ground for fish, and it has nothing to equal the cod and herring fisheries of the North Sea. But every year great shoals of tunny enter it from the Atlantic, and other edible species (notably mackerels, sardines, and cuttle-fish) reside permanently in it. An easy catch could be made of the dolphin, who seeks out ships and frolics around them; but Mediterranean seamen of all centuries have set a ban upon the killing of such a good companion. An accessory source of wealth is the murex shell, which in ancient times yielded a highly prized dye-stuff (p. 97).

The Iberian peninsula is a storehouse of all the principal metals, and Asia Minor does not fall far behind it in the variety of its mineral products. But the mineral resources of the Mediterranean lands as a whole are less abundant than those of central and northern Europe. At the present day the shortage of coal is a serious handicap upon Mediterranean industry. In ancient times the most noticeable deficiency was in tin, which had to be imported from the Atlantic seaboard. Greek and Roman industry, however, scarcely made use of coal, and its general consumption of metals was so modest that the indigenous supplies were almost sufficient for its needs.

2. GREECE

The history of Greece has been determined to a great extent by the character of its mountains.[1] It is isolated from the main

[1] The mountains of Greece are of recent formation, and the convulsions that brought them into being have not yet wholly subsided. In 464 B.C. Sparta was overturned by an upheaval of the earth; in 373 B.C. the Achaean cities of Helice and Bura were engulfed by a tidal wave. Destructive earthquakes have recently visited Corinth, Candia, and Cos.

In prehistoric times a volcanic eruption blew to pieces an Aegean island, of which present-day Santorin (ancient Thera) is a surviving fragment. Later volcanic activity on this site has been more alarming than dangerous.

body of the Balkan peninsula by a series of ridges which constitute a more effective obstacle than the moderate height of their peaks would seem to indicate. Their tallest summit, Mount Olympus, falls short of 10,000 feet; yet the chain out of which it rises securely bolts off Greece from Macedonia, and the Pass of Tempe, by which the River Peneius skirts its eastern edge, is a narrow and impregnable gorge. Further west, the highlands of Albania form a multiple barrier, which has seldom been penetrated before the days of the motor engineer.

But mountain ranges do not merely seclude Greece from the European continent: they also impede its internal communications. An irregular complex of minor chains runs across its face in every direction, and dissects it into a labyrinth of small compartments. Unlike other mountainous regions (such as Spain and Switzerland), Greece is not seamed with continuous valleys, and its rivers are for the most part mere winter torrents. Cross-country travel therefore necessitates a laborious ascent and descent of passes which are often snow-bound in the cold season. The mountain masses, it is true, are cut open by the Corinthian Gulf and by other deep fjords. But the water routes which these inlets provide are highly circuitous, and in ancient times they were little used during the winter.

The climate of Greece is typically Mediterranean. In winter torrential rains or icy blasts from Russia are succeeded by sunshine suggestive of a premature spring. Summer brings a sequence of almost cloudless days, during which no rain may fall for two, three, or four months. The sun's rays are reflected from the white-grey limestone with an intense heat and glare, but a frequent breeze from the north or north-east tempers the heat at the same time as it banishes the clouds. The bracing and exhilarating character of the Mediterranean climate is nowhere more apparent than in the Greek lands.

The landscape of Greece and of the adjacent Aegean area exhibits the special features of Mediterranean scenery at their best. It sets off the austere outlines of boldly sculptured mountain ranges against a sunlit sea, whose surface plays through every shade of colour from mother-of-pearl to a rich indigo-blue.

Nature has lavished beauty upon Greece, but has endowed her

less richly with worldly goods. The mineral wealth of the land is extensive and varied, but not copious. Its most enduring mineral asset consists of its white and coloured marbles, which still bring in a considerable revenue. In ancient times the excellent potter's clay of the river beds was an economic mainstay of certain cities (pp. 115-16). The principal deposit of metals was in the Laurium district of Attica, whose lead and silver mines contributed materially to the greatness of Athens (p. 36). Within easy reach of the Greek mainland lay the gold-fields of Mount Pangaeus in Thrace, and the copper beds of Cyprus. Iron lies so scattered about Greece in small pockets. On the other hand, Greece is barren beyond most Mediterranean countries. The mountains that lend it scenic charm sterilize the greater part of its surface. Below them extends a broad zone of evergreen bush and scrub. The patches of cultivable land in the plains comprise only a small percentage of the total area. Under intensive tillage the Greek lowlands may produce an illusion of riches. But Greece is a country of gardens rather than of fields, and husbandry is perforce on a minute scale.

Greece derives some compensation for the scantiness of its natural resources from the facilities which it enjoys for overseas trade. Of all Mediterranean waters, none is more enticing than the Aegean Sea. In the summer season it lies on the main path of the north-easterly trade winds. It is thickly strewn with islands—the emerging peaks of a sunken highland—which set the seafarer's course in any direction. From the promontory of Sunium at the tip of Attica you may survey the cluster of the Cyclades as far as Melos, from which in turn Crete rises into view. From Mount Ocha in Euboea you may glance across to Chios, on the margin of Asia Minor. As you near the coast of Thrace, you need never lose the peaks of Athos and of Samothrace out of sight. No other sea lures on the mariner like the Aegean, and none has been more continuously alive with shipping.

The most serious handicap under which the ancient Greeks suffered was the difficulty of their internal communications, which was part cause of their worst political failure—their incapacity to form a United States of Greece (pp. 31-2). The poverty of their soil was not an unmixed evil, for it stimulated them to become the principal traders and colonists of the ancient world (pp. 18–19). But Nature's best gift to Greece is its scenery and climate. The ancient inhabitants claimed that they enjoyed the most beneficial blend of weathers, and recognized therein a reason for their intellectual supremacy. This explanation contains a solid core of truth: the stimulating environment in which the Greeks lived undoubtedly helped to make them the most productive thinkers of the ancient world.

3. ITALY

Italy is fenced off from the mainland by the most massive chain of mountains in Europe. The barrier of the Alps, it is true, is notched with many gaps. Though its highest peaks rise to 15,000 feet, its passes for the most part do not ascend above 6000–8000 feet, and the col which gives access to Venetia from the Danube basin falls short of 4000 feet. The weak points of Italy's defences have often been utilized by invading armies. Yet the epigram that 'the history of Italy is the history of her invaders' bears hardly a semblance of truth, when applied to ancient times. While the Roman state and Italian civilization were still in the making, the Alps gave adequate (if not wholly unbroken) shelter from hostile intrusions. The comparative ease with which the Alps have been crossed since the Christian era has been mainly due to the Roman road engineer (p. 138), whose highways served to carry the matured Italian culture into the European continent.

The internal communications of Italy are less baffling than those of Greece. The peninsula is neatly sliced by a simple longitudinal chain, which leaves room for several extensive plains and commodious river valleys. Yet the Apennines occupy a large proportion of Italy's surface; by their diagonal course athwart the peninsula they cut across every route from north to south; and their passes are sufficiently high to impede winter travel. The state of political partition from which Italy has suffered continuously from the end of the Roman Empire until its reunion in 1870 has been due in no small degree to adverse geographical conditions. The early and lasting union of ancient Italy under the Romans could not have been achieved, any more than the

Roman conquest of the European mainland, without the aid of the Roman highway engineer.

In regard to climate, Italy is less characteristically Mediterranean than Greece. The basin of the Po, being cut off by Alps and Apennines from the warm winds of west and south, experiences severer winters than England; in summer it receives a moderate amount of convectional rainfall. Its weather therefore approximates to that of continental Europe. In peninsular Italy the climate conforms more closely to the Mediterranean type. The winter winds bring heavy rain to the western coast, and cover the Apennines thickly with snow; but the clouds disperse quickly, and sunless days are rare. In summer a cloudless northerly wind prevails: in latitudes south of Naples the rainless season may extend over four months. But the intensity of the sun's heat is tempered by regular sea-breezes; the drought lasts barely two months at Rome, and only four weeks at Florence.

The south and west of Italy are occasionally swept by a spring or summer wind from the Sahara (the 'scirocco'), which is also known in the south of Greece and of Spain, but blows with particular force in the central Mediterranean. It is superheated by compression in falling from a higher altitude, and it is laden with sand from the desert that clothes the sky with a leaden pall, and chokes the land with dust-clouds. But this unwelcome visitor never makes a prolonged stay.

Italian scenery lacks the unending variety which the intertwining of land and sea produces in Greece. Its landscape is bold and clear-cut; but a richer mantle of vegetation softens its contours and imparts to it a warmer tone of colour.

The comparative brevity of the summer drought in Italy is reflected in the greater wealth of its plant life. Deciduous trees grow more thickly on the mountain-sides, and in the clearings the provision of summer pasture is more abundant. The intermediate zone of bush and scrub is correspondingly narrow. The proportion of cultivable land is low, as compared with that of France or England. Yet Italy possesses several wide expanses of level land, and some of its plains are of exceptional fertility. In northern Italy the extensive basin of the Po and the Adige draws a double revenue from the Alps. The summer suns that melt the snow on the peaks of the Alpine giants, and the summer rains that descend on their flanks, ensure a copious supply of irrigation water throughout the hot season. In Lombardy and Venetia there is more danger of flooding than of drought, and until the Romans took possession of this district a great part of it lay waterlogged.[1] Furthermore, the melting snows and the rains bring down such masses of fertilizing detritus that the sub-Alpine lowlands can bear the strain of continuous intensive cultivation.

The western edge of peninsular Italy is seamed with a range of volcanoes which extends from southern Tuscany to Naples and is carried on through the Lipari Islands into Sicily. This volcanic zone is exposed to the usual twin hazards of earthquake and eruption. In ancient times, it is true, it was never overtaken by such a catastrophe as befell the city of Messina in 1908; but several smaller towns suffered severe havoc, and frequent tremors of the earth gave warning of a lurking danger. The northern end of the zone has been immune from eruptions throughout historical times, for all the craters in Tuscany and Latium were permanently sealed about 1000 B.C. But the southern half of the volcanic chain has been continuously active since the beginnings of history, and Vesuvius at its centre sprang a surprise on the unsuspecting town of Pompeii in A.D. 79, after many centuries of delusive restfulness. But volcanoes make amends for the destruction they cause by enriching the soil with the potash of their lava-dust. The neighbourhood of Naples (ancient Campania), which was thickly coated with the upcast of Vesuvius's prehistoric eruptions, was one of the most productive regions in the whole Mediterranean area, and the entire danger-zone of Italy was one of its most populous districts.

The mineral wealth of Italy, on the other hand, is deficient both in quantity and in variety. The quarries of Carrara are now the principal source of sculptors' marble; in ancient times they were not worked extensively until the age of Augustus. The iron mines of Elba are Italy's chief store of metal; they were actively exploited under Etruscan and Roman rule, and are still

[1] The inundations of the Po are, however, somewhat reduced by the lakes of northern Italy, which serve as natural regulating basins.

under operation. On the opposite mainland (near Populonia) lay copper beds which were a mainstay of Etruscan wealth and power; but these had apparently ceased to be productive by the time of Augustus.

The long seaboard of Italy suggests that this country is naturally suited to be a centre of maritime commerce. Yet in ancient times the Romans and the other native peoples of Italy never took kindly to salt water. The seas round Italy (especially the Gulf of Lions and the Adriatic) are regular tracks for winter cyclones; and the best stations for ships are not conveniently placed for trade. The mountain-locked pools of Genoa and Spezia have no natural economic hinterland; the commodious ports of Brindisi and Tarentum on the heel of Italy lay far from the chief centres of production in Roman times. But the shores of Italy were sufficiently accessible to tempt the mariners of other nations (notably the Greeks), and from the beginnings of its history Italy came under the influence of foreign peoples.

Italy is specially favoured among Mediterranean countries by reason of its relatively high fertility, which allows it to maintain a larger population than any of its Mediterranean neighbours. Its abundance of man-power and its central situation within the Mediterranean basin were two of the chief contributory factors to the political ascendancy of ancient Rome. In ancient times Italy also benefited by its proximity to Greece, which enabled its people to come into frequent contact with the more mature Hellenic culture, before its own indigenous civilization had become hard-set. This seasonable influence on minds naturally receptive brought it about that Italy achieved something far more enduring than a world-empire—that it became the principal seat of the Graeco-Roman civilization which is still living amongst us.

II

The Political Background

I. PREHISTORIC GREECE

THE GREEKS were a composite people, consisting in the main of an indigenous Mediterranean stock and of several intrusive elements from Asia Minor and the European continent. Their indigenous ancestors were the authors of a peculiar and precocious culture, which had its chief seat in Crete. The prehistoric Cretans or 'Minoans' were the first people to open up the Mediterranean by long seafaring voyages. Early contact with Egypt gave them the pattern of a civilization which they worked over with a free and bold hand, so as to create a peculiar and but lately deciphered script (p. 191, Appendix), and a distinctive naturalistic art. About 2000 B.C. they were brought under the rule of a miniature Pharaoh, whose palace at Cnossus was the earliest centre of political power in Greek lands.

The Minoans extended their influence and introduced their civilization into the Aegean area and parts of the Greek mainland. But here they were met by incomers from the north. Through the greater part of the second millennium successive waves of invaders from the Balkan lands or beyond overran Greece, and by the cumulative effect of their irruptions gave a new turn to its history. The newcomers brought with them a valuable gift to Greece, a language of an Indo-European type, out of which the Hellenic tongue of historical times was formed (pp. 180-1). But they also introduced more unsettled habits of life. About 1400 B.C. an 'Achaean' dynasty, which had established itself in the stronghold of Mycenae, ended the Minoan sovereignty with a destructive raid upon Cnossus. Two centuries later Achaean chieftains from many parts of Greece combined in an attack upon the fortress of Troy at the entrance to the Dardanelles.[1] This enterprise, which marked the climax of the

[1] The excavations of Schliemann at Troy have proved beyond question that the *Iliad* of Homer had an historical background. It

'Viking Age ' of Greece, overstrained the Achaean dynasts, and the coming of a further wave of migrants, the 'Dorians', brought on a prolonged period of confusion.

The northern invasions gave rise to a secondary current of migration from Greece to the west coast of Asia Minor, where some of the displaced populations found new homes. The western fringe of Asia Minor closely resembles Greece in climate and physical structure; by the end of the second millennium B.C. it had become an integral part of the Greek world.

About 1000 B.C. the age of invasions drew to a close. The component elements of the Greek people were now assembled, and a new nation was in the making. But this nation had to create a fresh civilization for itself, for the old Minoan culture had been destroyed under the stress of the invasions. Its art was forgotten; its script had been unlearnt; its trade was ruined; its command of the seas had passed into the hands of the Phoenicians; and the centralized monarchies of Cnossus and Mycenae had been dissolved into a chaos of petty tribal states. Like the Roman Empire at the end of the Germanic migrations, the Greek lands had been plunged into a Dark Age.

2. THE EARLY TRIBAL STATES

In some districts of Greece (Thessaly, Argolis, Laconia, and Crete) the invaders from the north converted the earlier inhabitants into serfs and kept themselves apart as a governing caste. But more commonly they settled alongside of the older population on even terms, and presently became amalgamated with it.

Among the Greeks (as we may henceforth call the dwellers in Greeks lands) the original unit of settlement was the village. Like all denizens of Mediterranean lands, the Greeks were compelled by the summer drought to cluster together near the perennial springs, or wherever the supply of water was unfailing. On the other hand, they did not at first feel the need of associating

remains uncertain whether Agamemnon and Priam were historical personages, and why the Achaeans set siege to Troy.

in larger centres of population, so as to form cities. Their earliest political units were groups of villages comprising, on an average, as much territory as a small English county (sometimes less than 100 square miles). In some parts of the country these 'tribal' states were loosely gathered into confederacies, each of which occupied one of the natural subdivisions of the Greek lands (Boeotia, Arcadia, etc.). But these larger associations did not come into active existence save on some special emergency, such as a major war, and they possessed no regular government. The tribal state was therefore the starting-point of Greek political development.

The franchise of the tribal states was the common heritage of all the freemen, and the entire *demos* (commonalty), or at any rate every able-bodied man, was entitled to attend the *ecclesia*, or Popular Assembly. But the tribal assembly as a rule merely gave or withheld a perfunctory assent to decisions taken elsewhere. The effective government lay in the hands of the larger landowners (descendants of the migration-leaders, who had been awarded a special domain at the time of settlement, or of pioneers who had improved tracts of waste land). These landlords had combined in each tribal state to form a local aristocracy. By using their wealth to surround themselves with retainers, and their leisure to acquire proficiency in arms, and by proclaiming their descent from gods and heroes, the nobles secured an undisputed ascendancy over the commons. In virtue of their lineage they occupied the posts of command and filled the seats in the *gerusia* or *boule* (the tribal council). By the same right the largest landowner held the title of *basileus* (king) and exercised the functions of Army Lord and High Justice. But despite the sharp cleavage between aristocracy and commonalty, the government of the tribal states was weak and intermittent. The king might call the folk to arms, but he could not compel their attendance. His jurisdiction amounted to no more than a voluntary arbitration between litigants who sought his court, and to the occasional punishment of a traitor or other serious offender against the community. He had no authority to order the reference of disputes to his tribunal, and no means of enforcing his award. The daily discipline of the community was therefore vested in the heads of the individual families, who retained their patriarchal powers and could enslave or even put to death their kinsfolk. But the writ of the family-heads did not run beyond their own household.

The early tribal government of Greece was inadequate to the barest needs of civilized life. Defence against roving bands of brigands or pirates was ill-organized and likely to be inefficient. Nay more, every tribal state was in itself a field of battle. In the absence of any compelling authority on the king's part to compose quarrels between individuals or families, each party to a dispute was prone to take the law into its own hands. The men of the early tribal states therefore always carried their weapons with them, and their chief care was to preserve their lives rather than to improve them. Under such conditions Greece remained condemned to barbarism.

3. COLONIAL EXPANSION

The Dark Ages of Greece lasted from 1000 to 800 B.C. In the following three centuries a renaissance ran its full course, and carried the Greeks to the highest point of civilization as yet attained in the world. The fundamental cause of this movement was a shift of population which revolutionized both the economic and the political life of the Greeks.

About 800 B.C. the Greeks began to heed the call of the sea, which never remains unheard for long in their country. They followed the tracks of Minoans and Phoenicians, and gained acquaintance with the whole of the Mediterranean basin. Their explorations gave rise to a new emigration from Greece and the Aegean area, which lasted until the middle of the sixth century. By 500 B.C. Greek settlements fringed the coasts of Macedonia and Thrace, of the Black Sea and its approaches, of Cyrenaica, of Sicily, and of Southern Italy.

This colonial movement opened a new epoch in Greek history. At its close the Greeks possessed the largest sea-front of all Mediterranean peoples; they shared with the Phoenicians the general carrying trade of the Mediterranean area; they provided its markets with the products of their own rising industry;

they became conversant with coinage and a money economy (p. 124).[1]

But trade and travel achieved something more than to furnish the Greeks with the material basis of a higher civilization; it opened their eyes and awakened their minds. Contact with foreign lands and peoples brought them new knowledge, and the knowledge thus won whetted rather than satisfied their curiosity. In the age of colonial expansion the Greeks borrowed from the peoples of the Near East an improved technical equipment. From the Egyptians and Babylonians they acquired the rudiments of mathematics; from the Phoenicians they derived better processes of shipbuilding and navigation, and an alphabetic system of writing, which they did not suffer to remain a secret of merchants, rulers, and priests, but made into a part of the general Greek heritage (p. 169–70). Above all, they conceived a wider interest in the world that was opening up before them, and set themselves to appreciate and understand it in all its aspects. By this self-imposed discipline they achieved an intellectual ascendancy that raised them above all other ancient peoples.

4. THE FORMATION OF CITY-STATES

At the same time as the Greeks were engaged in colonial expansion, they carried out a re-settlement of their population at home. The primary purpose of this movement was to obtain collective security. To this end they began about 800 B.C. to congregate and take up their permanent abodes on the natural strongholds in which the Greek lands abound—isolated bluffs that stand out from the plains, or mountain spurs that project into them—so that close-built urban settlements were formed at the natural rallying-points of the tribal states. With the growth of industry and commerce, these *synoikismoi*, or townward movements, received a fresh impetus.[2] In the more backward

[1] Against these gains must be set the growth of the slave trade and the diffusion of slavery (on which see Chapter III. 8).

[2] The sites of the early Greek towns, which usually stood at some distance from the sea, show that they were not chosen in the first instance to facilitate trade, but to provide security. The subsequent growth of trade sometimes led to the formation of a harbour-suburb, such as the Piraeus in relation to Athens.

GREECE AND
THE AEGEAN AREA

parts of Greece, and notably on its north-western border, the inhabitants were slow to take to city life, and continued to put their trust in their tribal confederacies (Aetolians, Acarnanians, etc.). But after 800 B.C. it became the general habit of the Greeks to dwell together in towns: only those whose fields or grazing grounds lay too far away remained on the open countryside.

But the Greek cities soon came to subserve other objects besides those of security and subsistence: they became centres of political life and testing grounds for new experiments in statecraft. When a *synoikismos* was effected, the king took up his residence on the citadel, the nobles built themselves town houses, and the whole machinery of the tribal government was transferred to the new city. In Medieval Europe the towns were the rivals of the country, in ancient Greece they became its masters. Indeed the city came to be so closely identified with the state that the same word, *polis*, was pressed into service to denote both of these terms.

5. ARISTOCRACY

The first political effect of the *synoikismoi* was to strengthen the hands of the aristocracy at the expense of the Crown. Unlike the medieval barons, who lived apart and could therefore be played off against each other by an astute monarch, the Greek city-nobles presented a common front to their king, and could therefore overpower him by their corporate influence. By a gradual and bloodless process they degraded the *basileus* to a titular tenure of a shadow monarchy, or swept away his office altogether. The overthrow of the city-monarchies began about 700 B.C.; by 600 B.C. they had been generally replaced by republics.

The constitutions of the early Greek republics were rigidly aristocratic. The duties of the king were put into commission among a board of annual magistrates elected by the nobles out of their own number. The seats in the *boule* were filled by a similar method of appointment, or by the admission of former magistrates *ex officio*: in either case the council remained a preserve of the ruling class. The commons might be convened from time to time to an *ecclesia*, but their only function was to give formal confirmation to the resolutions of the *boule*.

The change from monarchy to aristocracy induced a more energetic spirit into the government of the city-states. Applying their collective power to the strengthening of the state's authority, the city-nobles abolished the quasi-independent sovereignty of the families. They restricted the punitive powers of the family-heads (pp. 142–3), and prohibited private warfare between kin-groups. They compelled reference of all outstanding disputes to the courts of law, and made the courts into a regular instrument for the punishment of public offences.[1] By 600 B.C. the law which they applied had grown sufficiently complex and articulate to require codification, and one city after another compiled and published its law-book. In substituting the reign of law for that of force, the aristocracies established public security so firmly that the carrying of arms fell into general disuse in Greece. At the same time they taught the commons those habits of social discipline whose observance is a necessary pre-requisite to the enjoyment of political liberty.

But if the nobilities removed old abuses, they also created fresh grievances. Secure in the plenitude of their power, the ruling families forgot their responsibilities and offended against the rules of their own making. They resorted to violence in the pursuit of their private quarrels, and they stultified recourse to their own law-courts by selling justice to the highest bidder. Their 'gift-devouring' greed caused deep resentment among the peasantry, who could ill afford to see their slender earnings filched to swell the revenues of the rich. Yet the autocracy of the nobles was seemingly unassailable. Hedged in by the awesomeness of their divine pedigrees, well versed in the use of arms, and attended by numerous retainers, they could apparently afford to defy the timid and unorganized commonalty.

But the authority of the nobles was being undermined by the

---

[1] The procedure of the aristocratic courts remained rudimentary. Questions of fact were decided by ordeal, or by the rival oaths of litigants and witnesses. Penalties were harsh; for offences not expiable by a fine, death or exile was usually prescribed. More rational methods of trial were generally introduced into Greek courts in the sixth and fifth centuries.

concurrent movement of colonial expansion, and the consequent increase of trade and foreign contacts. In the seventh century the Greeks borrowed from the Oriental peoples a new military technique which eventually shifted the basis of power in the city-states. In the early days of the *polis* warfare on land had been an aristocratic sport, in pursuit of which the nobles and their retainers engaged in duels with single adversaries;[1] the ill-armed and untrained *demos* contributed little to the result, and was seldom called out in force. This method of combat was now replaced by 'hoplite' tactics (derived apparently from the peoples of Asia Minor), in which serried masses of armoured men sought to overpower their opponents by the collective impulse of their charge rather than by individual prowess. For this style of fighting high training was less essential, but numbers were indispensable. Consequently all citizens who could afford a suit of armour became liable to military service, and the greater part of the peasant population acquired some proficiency in arms. But a *demos* equipped and organized for war was in a position to bargain, and if need be to fight, for its political rights.

In their early naval encounters the Greeks had employed small galleys with not more than fifty oarsmen. The speed of these vessels was too low for effective manœuvring, and sea-battles at this stage could be decided only by boarding tactics. But about 700 B.C. Phoenician shipwrights conceived the idea of seating pairs of rowers side by side—one man a little above and in front of his neighbour—so as to double the ships' oarage without materially increasing their weight. Greek designers improved upon this device by seating three rowers abreast and fitting outriggers, so as to provide the correct leverage for each size of oar. A fleet of Greek 'triremes', manned by well-trained crews, could be manipulated so as to break through the enemy's line and sink his ships by ramming. But a full-sized trireme

---

[1] The early Greek aristocrats rode to battle and were consequently known as 'hippeis', or knights, but they did not as a rule fight on horseback. Cavalry never played an important part in Greek warfare, except among the Thessalians (p. 25). The small size of the Greek horses, and the lack of stirrups for the riders, prevented the development of shock tactics, and the mountainous nature of the Greek lands was unfavourable to light cavalry.

required no less than 180 oarsmen. To man a fleet of this type, therefore, heavy drafts had to be made upon the poorer citizens who could not find a suit of armour, but could offer the strength of their arms; and the proletarians eventually followed the peasants in demanding a reward for their services.

The ascendancy of the nobles was further threatened by the emergence of a new industrial and trading class, which possessed both the spirit and the material means to challenge the aristocracies. The leaders of this class were men whose wealth equalled or surpassed that of the nobles, and their political ambitions kept pace with their rising fortunes. Nay more, individual members of the ruling families, who had been tempted to supplement their rent-rolls with the proceeds of industry and commerce, acquired a fresh outlook as well as new riches, and turned against their own order. The solidarity of the nobles, which had been their chief source of strength, was crumbling under the new economic tide.

6. TYRANNY

In the seventh and sixth centuries the Greek cities passed through a critical stage of their development. In some districts the old order continued unchanged. In Thessaly, which remained for centuries a self-contained agrarian country, the nobles lived securely in the possession of large estates and the support of strong bands of retainers. On the only extensive plain of the Greek homeland their cavalry was the arbiter of battle; they seldom had need to arm the peasantry for hoplite warfare, and no reason to fear organized opposition on its part. In other inland regions the lesser proprietors, having been pressed into military service, demanded political concessions in return, and effected a peaceful revolution. In these states the powers of the *ecclesia* were extended, or political offices were thrown open to a wider class. But in numerous Greek towns, and particularly in those where industry and trade had become well established, the rule of the nobles was destroyed by violent methods.

The revolutions which put an end to aristocracy were not effected by mass risings of the *demos*, but by sudden *coups d'état* on the part of individual leaders of opposition. Enriched captains of industry or commerce, or aristocratic class-traitors, who had cast themselves for a more ambitious rôle, and had obtained the requisite armed force by hiring mercenaries, or by seducing the civic levy, would make a sudden pounce on the citadel, and hunt down or drive into exile the members of the ruling class. Having thus made a clean sweep of the aristocratic government, they replaced it by a personal despotism. Outwardly they made little or no change in the existing constitution; but they packed the magistracy and the *boule* with their own adherents, and they retained control of the citadel by means of mercenary troops. Their rule, in effect, was as absolute as that of any Eastern potentate, and they came to be known by a name derived from the dynasts of Asia Minor, 'tyrannos'.

The rule of the 'tyrants' conferred other benefits upon the Greek cities than the mere relief from aristocratic oppression. In order to justify their usurpation of power in the eyes of their subjects, many despots enlarged their range of functions beyond the established routine of keeping law and order. It was under the tyrants that the conception of the state as a general welfare worker, and something more than a mere policeman, came into existence. They remedied the land-hunger of the peasants by parcelling out among them the confiscated estates of the nobles, or by founding colonies overseas. They promoted trade by making alliances with other cities, and gave an impetus to industry by carrying out large programmes of public works, such as roads, aqueducts, and temples. The building activities of the tyrants opened a new chapter in the history of the Greek cities: towns which had been constructed in the first place for mere security henceforth became show-pieces of art and architecture. In extending their patronage to poets and arranging recitations or dramatic contests at the public festivals of their city the tyrants prepared for the golden age of Greek literature (p. 244). A few of the despots achieved lasting popularity; many others were so far successful as to found a dynasty.

Yet none of the tyrant dynasties outlasted a century, and most of them did not survive the second generation. If their governments showed enterprise, they also incurred expense. Whereas the aristocracies had kept house on a modest revenue from rents and tolls, the gentler despots had recourse to direct taxation, and the more unscrupulous ones raised funds by organized piracy or predatory attacks upon their neighbours. But the commonest causes of complaint against tyranny were its irresponsible character, which tempted the weaker dynasts, and more particularly those who had inherited their autocratic power rather than gained it by personal effort, to wanton outrages or acts of fiendish cruelty, and the atmosphere of general suspicion which absolute monarchy almost invariably engenders. Under the best of the tyrants the right of free speech, which to the Greek townsman was becoming a necessity of life, had to be exercised with discretion; under the worst despots a swarm of spies rooted out conspiracies, real or imaginary, which were punished with exemplary severity.

The counter-revolutions by which the tyrannies were abolished were usually led by surviving members of the displaced nobilities, who either fomented a popular rising or had recourse to the assassin's poniard. The earliest despotism was set up about 650 B.C. (at Sicyon, near Corinth); by 500 B.C. this form of government was fast becoming obsolete; and in course of time it acquired a singularly odious reputation. The word 'tyrant', originally a mere synonym of 'king', took on its modern invidious sense; tyrannicides lived on as heroes in popular tradition; and the mere rumour of plots to resuscitate autocracy would suffice to raise the public temper to fever heat. The greatest harm which tyranny did to Greece was to bequeath a tradition of physical violence as a recognized instrument of domestic politics. The successful use of force, both in making and in unmaking despots, set a precedent which the Greeks never lost out of sight, and acted upon all too frequently.

After the fall of the tyrants the liberated cities usually reverted to some form of government by a privileged minority, to which alone was given the right of holding office or membership of the *boule*. In some towns aristocratic prejudice lingered on in laws that disfranchised or disqualified from office all persons who had soiled their hands with petty industry or retail trade, or in a social stigma attaching to them. But a return to government by an hereditary caste was now ruled out. The basis of privilege was shifted from birth to wealth, and office was thrown open to all who commanded a certain income, or could equip themselves with a war-horse or a complete suit of armour. In a Greek 'oligarchy' (as these minority governments were called), men of ability could rise to high office, and the ruling classes were from time to time invigorated with fresh blood. But the fundamental difference between the early aristocracies and the later oligarchies was that the oligarchies conceded a more substantial share in public affairs to the *demos*. Although the commons at this stage still lacked the confidence or the leisure to take the whole burden of administration upon their shoulders, they were by now intent on securing firmer guarantees against misrule than the mere goodwill of the ruling class, and therefore claimed the safeguard of definite constitutional rights. The instrument by which the *demos* came to exercise its rights was a reconstituted *ecclesia*. In some cities the *ecclesia* acquired the power of electing the annual magistrates; in others it was constituted as a court of appeal, to revise arbitrary sentences by magistrates, or as a court of discipline, to punish abuses on the part of office-holders; in most towns it obtained the right of final decision on all important questions of state policy, such as the declaration of war and con-clusion of peace, or the extension of the city-franchise.

7. THE CITY-STATES AFTER 500 B.C.

By 500 B.C. the Greek city-state had passed through the main stages of its evolution. It had produced a system of strong yet responsible government, which gave magistrates adequate powers to enforce their lawful orders, yet provided sufficient means of curbing them if they exceeded their authority. It safe-guarded life and property both against the random violence of individual citizens and against the systematic oppression of persons in office. Nay more, it brought the people into partner-ship with the ruling classes. Membership of the *ecclesia* offered to the ordinary citizen regular and frequent opportunities of voicing his opinion, or at least of registering his vote; and since the total number of burgesses in a Greek state seldom exceeded

10,000, the individual voter was free to feel that he could make a difference to the pace of the boat if he were to pull his full weight. The constitutions of the city-states therefore had the effect of drawing out the plain citizen, and of keeping him continually interested in public affairs. The *polis* was something more than a creditably efficient piece of administrative machinery: it was also a practical school of politics and of social co-operation.

But the virtues of the city-state were apt to play over into vices, by cultivation to excess. Interest in its politics was prone to become an absorbing passion; and the clash of opinions in debate inflamed contending parties with a bitter spirit of faction. The commonest and most persistent of such causes of discord was a renewed conflict between the *demos*, which began to claim yet larger political rights as soon as experience of public affairs gave it confidence in its own powers, and the ruling class, which was bent on maintaining its own privileges. Under these conditions one city after another became the battle-ground of a democratic and an oligarchic party. The party contests, moreover, were not infrequently decided by actual physical force. The weapons that had served in turn to supplant aristocracies and tyrannies were now directed against each other by oligarchs and democrats, and it was accepted as a common doctrine that it might be justifiable to spill citizen blood in order to snatch a party advantage. Thus the internal peace and security which the city-states had established in the first instance was again imperilled by the spirit of *stasis* (faction gone mad).

Furthermore, the pride which the Greek felt in his own city tended to breed in him a disdain of other towns. The narrower loyalty to the *polis* eclipsed the wider obligation to the nation.

The growth of a Greek nation out of the diverse elements that inhabited Greece after the northern invasions was virtually completed between 1000 and 600 B.C. It was fostered by the racial fusion of the newcomers with the previous inhabitants, by the universal adoption of the Indo-European tongue which the former had brought with them, and by the institution of common religious festivals (p. 317). It received a further impetus from the early and brilliant rise of a Greek literature, whose first great work, the Homeric poems, soon attained the rank of a classic and spread the same ethical standards and ideals wherever the Greek tongue was heard (pp. 241–2). It was consummated by colonization and commerce, which brought home to the Greeks the fundamental differences between themselves and foreign peoples, and made them aware of their own individuality. There remained for a long while a considerable variety of dialects, religious cults and customs in the Greek lands; indeed these diversities served a useful purpose, in that they induced a healthy spirit of competition between the local cultures. Yet by 600 B.C. the Greeks had so far recognized their common characteristics as to adopt a national name, 'Hellenes', over and above their ethnic and civic designations, and had invented a complementary term, 'barbarians', to cover all non-Hellenes.

The common culture which the Greeks had achieved provided a durable basis for a national Greek state; and the practical need for closer political co-operation could not remain hidden from them for long. The Greek people was divided into several hundreds of separate and sovereign states, each possessing a territory as large as Leicestershire or as small as Rutlandshire. The opportunities of frontier quarrels or of mercantile disputes in this political ant-heap were almost endless. So long as each city closed its courts to all aliens, travellers and traders in Greece remained liable to spoliation; and the only method by which merchants could recoup themselves for unpaid foreign debts was by indiscriminate reprisals upon the shipping of all the debtor's compatriots—a practice scarcely to be distinguished from piracy.

By 500 B.C., accordingly, cities with large trading interests were beginning to make commercial treaties, by which they bound themselves to admit claimants from other towns to their courts, a practice which in course of time led to the growth of a general Greek 'law merchant'. To foreigners residing permanently in their midst they offered the status of *metoikoi* (registered and privileged aliens), which placed them on almost the same footing as citizens in matters of private law. In order to give practical effect to these conventions, mercantile cities entered into supplementary agreements with individual citizens of other towns to act as *proxenoi*, or consuls, who would undertake to exercise a general patronage over all visiting traders from the contracting town. A further step forward was taken when cities began to submit their collective disputes to arbitration, instead of fighting them out. The very multiplicity of Greek towns facilitated such a method of settlement, for the contending cities could hardly fail to find a third town which had no selfish interest in the matter at issue. Here and there, as in Boeotia, confederacies of cities were formed to set up a common front against enemies from outside, and to suppress warfare between the federating towns.

But these tentative and isolated approaches to a United States of Greece did not lead up to a comprehensive national confederation. The wide extent over which the Greek people was diffused, and the geographic difficulties of intercourse within the Greek homeland, offered an intitial obstacle to any such union. Yet physical impediments could have been overcome (as they have been surmounted by the Swiss and the North American Confederacies, and by the Union of South Africa), given the necessary goodwill. But the goodwill was lacking. The narrow patriotisms that now hinder common action between nations imposed a taboo upon any general and lasting co-operation between Greek cities. Though the cities went so far as to give protection to resident aliens, they clung obstinately to the archaic rule that citizenship must go by kin, and only in rare cases did they enfranchise an immigrant.[1] The arbitration of inter-city disputes remained an honourable exception, and the small local confederacies did not even succeed in extinguishing the mutual animosities of their constituent states.

In consequence of these failures, Greek history is largely made up of the records of inter-city warfare. Hostilities between towns, it is true, were not as a rule conducted with great bitterness or persistency. Since the peasantry who were the backbone of the armies would not consent to a prolonged absence from their homesteads, campaigns on land were of necessity limited to the slack seasons of the agricultural year. Since triremes were too frail to ride out winter storms, naval operations had to be confined to the fair-weather months. Besides, the aristocratic

---

[1] Emancipated slaves were also debarred from citizenship. They were enrolled among the *metoikoi*.

conception of war as a gentlemanly form of sport lingered on in Greece after the fall of the nobilities. Belligerent cities observed a code of established conventions. Field crops might be destroyed and fruit-trees felled, but wells must not be poisoned. Captives of war might be sold into slavery, but not until they had been given an opportunity of ransoming themselves. A defeated city might be crippled by severe terms of peace, but to raze it to the ground was not 'cricket'.

But if Greek warfare was tempered by a saving sense of decency, it had the supreme demerit, in a war, of being ineffective and indecisive. Since the troops were not sufficiently trained to remain in hand after a victory, a pursuit could seldom be pressed home; and if, for once, an enemy had been beaten out of the field, his city walls could be trusted to defy an assault with ineffective siegecraft. The rule therefore held good, that for each campaign there was a 'return match', and the feuds between cities were prolonged to the point of becoming hereditary.

Thus the Greek cities paid a ruinous price for their sovereign independence. The resulting strife among them was a constant drain on their resources and energies, and it disorganized their resistance to external enemies.[1]

8. THE DEFENCE AGAINST FOREIGN INVADERS

The Greeks had the good fortune of being immune from attack by foreign peoples in the early stages of their history. After the coming of the Achaeans and Dorians the tide of northern invasions was spent. In the western Mediterranean no strongly organized power had as yet appeared. In the east the formidable empire of Assyria remained out of striking distance; Egypt was decadent; the dynasts of Asia Minor were not unfriendly. The Greeks were therefore able to carry out their movement of colonial expansion, and to bring their political system and culture to maturity without disturbance by hostile

[1] The close resemblance between the histories of the ancient Greek cities and those of medieval Italy has often been observed. The Italian cities were the pioneers of modern civilization; but their interminable discord brought upon their country several centuries of foreign domination.

neighbours. But after 650 B.C. their capacity to organize a common defence was put to the proof.

About this time an ambitious new line of kings in Lydia (western Asia Minor) made war upon the Greek cities that barred their way to the Aegean Sea. These towns, acting in co-operation, should have had no difficulty in beating off the attack; but they allowed themselves to be subdued one by one, so that by 550 B.C. the greater part of Asiatic Greece had been incorporated in the kingdom of Lydia. But the Lydian kings had hardly completed the conquest of their Greek neighbours, when their own realm was annexed in its turn by the nascent empire of Persia. The Persian monarchy, which had risen on the ruins of the Assyrian Empire, was the most extensive, the wealthiest, and the best organized of the great Oriental principalities; it united the whole of the Near East under its sway, and it disposed of all the naval resources of Phoenicia and the Levant. The first serious trial of strength between Persians and Greeks took place about 500 B.C., when the Greek cities of Asia Minor, which had passed with the rest of the Lydian monarchy under the rule of Persia, rebelled against their new masters. With the important trading city of Miletus at their head, they created a war-confederacy which at first held the Persians at arm's length. But jealousy between the insurgent cities presently reasserted itself, the Greek league fell to pieces, and the revolt was suppressed. After this fiasco the Greek homeland was marked out for the next Persian advance.

In the homeland the Greeks beat off the Persians once for all, and by a voluntary effort, But they owed their delivery almost wholly to the exertions of two leading cities, Sparta and Athens. Of the two Greek champions in the Persian Wars, Sparta had risen to eminence by a path that diverged sharply from the main road of Greek history. Its citizens held dominion over the fertile valleys of Laconia and Messenia, the former of which they had conquered at the time of the Dorian invasion, the latter in the eighth or seventh century. Contrary to the usual Greek practice, they had not become fused with the previous inhabitants, but had reduced them to a condition of 'helotage', or serfdom, and so condemned themselves to stand ever after on guard over them. For the sake of security against the helots the Spartans abandoned all economic pursuits and the cultivation of art and literature (for which they had at first shown a true Greek appreciation), and they converted their city into a huge barracks. From their seventh to their sixtieth year they submitted themselves to a continuous training for war, and every detail of their lives was regulated with a sole view to military efficiency. Their method of government was equally adapted to this supreme end. The Spartans retained their kings as hereditary commanders-in-chief, but the real masters of their state were a board of five 'ephors', elected annually by the Popular Assembly, who exercised an almost unlimited disciplinary power over helots and citizens alike.[1]

In taking upon themselves this totalitarian dictatorship, the Spartans became the slaves of a soul-destroying machine, and renounced most of the benefits of Greek civilization. But they carried their servitude proudly. and upheld the rule of the ephors with steadfast determination. The Spartan constitution therefore attained a stability which excited the envy of thoughtful Greek observers. But the ascendancy which the Spartans came to exercise over the Greeks was mainly due to their military proficiency. Though their tactics were those of the ordinary hoplite column, they performed these with the precision and steadiness of professional soldiers, and invariably outmatched the half-trained militias of the other cities. In a series of campaigns, which they mostly undertook at the request of neighbouring states, bent on winning their local wars with borrowed armies, they brought the greater part of Peloponnesus into dependence upon themselves. They consolidated their victories by instituting the Peloponnesian League, a loose but effective federation which pledged the vassal states to render military aid to the Spartans for the maintenance of peace within the League's territory. By 500 B.C. Sparta had acquired an authority in Peloponnesus, and a prestige in all the rest of Greece, in virtue of

---

[1] The peculiar institutions of Sparta were commonly ascribed to an early lawgiver named Lycurgus. But they were probably the outcome of a gradual but inevitable development during the seventh and sixth centuries.

The Spartans had two co-ordinate lines of kings. The reason for this anomaly is not known.

which she was plainly cast for the rôle of captain-general in a national crisis.

The early history of Athens followed more closely the normal line of development of a Greek *polis*. About 700 B.C. its kings were replaced by an aristocracy, which gave to the city its first collection of laws, the code of Draco.[1] A century later the Attic nobles sought to appease the discontents of the commons, who at this time consisted for the most part of a poverty-stricken peasantry, and to forestall a threatened revolution, by constitutional reforms. Their lawgiver, Solon, now laid the foundations of the future Athenian democracy by transferring the ultimate controlling power in the state to the Popular Assembly, which henceforth elected the annual magistrates, heard appeals from their judicial decisions, and ratified all important acts of state.

The spirit of moderation and compromise in which Solon made his reforms was not lost on the Athenians, who never carried *stasis* to such extremes as other Greeks. But he failed to allay domestic strife completely, and in 560 B.C. the city fell into the hands of a tyrant. Fortunately the Athenian despot, Peisistratus, proved himself a benevolent autocrat. Under his rule Athens became a centre of industry and took the first steps to intellectual and artistic supremacy in the Greek world. After the fall of the tyranny in 510 B.C. another legislator, Cleisthenes, made a bold experiment in democracy by instituting a new *boule*, which was appointed by the annual drawing of lots among the men above the age of thirty, and was therefore bound by the logic of chance to consist for the most part of plain citizens. The constitution of Cleisthenes left the higher magistracies in the hands of the wealthy families, but it gave the *demos* a liberal share in the day-to-day business of government.

At this stage the Athenians still stood far below the Spartans in general reputation. But in 490 B.C. they suddenly leapt into prominence by defeating single-handed a Persian corps which had been sent to chastise them for assistance given to the rebel Greek cities in Asia Minor (p. 33). On the field of Marathon the Athenian general Miltiades taught the Greeks to 'look the

---

[1] This code eventually obtained a bad reputation for its severity. Probably it was no more harsh than any of the early Greek codes.

Persians in the face', and proved that Greek hoplites, firmly led, could overpower the archery of the East.

But this campaign was merely a preliminary skirmish. The real test for the Greeks came in 480–479 B.C., when a Persian army and fleet of unprecedented magnitude set out to subdue them systematically. In this crisis the Spartans took the lead in summoning delegates from the homeland cities to form a war congress at Corinth, and at this convention they were entrusted with the command of all the Greek forces. In the land-warfare they won a moral triumph for Greece by their last defiant stand in the disastrous battle of Thermopylae (480), a deed which in the eyes of the Greeks ranked as Sparta's supreme achievement. At Plataea (479) they turned an imminent Greek disaster into a complete and final Persian rout.

The main issue of the Persian Wars, however, lay on the sea. With rare foresight an Athenian statesman, Themistocles, had carried a proposal in 483 B.C., that a windfall revenue from some recently developed silver mines at Laurium (p. 10) should be appropriated to the strengthening of the Athenian navy. In 480 he brought on a naval engagement in the bay of Salamis, in which the augmented Athenian fleet, reinforced by contingents from the other maritime states, put the Persian armada out of action. By this victory the Greeks stopped dead the entire Persian advance and prepared the way for a counter-offensive. After the battle of Plataea, and the consequent liberation of the Greek homeland, the Athenian navy carried on a thirty years' war, in the course of which it detached the Greek towns of Asia Minor from Persian rule and swept the Aegean clear of Persian craft. By 450 B.C. the Persians had been fought to a standstill, and Greece had been definitely freed from the risk of further invasion from that quarter.

In the sixth century the tide of Greek expansion in the west was turned by Carthage, a colony of Tyre, which rallied all the Phoenician settlers in North Africa and Spain against the Greek immigrants. Like their compatriots in Asia Minor, the Greek colonists in the west had amply sufficient man-power to cope with their foreign rivals, but frittered it away in spasmodic and disunited action. By 500 B.C. they had been thrust back to the confines of the western Mediterranean, and the Carthaginians were preparing to take possession of Sicily, so as to close the gate of the western seas to all comers.

In Sicily the Carthaginians delivered their attacks at regular intervals during the fifth and fourth centuries. They were beaten off by a succession of tyrants (Gelo, 485–478 B.C., Dionysius, 405–367 B.C.; Agathocles, 317–289 B.C.), each of whom in turn made himself autocrat of the principal city, Syracuse, and then proceeded to subjugate the remaining Greek towns by a policy of systematic aggression. By virtue of this forcible union the Syracusan despots were able to meet the Carthaginians on level terms, and to save their subjects in spite of themselves. In the third century the Greeks were finally rid of the Carthaginian peril by the intervention of the Roman Republic (pp. 63–4). But in accepting Roman protection against Carthage they merely made a wise choice of masters.

9. THE PREDOMINANCE OF ATHENS

The victory of the Greeks over the invincible Persians placed them on top of the whole world. With calm confidence in their own powers, they now looked life steadily in the face, and set themselves to solve its deepest problems. The world-wide importance of the Persian Wars resides in the fact that they brought on the Golden Age of Greek culture. Their immediate political significance lay in the light which they cast upon the strength and the weakness of the Greek city-state. In giving to its burgesses a sense of active partnership and a direct interest in its welfare, the Greek *polis* nurtured in them a more deep-seated patriotism than the subjects of an Oriental monarchy could ever conceive, and built up in them a larger fund of moral reserve. Once the fortune of war began to turn against them, the subjects of Persia lost heart; the Greeks, when pressed back, recoiled upon the invaders with redoubled strength. On the other hand the *polis*, in aiming at complete and sovereign independence, was a danger to itself and to the whole of Greece. The Persian Wars had revealed the imperative need of concerted action by the cities, and the chief political problem of the future was to associate them permanently in a comprehensive confederacy.

A nucleus for such a confederacy was at hand in the war-coalition which the Spartans had improvised at Corinth. But as soon as the Persian peril was past, the Spartans allowed the League of Corinth to fall into abeyance. Deterred by the ever-present danger of a helot revolt from taking on new commitments, they again restricted their interests to Peloponnesus, and left the rest of Greece to fend for itself. This self-eclipse of Sparta, however, gave a free hand to a city of more generous ambitions. By common consent the chief credit for the victory over Persia went to Athens, and the Athenians were being spurred by their past performance to yet greater efforts. In the years that followed the Persian Wars they achieved an ascendancy in art and literature which raised their name once for all above that of all other Greek cities (pp. 245-7). They supplemented their industrial pursuits with a commercial activity which extended over the greater part of the Mediterranean and Black Seas, and made their harbour, the Piraeus, into the emporium of all Greece. Furthermore, they gave themselves the most democratic form of government that had as yet been attempted in a Greek state.

During the Persian Wars the Athenian people had been well served by the men of high rank who led them to victory. But the chief instrument of this victory had been the new Athenian navy, and the crews of the Athenian galleys had been recruited from the poorer citizens. These proletarians now gained a confidence in themselves such as seldom comes to men of ordinary station. They demanded that political rights and duties should be shared out equally among all, and their claims were presented with compelling force by a nobleman named Pericles, who carried on the democratic tradition of his great-uncle Cleisthenes. The two chief reforms which were now introduced into the Athenian constitution concerned the judiciary and the executive. Jurisdiction had hitherto been in the hands of single magistrates, subject to an appeal to the Popular Assembly. Henceforth all important cases, both civil and criminal, went directly before juries selected by lot from all citizens above the age of thirty. The procedure in these *dicasteries* was kept studiously simple. The parties conducted their case in person and the juries proceeded straightway to their verdict, without instruction from the presiding magistrate. To discharge the current business of a rapidly expanding state, the executive was enlarged by the addition of many new boards of officials with specialized functions, and the boards were annually appointed by lot in the same manner as the *boule* and the *dicasteries*. With the exception of a few posts, such as the high military offices, in which technical knowledge was obviously essential, the entire administration was confided to the hands of ordinary citizens. In order to facilitate the attendance of every citizen at his public post, a small fee was paid to councillors, jurors, and executive officials.

This audacious new constitution at once drew the fires of criticism, and political experts, ancient and modern, have never wearied of dilating on its errors and absurdities. Indeed its weak points lay on the surface, and they manifested themselves at once. Miscarriages of justice resulted from a system by which litigants were permitted to play unchecked on the anger or pity of the jurors, and the mere multitude of the dicasts (who never numbered less than two hundred and one) was in itself an incitement to surrender to herd impulse. Particular harm was done by the *sycophants*, or professional blackmailers, who abused the right of every citizen to act as common informer in criminal proceedings. But the worst blunders were perpetrated in the field of foreign policy, in which were goodwill and mother-wit, uninformed by special knowledge, proved an insufficient guide. On such questions the *boule*, a body of plain citizens which changed its membership from year to year, could give no authoritative lead; and the *ecclesia* was precluded by its unwieldy numbers from a close scrutiny of any complex issue.[1]

Nevertheless the Periclean democracy was, at least, an experiment well worth making. If it took up much of the citizens' time, under Athenian conditions of life the time was there to

---

[1] The total number of Athenian citizens in the days of Pericles had risen to 40,000–50,000. The attendance at any important meeting of the *ecclesia* must have been numbered by thousands.

spare. If justice was sometimes erratic, it was also incorruptible and prompt, and within easy reach of the poorest citizen. The general standard of efficiency would certainly bear comparison with that of other Greek states. Athenian finances, which dealt with large sums of money, were characterized by the strictness of their accounting, and they made better provision than those of other cities for the accumulation of reserves. The Athenian navy surpassed all the rest, not only in size, but in training and organization. Moreover, the Athenian democracy set a new example of humane legislation. It protected slaves against wanton ill-treatment; it devised a painless method of carrying out capital sentences; it provided pensions for disabled men. Lastly, the characteristic merit of the city-state, that it gave a never-ending education to its citizens, attached in a pre-eminent measure to Periclean Athens. Indeed, it was Pericles' chief boast that he had made Athens into the 'school' of Greece. In the Funeral Speech in which he bequeathed his political faith to posterity[1] he claimed that the Athenian democracy not only gave free scope to the energies of all citizens, but positively drew them out by a kind of political conscription, and trained them in an invisible class-room to excel in every walk of life. In any case, whatever the actual merits and demerits of the Periclean constitution, the Athenian people were so well satisfied with it, that they made scarcely any further alteration in it. Moreover, as the general current of opinion in Greece during the fifth century was setting towards democracy, the new Athenian constitution found imitators and sympathizers in other cities.

10. THE BREAKDOWN OF CITY-STATE IMPERIALISM

After the Persian Wars Athens gave promise of becoming not only the school of Greece, but also its chief political centre. In the course of these wars the Athenians had enrolled the towns detached by them from Persian rule into a confederacy which eventually comprised nearly all the states of the Aegean seaboard. This league (usually known as the Confederacy of Delos,

[1] The substance of this speech (but not its actual text) has been reproduced in Thucydides ii. 35–46.

from the island which served as the meeting-place of the federal parliament) proved an effective guardian of peace in Aegean waters; it eventually included some 175 states; and, with wiser statesmanship, it might have been the starting-point of a more comprehensive union of Greek cities.

But the Athenians, rendered over-confident by the seemingly irresistible power of their navy, embarked on courses which destroyed their chance of a wider political leadership. A prime condition of any durable alliance of Greek states was that all its partners should have a voice in the discussion of federal affairs, and, above all, that they should retain their 'autonomy' (freedom in regard to their domestic government). In discontinuing the congress at Delos, and in usurping an overriding control over the internal administration of their allies, the Athenians earned the name of 'tyrant city' and lost the goodwill on which their league had been founded. At the same time they allowed a trade rivalry with the city of Corinth to lead on to open hostilities, and thus antagonized Sparta, on which Corinth, as a member of the Peloponnesian League, had a claim for protection.

The 'Peloponnesian War', in which Athens and Sparta fought out their quarrel, lasted from 431 to 404 B.C., and drew the greater part of Greece into its orbit. It was waged with a growing disregard of the traditional sportsmanship of Greek warfare, and with a low standard of generalship; but it was decisive in its issue, and the side that possessed the winning assets sustained defeat. With their command of the seas and ampler financial resources, and a system of fortifications which rendered their city impregnable to attack by the stronger Spartan land forces, the Athenians appeared to hold ultimate victory in their hands: by the sure if slow expedient of sitting still they could count securely on wearing the enemy down into submission. But they frittered away their advantage in spasmodic attempts to force the pace, and they finally tilted the balance of power against themselves by engaging in an unnecessary side-war in Sicily. The result of this ill-conceived and ill-managed adventure was that the greater part of the Athenian navy lay sunk in the harbour of Syracuse, and that the Spartans, assisted by shipbuilding subsidies from Persia, were able to wrest control of the sea from their adversary. With their allies in revolt, and their city under blockade on every side, the Athenians capitulated to Sparta, and were reduced to the rank of a vassal state.

The immediate result of the Poleponnesian War was to knit Greece together more closely than ever before. The Spartans, finding themselves in possession of the entire Athenian Empire, retained it in their hands, and during the war they had acquired new allies in the Greek homeland. For the time being, therefore, only the outlying parts of the Greek world stood outside their control. But they promptly estranged their dependants, old and new, by high-handed methods of government which made the former Athenian 'tyranny' seem mild in comparison. A general uprising against Spartan rule was fomented by the Persians, who were offended by Sparta's refusal to pay the agreed price for their recent subventions—the retrocession of the Greek cities of Asia Minor. After another round of widespread warfare (395–386 B.C.) the Spartans bought off the Persians by ceding to them the Greek towns according to the bond. In honouring this dishonourable bargain the Spartans salvaged their ascendancy in the homeland, but their new lease of power in Greece ran out before long. In 371 B.C. they suffered a fatal defeat at the hands of a former ally, the city of Thebes in Boeotia, whose general, Epameinondas, had improved upon the stereotyped hoplite tactics of the last three centuries, and now completely outfought the magnificent but orthodox Spartan grenadiers. The spell of Spartan invincibility was broken for good, and the former masters of Greece lost everything except their native Laconia.

After the downfall of Sparta the prospect of any permanent Greek union under one of the more powerful cities receded out of sight. Though the Thebans played with the idea of setting up a protectorate over the Greek homeland, they soon abandoned this project; and a second naval confederacy which the Athenians extemporized in the Aegean area presently fell to pieces. By 350 B.C. Greece was rid of its 'tyrant cities', and every town enjoyed its autonomy. But the mere possession of autonomy afforded no remedy for the two most deep-seated diseases of the

Greek *polis*. The strife between oligarchic and democratic factions continued to flare up now here now there, and it grew none the less violent as it became more and more divorced from any political principle, and degenerated into a mere scramble between Haves and Have-nots. The ancient feuds between city and city were rekindled now and again, and Greece once more lay exposed to attack by a foreign invader.

II. THE MACEDONIAN CONQUESTS

The danger to the Greeks was now no longer from the Persians —though these had recently obtained the Greek cities of Asia Minor as a gift from Sparta, they lacked the strength to help themselves to more—but from their northern neighbours in Macedonia. The Macedonians were related to the Greeks by race,[1] but had not been in close contact with them and were regarded by them as barbarians. A self-contained folk of plough-men and woodcutters, they had not shared the city life of the Greeks, nor their political development. In the fourth century they were still governed in patriarchal fashion by a king and a semi-independent nobility, and their army was a loose aggregate of royal and baronial levies. But a new era began in Macedon in 359 B.C., when a king named Philip proceeded to create a centralized monarchy, and a national army with an organization more perfect than that of any Greek state. The remodelled army contained a *phalanx* or 'steam-roller' of heavy infantry, but it was also provided with light troops, with excellent cavalry and with much-improved siege-weapons: from a mere militia it had been converted into an instrument of foreign conquest. In the next twenty years Philip took advantage of renewed dissensions between the Greek cities to intervene in their affairs and reduce them to vassalage. The only serious resistance to his progress was offered by a coalition of Athens and Thebes, which the Athenian orator Demosthenes brought about at the last moment. But this extemporized alliance was shattered by Philip at the

[1] The Macedonian kings gave themselves out as Greeks on the score of their pretended descent from the legendary Greek hero Heracles, and this claim was generally admitted in Greece.

battle of Chaeroneia (338 B.C.), which laid the whole of the Greek homeland at his feet.

The Greeks had provided themselves with a master. But Philip made his control as invisible as possible. He exercised his authority by means of a parliament of delegates from all the cities of the Greek homeland, which he inaugurated at Corinth. The duties of this parliament were to furnish the king with troops when required, and to keep the 'common peace' among the Greek states. The latter object was to be attained by placing a ban on inter-city warfare and providing arbitrators for inter-city disputes.

In 338 B.C. Philip called into being those United States of Greece which the Greeks had been unable to create for themselves. The new federal constitution, it is true, was never given a fair trial (p. 46). Nevertheless the association between Greece and Macedon which Philip brought about became an enduring one, and in this society the Greeks soon became the senior partners. By virtue of their superior culture they absorbed and hellenized the Macedonians, and they reaped the chief benefit of the conquests which the Macedonians proceeded to make at the expense of the Persian Empire.

It had been the intention of Philip to invade Persia, in order to liberate the Greek cities in Asia, and to annex Asia Minor, in whole or in part. This invasion was carried out after his death by his son Alexander, but on a vastly greater scale than Philip had envisaged. With a combined force of Greeks and Macedonians Alexander inflicted such a succession of defeats upon the antiquated Persian army that the Persian Empire fell to pieces under the shock. Lured on from victory to victory, he made a nine years' progress (334–325 B.C.) through the Asiatic continent, during which he incorporated all the territories this side of the Iaxartes (in Turkestan) and Hyphasis (in the Punjab). On his return from the East he traced out a plan for the government of the new empire. His leading idea was the 'marriage of Europe and Asia', by which he meant, in the first instance, the co-operation of Graeco-Macedonians and Persians on equal terms in the imperial administration, and the eventual fusion of European and Asiatic peoples.

12. HELLENISTIC GREECE

With the death of Alexander in 323 B.C. a new period of Greek History, usually known as the Hellenistic Age, begins. The suddenness with which the king fell ill and died had the effect of wrecking his plans and of throwing his dominions back into the melting-pot. Since he had left no heir of sufficient age or mental capacity to carry on his work, the destinies of his empire fell into the hands of the Macedonian nobles who had held the high commands in his army. These marshals of Alexander swept aside his family and scrambled among themselves for the whole or part of his dominions. A confused struggle ensued, and it was not until 275 B.C. that the succession-states which were carved out of Alexander's realm took definite shape. While this conflict was going on, the cities of the Greek homeland made repeated attempts to shake off the authority of Alexander's officers, only to be defeated by their own faulty co-operation. Nevertheless the greater number of them had slipped back into independence by 275 B.C.

At this stage one first-class power had emerged on each of the continents. Egypt (with a few outlying possessions) had fallen to the share of a Macedonian house, all of whose members carried the name of Ptolemy. The greater part of Alexander's Asiatic dominions was gathered into the hands of a dynasty founded by an officer named Seleucus. Macedonia was reconstituted as a separate kingdom by Antigonus Gonatas, who held in addition a scattered group of vassal cities in the Greek homeland. The new Great Powers, however, became engaged in further rounds of wars arising out of dynastic feuds or frontier disputes. The Ptolemies and Seleucids repeatedly came to blows over the possession of Syria and Palestine, while Ptolemies and Antigonids kept up a running conflict for the mastery of the Aegean Sea.

While the successors of Alexander were absorbed in their mutual rivalries, the Asiatic continent slipped out of their control. India broke away about 300 B.C.; Bactria and Persia gradually detached themselves bewteen 300 and 150 B.C.; between 150 and 100 B.C. Mesopotamia followed suit. In the north of Asia Minor a number of small native principalities established themselves. The permanent Greek acquisitions thus came to be restricted to the fringe of the Mediterranean Sea, and the Seleucid Empire eventually shrank into Syria and a few adjacent territories. The loss of Alexander's continental possessions, however, was in any case no more than a matter of time: they were too remote for successful administration by a Greek ruling class, and too alien in culture to be assimilated into Hellenic civilization. For a maritime people such as the Greeks, the limits of effective and enduring penetration lay not far distant from the Mediterranean seaboard; and it remained no less true after Alexander's conquests than previously, that the political centre of the Greek world was in the homeland and the Aegean area.

On the eastern border of the Aegean a new principality was formed about 260 B.C. by a line of Greek rulers, the Attalids, who detached the north-western portion of Asia Minor from the Seleucid dominion and set up their capital at the city of Pergamum. About this time the city of Rhodes, which had become an important centre of trade since the time of Alexander (p. 122), rose in political importance on the strength of its small but efficient navy.

In the Greek homeland the cities missed an opportunity, which came to them after the death of Alexander, of taking over and converting to their own uses the federal parliament that Philip had provided for them. They simply allowed the confederacy to lapse, and reverted to their former separatism. Oligarchs and democrats resumed their faction-fights and took their turn of power. Their established routine of revolution was broken now and then by the resurgence of tyrants; but these latter-day despotisms endured no longer than those of previous centuries. At the same time the common peace was violated by renewed outbreaks of inter-city wars. Nevertheless the Greek cities made some attempt to put their houses into better order. They exchanged franchise more readily; they resorted more frequently to arbitration; they reintroduced a more humane code of war.

A partial substitute for Philip's general confederacy was found in two sectional leagues, of which one came to include most of central Greece, and the other the greater part of Peloponnesus. In central Greece the Aetolians, a backward people who had long retained their early tribal organization, but took to town life after the time of Alexander, associated their towns into a confederacy and threw open their league to the neighbouring cities. About 250 B.C. the old-established local league of the cities of Achaea was remodelled so as to admit all Peloponnesians. Under the constitution of these two confederacies an *ecclesia*, which stood open to all citizens of the affederated towns, was convened to elect federal officials and to decide important questions of general policy. But the chief organ of federal government was a *boule*, consisting of deputies from the constituent states.

But these steps towards unity were taken too late, and did not carry far enough. The Aetolian and Achaean leagues made an ingenious attempt to bring together large numbers of cities without recourse to the overriding control of any one town, and the consequent risk of this town turning 'tyrant'. But so far were they from being able to guarantee the common peace, that they occasionally went to war with one another, or with isolated cities outside their group.

Of these separate cities, Athens now enjoyed an undisputed intellectual primacy in the Greek world, but its hopes of renewed political leadership were dissipated once for all. Immediately after the death of Alexander the Athenians headed a revolt against Macedonian overlordship, but they sustained defeat and suffered the complete and final destruction of their navy. In the third century their economic prosperity was undermined by the gradual exhaustion of the mines at Laurium and the eastward shift of Greek commerce (p. 122). With the loss of the fleet and of sea-going trade went the predominance of the Athenian *demos*, which allowed the control of the state to revert by a silent revolution into the hands of the wealthier classes. By 250 B.C. Athens had resigned itself to a dignified neutrality.

On the other hand, Sparta clung tenaciously to the chance of recovering its former ascendancy. Since the disasters of the fourth century its military power had been further reduced by a decline of population, due to a gradual concentration of landed property in fewer hands. But about 230 B.C. a king named Cleomenes effected a revolution, by which he redistributed the land in Laconia, abolished the ephorate, and invested himself with autocratic power. With a remodelled and augmented army Cleomenes challenged the Achaean League for supremacy in the Peloponnesus, and he pummelled it to such effect as to bring it to the verge of collapse.

The Greeks had failed once more to keep themselves free from internecine war, and so played themselves again into the hands of Macedon. The new Antigonid dynasty in Macedonia had not revived the claims of Philip and Alexander over the Greek homeland, but it retained a few dependencies in Greece, and the need to defend these outlying posts obliged it to intervene occasionally in the affairs of the other cities. Finally, in 225 B.C. King Antigonus Doson was presented with an opportunity of restoring Macedonian authority over Greece, when the leading statesman of the Achaean League, Aratus, invoked his assistance against Sparta. At the battle of Sellasia (222 B.C.) Doson destroyed the forces of Cleomenes and set the Achaean League on its feet once more. At the same time he reinstated, in a modified form, the federal constitution of Philip.

For the moment Macedon and Greece presented a common front to the world. But Doson's successor, Philip the Fifth, alienated his Greek allies by a high-handed policy which suggested that he intended to rule them as his subjects. The new Graeco-Macedonian league therefore collapsed, when Philip entangled himself in a war with the Roman Republic, and the disunited Greek states fell piecemeal into Roman hands (200–146 B.C.: see pp. 65–6). From this point onward the political history of Greece becomes merged in that of Rome.

13. HELLENISTIC STATECRAFT

The century and a quarter that elapsed from the death of Alexander witnessed the collapse of his empire, the renewed failure of the Greeks to achieve a durable union, and the advent of a foreign Power which made an end of Greek independence.

Setting out in the wake of Alexander, the Greeks embarked on a new movement of colonial expansion which did not stop short at the Mediterranean coast, but carried them to the farthest limits of the Macedonian's conquests. Old soldiers of Alexander, recruits attracted to the armies of his successors by the promise of land-allotments, civilian administrators in the employ of Hellenistic rulers, and merchant venturers, settled down in every part of the new world which Alexander had opened. The more distant of these colonies, it is true, did not long survive the restoration of native rule; but a large number of Greek cities was permanently established in the interior of Asia Minor and Syria, and the Greek foundations in Mesopotamia maintained themselves until the second or third century of the Christian era. The colonial movement of the Hellenistic period secured the ascendancy of the Greeks in Syria until the coming of the Saracens, and in Asia Minor up to the advent of the Turks. Of the new Greek cities Alexandria, which was the capital of the Ptolemies, Antioch, where the Seleucids established their court, and Seleucia-on-Tigris, the predecessor of Baghdad, ranked among the largest of ancient towns.

In the Hellenistic period Greek warfare reached its highest level of technical proficiency. The elephant corps which Seleucids and Ptolemies introduced into their field armies were, to be sure, a reinforcement of doubtful value. But the artillery of the Hellenistic kings (catapults and stone-throwers) opened a new chapter in the history of ancient siegecraft; and they provoked a corresponding improvement in the fortification of cities, whose ring-walls were rebuilt so as to derive the utmost advantage from the natural strength of the site. New methods of ship-construction led to the replacement of the trireme by the more powerful quinquereme (with five oars in adjacent portholes).

The Ptolemaic, Seleucid, and Attalid monarchies made some notable experiments in the adminstration of large territorial states. Like the Persian Empire which they superseded, the new kingdoms were undisguised despotisms; and they followed the Persian pattern in maintaining a sharp distinction between ruling people and subject nations. They deliberately reacted against the cosmopolitan tendencies of Alexander; they reserved most higher offices for Greeks, and mostly recruited their armies from the same element; they regarded the natives chiefly as sources of revenue. But their government attained a higher degree of complexity than that of the Persians. The Hellenistic principalities were more centralized monarchies, in which the king personally directed every branch of the administration, and enforced his authority by means of a staff of permanent officials. In Egypt, a country that lends itself well to centralized government, the Ptolemies instituted the most extensive bureaucracy of ancient times. They imposed innumerable taxes and constructed an elaborate apparatus for the collection of these imposts, and for the strict accounting of all public moneys.

On the other hand, the Hellenistic kings conceded a greater or lesser measure of self-government to their Greek colonies, in which the spirit of local patriotism waxed as strong as in Old Greece, and the demand for autonomy was scarcely less insistent. The new Greek cities were required to pay taxes and to obey occasional ordinances from the royal chanceries. But they were as a rule allowed to administer their internal affairs with little interference, and to set up the usual organs of a Greek *polis*, annual magistrates, a *boule*, an *ecclesia*, and courts of law.[1] The most favoured ones were also endowed with large pieces of territory, over which they exercised unfettered control.

Lastly, the conquests of Alexander had a profound influence upon Greek economic life and culture. They diffused the Greek type of money economy over the Near East lands, and they brought about a wide extension of Greek culture (p. 256). This spread of Greek civilization was the most permanent and important result of Alexander's career. The Romans put an end to Greek political liberty, but they capitulated to Greek culture. One main reason for their strange and momentous surrender was that they found this culture already holding dominion over half the Mediterranean area. Alexander and his successors had at least made the world safe for the survival of Greek life and thought.

[1] A tighter hand was naturally kept by the kings over their capital cities. This was especially the case at Alexandria, which contained large native and Jewish elements in its population and was notoriously unruly.

(b) ROME

I. EARLY ITALY

The population of ancient Italy was of similar composition to that of Greece. An apparently indigenous folk was overlaid and eventually amalgamated with immigrants who entered Italy from the north during the second millennium B.C.[1] The native folk, however, produced no civilization to match that of the Minoans in Greece, and the invaders did not bring on a 'Viking Age'. In prehistoric times Italy remained a self-contained country, and the progress of its inhabitants to civilized life was gradual and slow.

About 1000 B.C. the Italian peoples had attained, albeit by a different path, a similar level of culture to that of their Greek contemporaries. They lived in village communities, which were grouped together to form tribal states or '*pagi*'.[2] In special emergencies they might associate in wider confederacies, whose names ('Umbrians', 'Samnites', 'Lucanians', etc.) often meet us in Roman history; but in ordinary times the chief political unit was the *pagus*. A distinguishing feature of early Italian society was the 'ius fetiale', a code of inter-tribal usage which bound the states to seek peaceful redress for damages before resorting to open hostilities, and defined the rights of belligerents. But since no authoritative tribunal was at hand to interpret this code, the fetial law could not altogether prevent recourse to war.

Before 800 B.C. the Italians hardly came into contact with the more advanced civilizations of the eastern Mediterranean. In the eighth century Greek settlers took possession of the southern coastlands of the peninsula from the Gulf of Otranto to the bay of Naples (p. 18). These colonists introduced into Italy the

[1] Presumably the northern immigrants introduced the Indo-European languages (Latin, Oscan, etc.) which were spoken in Italy in prehistoric times.

[2] An intermediate unit between the *pagus* and the individual household was the *gens*, which appears to have been originally an association of families for the common tenure of land. The *gens* had lost all practical importance in historical times, but it was perpetuated in the peculiar Italian custom of carrying a 'gentile' name ('Iulius', 'Tullius', etc.) in addition to a personal one.

nascent culture of Greece, with its city life and hoplite warfare, and its alphabetic writing. But their absorption in the usual Greek inter-city quarrels incapacitated them alike for the conquest and for the peaceful penetration of Italy; indeed their influence scarcely extended beyond the southern seaboard.

The first centre of political power and focus of a higher civilization in Italy was Etruria. This district, which possessed a fertile soil and the chief mineral resources of Italy (p. 13), was colonized about 800 B.C. by immigrants from Asia Minor, who brought with them a peculiar tongue (which still awaits interpretation) and a civilization partly modelled on that of Greece. By 650 B.C. these settlers had set up their fortified cities in every part of Tuscany, in the next hundred years they conquered parts of Latium and Campania, and a large portion of northern Italy. About 550 B.C. the whole of Italy seemed destined to fall under the rule of the Etruscans and to receive the impress of their culture. But they failed to assimilate or conciliate their dependants; their ascendancy rested on mere force, and it was undermined by the feuds of the Etruscan cities, which had no more capacity to co-operate than those of the Greeks. About 500 B.C. they were driven back from Latium and Campania; a century later they lost their hold on northern Italy (p. 59). After 400 B.C. Etruscan culture fell into decay, and was gradually supplanted by the more vigorous and adaptable civilization of the Latins.

The Latin people was a branch of the ordinary Italic stock, whose territory extended along the western seaboard between the rivers Tiber and Liris. The coast of Latium was low-lying and liable to become waterlogged; but the plain of the Tiber and the volcanic hill-country round the Alban Mount were fertile tracts and could give subsistence to a relatively large population. Moreover, under Etruscan influence the Latins took to city life; and in founding the city of Rome they built for all time.

The city of Rome was situated, like London, at the lowest convenient point for crossing an important river. Its hills provided dry building-space above the flood-level of the Tiber valley, and firm abutments for bridging its waters. It also

ITALY AFTER THE ROMAN CONQUEST

resembled London in having easy access to the sea. But the chief natural advantage of Rome was that it lay at the centre of road communications in peninsular Italy. It was founded about 600 B.C. by the amalgamation of the villages which had previously been formed on the separate hill-tops.[1] Its centre lay in the valley enclosed by the Palatine, Capitoline, Quirinal, and Esquiline hills, where the Forum Romanum was laid out. In area it was the largest town of central Italy, and its foundation was probably due to a special effort on the part of the neighbouring Latin communities, which needed a stronghold on the lower Tiber in order to defend its passage against the oncoming Etruscans. We may therefore regard Rome, the greatest founder of military colonies in ancient history, as being itself a military colony of the Latins.

2. ROME UNDER THE EARLY KINGS

For the first hundred years of its existence Rome was little more than a large market town, and its early government conformed in most respects to that of any ordinary city-state. The commonalty or *plebs*, consisting mostly of the lesser peasantry, was convened on occasion to a general assembly known as the *Comitia Curiata* (in which the citizens were grouped according to the *curiae* or districts in which they resided). But the Comitia Curiata did little more than give assent to the decisions of the Council or *Senate*, to which none but *patricians*, i.e. the aristocracy of larger landowners, were admitted; and the ascendancy of the patricians was confirmed by the bond of clientship which tied many of the small holders to the greater landlords. Jurisdiction and the command of the armed forces

---

[1] The traditional story of the foundation of Rome in 753 B.C. by Romulus, a prince from the Latin town of Alba Longa and a remote descendant of the Trojan hero Aeneas, is now generally discredited. It was mainly a product of Greek and Roman antiquarians of the fifth, fourth, and third centuries, to which Vergil and Livy gave final shape in the days of Augustus. Archæological evidence, which is our only sound source of information concerning the beginnings of Rome, indicates that soon after 1000 B.C. small villages were formed on several of the hill-tops, but that these did not amalgamate into a city until c. 600 B.C.

were in the hands of a *rex* or king. The Roman king did not reign by hereditary right; he was an elective official who owed his authority to the choice of Senate and Comitia. But, once appointed, he wielded an unlimited power of coercion, of which the *fasces* or bundles of rods and axes in the hands of his attendants were not merely a symbol but the actual instrument. The king's *imperium* or power of life and death over the citizens was the most characteristic feature of the first Roman constitution. It is no mere accident that in the early history of Rome we never hear of blood feuds and private wars between the individual families. But the same causes which put an end to monarchy in early Greece were also at work in the cities of Italy: the aristocracies dispossessed the kings and shared out the royal power among themselves. At Rome the monarchy was discredited by the arbitrary and despotic rule of an alien king of Etruscan origin, Tarquin the Proud. It was swept away about 500 B.C. by a revolution which set up an aristocratic republic, and fostered an enduring prejudice against kingship among the Romans.

3. THE EARLY ROMAN REPUBLIC

The authority of the kings at Rome was transferred to a pair of annual magistrates, the *consuls*. These officials were elected by the Popular Assembly, but they belonged to the patrician families and exercised their power in the patrician interest. They imposed upon the plebeians a more regular military conscription, and rigorously enforced against them a harsh law of debt, which bade a defaulting borrower to be handed over to his creditor as a slave.

The grievances of the plebeians under patrician rule gave rise to a long political duel, the 'Conflict of the Orders'. This struggle took a course far different from that of the revolutionary movements which led to the downfall of aristocracy in the Greek cities (pp. 23–4). The plebeians at Rome fought out their battles for themselves, without recourse to the interested championship of a tyrant, and they conducted their class-war with bloodless weapons. They organized themselves into a state within a state, and by collective action they made their weight of numbers irresistible. They formed an unofficial but orderly popular assembly, the *Concilium Plebis*, in which they grouped themselves according to their *tribus* (a larger local division which henceforth displaced the *curiae* for political purposes), and in this convention they appointed their own officials, the *tribuni plebis*, who were presently constituted as an annually elected board of ten members. They commissioned the tribunes in the first instance to negotiate or remonstrate with the consuls. If the consuls proved obdurate to their demands they had recourse to a novel weapon, the political strike, which took the form of a mass-refusal to perform military service. By organized passive resistance, or by the mere threat of collective disobedience, they extorted concession after concession from the patricians.

The plebeians first obtained the publication of the law administered in the patrician courts, in the 'Code of the Twelve Tables'. Next, they secured the right of appeal from any severe judicial sentence by a consul or other magistrate, and of re-trial before a popular assembly acting as a final court of law. To ensure observance of this rule they set the tribunes to act as watchdogs on the consuls. Nay more, the tribunes, armed with the right of interceding on behalf of ill-used plebeians, enlarged this right from precedent to precedent, until it grew into a general power of veto on any public act, on the tacit assumption that this was in the interests of the plebeians. By means of this arbitrary but effective expedient the tribunes placed the persons and property of the commons beyond the reach of official oppression. Henceforth the mere words 'civis Romanus sum' acted as a magical formula for upholding the liberty of the subject.

Thus safeguarded in their fundamental rights, the plebeians pressed on to obtain for themselves a larger share of political power. They secured the right of legislation for the Concilium Plebis, and for yet another Popular Assembly, the *Comitia Centuriata*, which had grown out of the Roman army, and always retained a quasi-military grouping by *centuriae* or companies.[1]

---

[1] The origin of the Comitia Centuriata is extremely obscure. Roman tradition was probably at fault in dating it back to the regal period. There is no certain trace of it before the later years of the fifth century B.C.

For the Comitia Centuriata they also gained the right of electing the consuls and other higher magistrates, and of revising judicial sentences on appeal. Finally, the leading men of the plebeian order demanded admission to the magistracies and the Senate. In 366 B.C. their right to stand for election to the consulship was acknowledged, and this concession carried with it their eventual entry into all the other magistracies. Their claim to seats in the Senate—which hitherto had been in the gift of kings, consuls, or censors—was granted indirectly by a new rule, which gave a preferential right of membership to all persons who had held one of the greater political offices (c. 312 B.C.). Consequently, as plebeians won their way into the higher magistracies, they passed *ex officio* into the Senate.

About 300 B.C. the Conflict of the Orders ended with the general abolition of patrician privilege at Rome. This end had been attained by a series of piecemeal reforms which left the Roman constitution in a singularly untidy condition. To say nothing of the Comitia Curiata, which gradually fell out of use, there existed two co-ordinate popular assemblies, the Comitia Centuriata and the Concilium Plebis, whose spheres of competence were not clearly defined.[1] The magistracy also harboured many possibilities of conflict. Since the foundation of the Republic the number of executive offices had been considerably increased. The consuls were now mostly occupied with military duties; their civil jurisdiction was taken over by a *praetor*, their financial functions by four or more *quaestors*. Four *aediles* attended to the municipal services of Rome (maintenance of streets, markets, etc.); two *censors* (appointed only at intervals of four years) numbered the people and made up the list of the Senate. These magistrates were arranged in a hierarchy that led from the quaestorship and the aedileship to the three higher offices, the praetorship, consulship, and censorship. But their functions overlapped to some extent, and the work of any of them was liable to be obstructed at any moment by the veto

[1] The catalogue of popular congresses at Rome included another assembly, the *Comitia Tributa*, which was usually convened by a consul and nominally at least was open to patricians as well as to plebeians. But in practice the Comitia Tributa came to be scarcely distinguishable from the Concilium Plebis.

of any of the ten tribunes. To prevent a deadlock at a time of crisis, such as a foreign invasion, the consuls were empowered to nominate an emergency official, the *dictator*, who assumed authority over all the other magistrates. The dangerous expedient of the dictatorship proved remarkably successful, for all its holders had sufficient strength of character to abdicate their office when the crisis was over. But the recurrent need for the suspension of the ordinary machine of government showed up the faultiness of its structure.

Nevertheless, the constitution of the Middle Republic gave general satisfaction. It struck an effective if rough-and-ready compromise between the authority of the magistrate and the personal rights of the citizen. It gave an adequate measure of control over the government to the people, who elected the magistrates and heard appeals from them, made the laws and decided all important questions of policy, such as the declaration of war and the conclusion of peace. Moreover, the people, who at this stage consisted for the most part of an economically independent peasantry, living within easy distance of Rome, exercised their powers with more than the usual confidence and discernment. The constitution also provided for the occasional freshening up of the governing class by the admission of plebeians into the magistracies and Senate; and the Senate (a body of ex-magistrates holding their seats for life[1]) became a reservoir of the best talent and the ripest experience in the state. Moreover, the amicable manner in which the Conflict of the Orders had been resolved left an atmosphere of goodwill, and a general determination to work the constitution to the best advantage. In actual practice, the two chief popular assemblies shared out their field of work so as to avoid a clash; the magistrates and tribunes came to terms with one another or sought the arbitration of the Senate. Lastly, the economic distress out of which the Conflict arose had in the meantime been dispelled by the wars that started Rome on her career of conquest.

[1] In the third and second centuries the Senate contained about three hundred members. From the time of Cornelius Sulla (p. 73) its numbers were raised to five or six hundred, so as to correspond with an increase in the number of the magistrates.

4. THE CONQUEST OF ITALY

The Roman army was at first constituted like that of other early city-states (pp. 22–3). The patricians and their retainers contributed a nucleus of trained fighting men, but the commons were not yet called upon for regular service. Such a force was better adapted for border warfare than for systematic conquest, and it gained no victories of permanent importance. Under one of the later kings, or more probably in the days of the early Republic, it was remodelled on the pattern of the Greek hoplite forces (p. 24). Military service was henceforth made compulsory upon the whole citizen body, and about 450 B.C. a special pair of magistrates, the censors, was created, primarily for the purpose of keeping the National Service Register (p. 57). Nevertheless in the fifth century the Roman forces were hard put to it to repel the incursions of nomadic tribes from the Central Apennines, the Aequi and Volsci; and in 390 B.C. the history of Rome was almost brought to an end, when a roving band of Gauls—Celtic immigrants from France, who had taken possession of northern Italy since the fifth century—routed the Roman army, captured the lower city, and penned up its inhabitants on the Capitoline hill of refuge. The Gauls, however, being more intent on plunder than on conquest, allowed themselves to be bought off.

The Romans profited by their narrow escape to improve their warcraft by systematic study and experiment. They replaced the hoplite's thrusting-spear with a sword, which was suitable alike for hewing and thrusting. They broke up their *legions* or infantry columns into separate *manipuli* or companies, which were trained to manœuvre independently on the field of battle. These reforms entailed a more rigorous course of drill than was usually practicable in a city-state militia. But the Roman people, however intent on curbing the consular imperium in domestic affairs, never imposed any limits upon it in the sphere of war, and submitted uncomplainingly to an exceptionally severe discipline. The Roman legions thus became the most versatile of ancient infantry formations; by their capacity to fight equally well in close or in open order they proved themselves wellnigh invincible in battle. In addition, the Roman soldier was inured to hard digging and marching, and in the later years of the fourth century the Roman road engineers began to construct the system of metalled roads which eventually placed their city within easy striking distance of every part of Italy (p. 138). These roads enabled the legions to be rapidly moved to any critical front; and the entrenched camps which the soldiers were compelled to construct whenever they changed their quarters gave them a secure rallying-point in the rare event of a lost battle. Finally, the Romans consolidated the ground won in their campaigns by the foundation of military colonies.[1] At the end of a successful war they appropriated a piece of enemy territory and settled a permanent garrison upon it. These colonies served, in addition, to relieve economic distress and to appease the land-hunger of the Roman peasantry; but their main object was to secure strategic points such as river-crossings and exits from mountain-passes. The number of these fortresses eventually grew to seventy-five, and their network enmeshed the whole country.

The Romans had now equipped themselves with an instrument which made them masters of all Italy in a century and a half. The first large stride towards the Roman conquest of Italy was the Great Latin War of 340–338 B.C. From early days the Latin people had been bound to Rome not only by racial ties, but by the need of common defence against the Etruscans, the Aequi, and the Volsci. In 494 B.C. an equal alliance had been made between Rome and a confederacy including most of the other Latin cities; but the growing military preponderance of Rome in the fourth century gave alarm to her partners and prompted them to demand fresh safeguards for their independence. Upon refusal of this request they made war upon Rome, but were decisively beaten. The Romans dissolved the Latin League and entered into new compacts with the individual Latin towns, by which these were definitely reduced to a dependent status.

About this time the Romans were drawn on by an appeal for assistance which was a tribute to their rising military reputation.

[1] A Roman colony was a town with a small tract of country attached to it. It had no resemblance to a modern British or French 'colony'.

In 343 B.C. Capua, a prosperous city of Campania, solicited Roman aid against the marauding Samnites of the southern Apennines. By acceptance of this call the Romans involved themselves in a series of hard-fought wars (343–290 B.C.) which they won by building roads and planting colonies as much as by their prowess in the field. In 282 they answered a similar summons from the Greek town of Thurii, which was being molested by native Lucanian tribes, and in so doing became embroiled with Tarentum, the most powerful of the Greek cities of Italy, which resented Roman interference in what it considered its sphere of influence (282 B.C.). For the war against Rome the Tarentines engaged King Pyhrrus of Epirus (a small principality on the east side of the Adriatic), who was a master of the Hellenistic system of combined tactics with infantry, cavalry, and elephants. The Roman legions were repeatedly outmanœuvred by Pyrrhus, yet by their dogged resistance they won the whole war, for the Epirote king lost patience with his slow progress and deserted the Tarentines. After the fall of Tarentum in 272 the Romans had established their ascendancy over all the south of Italy and in the mountain districts of the central Apennines. In the recent wars all the cities and tribes of these regions had been drawn in, and had either been subdued by force or had become dependent allies of Rome.

In the meantime the Romans had also been involved in occasional wars with the cities of Etruria, arising for the most part out of frontier disputes. Faulty co-operation on the part of the Etruscans gave the Romans the opportunity of a piecemeal conquest of their country. By 265 B.C. the whole of peninsular Italy had fallen under Roman control.

The conquest of northern Italy followed in 225–220, as a counter-offensive to a sudden and alarming incursion of the Gauls into central Italy. With the resources of the entire peninsula now at their command, the Romans annihilated the invading bands and easily subdued the disorganized Gallic tribes.

The conquest of Italy imposed upon the Roman Republic a problem of organization such as neither Athens nor Sparta among the leading cities of Greece had been able to solve. In the earlier stages of their expansion the Romans usually annexed the territory of defeated states and enrolled their inhabitants into their own citizen body, thus bringing them under the imperium of the consuls and rendering them liable to military duty in the Roman legions. But they left to the incorporated communities a large measure of self-government: indeed, but for an occasional requisition of recruits by the consuls, and periodic visits by the *praefecti*, or itinerant justices whom the praetor at Rome commissioned to hold local assizes, these communities scarcely felt the burden of their new allegiance. Furthermore, the newly enlisted citizens invariably received the basic constituents of Roman franchise, the full protection of the Roman law for themselves and their property; the burgesses of the annexed cities in Latium obtained the Roman franchise entire, so that members of the local aristocracies, e.g. the Porcii Catones of Tusculum, were able to enter the Roman Senate and to attain the consulship.

When the Romans came to assume control over the remoter parts of Italy they abandoned the practice of incorporation, for this would have extended their territory beyond the limits which they could conveniently supervise at this period, and would have injected into their citizen body large masses of people who were as yet alien to them in speech and culture. They therefore secured the outlying cities and tribes by the looser bond of treaties. Although the Italians bound by treaty were termed 'socii', or partners, their partnership was purely passive. They were not consulted on matters of common policy, and they were pressed into wars in the making of which they had no choice. While the terms of the treaties varied considerably from case to case, they invariably included the obligation to provide military contingents to Rome up to a stipulated maximum. To this extent the 'socii Italici' were worse off than the members of the Peloponnesian League (p. 34) or of Philip's confederacy (p. 44). On the other hand, they retained their full autonomy in domestic matters, they paid no taxes to Rome, and they scarcely realized their dependence except in times of war. In return for their obligation to render military aids to Rome they enjoyed the 'common peace' of Italy; the settled populations were no longer exposed to the raids of the Apennine highlanders, and peninsular Italy as a whole was relieved of the Gallic peril. Moreover, in extending their franchise to Latins and other neighbouring peoples, the Romans held out a prospect of an eventual real partnership to the 'socii', once these had served their term of apprenticeship to Roman warcraft and Roman culture.

Under such conditions the Roman organization of Italy proved an enduring success. The Italian peoples stood firmly by their partnership in arms with Rome and played their full part in the founding of the Roman world-empire. Under the influence of comradeship in arms they gradually adopted Roman habits of life; they replaced the surviving tribal organizations by miniature city-states on the Roman pattern, and they discarded their native dialects in favour of the Latin tongue. Thus the Romans acquired for their free disposal a man-power such as no other Mediterranean state could muster, and the union of all Mediterranean lands under one political overlord now became feasible for the first time.

5. ROME'S FOREIGN CONQUESTS, 264–100 B.C.

The Romans had not consolidated their dominion in Italy before they were drawn into an overseas adventure which was the starting-point of their interminable foreign conquests. A casual collision with the Carthaginians over the possession of the Sicilian town of Messana, which had asked for Roman intervention in a war against its neighbour Syracuse, developed into a struggle for the possession of all Sicily. In this 'First Punic War' (264–241 B.C.) the Romans engaged their forces unsparingly; they improvised a war-fleet, and, undismayed by heavy losses, finally gained the mastery over the Sicilian seas. By the peace of 241 they acquired Sicily and made it into the first Roman 'province' (p. 68). Three years later they resolved by an afterthought to take Sardinia and Corsica into the bargain, and deprived Carthage of these possessions on a flimsy pretext. This action led to the 'Second Punic War', which was the Carthaginian reply to the new Roman policy of 'grab'. In preparation for this conflict the Carthaginian general Hamilcar

subdued the discordant and ill-organized peoples of southern
Spain, so as to gain a fresh recruiting ground for the Punic
army. In 218 his son Hannibal opened the Punic counter-attack
by invading Italy with a picked force of Spanish and North
African natives.

The Second Punic War (218–201 B.C.) was the severest test
of Roman fortitude in battle. By a masterly application of
Hellenistic warcraft Hannibal took an unprecedented toll of
Rome's military strength; on the field of Cannae, with numeri-
cally inferior forces, he encircled and destroyed a Roman army
of more than 50,000 men. But the Romans, drawing upon their
last reserves, repaired their losses, and the greater number of
their Italian dependants stood in with them. Avoiding further
pitched battles, they used their still superior man-power to
wear down the invader in a war of attrition. The eventual
Roman counter-offensive was undertaken by a young officer,
P. Cornelius Scipio, who had studied Hannibal's methods and
proceeded to apply them against the Carthaginians. In 210–206
he drove the Punic forces out of Spain; he then carried the war
into North Africa, and in 202 he inflicted a final defeat upon
Hannibal's veterans at the battle of Zama.

The Carthaginians, who had staked everything on Hannibal's
venture, were now reduced to impotence and sank into a state
of dependence on their conquerors. But the Romans, with
unreasoning apprehension of a second Punic *revanche*, regarded
their victory as incomplete. Fifty years later they took advantage
of a technical infraction of the peace of 201 by the Carthaginians
to open the 'Third Punic War' (149–146 B.C.). Taking Carthage
after an obstinate siege, they destroyed the city completely and
sold the remnant of its population into slavery. The territory
of Carthage (modern Tunisia) was converted into a Roman
province, named 'Africa'.

The First Punic War gave the Roman Republic its first overseas possessions, the Second War paved the way for a general
Roman dominion over the western Mediterranean. In the course
of the Second War Scipio won over to the Roman side the native
king of Numidia (Algeria), which became in consequence a
Roman dependency. A punitive expedition which the Romans

subsequently directed against a refractory member of the Numidian dynasty brought them into touch with the king of Mauretania (Morocco), which was added to the list of Roman client-states in 106 B.C.

By the peace of 201 B.C. the Romans took over the Carthaginian territory in Spain, to make it safe against a Punic reoccupation. Like the British in India, they found themselves obliged to make their new possession more secure by extending it from sea to sea. At the end of two long wars (197–179 and 154–133 B.C.), in which the natives fought with all their usual obstinacy and their usual incapacity for united action, the Iberian peninsula passed into Roman hands.

During the Second Punic War the Romans obtained a footing in Gaul by making an alliance with the Greek colony of Massilia (mod. Marseille). In 125 B.C. the Massilians invoked Roman aid against the hinterland tribes, and the Romans were tempted by some easy victories over these to overrun all south-eastern France, which was now made into a province. By 120 the western Mediterranean had become a Roman lake.

The Second Punic War further had the effect of drawing the Republic into the orbit of the Hellenistic states, and of initiating a parallel course of Roman conquests in the eastern Mediterranean. Previous to this war the Romans had in general kept themselves aloof from Greek politics. But an ill-judged intervention by Philip the Fifth of Macedon (p. 48) in the Second Punic War, which he made in the hope of sharing the fruits of victory with Hannibal, forced the Republic to form a front against him. Thanks to the Roman fleet, Philip was held at arm's length and could render Hannibal no effective assistance. But his attempted invasion of Italy was not forgotten. In 200 B.C. the Romans entered into an alliance with the King of Pergamum and the city of Rhodes (p. 46), which had in the meantime become embroiled with Philip, and in so doing became inextricably entangled in Eastern affairs.

The 'Second Macedonian War' (200–196 B.C.) resolved itself into an old-fashioned infantry duel. In the final encounter at Cynoscephalae, in Thessaly, the more adaptable Roman legions won the day by holding their formation, while the rigid Macedonian 'phalanx' broke into pieces under the stress of a fluctuating battle. After this victory the Romans withdrew their troops, in the belief that Philip was now innocuous, and that the Greeks could be safely left to their own devices. Presently, however, their suspicions were reawakened, and without adequate reason they made a preventive attack upon Philip's successor Perseus. The 'Third Macedonian War' (171–167 B.C.) culminated in a battle at Pydna (in Macedonia), in which the legions repeated the victory of Cynoscephalae. Still loath to assume permanent control over Greek peoples, yet unwilling to trust them further, the Romans after some hesitation reduced Macedonia to the condition of a province (148 B.C.).

At the end of the Second Macedonian War the Romans freed the cities of the Greek homeland from Macedonian tutelage. The Greeks were thus given one last chance of taking the federal constitution which the Macedonian kings had provided for them (pp. 44, 48) into their own hands. They neglected this chance, yet they would not fight out their quarrels for themselves, but repeatedly solicited Roman intervention against one another. After several vain attempts at a diplomatic pacification the Romans coerced the recalcitrant Achaean League with a punitive expedition (146 B.C.) and dissolved all the sectional federations, so that the Greek homeland was once more resolved into a powder of isolated city-states. With this forcible settlement the political history of the Greek homeland came to an end. The Greek cities were at last overawed into keeping the common peace which they had been unable to compass by their own effort. But the shock inflicted upon the national pride of the Greeks, when they discovered that they had played themselves irrevocably into the hands of an alien master, was scarcely mitigated by the respect which their master showed for Greek culture. The spirit of self-confidence that had been the mainspring of this culture was broken beyond repair, and Greece ceased to be the pioneer of ancient civilization.

The rulers of Pergamum, who had been the first to invite the Romans into Greece, drew them on into Asia with a renewed call for help. Taking alarm at the growing power of an energetic ruler, Antiochus the Third, who was recovering one by one the lost territories of the Seleucid Empire (p. 45), King Eumenes invoked the Republic to stay his progress. The Romans showed little inclination to entangle themselves in the affairs of Asia, but Antiochus forced their hands by invading Greece and challenging the Roman protectorate of that country. Their first campaign in Asia Minor ended in a battle at Magnesia (190 B.C.), in which Antiochus attempted combined tactics with an insufficiently trained army, and thereby exposed it to complete destruction at the hands of the Roman legions. Though the Romans now withdrew their forces and attempted to resume a policy of non-intervention in Asia, they could not escape the consequences of their victory. While the Seleucid Empire crumbled to pieces under the shock of Magnesia, and its eastern districts definitely reverted to Oriental rule (p. 46), all the dynasties of the Near East, both Greek and barbarian, voluntarily entered into a relation of dependent alliance with the western Republic. The Ptolemies, who had cultivated friendship with Rome since the Republic's victory over Pyrrhus, were now content to sink into a condition of clientship, and the newly established dynasty of the Maccabees in Judaea, which had led a successful rebellion against Seleucid rule (c. 160 B.C.), at once put itself under Roman protection. By 133 B.C. the Romans had grown so well into their new part as overlords of the Near East that they accepted an eccentric bequest from the last king of Pergamum, who made over his estates to them by testament, and under cover of this will they converted his realm into the province of 'Asia'.

By 100 B.C. the Heroic Age of Roman conquest came to an end. The Roman Empire now extended all round the Mediterranean; and, if exception be made of the subsequent advance into the European continent, the later wars were waged to consolidate rather than to enlarge the Roman dominions.

6. THE GOVERNMENT OF THE ROMAN PROVINCES

The acquisition of Rome's world-empire was not the result of a set policy of aggrandisement. Though the desire for war-spoils on the part of the people, for military distinction or for new sources of revenue on the part of the governing class, exerted an influence on the Republic's foreign relations, self-protection against aggressors, real or imaginary, and the defence of allies, old or new, had been its main determinants. The Romans had not wholly lost sight of the old Italian convention, that war should not be declared without adequate cause (p. 51), and they had embarked on their career of conquest, not with a light heart, but with frequent misgivings. Moreover, it was their regular practice to lighten the burden of their commitments as far as possible, and the organization of their overseas dominion was largely directed to this end.

Wherever the Romans thought that they could count on the loyalty and the competence of their overseas dependants, they contented themselves with a loose treaty of alliance, by which the latter became 'socii et amici populi Romani'. Under these treaties the allies undertook to maintain friendly neutrality, or to render occasional military aids, but they retained complete liberty in their internal affairs. On the other hand, the Romans offered their protection, but this took the form of diplomatic more often than of military intervention. The method of control by alliance was at first applied universally to Rome's dependants in the eastern Mediterranean. But in the west the fear of Carthage impelled the Romans to make sure of their overseas acquisitions by 'reducing them to the form of a province', i.e. by assuming direct control over them; and the provincial system of government was gradually introduced into the east after 150 B.C.

The distinctive feature of this method of government was that the Romans undertook the military protection of the provinces by means of Italian troops, and that instead of exacting military service from the native population they imposed taxation upon it. The governors of provinces also exercised a general supervision over the domestic affairs of the native cities or tribes, and they held a court for the hearing of the more important lawsuits. But as a rule the native communities suffered little restriction in their autonomy, and they were allowed to retain the use of their own customs, religions, and languages. In the east the Greek tongue remained a lingua franca under Roman rule, as it had been under the Hellenistic kings.

The normal method of staffing the provinces was to send out as governors the consuls and praetors whose term of office at Rome had just expired. These *proconsuls* and *propraetors* ('acting consuls and praetors') took with them a quaestor in charge of their money-chest, and a few *legati* or general adjutants. The collection of taxes was left to the native communities, or was entrusted to private syndicates of Roman capitalists, who paid in advance the expected yield of an impost (minus a small margin for their profit) and recouped themselves at the expense of the provincials.

This system of administration proved at first less successful than the Roman organization of Italy. The governors, whose term of office did not as a rule extend beyond one year, were not given adequate time to acquaint themselves with the country under their charge; they were not paid a regular salary, and they were insufficiently provided with assistant officials. In consequence, they could not exercise a strict control over the *publicani*, or tax-farmers, who took advantage of their freedom from supervision to extort more than their due from the provincials. Nay more, the governors were tempted to pay themselves for their services by all manner of illegal exactions on their own account, or by connivance at the malpractices of the publicani. But the fundamental defect of the Roman régime was that it disbanded the native armies and did not train the provincials for service in the Roman forces. The native populations therefore stood in the position of subjects rather than of partners in the Roman Empire, and they were helpless in the face of oppression by the Roman residents, official or otherwise. Yet the Roman administration of the provinces should not be judged by a few sensational cases of misrule, or by the vehement denunciations of some guilty officials on the part of the orator Cicero. Under normal conditions the provincials were probably no worse off than under the previous rulers. They retained their local self-government almost intact; their regular taxes were not heavy; they were protected against foreign invaders and enjoyed immunity from intestine warfare.

6

7. DOMESTIC AFFAIRS IN THE SECOND CENTURY B.C.

The outstanding importance of the Roman conquests resided in the fact that they introduced an era of world-peace, that under the shelter of the *pax Romana* a new world-economy grew up (p. 122), and a Graeco-Roman civilization matured, of which we are the heirs. But these benefits were bought at a heavy price. The Greek genius declined in productiveness under Roman rule. The immediate economic effect of the Roman victories was a sudden and harmful concentration of Mediterranean riches in Roman hands, and a growing disparity between rich and poor within the Roman community. Rome's subjects in the provinces were exposed to oppression, and the ruling people itself was filled with discontent and discord. The stability which had characterized the Roman constitution during the age of conquest broke down, and the Republic drifted through political crises into civil wars.

During the third century the ruling class at Rome was being quickened with a slow but continuous infusion of fresh blood, and it performed its work under a healthy sense of responsibility to the general body of the Roman people. In the second century, however, the Comitia, through which the people exercised its control, underwent a transformation. The Roman peasantry, which had hitherto been the backbone of the Comitia, was being reduced and impoverished under the excessive burden of prolonged military service in foreign parts, and so lost its preponderance in the Assemblies. These now fell more and more into the hands of the urban population, which was being rapidly augmented by an influx of immigrants, both free and slave. The servile element, consisting largely of war-captives, was particularly numerous, and since the Roman law, more liberal in this respect than that of the Greek cities (p. 31), gave the suffrage to slaves as soon as they were set free by their masters, the Comitia came to include large numbers of freed-men of alien origin. The elements that now frequented the Assemblies were economically less independent than the rural voters, and less confident in their own judgment. They therefore lent themselves to political management, and actually fell under the control of a coterie of some twenty-five leading families, who kept them amenable by personal patronage, by collective bribery, and by a lavish outlay on public amusements (pp. 160–2) In return, the ruling class regularly contrived the election of its own nominees to office, and through office to the Senate; and it ensured that the resolutions passed on its initiative in the Senate should be almost automatically confirmed by the Comitia.

The Republic thus relapsed into the power of an exclusive aristocracy, which deliberately closed the door on 'new men'. But this nobility proved unequal to the task of governing an empire. It was corrupted by a hard scramble for riches; and it was half-hearted and dilatory in the urgent business of enlarging and improving the machinery of government, so as to adapt it to the growing needs of an imperial state.

The most successful reforms of this period were carried out in the sphere of jurisdiction. About 240 B.C. a second praetor was appointed to deal with the growing number of cases (mostly of commercial character) in which one party was not a Roman citizen. The Roman nobles who judged in the praetor's court rose to their new responsibilities, and adapted the law to suit the needs of an international capital. About 150 B.C. the system of trial by jury was introduced for the more important criminal cases. The jurors, usually about fifty in number, were selected from the members of the Senate or other privileged bodies (p. 72); the procedure of the courts was more methodical, and gave more opportunity to the trained jurist, than that of the Athenian dicasteries (p. 39).

Other measures of reconstruction which were falling due were evaded or actively opposed by the nobility. The city of Rome, which had grown into a cosmopolitan capital, needed a system of public assistance to relieve the distress of its floating population, and a regular police force to control its turbulent elements. The 'socii Italici', who had given staunch support to Rome in war, and were now being romanized apace, were presenting a justifiable claim to the Roman franchise. The Roman army was proving inadequate to the new conditions of continuous service abroad, and the time had come to replace the conscript militia by professional soldiers. The failure of the nobility to grapple with

these problems brought on political crises that led to the overthrow
of the aristocratic régime and the downfall of the Republic.

8. THE DECLINE OF THE REPUBLIC

The first stage in the Roman revolution was reached in 133 B.C.,
when a tribune named Tiberius Gracchus succeeded in enact-
ing a land-allotment bill—itself of no great importance—over
the heads of the Senate, but was killed shortly afterwards in a
street uproar. In 123–2 his brother Gaius similarly carried
an extensive programme of new laws. But Gaius' principal
measures were reforms in the wrong direction. His attempt to
play off against the senatorial nobility a new class of financiers
and contractors who had acquired riches in the wake of the
Roman foreign conquests, by giving them seats on the jury
courts and other political privileges, did more harm than good,
for the *Equites*, as this new bourgeoisie was called, used their
political power in their own selfish interests. A scheme of Gaius
for lowering the price of corn in Rome, though well considered
in itself, stimulated later reformers to bring forward a series of
supplementary laws which ended in the free distribution of food
to the entire urban proletariat—an insitution which survived to
the end of the Roman Empire. Finally, Gaius was involved in a
renewed outbreak of rioting and shared his brother's fate. The
chief significance of the history of the Gracchi lies in the manner
of their deaths, which showed that domestic disputes at Rome
would in future be waged with less restraint than during the
Conflict of the Orders, and that the deciding factor of future
conflicts would be physical violence.

In 91–89 B.C. the Republic was overtaken by its most critical
war since Hannibal's invasion, when a confederacy of the
Apennine peoples made an attempt to extort the Roman franchise
by force of arms. The rebels took the Roman government by
surprise, but missed their chance of a decisive attack upon the
city, and eventually succumbed to Rome's greater man-power.
Even so they carried their point, for the Roman nobility, by a
unique example of statesmanship, conceded the franchise to all
'socii Italici', not excluding the defeated insurgents. A new

nation-state was thus brought into existence, and a closer partnership between Rome and Italy was established, which bore good fruit in due course. But the enfranchisement of Italy had little immediate effect upon the course of Roman politics. No polling stations were set up in the outlying parts of Italy, so as to make the votes of the new citizens effective, and the 'old gang' retained control of the government.

But in the meantime the weapon which was to destroy the Republic had been forged. In the closing years of the second century a general named C. Marius carried out on his own authority a military reform of fundamental importance, by enlisting an army of volunteers on terms of long service. The New Model army at once proved its worth by defeating and destroying a host of roving Germans or Celts (the Cimbri and Teutones),[1] who had made an alarming incursion into southern France and Italy (102–1 B.C.), and henceforth the Roman forces were regularly recruited on a voluntary basis. But the professional soldiery, who were mostly landless men 'without a stake in the country', and ready for any profitable adventure, proved a dangerous instrument in the hands of ambitious politicians who no longer scrupled to gain their ends by private war. In 88–2 B.C. Marius and his supporters fought out a round of sanguinary civil wars against a rival named Cornelius Sulla. Each commander in turn captured Rome with his personal army, and Italy was trampled under by the contending forces.

The first Roman civil war ended in a complete victory for Sulla, who now assumed the position of dictator and could have ended the Rupublic by a stroke of the pen. But Sulla merely used his autocratic power to buttress the authority of the Senate with some perfunctory reforms. When the crisis was past, he resigned his office, like the dictators of old.

9. THE FALL OF THE REPUBLIC

The thirty years that followed the first civil war marked a new stage in Rome's achievement. The effects of Roman contact

---

[1] The Cimbri were probably Germans from Jutland; it is uncertain whether the Teutones were Germanic or Celtic.

with Greek civilization were now showing through. The Golden Age of Roman Literature set in, and Latin took its place beside Greek as a classical language (p. 260 ff.). The leisured classes of Rome and Italy were absorbing Greek culture, and were educating themselves to become the teachers of western and central Europe.

In the field of war the new professional armies gained further distinction. In Asia Minor an ambitious Oriental dynast, King Mithridates of Pontus, had taken advantage of the recent dissension in Italy to overrun the province of Asia and to invade the Greek homeland. He was checked by Sulla, who temporarily left the Italian scene of war in order to recover the lost ground (87–4 B.C.); but he returned to the charge shortly afterwards, and drew in his neighbour, King Tigranes of Armenia. He was now driven out of the field by L. Lucullus, who overran the greater part of Pontus and Armenia, and was finally disposed of by Lucullus' successor, Cn. Pompeius (74–63 B.C.). After the Mithridatic Wars Pompey made a new settlement of the Near East. He added Armenia to the list of Roman client-states, and he made a province of Syria, which had sunk into a state of anarchy under the last Seleucid rulers.

A more important extension of the Roman Empire took place in Gaul, where a weak frontier and the dissensions of the hinterland tribes prompted an advance beyond the confines of the existing province. In 58 B.C. an enterprising proconsul, C. Iulius Caesar, who had been invoked by some of the free Gallic peoples to repel a German invasion of Gaul, seized the occasion to move the Roman boundary forward to the Rhine, and so to annex all Gaul to the Roman dominions. Despite the vigorous resistance of the Gallic tribes, culminating in a final rally under a chief named Vercingetorix, Caesar completed the conquest by 50 B.C. The Roman Empire was now no longer a purely Mediterranean state, and henceforth its European constituents obtained a definite preponderance over the rest.

But while the Republic was enlarging its foreign dominions, it became progressively less capable of maintaining order within its own house. The senatorial nobility profited little by Sulla's reforms. Pompey and Caesar alike conducted their campaigns with a general disregard of the Senate's authority, and the destiny of Rome was again transferred into the hands of the military chiefs. But so long as army commanders were free to turn their forces upon one another, no settled government was possible. Pompey and Caesar eventually became embroiled over a trivial issue and plunged the Republic into a second period of military anarchy.

The Second Civil War (49–5 B.C.) was won by Caesar in a series of whirlwind campaigns that extended over the whole of the Roman Empire and revealed him as the greatest infantry general of ancient times. On his return to Rome Caesar followed the example of Sulla in assuming a dictatorship. But he wielded his dictatorial powers with far greater energy and insight; he carried out a comprehensive programme of minor reforms and enacted several new measures of far-reaching importance. His most enduring act was the introduction of a solar calendar which survives to the present day in a slightly modified form (p. 140). But his constructive statesmanship was best exemplified by his grants of Roman citizenship to numerous individuals of provincial origin, and to the entire free populations of certain provincial towns. This extension of the Roman franchise beyond the bounds of Italy was the starting-point of a process that transformed the Roman Empire from a military dominion into a commonwealth of equal partners (p. 87).

In 44 B.C. Caesar disclosed to a startled world that his ultimate purpose in assuming a dictatorship was not to mend but to end the Republic. Instead of resigning his office when his programme of reforms was completed, he converted it into a 'perpetual dictatorship', which was but another name for a legalized permanent autocracy.[1] Thirty years of recurrent disorder since Sulla's attempt at a Restoration had convinced him that the senatorial aristocracy had forfeited its right to rule. and he took the shortest cut to an alternative form of government. But the abruptness of his usurpation so affronted the nobility that he took on the shape of a Greek tyrant in their eyes, and so tempted them to tyrannicide.

---

[1] It is not known whether Caesar intended to assume the title and insignia of a king. But he showed beyond doubt that he was resolved to establish a monarchy in some form.

The assassination of Caesar, far from giving a new lease of life to the Republic, brought on a new and prolonged period of military anarchy. An attempt by the veteran orator Cicero to play off the two principal war-lords, Caesar's chief lieutenant, M. Antonius, and an adoptive son of the dictator, C. Iulius Caesar Octavianus, against one another, ended in their joining hands to suppress him. In 43 B.C. Antony and Octavian, together with a lesser general, Aemilius Lepidus, had themselves appointed 'triumvirs for the reconstitution of the Republic'; but under this fallacious title they exercised an undisguised autocracy, and for twelve years the masters of the Roman legions disposed freely of the empire. In a succession of further civil wars the triumvirs swept away the chief tyrannicides, M. Brutus and Cassius, and other belated defenders of the Republic. But the requisitions which they imposed for the upkeep of their enormous military forces were intolerably severe, and their own rival ambitions ensured the eventual collapse of their syndicated despotism. Lepidus was soon elbowed out, and Antony, who had taken the eastern half of the empire for his special sphere of operations, exposed himself to an attack from his remaining partner by his subservience to the enchantress Cleopatra. Unlike some of her male predecessors, this captivating queen was not content to hold Egypt at Rome's pleasure, but sought to recover the un-diminished empire of the earlier Ptolemies, and she seduced a Roman general to transfer the adjacent Roman territories to her dominions. Octavian took full advantage of Antony's blunder to discredit him in the eyes of Rome and Italy; in 31–30 B.C. he made open war upon his colleague and won a runaway victory by the desertion of his adversary's army.[1] With Octavian's victory over Antony the age of military usurpations and civil wars came to an end for the time being.

10. THE SETTLEMENT OF AUGUSTUS

Shortly after his return to Rome Octavian assumed the new name of Augustus ('he who rules by divine approval'). The

---

[1] The culminating naval action at Actium was indecisive in itself, but it accelerated the 'rot' which had set in among Antony's forces.

political settlement which he now made lasted in its main outlines for three centuries. Unlike Caesar, Augustus respected the continuity of Roman tradition and sought to preserve time-honoured institutions, so far as they could be put back into working order. He therefore (in his own words) 'restored the Republic', by taking the magistrates and Senate into partnership with him. Under the new division of work the magistrates took charge of the administration of Rome, of the supervision of Italy, and of ordinary jurisdiction. The Senate recovered a position not merely of dignity but of considerable authority. It was consulted by Augustus on matters of high policy, and it was invested with additional powers. It was constituted into a high court of criminal jurisdiction, to which accused persons of exalted rank were henceforth to be presented; it took over the legislative and (under Tiberius) the electoral functions of the Comitia (which now fell into abeyance); and after the death of Augustus it appointed his successor.[1]

At the same time the magistracy and the Senate were thrown open to a wider field of candidates. During the civil wars the ranks of the republican nobility had been so depleted that it could now supply no more than a fraction of the required number of office-holders. Picked men from the governing classes of the Italian municipalities were therefore admitted to the magistracy at Rome, and passed on into the Senate.[2] The magistracy and Senate thus became more truly representative of the Italian nation, and their personnel no doubt was of higher average ability than that in the days of the later Republic.

For his own part Augustus retained certain reserved functions, and with these he combined a general supervisory authority over the magistracy. The main constituents of his prerogative were

[1] The Senate's constitutional position was not definitely fixed until the reign of Augustus' successor Tiberius. But Tiberius merely completed the reforms which Augustus had contemplated.

[2] Admission to the magistracy and Senate was henceforth restricted to the members of a *senatorius ordo*, or panel of candidates, which was drawn up by Augustus himself. In addition to the sons of existing senators, who were inscribed on the list as a matter of course, the cadets of the leading municipal families readily gained access to the *ordo*.

A moderate property qualification was prescribed for membership of the Senatorial Order.

to be henceforth a proconsular imperium, in virtue of which he became governor of a group of provinces (about half of the total number), a *maius imperium* or overriding control over the governors of the remaining provinces, and a tribunician power which gave him a right of veto over magistrates at Rome. Although it was contrary to normal republican usage that one man should gather into his hands such a wide range of powers, and should hold them by a life tenure, Augustus could plausibly assert that he was but a senior partner in a team of republican officials. Moreover, he gave colour to this theory by summing up his functions under the modest title of *princeps*, or 'First Citizen', and by maintaining a style of life scarcely distinguishable from that of any great nobleman.

But Augustus reserved for himself a power of paramount importance, the chief command over all the military forces, for by relinquishing or even sharing his authority over them he would have opened the door to fresh civil wars. He therefore continued to exact an oath of allegiance from the soldiers to his own person, and he stationed his forces in the provinces over which he had direct authority as proconsul. The controlling fact in Augustus' settlement was that he remained *imperator* or supreme chief of the fighting forces: the name of 'emperor', by which he is now generally known, correctly conveys the essence of his position.

As permanent chief of the Roman army Augustus held the issues of war and peace in his hands, and he became, in effect, the sole director of Roman foreign policy. As paymaster of the forces he required a liberal appropriation from the public funds for his *fiscus* or departmental chest. A large share of the revenue was therefore set apart for his use, and he thereby virtually assumed responsibility for the empire's finances.

Moreover, the reconstituted Senate and magistracy accomplished less than Augustus expected of them. The Senate in particular had lost its capacity for leadership during the period of military usurpations, and could not recapture it under the new régime. Extremely jealous of its outward dignity, it nevertheless shrank from any bold exercise of its undisputed powers, and waited on the emperor's initiative in all matters of importance.

As an organ of enlightened public opinion the Senate still carried weight, but as a director of public affairs it effaced itself.

Thus in the long run the burden of government came to rest almost wholly upon the shoulders of the emperor. In order to discharge the ever-increasing tale of his duties, Augustus laid the foundations of a new executive, which he created by the simple process of nominating suitable men to be his delegates in some particular sphere of work. To each of the provinces of which he was the titular proconsul he appointed an acting governor (*legatus Augusti*) and a staff of financial commissioners (*procuratores*). For the administration of the city of Rome, which passed back into his hands, he set up *praefecti* and *curatores* who took charge of the corn supply, of the fire and water services, and of a newly formed police corps. A secretariat and a staff of accountants busied themselves with Augustus' correspondence and drew up his departmental budget, and the *praefectus praetorio* or commander of the imperial Guards developed under Augustus' successors into a general adjutant. The secretariat and the financial staff were recruited under the early emperors from their own domestic establishment, but the executive posts were mostly filled with members of the senatorial or equestrian class, the former of which held most of the provincial governorships, while the latter exercised the procuratorial functions. Each of these offices was ordinarily held for a term of several years, and carried a regular salary; promotion ladders were established, and men of ability were encouraged to make their careers as professional administrators. Under Augustus' successors the new imperial service grew steadily in numbers, and it encroached continually on the remaining functions of the magistracy.

Lastly, in virtue of his varied prerogatives Augustus was invested with an extensive jurisdiction, and by a natural development, rather than by any statutory enlargement of his powers, the emperor's tribunal grew into a general court of appeal for the whole of the Roman dominions. To assist him in his judicial duties Augustus constituted a *consilium principis*, or Privy Council, in which subsequent emperors allotted an increasing number of seats to expert lawyers.

Augustus not only stabilised the Roman constitution, but he reformed the Roman army and rectified the Roman frontiers. The Roman army received from him a new organization which it retained in all essentials for the next two hundred years. The total number of the armed forces was now fixed at 250,000–300,000 men. In order to maintain this establishment at a uniform level the soldiers were enlisted for a definite number of years (sixteen or twenty or twenty-five), and the legions and other units into which they were drafted were converted into permanent bodies like modern regiments.[1] The greater part of the army was quartered in standing camps on the frontiers or in the vicinity of unruly subject populations. Under the early emperors the main concentration of Roman forces was on the Rhine and Danube, where whole divisions were kept together in large base camps. From the time of Nero a gradual shift of troops took place from Europe to the Euphrates frontier, and in the second century the various units were cantoned out more widely in smaller camps. The actual frontier line was henceforth closely picketed with detached but closely inter-connected forts, or shut off with continuous barriers, such as the stone wall of Hadrian in northern England, the turf-and-clay wall of Antoninus in Scotland, and the turf-and-log wall in western and southern Germany.

The enlistment of soldiers continued to be mainly voluntary, as in the later age of the Republic. But in order to obtain the requisite number of enrolments Augustus was compelled to look beyond Italy, for this country had been overburdened with military service under the Republic and could no longer carry on its shoulders the entire weight of empire defence. He therefore threw open the ranks of the army to the more warlike populations of the provinces (Gauls, Spaniards, Illyrians, Galatians, Mauretanians, and others). Although the provincials were technically known as 'auxiliaries', they were in actual fact professional soldiers like the legionaries, and they contributed a full half of the total establishment. The legions still provided the greater part of the heavy infantry, while the auxiliaries

[1] The legions henceforth carried permanent numbers and distinctive names (e.g. Nona Hispana, Vicesima Valeria Victrix).

furnished an increasing number of light infantry and horse. The conditions of service were made more attractive by an increase of pay (since the time of Caesar), and by the provision of regular pensions for time-expired men. The auxiliaries were not entitled to pensions, but they received Roman citizenship at the end of their service.

A complete corps of regular officers was not instituted. But many of the provincial governors who commanded *ex officio* the army divisions within their jurisdiction were men of wide military experience, and the centurions who acted as company officers were long-service men promoted from the ranks.

Augustus also instituted a permanent Roman navy. After the destruction of the Carthaginian and the Hellenistic navies the republican government had disbanded the war fleets which it had created in the third and second centuries, and it took no other measures to deal with the growing scourge of piracy in the Mediterranean seas than to organize an occasional drive against the corsairs with improvised flotillas.[1] From the time of Augustus the Mediterranean was regularly patrolled by squadrons of light cruisers, and after the conquest of Britain a 'classis Britannica' was stationed in the English Channel. The crews of the imperial navy were mostly drawn from the provincial population.

Augustus' reorganization of the military forces gave the Roman emperors a highly expert and well-disciplined instrument for the defence of the frontiers and for their occasional extension. The weakest part of the existing boundaries was on the northern and north-eastern sectors, where Italy, Dalmatia, and Macedonia lay open to border forays. In the early years of his reign Augustus directed his subordinate commanders to carry out a series of campaigns, by which the Alpine lands, the Balkan peninsula and all the intervening territories were brought into the empire, so that its European boundary was extended to the Danube. After these conquests he planned to shorten the frontier by annexing western Germany and Bohemia, and he had almost completed the conquest of Germany as far as the Elbe,

---

[1] One such operation which Pompey undertook in 67 B.C. was brilliantly successful; but it was no more than a palliative.

when a disaster to one of his expeditionary forces, which was trapped in the forests and swamps of Westphalia, induced him to fall back to the Rhine and Danube. Despite the loss of Germany, Augustus could claim that he had provided the empire on all sides with clearly defined and easily defensible frontiers, with oceans, deserts, and large rivers. The empire also appeared by now to have reached the limits of profitable expansion in an economic sense, for the territories beyond the border were for the most part in a backward condition, and seemingly not worth developing. In his political testament Augustus called upon his successors not to adventure themselves beyond the boundaries which he had marked out for them, and this injunction was generally obeyed.

II. THE ROMAN EMPIRE AT ITS HEIGHT

Though Augustus left many details to be filled in by his successors, the general outline of his new system of government had been completed at the time of his death (A.D. 14). The next hundred years showed up some serious defects in his constitution. While the legal appointment of new rulers rested with the Senate, the actual arrangements for the succession were usually made in advance by the reigning emperors, and their choice was sometimes influenced by family considerations or palace intrigues. On several occasions the soldiers took a hand in the game of emperor-making (see next paragraph), and imposed their nominee upon the Senate. Under this system, or lack of system, the imperial power repeatedly devolved upon men who were ill qualified to exercise it. Capricious rulers idled away their time in silly and sometimes disreputable amusements, or misappropriated large sums of public money to gratify themselves and their favourites; weak characters put themselves into the hands of their wives or other domestic confidants, and admitted sneaks and sycophants into their court. Above all, the successors of Augustus were habitually haunted by a sense of fear, arising partly from a remembrance of Caesar's assassination, partly from distrust of the generals in command of the frontier forces. It is true that their suspicions were sometimes well founded; but they carried their precautions so far, that now and again high society at Rome lived under the shadow of a reign of terror.

But the chief symptom of weakness in the rule of the early emperors lay in the renewed intrusion of the soldiers into politics, as the traditions of stricter discipline which Augustus had succeeded in imposing again became relaxed. A pernicious example was set by the *cohortes praetoriae* (the Corps of Guards), who took advantage of their presence at the seat of government to make their own choice of emperors—usually in consideration of a promised bounty—and to force them upon the Senate. The praetorian troops mostly carried their point without resistance, but their very success prompted the troops on the frontiers to follow suit. A.D. 68–9 witnessed an orgy of emperor-making, in the course of which four successive changes of ruler were made by different divisions of the army, and Italy twice became the scene of regular warfare between the contending sections. The final winner in this scramble, T. Flavius Vespasianus, was strong enough to restore orderly government and to beat back the troops to their proper quarters. But the discovery 'that Rome was not the only place where emperors might be made' eventually proved fatal to the empire.

None the less the initial difficulties of the new régime were gradually overcome. After A.D. 69 the Roman state enjoyed a long immunity from civil wars, and from 98 to 180 it was governed by an unbroken succession of good rulers (Trajan, Hadrian, Antoninus Pius, and M. Aurelius). No other great monarchy of ancient times was better governed than the Roman Empire in the second century of the Christian era.

After the death of Augustus the Roman Empire underwent little further expansion. In Tunisia and Algeria the limit of Roman occupation was gradually carried across the coastal plateau towards the edge of the Sahara; but this advance was made with the plough rather than with the sword. A similar extension to the fringe of the Arabian desert was made in Transjordania. The German frontier was rectified by pinching off the angle between the Rhine and the Upper Danube. But the only substantial additions to Roman territory were made

THE ROMAN EMPIRE
IN IMPERIAL TIMES

Frontiers of Roman Provinces ....
Provinces temporarily held ---------
Numbers signify dates of annexation
Plain numbers refer to dates B.C.

Caspian
Sea

D A C I A
106-270 A.D.

R. Danube

Black Sea

114 A.D.

MOESIA
11

46 A.D.

ssus

THRACE

Philippi

MACEDONIA
Dyrrhachium
146

Pharsalia

rcyra

Actium

ACH-
AEA
15

Byzantium

Nicomedia

BITHYNIA

ASIA
133

74

GALATIA

25

LYCAONIA

LYCIA
43

PAMP.

CILICIA 64

PONTUS
63

Zela

CAPPADOCIA
17 A.D.

ARMENIA
114-117 A.D.

MESOPOTAMIA
115-117 A.D.
& 165 A.D.

ASSYRIA
115-117 A.D.

R. Tigris

Antioch

SYRIA
64

Palmyra

R. Euphrates

CYPRUS 27

CRETE 67

74

CYRENAICA

Alexandria

30

74

ARABIA
PETRAEA
105

JUDAEA
70 A.D.

E G Y P T

30

R. Nile

7

in Britain and Dacia (Transylvania). Britain, which Caesar and
Augustus had renounced as not worth the bones of Roman
soldiers, was invaded in A.D. 43 by the Emperor Claudius—
probably for economic rather than for military reasons—and
was reduced by slow and methodical stages. After two tentative
advances into Scotland (c. A.D. 80 and 140), the Roman boundary
was finally (c. A.D. 185) established between the Tyne and
Solway estuaries, where Hadrian had previously (c. A.D. 125)
constructed an elaborate set of fortifications. Dacia, where a
native king had built up a formidable power, was annexed in
A.D. 106 by Trajan, as a safeguard for his Balkan provinces.
These conquests did not add to the strength of the Roman
frontier; yet on the whole the empire remained a compact and
easily defensible ring of territories. Moreover, the actual
boundary zones were systematically reinforced with forts and
signal towers, or with continuous barriers (as in Britain, Germany,
and Roumania), which served to keep out the more dangerous
mounted raiders; large base camps were established within
easy reach of the frontier-line; and the defences of the entire
empire were rendered coherent by an ever-tightening network
of roads (p. 138). To meet the needs of a more static warfare,
the Roman army was partly remodelled. While the legionary
infantry still provided its core, at least one half of the total
establishment came to consist of 'auxiliary' companies of light
infantry and mounted troops. But while the details of drill and
equipment changed, the professional spirit of the force remained
as high as ever.

Under the shelter of the imperial armies the Roman territories
enjoyed a long immunity from invasion. Outside the frontier
regions many towns dispensed with their ring walls, and an atmosphere of security pervaded the empire, such as its constituent
countries have never recaptured since its fall.

The benefits of the imperial régime were nowhere more
manifest than in the Roman provinces, whose number underwent a steady increase, whether by fresh conquest or, more
commonly, by the gradual absorption of the dependent kingdoms.
In the 'imperial' provinces (of which the emperor was the
titular proconsul) the acting governors held their posts for an

adequate term of years (usually three to five), and they had at their side trained staffs of procurators, who either collected the revenue directly or exercised a close control over the tax-farmers. The network of roads which now bound the empire together also served the needs of an improved administration. By the institution of a *cursus publicus* or government postal service Augustus was able to make a closer contact with his agents in the provinces and to keep them constantly under his supervision. In the provinces which remained under senatorial control the governors were recruited, as before, from the ex-consuls and ex-praetors, and the terms of office remained short. But the failures of senatorial nominees could now be made good by the emperor's exercise of his *maius imperium,* and the governors, senatorial as well as imperial, had now to reckon with the *concilia* or parliaments of the provinces. These assemblies, consisting of deputies from the several towns or districts of each province, were convened annually to discuss matters of general concern to their constituents; and they proved an effective instrument for collecting evidence against bad governors and forwarding it to Rome. Though extortion in the provinces was never quite suppressed, the standard of administration under the emperors was appreciably higher than under the Republic. The local self-government which the provinces had enjoyed in republican times remained undiminished, and newly formed cities had no difficulty in obtaining charters to safeguard their liberties.

Nay more, the status of the provincials underwent a profound change, in consequence of their progressive absorption of Greek or Roman culture, and of their admission to service in the Roman army (p. 80). Following the lead which Caesar had given in this matter (p. 75), the emperors gradually extended the Roman franchise to non-Italian peoples; and they admitted selected individuals of provincial origin into their professional service, or enrolled them by a newly assumed power of adlectio or direct nomination into the Senate. The process of enfranchisement was accelerated after A.D. 98, when Trajan, a native of Spain, was raised to the seat of Augustus; in 212 it was completed by the Emperor Caracalla. Henceforth every free native of the Roman dominions was *ipso facto* a Roman citizen, and if he possessed a certain standard of wealth and education he could rise to the highest offices of state, irrespective of his origin. Thus the Roman Empire, which had taken its rise in military conquest, like the Hellenistic monarchies, ended by realizing the forgotten dream of Alexander about a partnership of victors and vanquished (p. 45).

The general sense of security within the empire, and the wide extension of its road system, combined to stimulate every branch of economic production and to create a new world-trade (pp. 122–3). This spurt of economic activity was reflected in the growth of new towns, especially in provinces where urban life had hitherto not struck roots,

Lastly, the rise of material prosperity, the growth of city life, and the more rapid movement of population brought about a wide diffusion of Greek and Roman culture. In the eastern provinces the process of hellenization which had begun under Alexander's successors gained fresh impetus under the Roman emperors. In western and central Europe and in North Africa the spread of Roman civilization went on at an even greater pace. In these regions the Roman garrisons, and the settlements of veterans, many of whom were grouped together in colonies of the old Italian type (p. 60), contributed powerfully to the adoption of the Latin tongue and of Roman habits of life. At the same time Roman civilization was now attaining a position of parity with that of Greece, and the combined Graeco-Roman culture which has been transmitted to us was taking definite shape (p. 260 ff.).

12. THE DECLINE OF THE ROMAN EMPIRE

In the later years of the second century the Roman world was showing signs of becoming hard-set. New land was no longer being brought into cultivation, and in the absence of fresh technical inventions economic production achieved no further growth. In art and literature new ideas were no longer finding expression. This arrest of progress, it is true, had not yet passed over into the stage of actual decay, and need not have done so, if the Roman Empire had continued to enjoy political stability. But in the third century the Roman state was shaken to its foundations.

The Second Roman Revolution, like the previous one that destroyed the Republic, was set in motion by the Roman army. After a hundred years of improved discipline the soldiers resumed the game of emperor-making, in pursuit of which they fought another round of civil wars (A.D. 193–7). They were temporarily reduced to order by the winner of this competition, Septimius Severus, who repeated the work of Vespasian, but with less enduring success. In A.D. 235 the troops threw away all restraint, and during the next fifty years they set up and knocked down emperors like ninepins.

The military anarchy of this period proved a turning-point in Roman history, because it brought on the age of the Germanic invasions. These inroads were not so much due to any growing pressure of population or rising political ambition among the Germanic tribes, as to the standing invitation which the Roman army gave to intruders by its absorption in domestic warfare, and the consequent depletion of the frontier garrisons. With an open road before them, the Goths overran the Balkan peninsula and penetrated into Asia Minor; the Alamanni poured into northern Italy; the Franks made their way across France into Spain (A.D. 250–268). The final collapse of the Roman Empire seemed at hand, when a fortunate hazard produced a succession of Rome's greatest emperors. Among these Aurelian (A.D. 270–5), the 'Restitutor Orbis', repeated the labours of Hercules by marching indefatigably from one war zone to another and mending all the broken fronts. Diocletian (284–305) spent twenty years in reorganizing the disordered government, and Constantine (323–37) enlisted the spiritual forces of the Christian Church to knit the empire together again. But for the loss of the outlying territory of Dacia, the Roman Empire of Constantine's day stood virtually undiminished in extent.

Nevertheless the crisis of the third century left an indelible mark upon the Roman world. Under the stress of the military anarchy and the barbarian invasions the constitution of Augustus broke down; Diocletian and Constantine did not destroy it, but merely swept away its fragments. The republican magistracies were discontinued or faded into mere titles of honour, and the sessions of the Senate were reduced to pure formalities. More serious, the traditions of local self-government which had been preserved since the days of the Republic died out, as the impoverished municipal aristocracies were driven to shirk the offices which they had formerly coveted. The emperors assumed the absolute power of Oriental despotism and introduced the pomp and ceremonial of Asiatic sultans into their Court. The professional executive, which had grown to enormous numbers and had acquired a rigid organization, exercised a pervasive control over the helpless citizen body. But a collateral authority to that of the emperors and their professional staff was now growing up in two quarters. The principal landowners, who had profited by the recent confusion to accumulate vast territories into their hands, began to constitute these as quasi-independent states within the larger state. The Christian clergy, who had received full liberty of worship from Constantine, were raised by his successors into a privileged class and became a political power. The Roman Empire was entering on that process of transformation which gave rise to the Medieval state.

III

The Material Background

I. FOOD AND DRINK

THE DIFFERENCE between the civilization of the Greeks and Romans and that of the present world rests not so much on the disparity of their political activities, of their intellectual life and moral habits, as of their material equipment. The imperfect control of the Greeks and Romans over the forces of Nature was a fundamental handicap which they never overcame. Consequently the forms of their private life and their economic structure never attained that high degree of elaboration which characterizes the culture of the present day. But this deep-seated contrast between their civilization and ours is the result of a comparatively recent event, the Industrial Revolution of the eighteenth and nineteenth centuries. From the material point of view, the dividing line between Ancient and Modern should be drawn in the age of Watt and Lavoisier. The material basis of ancient life was not radically distinct from that of the Middle Ages, or even of the Tudor and Stuart periods of English history.

The climate and general conditions of life in Mediterranean lands are conducive to frugal habits of diet. But in ancient times such habits were as much a matter of necessity as of preference, for the variety of foodstuffs was then far smaller than that which the modern world commands. Many kinds of food and drink which now are objects of mass consumption were either wholly unknown to the Greeks and Romans, or remained articles of luxury to them, because difficulties of transport and preservation raised their price beyond the reach of the ordinary purse.

The principal nourishment of the Greeks and Romans consisted of grain. Their daily ration of cereal food was more generous than that of most Britons. The daily allowance of bread in the British army is sixteen ounces. Roman soldiers and slaves engaged on active work, received two Roman pounds (*c*. twenty-six ounces avoirdupois); and the Law of the Twelve Tables prescribed a minimum ration of one Roman pound to an enslaved debtor. If barley (a less nutritious and digestible grain) was served out, the daily quantity was double that of wheat.

But the variety of their cereal foods was relatively restricted. Maize, an American plant, was unknown to them. Oats, which are ill suited to the dry Mediterranean summer, were not cultivated on any large scale, and rye was looked upon with disfavour. Rice was imported from India, but not in large quantities, and partly for manufacture into face-powder. Barley was the regular animal fodder, and it also served as the staple foodstuff in the Greek homeland, whose soil is mostly too thin to support other cereals. But wheat was consumed by such Greeks as could grow it, or could afford to import it from abroad; and it was the universal breadstuff of Italy.

In the preparation of barley the husks were first steamed off on a hot-plate; the resultant 'pearl-barley' was ground, and then moulded into a paste with an admixture of milk, oil, or honey. The paste was formed into cakes, which were toasted but not baked. The wheat of the early Italians ('far'), being a coarse and husky grain that did not lend itself to baking, was boiled into a porridge resembling the 'polenta' of the modern Italian peasant. The Greek wheat (Lat. *frumentum*) was of a finer texture, and suitable for making into bread. It was transplanted by the Greek colonists to Italy and Sicily, and by the third or second century B.C. it had generally displaced the native 'far'. The *frumentum* was ground with stone rollers which produced a wholemeal flour; for fastidious folk who preferred a dead-white bread the flour was mixed with chalk or bleached with sea-water. The bread was baked into flat loaves, with wine-lees for leaven. Cakes and biscuits were also made in the baker's oven; but macaroni was unknown, and puddings of a starchy consistency were not prepared.

The commonest adjunct to the cereal food was a vegetable. The two American plants, the potato and tomato, were unknown; but leaf vegetables and legumina (peas, beans, lentils) were consumed in many varieties. The bulbous plants (onions, leeks, garlic) were much relished by the poorer people; and olives, fresh or pickled, were almost a necessity of life.

Of the animal foods, meat was not in regular demand, except among the well-to-do. Under the Greek and Roman system of pasturing (p. 109) there was no lack of winter food for grazing beasts, and no need to slaughter off the herds in autumn, as in Medieval England; but the Mediterranean climate does not induce a large appetite for animal fats. Roman soldiers previous to the third century A.D. received no regular meat ration, and in many households the only flesh consumed was that of a sacrificial animal on occasional festival days. Poultry was a fashionable fare of the rich; pork and ham were the popular favourites. Eggs, being difficult to store, were a seasonal food or a luxury.

Among the seaboard populations fish and the smaller marine animals (*It.*: 'frutti di mare') formed a big part of the popular diet. Fishing for tunnies or sardines was the staple industry of many small coastal towns, which pickled their surplus catch for export. But the inland populations rarely tasted fresh fish. Wealthy gourmets reared lampreys or mullets in their private ponds, or imported oysters from countries as far distant as Britain.

The consumption of milk in the cities was severely restricted by the difficulty of transport and preservation. On the country-side it was naturally more plentiful, but the milking herds consisted of goats and sheep rather than of cows (p. 109). A large proportion of the milk was converted into cheese. The softer cream-cheeses were a luxury of the rich; the more durable goat's-cheese provided the popular fare. Butter was not made, except for external application as an ointment. Its place as a cooking ingredient was taken by olive oil, which was easier to conserve. The 'butter-eating' Thracians were an object of amusement or disgust to their Greek neighbours.

The dessert-tables of the Greeks and Romans were not so well garnished as the present-day export trade of fruit from Medi-terranean lands might suggest. The summer sunshine of the Mediterranean produces fruit of the choicest quality, but its summer drought is unfavourable to mass-cultivation (p. 6). For this reason native species like the apple, pear, and plum, and

Asiatic plants that had been successfully acclimatized, the cherry, peach, and apricot, were relatively scarce. Of the other Oriental fruits, oranges were as yet unknown, and the only species of lemon under cultivation was a bitter citron.[1] Neither were the European berry fruits widely grown. Mass-consumption of fruit was therefore confined to the fig and the grape, or raisin. In the remoter uplands the sweet chestnut served as a popular foodstuff.

For the predominantly vegetarian fare of the Greeks and Romans seasoning materials were an essential adjunct. The shallow lagoons that fringe part of the Mediterranean coast are natural factories of solar salt: the traffic in this condiment was one of the earliest bonds of union between the seaboard and the inland. Aromatic herbs grow in abundance on the Mediterranean hill-sides, and vegetable spices of many varieties were cultivated in the ancient kitchen-gardens. The relative scarcity of pepper, which was little known before the opening up of trade with India (p. 123) was therefore of little account. The sugar-cane was discovered by Alexander's army in India, but it was not acclimatized in Mediterranean lands; and the extraction of sugar from beet remained a secret to the ancient world.[2] But the Mediterranean uplands, being rich in strongly scented flowers, are a natural haunt of bees, and the intensive apiculture of the Greeks and Romans (p. 110) gave rise to a large production of honey.

The list of Greek and Roman beverages was even more restricted than that of their foodstuffs. The modern infusion drinks were altogether unknown. The coffee berry escaped the attention of Greek travellers in Arabia, and tea was not included among the commodities of trade with China (p. 121). The process of distilling spirits also remained undiscovered. Beer was a popular drink in Egypt and Babylonia, and among the peoples of central and western Europe; but since it was brewed

[1] The bitter orange was introduced into the Mediterranean by the Saracens, the sweet variety by the Portuguese. The currant-vine was not grown in Greece until modern times.

[2] Mediterranean cane was the principal source of sugar in Europe from the time of its introduction by the Saracens until the eighteenth century, when the process of extraction from beet was discovered.

without hops, like the ale of the Middle Ages, and therefore was insipid to the taste, it did not gain favour among Greeks and Romans. The only common beverages of the Greek and Roman world were therefore water and wine.

The spring water of Mediterranean lands is not only copious but highly palatable, and where a good local source was not available the Greeks and Romans would go long distances to find a plentiful supply (pp. 105–6). Like their modern descendants, they recognized the medicinal value of water-drinking: the proverb 'Water is best' has a Greek origin. But even among the poorest the water was frequently flavoured with wine, which was produced on such a scale as to come within the reach of the slenderest purse (p. 111). The cheapest brands, it is true, were so sour as to resemble vinegar, and they kept so badly that they were sometimes strengthened with an admixture of resin (a practice which survives in modern Greece). But the inferior varieties were made more palatable by spicing and sweetening, like the 'mulled wine' of the Middle Ages, and when served with hot water they made a tolerable substitute for tea and coffee. The choicer Greek and Italian wines were probably quite comparable with good modern ones. The best vintage years were red-letter dates in the calendars of connoisseurs, and ancient Romans smacked their lips over the product of 121 B.C. ('when Opimius was consul'), as we do over 1893 champagne or 1934 hock. But even the best wines of the ancients were usually diluted with water: two parts of water to one of wine was a not uncommon ratio.

The frugality of Greek and Roman diet simplified the task of preparing meals. In the towns the bread was made at bakehouses, and cooking operations in the poorer homes required nothing more than a small hearth or brazier. The well-to-do households had their separate kitchens, and slaves to dress and serve the food; on special occasions they might hire a professional chef to prepare a dinner and to write out the menu in Doric Greek (corresponding to our culinary French). The number of set meals did not as a rule exceed two. Breakfast usually consisted of a morsel of bread, a relish, and a sip of wine—the ancient equivalent of our coffee and rolls. Lunch was a more

substantial repast, which might include eggs, fish, or meat.
But the principal meal was dinner, which came after the day's
work or afternoon exercise, and might be served at any time
after three o'clock. Even in simple bourgeois households
dinner might consist of four or five courses—an hors-d'œuvre,
two or three substantial dishes, and dessert. When guests were
present, a drinking bout sometimes followed, at which the wine-
cup might be passed round until long after nightfall (pp. 148–9).

The Greeks adopted from the Orientals, and passed on to the
Romans, the curious custom of reclining on a couch at the
principal meal. The diners, being propped up on their left
elbows, had only one free hand, and could not cut up their food
at the table. All the necessary carving was therefore done
beforehand by the attendants; knives and forks were not laid,
and spoons were provided only for eggs and snails and other
elusive foods. The more solid fare was taken with the fingers,
which were afterwards wiped on a napkin or a piece of dough,
or rinsed in a rosebowl. The plates and cups of the poor were
made of earthenware; the wealthier classes used fine pottery,
silver, or glass, and spread a cloth upon the table.

2. DRESS

The commonest dress material among the Greeks and Romans
was wool. A short-staple silk was spun from the cocoon of a
native silkworm in Asia Minor, and small consignments of the
finer Chinese thread were imported under the Roman emperors
(p. 123). But silken garments, even when mixed with linen,
always remained rare articles of luxury. Cotton was discovered
by the Greeks in India, and was perhaps acclimatized by them
in Egypt. But despite its suitability to the Mediterranean
climate it was never more than a 'fancy' stuff: perhaps it could
not be drawn into a sufficiently firm thread by ancient hand-
spinning methods (p. 116). Flax is indigenous in Europe, and
linen cloth was prepared from it since prehistoric times. In the
Greek and Roman world it was the chief substitute for wool;
but it was regarded as a treacherous material, on account of
its non-absorbent character. Its use was mainly confined to

women, and it was avoided by those who spent much time out of doors. Wool, on the other hand, was both a safe and a cheap material. Sheep are particularly well adapted to Mediterranean conditions of pasturage (p. 109), and they were the commonest of ancient grazing beasts. For workaday wear the Greeks and Romans left the wool in self-colour; the poorer folk preferred a fleece with a dark strain in it, so as to produce a grey or dun cloth. On festal occasions both sexes wore brightly coloured costumes. Their most highly prized dyestuff was extracted from the purple shell, whose juice could be boiled to various intermediate shades between red and blue, or to a *sang-de-bœuf* colour with a rich lustre. Their ordinary dyes were of vegetable origin (saffron, madder, woad). The festal attire of men and women was also decked out with embroidery.

Magistrates and priests usually wore a distinctive dress. At Rome only citizens appeared in a toga (pp. 98); the higher officials (including the emperors) had a purple edging round their toga, and consuls or emperors celebrating a triumph (p. 152) were resplendent in full purple costume.[1] But in general the cut of Greek and Roman clothes showed no great diversity between the sexes, or between rich and poor; and the play of fashion was less rapid and less fanciful than at the present day.

The most universally worn garment was a long shirt or gown, which was either fastened at the side with pins or (more usually) passed over the head (Lat. *tunica*). It was worn by men down to the knees. and by women to the ankles, but it could be shortened by rucking up the skirt through a belt. It was made with an overlap at the top, so as to give a double thickness of material over chest and shoulders, but it had no sleeves, or only short ones.[2] It was usually the sole garment of slaves, of workers requiring the free use of their limbs, and of leisured persons in the privacy of their homes.

[1] A purple-bordered toga was also worn by Roman boys, at any rate of the wealthier classes. A 'toga candida', i.e. a garment made snow-white with pipe-clay was the special dress of Roman canvassers for office. Hence they were called 'candidati' ('whited men').

[2] The Greek 'chiton' (as the inner garment was called) was of either 'Doric' or 'Ionic' type. The former was a woollen garment that fell in heavy folds, the latter was a looser costume of linen which bunched into many small crinkles.

For out-of-door wear, those who wished to be correctly dressed put on an ample outer raiment (Lat. *pallium*), which was draped over the body like a plaid or shawl. In its most usual form it was a rectangular piece of cloth, about 12 by 5 feet, which the wearer first folded lengthwise down the middle, then passed over the left shoulder, round the back and front, and again over the left shoulder. The 'toga' worn by the Roman men had cut-away edges, but was broader in the middle and longer—under the early emperors its measurements grew to 12 or 15 by 9 feet—and consequently trailed down to the feet in heavy bunching folds. Though it was long cherished as a distinctive national garb, and remained *de rigueur* for all public occasions, it was gradually discarded for daily wear in favour of the shorter and less unwieldy pallium: some Romans even went so far as to reserve their toga for the day of their burial. The draping of toga and pallium alike required considerable skill, and the mark of a well-dressed person lay in his ability to make them 'sit' easily.

During spells of cold weather an inner tunica would be worn, and for protection against rain a poncho of thick felted wool would be slipped over the head. Soldiers carried capes, under the Roman emperors the troops in Britain and other northern countries adopted the native custom of wearing *bracae* or trousers.

The Greeks and Romans ordinarily went bare-headed; but travellers and workers in the open air wore broad-brimmed hats of felt and straw, or caps of leather, and ladies carried parasols. Neckwear, gloves, and stockings were not in use, except among invalids. Rustics shod themselves with stout boots or clogs. Townsfolk preferred foot-gear with open-work uppers;[1] indoors they went barefoot, or in light slippers.

Rings were common to both sexes; men wore them with seals attached, or as amulets, or (at Rome) as marks of rank.[2] Jewellery was an essential part of the wealthier women's outfit: with the growth of eastern commerce (p. 123) the importation of precious

---

[1] Boots with solid uppers were considered *comme il faut* for senators and other persons of rank.

[2] At Rome betrothal rings also were worn.

stones into Rome at times upset the balance of trade and gave point to the inevitable complaints about female luxuriousness.

Greek women of all ages were in the habit of 'doing up' their hair with the help of pins or combs or nets. Roman women of the republican period made more sparing use of such aids, but under the emperors society ladies adopted elaborate coiffures, with frequent changes of style. The men of early Greece and Rome wore their hair long and were bearded. After the Persian Wars the Greeks gave their skulls a moderately close crop, and Alexander of Macedon introduced among them the custom of shaving the chin. The Romans began to wear their hair short about 300 B.C., and not long afterwards they copied the new Greek habit of clean-shaving. A reaction to hirsuteness was instigated by the Emperor Hadrian, who grew a beard to conceal a scar on his cheek, and the Roman world in general made a virtue of its ruler's necessity. But fashion was reversed once more by Constantine, who returned to clean-shaving.[1] The Romans never adopted the Celtic custom of wearing a moustache only.

The only soap known to the ancients was a preparation made with potash from sea-kelp. But this substance was apparently used as a hair-dye, by means of which dark tresses were turned into blonde or Venetian gold, rather than as a detersive agency. The place of soap among the Greeks and Romans was taken by olive oil, which also served as an embrocation. Powdered pumice-stone did duty as a dentifrice. The use of perfumes attained a wide vogue, especially after the growth of trade with the eastern countries, and it was not wholly confined to one sex.

Linen clothes were simply scoured and soused in water. The more absorbent woollen articles could not be properly washed at home, but had to be sent to professional cleaners, who treated them with fuller's earth or other alkaline substances. But the whole problem of ablutions was simplified for the Greeks and Romans by the dryness of the Mediterranean summer, and by the general absence of smoke-pollution in their cities.

[1] The Emperor Julian (A.D. 360–3), in his futile endeavour to revert to old-fashioned paganism, not only wore a beard, but allowed it to collect vermin. The fashion did not survive him.

3. HOUSING

In the Greek and Roman world the peasantry mostly dwelt in cottages of wood or rammed clay, the poorer townsfolk in tenements or garrets of timber. The wealthier classes in early times built houses of sun-dried brick on stone foundations; but from the fourth or third century B.C. they used more durable materials. The surviving Greek houses (mostly at Olynthus, Priene, and Delos), and the earlier ones discovered at Pompeii, were made of stone. From the second century the Italians used concrete with stone linings for their walls; under the emperors they replaced the stone facings with burnt brick.

In view of the general disappearance of the poorer dwellings, only those of the more well-to-do classes can be described in detail. The Greek houses were mostly of the quadrangle type, with rooms opening on an inner court of oblong shape. The principal living-rooms and bedrooms were usually on the side farthest from the street entrance; the other sides contained the offices, storerooms, and servants' quarters. Except in the larger towns, the houses were mostly built in one or two storeys. A suite of rooms on the upper floor or at the back of the house was sometimes set apart as a women's quarter.

The Pompeian houses were also of the inward-facing type; but the earlier ones were more square in plan, and the place of the Greek courtyard was taken by a tank, corresponding to an opening in the roof which let in both sun and rain. In the second century B.C. the wealthier residents began to expand their premises, so that henceforth the typical large house at Pompeii was of a composite type, with a front part ('atrium') on the old Italian plan, and a rear portion consisting of a Greek courtyard dwelling ('peristylium'). In such double houses the atrium was reserved for receptions, and the living apartments were grouped round the peristyle. Pompeian houses sometimes rose to two or three storeys, but were generally built low. In Greek and Roman towns the house walls usually bordered on the street, but a small garden was sometimes laid out at the back, and a shrubbery and fountains would adorn the centre of the peristyle.

At Ostia, where a rapid growth of population in the first two centuries A.D. caused a pressure upon house-space, the more well-to-do residents took suites of rooms in blocks of flats with four or five storeys, whose general appearance probably bore a close resemblance to the residential flats of modern European cities. At Rome the dwelling-houses rose continually in height, until the emperors fixed the building limit at sixty or seventy feet. It is not unlikely that in the larger towns of the Roman Empire the tall-fronted type of house became the more usual.

The country villas naturally exhibited a wide variety of plan. The majority were plain farm-houses with a central court. Others, which served as holiday residences for men of wealth, were elaborately furnished, with multiple suites of rooms, and stood amid extensive grounds laid out in formal style with pergolas and hedges of box-wood.

The ground floors of Greek and Roman houses were not made of timber (which in a hot summer climate tends to become a breeding-place for vermin), but consisted of beaten earth overlaid with concrete or stone paving. In the larger rooms small coloured stones were often arranged in mosaic patterns—a custom that originated in Greece but also became popular in Italy and the western provinces.[1] In winter carpets or rugs were laid down.

The courtyard houses, which received an abundance of daylight from inside, had only a few windows, which in earlier days were filled with lattice-work, but from the time of Augustus were often provided with glass panes (p. 116). The outer walls of this type of house were mostly finished with a plain coating of plaster or limewash. The façades of the blocks at Ostia, on the other hand, were diversified with large windows and balconies. The inner walls of the more important rooms were coated with fine stucco and adorned with fresco painting. In the earlier Pompeian houses the painting was executed in formal patterns; in the later ones, and in a few surviving residences at Rome, it included landscapes, portraits, and more especially scenes from

---

[1] The recent American excavations at Antioch have brought to light many fine mosaics in the houses of the Roman period.

Greek mythology (p. 234). To meet the needs of a hot summer climate, the rooms were built high: in some of the larger apartments they measured twenty-five feet in height.

The roofs, which covered the sides of the house only, were flat or low-pitched; they were lined with interlocking tiles.

The earlier Greek and Italian houses had no internal water-supply, except perhaps a well or cistern in the courtyard, and their sewerage was collected in cesspools. By the first century B.C., however, water was commonly laid on to the ground floor from street pipes; latrines were fitted with a water-flush, and the waste was carried off to the street drains. Under the Roman emperors even the camps on remote frontiers were provided with good sanitation.

Heating arrangements were usually inadequate. The early Italians burnt logs on an open hearth in the atrium; their descendants made shift with portable charcoal braziers. Roman residences in northerly climates were commonly fitted with a 'hypocaust' system of central heating, which circulated hot air from a cellar-furnace underneath the hollow floors of the principal apartments and conveyed it up the walls by means of pipes. But the ancient Mediterranean peoples, like their modern descendants, were inured to an occasional spell of cold weather, and as a rule they made no elaborate provision against it.

The commonest form of artificial lighting was by means of small lamps of clay or bronze resembling covered saucers, and burning olive oil through a woollen wick; they were lit with sulphur matches or a flint-and-steel apparatus. They produced a dull and murky flame and were apt to make a reek, so that the composition of ancient authors who burnt the midnight oil might literally smell of the lamp. But the lack of better illuminants was not felt severely, for the general habit was to rise with the sun and to retire not long after its setting.

The furniture of Greek and Roman houses was scanty, but the surviving pieces are mostly of good workmanship and elegant shape. Men of wealth would pay fancy prices for tables of marqueterie and fine bed-linen.

4. TOWNS

The civilization of the Greeks and Romans was essentially urban. The practice of clustering together into cities, which originated in the requirements of common defence (p. 19), lived on in days when the shelter of ring walls was no longer needed, for the social and economic advantages of city life made a strong appeal to Greeks and Italians, and they also commended themselves in varying degrees to the foreign peoples who came under their influence.[1] The eventual number of towns in the Roman Empire therefore rose to several thousands. But the very multitude of these towns indicates that as a rule they were not of large dimensions. In the ancient world there was no need for the concentration of machine-power, which has been the prime factor in the making of monster modern cities; and ancient methods of transport were hardly adequate to the feeding of great multitudes. Athens in the days of Pericles is estimated to have contained at most a quarter million inhabitants; Syracuse and Carthage probably rose to the same total; Alexandria surpassed the half-million mark; and Rome under the emperors had a population of a million or over. But these towns owed their size to political considerations or to a specially favourable situation for commerce. The area of most Greek and Roman cities did not exceed four hundred acres (the size of Hyde Park), and did not contain more than fifty thousand inhabitants.

The earliest towns of Greece and Italy were built with a view to military strength rather than to convenience or fine appearance. Their streets were narrow and irregular, without pavement or drains. Apart from the market-place, they had few open spaces in the centre, and no public buildings, save perhaps a temple or two, to attract the eye. But the wealth which they acquired, and the municipal patriotism which they fostered, eventually brought about a transformation in them.

The planning of towns suggested itself to the Greeks and Romans as a result of their colonizing activities: the systematic

[1] The growth of towns was especially vigorous in North Africa. The Celtic and Danubian peoples took less kindly to urbanization.

apportionment of allotments in the colonial settlements led by an easy progression to the public control of building sites. An example of comprehensive planning was set by the Athenians in the fifth century, when they laid out their new harbour, the Piraeus, on a virgin site; and their lead was extensively followed in the Hellenistic age, when Greek cities sprang up in mushroom fashion in the lands conquered by Alexander. At Alexandria, and on other level and open sites, the city architects laid down a simple checkboard pattern; but elsewhere they showed great skill in adapting their schemes to the natural framework provided by mountains or rivers. Under the Roman emperors the tendency to regularity and symmetry in town plans tended to become excessive. In old-established cities a comprehensive re-alignment of the streets was not practicable, and neither Athens nor Rome succeeded in straightening out all its labyrinths. But at Rome Caesar and various emperors took in hand the patching of the central areas, and Nero made good use of the opportunities afforded by a great conflagration in A.D. 64, which burnt out several quarters of the city.

The ancient town-planners made their streets run straight, but they left them narrow. They usually provided one capacious main road across the centre of the city: at Alexandria a boulevard one hundred feet in width ran the whole length of the town, and at Rome a 'Via Sacra' was laid out for the use of processions to the Forum and Capitol. But the main streets as a rule did not exceed twenty to thirty feet in width, and the side roads were mere alleys.[1] Wheeled traffic was therefore prohibited or restricted in some towns, and carriages were replaced by litters; at Rome the streets were closed to wheeled vehicles in the daytime. But the narrowness of the roads gave shelter from the sun—an important consideration in Mediterranean lands, and one which in ancient times at least outweighed the inconvenience of traffic restrictions.

In every town which could afford the outlay, and in some which could not, the public buildings made a brave display. The pride of the whole city was engaged in them; public money

[1] On hilly sites the side streets were often cut into steps, as is still usual in smaller Mediterranean towns.

was freely expended on them, and the wealthier residents would seek to immortalize themselves by lavish contributions to the building funds. The earliest showpieces of Greek and Roman architecture were temples. Then followed porticoes and basilicæ (covered halls, usually constructed with internal rows of columns to hold the roof); next came gymnasia, race-courses, theatres and amphitheatres, and baths. Under the Roman emperors it became the fashion to flank the main streets with continuous colonnades. In the ruins of Palmyra a pillared street extending over more than half a mile may still be seen; another, at Antioch, is said to have measured three miles.

The material for public buildings was usually the best available stone. Only a few cities could afford temples constructed wholly of marble, such as the Parthenon and Erechtheum at Athens, and the shrine which Augustus raised to Apollo on the Palatine, or to line their edifices with marble façades. But the limestone formations of the Mediterranean lands provide an abundance of durable material for masonry, and where inferior stone was used it would be overlaid with stucco or terra-cotta revetments. At Rome the emperors also made some notable experiments in the use of concrete and linings of stone or burnt brick (pp. 222–3).

At Athens the Golden Age of public building began under Peisistratus, and reached its climax under Pericles. Rome in the republican era made only sporadic attempts to beautify itself; but between the time of Caesar and that of Hadrian it became the chief showplace as well as the capital of the empire. A special feature of imperial Rome was the chain of new *fora*. (open spaces flanked with porticoes and shops) which extended from the old republican Forum to the Campus Martius. In general, the age of Hadrian and Antoninus was the period at which the cities of the empire attained their greatest outward splendour.

One of the earliest and latest objects of public expenditure in Greek and Roman cities was a good supply of water, which in some cases was brought in from a distance of thirty or even fifty miles. The water was sometimes conveyed in pipe-lines following the rise and fall of the ground; but to save the risk of bursting pipes[1] the ancient engineers preferred to keep the water flowing at a uniform rate, and to this end they would tunnel through hills and span the valleys with arcades, like the makers of modern railway tracks.

At Rome the construction of aqueducts went on intermittently from 300 B.C. to A.D. 100; the Aqua Marcia, built *c.* 150 B.C., remains in use at the present day. It is estimated that the eventual daily inflow of water into Rome amounted to eighty gallons per head of population, or twice the present ration of residents in London. In the provinces the 'puente' of Segovia in Spain, and the Pont du Gard near Nîmes (both of uncertain date), still bear eloquent testimony to the material benefits of Roman rule.

The provision of drains for the off-flow of waste water was mainly a work of the last three centuries B.C. Underground systems had become the general rule by the time of Augustus.

The paving of the town streets mostly fell within the same period. The streets of Rome were laid with stone flags between 250 and 150 B.C. At Pompeii raised footwalks were provided alongside the carriageways.

In some cities lamps were hung up to illuminate the streets after nightfall: the city of Antioch, it is said, 'took the sunlight in small change' by night. But it is doubtful whether street lighting became common. In view of the early-to-bed habits of ancient peoples, it was not urgently necessary.[2]

After the Persian Wars the Athenians began to plant copses of plane-trees on the outskirts of their city. Their example was followed in the Hellenistic towns. The palace quarter at Alexandria stood inside a large park, and Antioch was famous for the garden suburb of Daphne. Rome was fringed with a garden area since the later days of the Republic, when wealthy personages laid out pleasure-grounds for themselves on several sides of the city. In the days of Caesar and Augustus part of this garden-belt was converted into public parks.

---

[1] The Greeks and Romans, being unable to manufacture cast iron (p. 117), lacked a material for water-mains that was at once strong and inexpensive.

[2] Nocturnal travellers sometimes had a 'link boy' with a torch to escort them.

At the time of their highest development the towns of the Greek and Roman world would probably have borne comparison with those of Europe in the eighteenth or early nineteenth century. But in the age of the barbarian invasions that followed they suffered a general decline. Their inhabitants were able to defy the invaders behind their ring walls, which they had repaired after a long period of neglect. But they were the chief losers by the economic decay which now set in (p. 123). The public-spirited municipal aristocracies which had been their financial mainstay were ruined, and the territorial magnates who survived from the economic wreckage retired from the towns to their self-contained estates. In the eastern provinces, which lay off the main track of the invasions, the towns maintained something of their former style under the early Byzantine emperors; but in Italy and the greater part of Europe they reverted to what they had been at the outset, fortresses in a war zone.

5. AGRICULTURE

By far the most important source of wealth for the Greeks and Romans was agriculture. Their population was chiefly engaged in work on the land; the ownership of real estate was held by them in the highest esteem; colonization was mainly directed to lands awaiting development; and the cry of the discontented was not 'more wages and shorter hours,' but 'more land allotments'. In the Roman world more especially the landowner was preponderant both in the economic and in the political sphere.

The greater part of the cultivable land was used for the production of the cereal crops which were the staple articles of consumption in the Greek and Roman diet. The ordinary method of tillage was by a two-year shift, a system which is still common in Mediterranean countries. After the taking of a crop the land was left untouched during the autumn and winter. In the following spring it was cut open with a shallow ox-drawn plough, and this operation was repeated before the hardening of the ground under the summer drought, and again after the first autumn rains. This manifold preparation of the soil was all the more necessary, because the ploughshare, not being fitted with a shoulder, did not overturn the sod, and because the work of the plough was not supplemented with a harrow. Besides, by keeping the surface soil in a rough condition, it had the effect of conserving moisture and retarding evaporation under the summer sun.

As soon as the land had been made ready, it received the seed. Both wheat and barley were autumn-sown, and spring seed was used only in emergencies. The casting was done by hand, but the seed was subsequently drawn into rows with hand-rakes, or with a tail-board attached to a plough. This terminated the work of the fallow year.

In the spring of the harvest year the ground between the rows of sprouting corn was hoed and weeded. The harvest followed in early summer; June was the usual harvest month in Greece, and July in Italy. The ears were cut off near the top of the stalk by means of a hand-sickle, and were threshed with sticks, or under the hooves of oxen. The chaff was winnowed away by tossing the grain on a breezy day. The harvesting operations took a long time to complete, but in the set-fair weather of a Mediterranean midsummer there was no need to hurry them.

Improving landlords introduced many variations into the normal practice. They used ploughs with shoulders and deep-cutting blades, and covered the ground with these four or five or even nine times. They followed up the work of the plough with a harrow or a roller. They imported harvest machinery—rotary sickles from Gaul and threshing sledges from Carthage. They took a catch crop of vegetables or of some quick-growing cereal species after the main harvest. To restore the productivity of the soil they ploughed in autumn crops of fertilizing plants (beans or lupines.) But these experiments did not bring about a revolution in the standard methods of cultivation, which underwent little change from century to century.

The average yield of Greek and Roman cornfields is difficult to determine. Under a system of frequent ploughing and hoe cultivation it is probable that it at least equalled the modern average of twelve to fifteen bushels per acre in Mediterranean countries.[1] But the land produced a crop in alternate years

[1] The starting-point of improved cultivation in Britain during the eighteenth century was the introduction of the Mediterranean system of hoeing by Jethro Tull.

only, and the methods of tillage were so expensive in labour that a large exportable surplus could be produced only in districts of exceptional fertility such as the Nile valley, the 'black earth' region of Southern Russia, and the volcanic zones round Etna and Vesuvius. It is also not unlikely that the Greek and Roman system of cultivation had the effect of slowly impoverishing the land. The soil was protected against erosion in winter by careful ditching and draining, and by terracing the hill-sides. It was supplied with all the available fertilizers: all manner of vegetable manure was applied, and grazing animals were folded in winter on the stubble of the harvest-fields, or on the rough herbage that grew spontaneously on the fallow. But continuous cropping with wheat or barley, and the absence of any balanced system of rotations, probably caused a gradual loss of productivity.

In the Greek and Roman economy tillage was kept more separate from grazing than in modern countries where 'mixed farming' prevails. As a rule the only stock that was permanently carried on the crop-land consisted of the oxen required for draught work, and the mules or donkeys employed in odd jobs. For the greater part of the year these animals were stall-fed with barley or vegetables or chaff, and no special grazing-fields were set apart for them. Horses and cows were pastured in meadows irrigated by rivers or canals, but not in large numbers. Horses were in demand for warfare and racing, and for the traction of carriages and coaches, but on the farm and for the general work of transport they were replaced by oxen, asses, or mules; and cows were not required to any great extent as milk-producers (p. 93). Besides, the irrigable meadow-land in Mediterranean lands is severely limited: for the feeding of their dairy herds some enterprising landowners had recourse to cultivated grasses like alfalfa (as is now done in the dry regions of South Africa and America). Pigs were left free to feed on oak and beech mast in the woodlands, or were fattened in sties on millers' offal.

The principal grazing beasts were sheep and goats. These animals, being naturally adapted to a nomadic life, and being able to thrive alike on the wiry grass and scrub of the Mediterranean uplands and on the stubble and rough herbage of the winter fields in the plains, fitted excellently into the agrarian economy of the Greek and Roman world; and there was always a market for the sheep's fleeces and the goats' hair. Goats formed the principal stock of the small crofters; sheep were kept in large flocks by the more substantial landowners. Wherever political conditions permitted, the sheep were driven in springtime to the summer pastures of the uplands; in autumn they made a return journey to the valleys. On this system of alternate winter and summer grazings (which is still prevalent in Mediterranean countries) the flocks could be kept all the year round in the open, and the cost of steadings was thereby saved.[1] After the Roman conquest of Italy, which broke down the old antagonism between the hill and the plain, and gave rise to a regular code of rights of way, it became a not unusual practice to set a thousand head of beasts in movement in one drove, and their journey sometimes extended from the summer grazings of the Samnite mountains to the winter pastures of the Apulian coastlands.

While cereals in the Greek and Roman world were mostly cultivated for subsistence, pasturage was partly organized with a view to high profits. The grazing industry was attended with big risks, for ancient veterinary science had no adequate means of coping with outbreaks of disease among the herds; but under favourable conditions it was more remunerative than tillage.

The semi-nomadic conditions of Greek and Roman pasturage gave little scope for scientific stock-breeding. Pedigree rams were imported from Miletus, and stud horses from Cappadocia (a natural grazing-land in eastern Asia Minor). But the value of the Arab strain was not yet recognized, and it was left to the Byzantines to introduce into Europe the heavy war-horse of the Parthians and Armenians.

The baking sun of the Mediterranean summer ripens fruit to

---

[1] This system of grazing is to be found in modern Mediterranean lands; it is also practised on the East Highveld of Transvaal.

perfection, but the seasonal drought limits the area available for orchards. In ancient times the only fruit-trees to be planted on a large scale were the three drought-resisting species, the fig, the olive, and the vine; and of these the vine and the olive received particular attention.

The vine was introduced in prehistoric times from the Near East into Greece and was brought to Italy by the Greek colonists. Under Greek and Roman influence it eventually attained a similar range of cultivation as at the present day. In Mediterranean latitudes it is not limited to southward aspects, and it thrives alike on hill and on plain. Of all fruit plants it requires the most continuous and the most skilful tendance. The labour of the vineyard began in spring with the tying of the plants to their supports. For this purpose the ancient Italians, like their modern descendants, sometimes trailed the vines across the branches of live trees, but stakes or pergolae of dead timber were the more ordinary form of prop. The work went on through the summer with the hoeing or trenching of the soil round the roots, and with selective pruning of the tendrils: and the vintage operations lasted into October. But viticulture was the chief pride of the Mediterranean husbandman (as it remains to this day), and it was carried on so extensively that while its choicer products commanded a good return, the cheaper brands sometimes glutted the market and had to be disposed of at knockdown prices. In the Greek lands the finest wines were produced in the Aegean islands (notably in Thasos, Chios, Cos, and Rhodes). These vintages had no rival until the first century B.C., when the wines of Campania attained a similar standard of excellence.

The olive, which accompanied the vine on its travels from east to west, has a more restricted range of cultivation. Being unable to withstand frost, it is confined to the coast-lands and to the sheltered inland valleys. As it requires some twenty years of growth before it yields a full harvest, its production on a large scale entails a heavy outlay of capital. But it thrives even on thin and stony soil, such as the Mediterranean peasantry still collect in artificial terraces on the hill-sides; and its long tap-root reaches down to water-level in the driest of summers. Once established, it needs no further attention than an occasional pruning of branches and roots. The fruit is ready for picking in midwinter, a season at which farm hands might otherwise go unemployed, and in ancient times it had such a variety of uses that it could always find a market. The oil was consumed at table, in lamps, and at the gymnasia; the pulp was fed to cattle, and the lees were used as a disinfectant. The best olives were grown in Attica and (since the first century B.C.) in Campania and Apulia. Under Roman rule cultivation spread to Provence, to Valencia and Andalusia, and to Tunisia; eventually large quantities of oil were shipped to Rome from Spain and North Africa.

The large cities of the ancient world created around themselves the usual zones of intensive cultivation by market-gardeners and poultry-keepers. Their products included cultivated flowers, which the townsfolk required to brighten their banquets and carnivals, and to deck their graves. The strongly scented wild flowers of the Mediterranean countryside provide unlimited food for bees, and the Greeks and Romans not only took an imaginative interest in bee-hives as microcosmic city-states, but showed a practical concern for them as the source of their only sweetening material. Apiculture was therefore an important minor branch of land work, and care was exercised in providing the bees with clean and warm homes.

The Greeks and Romans acclimatized in their countries shade-giving trees such as the Oriental plane, which served to ornament their parks and gardens. But they gave no thought to the conservation of their natural supplies of timber by scientific forestry. Their lumbermen mined the forest areas, and after they had laid bare one mountain-side, they went on to despoil another. In ancient times the natural standings of timber sufficed to cover the needs of the towns for the purpose of house-construction and shipbuilding. The Greeks took toll of the woodlands of Macedonia, and when the city of Rome had exhausted the beech and chestnut copses of Latium and Etruria, it found alternative sources of supply in Corsica and North Africa. But conditions of soil and climate retard the growth of forest trees in Mediterranean lands: a cleared area, left to itself,

becomes a waste of stunted bush or scrub. The present denuda-
tion of the Mediterranean countries is to a large extent a legacy
from the ancient Greeks and Romans.[1]

Greek and Roman land was for the most part held in private
ownership. The system of joint tenure by groups of kinsmen
died out before the beginnings of Greek and Roman history, or
in its earliest days. The more important temples possessed
domains, but these were rarely extensive. The less productive
territories, such as the mountain pastures and forests, remained
unappropriated, or were treated as state property. The Hellenistic kings converted large tracts of conquered territory into
Crown property, and the whole of Egypt under the Ptolemies
was technically 'king's land'. The Roman emperors acquired
domains in many provinces by inheritance or confiscation.
Nevertheless private ownership and individual exploitation
remained the general rule, and with rare exceptions (as at Sparta)
the market in land was not restricted by entails.

In early times the holdings in land were mostly small. In
Attica the great majority of cultivators owned less than fifty
acres, and the individual allotments in some of the early Roman
colonies did not exceed five acres. Moreover, the natural play
of economic forces did not give any strong impetus to the concentration of properties. The current methods of cultivation
did not require the use of much machinery or the outlay of a
large capital, and the general effect of mass-production would
merely have been to glut the markets. In addition, governments
dependent on their military man-power had an interest in keeping
up the numbers of the small peasantry, from whom they drew
their best recruits. Consequently the Hellenistic kings pursued
an active policy of colonization by small holders, and the Roman
republic created some hundreds of thousands of small allotments.

On the other hand, the lesser proprietors suffered more from
bad seasons and the ravages of war, and they seldom had facilities
for borrowing materials or money at easy rates. In some cases,
as under the Roman republic during the great period of foreign

[1] Soil erosion constitutes a serious problem in several districts of
South Africa and of North America.

conquests, the exigencies of military service compelled the peasantry to absent themselves for long periods from their homesteads, and the lure of easy subsistence and free entertainments at Rome tempted them not to return to the land. At the same time contractors and speculators who had done themselves well out of the wars eagerly bought up the derelict small holdings, because land gave social prestige and was the only secure form of investment. In the second century B.C., accordingly, a gradual concentration of property set in. Under the early emperors this process sustained a check; but it gained a fresh impetus in the age of the barbarian invasions, when many small proprietors surrendered their freeholds to their more powerful neighbours in return for their protection. Yet in the Greek and Roman world, taken as a whole, large and small estates balanced one another in due proportion, and in no age or country did the peasant proprietor die out altogether.

6. MANUFACTURES

The industry of the ancient world was literally a process of 'manufacture', or production by hand. It had at its disposal most of the ordinary hand tools, but was ill provided with machinery. Though Greek ingenuity invented many small pneumatic and hydraulic machines, and a toy steam-engine, it rarely applied itself to the practical exploitation of mechanical power. The mathematician Archimedes designed balanced cranes and compound pulleys, and a suction screw for raising water, but his achievements did not lead on to an industrial revolution. Water-mills had come into use by the time of Augustus, and were subsequently installed in the Tiber to grind Rome's grain-supplies, but the uneven flow of Mediterranean rivers restricted the use of such machinery. Of wind-mills we hear nothing. Altogether, the mechanical equipment of the Greek and Roman world was considerably inferior to that of the later Middle Ages.

Furthermore, the processes of ancient industry remained almost static. Philosophers speculated on the ultimate problems of chemistry and physics (pp. 197–8), but in the absence of systematic observation and experiment they made no discoveries of practical importance. Craftsmen now and then worked out a practical problem by empirical methods, or happened upon its solution by accident, but they kept their new knowledge to themselves.

With their simple tool equipment and unchanging processes ancient manufacturers could turn out articles of high quality, but only at a high cost in labour and materials; and they could not greatly extend the range and variety of their products.

Of particular industries, the Greeks and Romans understood none better than that of building. But for their ignorance of steel construction, their processes were essentially the same as those of the present day. The excellence of their workmanship is attested by the perfect join of blocks laid without mortar, which characterized Greek stonework of the fifth and fourth centuries B.C., and by the unsurpassed tenacity of Roman concrete. The chief deficiency of the Greek and Roman builders was the lack of mechanical power for hauling heavy materials. The labour costs of construction were therefore high, unless a cheap supply of workers, such as prisoners of war or peasants impressed by force, was available. The Parthenon, which measures only 225 by 100 feet, is reputed to have cost 1000 talents (say £230,000).

Another industry in which Greeks and Romans attained a high standard of proficiency was pottery. The finer sorts of ceramic ware were either produced with moulds, or (as in the case of the best Greek vases of the sixth and fifth centuries) were thrown on the wheel and received their final shape by turning on a rudimentary lathe. The process of firing had been mastered by long experience. By skilful manipulation of the air supply the iron in the clay was converted to ferric oxide, which gave to the vases the bright red colour characteristic of the finer Greek and Roman ware. By a similar process of air control the Attic potters produced a lustrous black glaze whose constituents (iron and soda) required delicate handling to bring about the correct degree of fusion.[1] On the other hand, the ancient ceramic

[1] The method of producing Attic black glaze is explained by C. F. Binns and A. D. Fraser in the *American Journal of Archæology*, 1929, pp. 1–9.

workers were not acquainted with the tin-glazing processes of medieval and modern times, and they could not produce the high temperatures required for making the salt-glazed stoneware of the present day.

The Greeks and Romans for many centuries left the manufacture of glass in the hands of its inventors, the Egyptians. But about the time of Augustus they acquired the technique of glass-blowing, which had been recently discovered by Phoenician craftsmen, and produced lighter and more transparent ware than the Egyptian moulded glass; and they subsequently learnt how to remove discoloration by impure sand. Under the Roman emperors glass became a fairly common material for window-panes and for jugs and bottles. But it was never manufactured on a scale comparable to that of pottery, and it appears to have been used less extensively in its native East than in the western and northern provinces. Greek and Roman craftsmen also acquired proficiency in cutting glass or precious stones, but they made no systematic study of lenses, and therefore failed to invent any optical instruments. This failure greatly restricted their field of scientific discovery.

The lack of mechanical inventiveness among the Greeks and Romans is clearly illustrated in their textile industry. The preliminary combing of wool for worsted cloths was done by hand. In the absence of spinning-wheels (an invention of the later Middle Ages), the yarn was prepared by drawing out the wool or flax from the distaff and winding it on a spindle attached to a disk of stone or clay, which was then set into a spin and dropped to the ground, so as to pull the material into a tight thread and to give the necessary twist. The weaving-looms were fitted with rudimentary harnesses which drew out the warp threads singly or in regular groups and thus allowed the shuttle to be thrown from end to end of the piece. But for the weaving of any complicated pattern it was necessary to pass the shuttle from hand to hand, or to use an embroidering needle. By this process it was possible to manufacture cloth of the finest quality, but even the simplest textile operations were slow and laborious.

Mining operations were conducted partly on the surface, partly by excavation. In ancient times surface supplies of gold and tinstone were still available. These minerals therefore were usually obtained by sifting or washing. The other metals were extracted from pits and galleries. Remains of ancient workings, e.g. at Laurium in Attica, on the isle of Elba, and at Rio Tinto in Andalusia, show that the miners were not afraid of driving long tunnels into the mountain flanks, propping up the roofs as they went, and that they could bale out the sump water with dredge-buckets or Archimedean screws (p. 210). But their galleries were often narrow and ill ventilated.

In the reduction of the ores the Greeks and Romans were handicapped by their ignorance of chemical reactions and their incapacity to produce or maintain high temperatures (1000–1200° C. or over). The charcoal which they used for firing was a good if wasteful fuel; but when burnt on an open hearth or in a diminutive furnace, with an intermittent blast from hand-bellows or a natural wind down a funnel, it seldom liquefied the metal completely. Though the percentage of metallic residue in the slag varied greatly, it rarely fell below ten per cent and sometimes rose to fifty per cent. The ancient metallurgists, however, could afford this imperfect procedure. In their day the world's mineral resources had as yet been scarcely tapped, and they could pick out the richest and most tractable ores.

Remains of ancient gold- and silversmiths' work show that in the hand-finishing of these metals the ancient craftsmen were unsurpassed (see p. 236). Of the various copper alloys, brass was little used, because of the difficulties of zinc reduction. But bronze was produced in large quantities from copper and tin, and the abundant remains of Greek and Roman statuary are witnesses to the high degree or proficiency attained in the difficult art of bronze-casting.

The Greeks and Romans did not manufacture cast iron, because they could not command the high temperature required for this purpose. The iron produced on their open hearths was easily malleable on a hand forge, but its softness greatly diminished its utility. For weapons and cutlery, the ancient metallurgists reheated forge iron for long periods in a reducing atmosphere, a process by which a good quality of steel could be obtained. The steel was further hardened by sudden cooling in

9

water, and was rendered elastic by annealing in a slow flame. The highest skill in steel-production was exhibited by the armourers of Gaul and Spain, whose swords neither cracked nor warped when stretched across the head from shoulder to shoulder.[1] But these processes entailed a great expenditure of fuel and labour. The manufacture of iron goods was therefore on a limited scale; indeed it hardly extended beyond the making of war material, cutlery, and agricultural implements.

The technique of Greek and Roman industry to a large extent determined its organization. Depending in a great degree on manual skill, it favoured specialization of labour, wherever there was a market for highly finished goods. In the early days of Greece and Rome such specialization was not yet possible. The general standard of life of all save a small ruling class was too low to create an efficient demand for well-made and therefore costly goods. Similar conditions prevailed in the declining days of the Roman Empire, and especially in the western provinces, where the remnant of the wealthier population entrenched itself in its self-contained country estates. But an impetus was given to specialization in Greece by the colonial movement, which diffused riches more widely and raised the standard of taste through intercourse with the old civilization of the Near East (p. 19). In the Homeric poems no skilled craftsmen appear except smiths, potters, carpenters, and shipwrights;[2] in the seventh and sixth centuries the number of specialized industries underwent a rapid increase. A similar fillip was given to Roman industry by the wars of conquest in the third and second centuries, by reason of the new wealth which they brought to Italy, and of the fructifying contacts between Romans and Greeks. In the first and second centuries A.D., when economic output reached its highest point under the shelter of the Pax Romana, and prosperous bourgeoisies established themselves in every province, the specialization of labour also attained its maximum. But at all times it was mainly confined to the higher-priced articles,

[1] The finest of all ancient steels was made in India and China by the crucible process.

[2] Various passages in Homer suggest that the specialized stonemason was known in his day also.

and under the Roman emperors it was partly counteractcd by a tendency to standardize manufactured goods.

The high labour costs and consequent high prices of ancient manufactured articles tended to restrict their markets; and work for export was hindered by the expensiveness of transport, and by wars and political disorders. Mass-production would usually have meant over-production, and large establishments had little advantage over small ones. The heads of individual firms were therefore mostly small masters who worked with their own hands in the company of a few assistants, and in many cases made to order rather than for stock. Even mining operations were largely in the hands of petty entrepreneurs who drove separate adits into the minefields. General prosperity and freedom from political disturbances under the early Roman emperors created a wider market, and this, together with increasing standardization of output, gave rise to some closer concentrations of industry. The ceramic industry in particular was organized for large-scale production of uniform goods, and the 'terra sigillata' (glossy red table-ware) of the Gallic potteries of this period bore some resemblance to the mass-produced plates and cups of the present day. But the general rule held good, that the unit of ancient industry was the shop rather than the factory.

The small scale of ancient workshops did not allow much opportunity of amassing wealth by manufacture. But the industrial class as a whole was prosperous. In many Greek states, and under the Roman Republic, craftsmen stood under a social stigma; but under the Roman emperors industrial entrepreneurs often made their way into the ranks of the municipal aristocracies.[1]

The lack of machinery created a large demand for manual labour, and this was met only in a small degree by the women workers, whose sphere of industry was almost wholly domestic. The men wage-workers should therefore have been able to command good rates of pay. But they failed to do this. Though detailed information about the remuneration of workmen in the

[1] This snobbish attitude tainted the writings even of philosophers like Plato and Cicero. But Cicero conceded that business might be respectable, provided that it was Big Business.

Greek and Roman world is scanty, it suffices to show that they seldom rose far above subsistence level. The main reason for their low rates of wages was that they were exposed to the competition of slave labour (pp. 133-4).

Greek and Roman industry was not subjected to any rigorous collective control. The free workers were not in a position to exercise pressure on their employers through trade unions. They were dispersed in many small establishments, and were liable to be replaced by slave labour. The masters, who often lived together in the same street or quarter of a city, had better opportunities of collective action, and they frequently associated themselves in gilds. They would occasionally join forces to canvass on behalf of a candidate for municipal office, or to call a strike by way of protest against a vexatious ordinance by a magistrate; but they did not frame and enforce any elaborate codes of craft rules. Indeed the object of the craft gilds was largely, perhaps mainly, social.

State action in control of industry was likewise infrequent. Both territorial states and cities sought to acquire mines and quarries for their own use, and in some instances they exploited their properties directly. The kings of Pergamum operated their own tile-kilns and textile factories, and the later Roman emperors (from Diocletian onwards) produced in state establishments part of the armour and uniforms required by them for their military forces. But more commonly the monarchs and cities leased their industrial properties to private entrepreneurs for the sake of revenue.

Interference in industry by legislation was inspired to a large extent by fiscal considerations. Greek cities sometimes set up monopolies in certain branches of manufacture for the sake of the licence fees which they imposed upon the producers, and already under the early Roman Republic the salt-pans of Ostia were worked under a state permit. In Egypt the Ptolemies established a pervasive system of industrial monopolies, which they safeguarded by drastic regulations and high customs tariffs. In order to ensure the requisite supplies of bread for the capital city the late Roman emperors tied down the bakers to their occupations, and it is not unlikely that they imposed a similar industrial serfdom upon other essential crafts. In other instances government regulations were issued on sanitary grounds. Brick-works, pottery-kilns, and tanneries were usually relegated by law to the outskirts of towns.

But in all these cases the state authorities showed little concern for the welfare of the workers. Being mostly drawn from the landowning classes, they took but a slight interest in what they regarded as menial occupations. The urban craftsmen seldom exercised their political power to improve their status. If they felt discontented, their demands were more commonly directed to a change of occupation, by the provision of land allotments, than to an improvement in its conditions. The point of their grievances, moreover, was blunted by distribution of free or cheap corn, and by free entertainments—a method of 'doping' which the Greek cities introduced experimentally, and the Roman Republic, with the emperors to follow, developed on a right royal scale.

7. COMMERCE

The history of Greek and Roman commerce ran a parallel course to that of industry. Under the general conditions of political insecurity and self-contained economy that marked the beginnings of Greek history, trade could scarcely progress beyond occasional exchanges in a neighbouring market and rare transactions with venturers bringing raw metal or 'Birmingham goods' from overseas. The colonial movement, which opened up the Mediterranean to the Greeks and promoted the specialization of their industry, created a regular flow of commerce which was not wholly confined to the Hellenic lands, for the Greeks now gathered no small part of the general carrying trade of the Mediterranean into their hands. Their commercial development was assisted by the invention of coinage (p. 124), which coincided with the colonial movement, and by the growth of war fleets, which set a check upon piracy. In general, the Greek traders imported raw materials (grain, timber, metal, slaves) from the colonial areas or from foreign countries, and exported the industrial products of the homeland and Aegean area, which by reason of their high finish and artistic excellence found their way into every Mediterranean market. The volume and diffusion of Greek overseas trade since the sixth century may be gauged by the ever-increasing finds of Greek pottery, of which vast quantities have been unearthed in Tuscany and southern Russia, and lesser but not inconsiderable amounts in Carthage and Spain, in Egypt and Syria.

Greek expansion was checked by the Persian and Carthaginian invasions (pp. 36–7), and was not resumed on any great scale in the fifth and fourth centuries. The mercantile ascendancy of Athens at this period was largely gained at the expense of the older trading cities, Miletus, Aegina, and Corinth. The conquests of Alexander further widened the range of Greek commerce and gave rise to new trading centres, such as Rhodes, Seleucia-on-Tigris, and, above all, Alexandria, whose turn-over exceeded that of any other ancient port. But the Greek merchants did not obtain a secure foothold beyond Mesopotamia and the Red Sea. About 300 B.C. a Massilian captain named Pytheas made a bold voyage of exploration in the Atlantic, in the course of which he circumnavigated Britain and skirted the continental coast as far as Heligoland. But his cruise had no economic result, except to create a new trade route for Cornish tin across Gaul, in competition with the Carthaginian traffic through the Straits of Gibraltar.

In the meantime the Roman Republic remained an essentially agrarian state. Though the wars of the third and second centuries carried Roman arms to all parts of the Mediterranean, they did not give rise to an extensive Roman trade, except in money (p. 127). The destruction of Carthage broke down the Phoenician trade monopoly in the west; but the new freedom of the western seas was offset by a recrudescence of piracy in the Levant, consequent upon the decay of the Hellenistic monarchies and the neglectfulness of the Roman government, which disbanded its war fleets and left the merchantmen to shift for themselves. Under the early emperors, however, commerce developed even more rapidly than agriculture and industry. The general security of land and sea, the wider diffusion of wealth, and the standardization of weights and measures (p. 139), gave a special impetus to mercantile activities. A further stimulus was provided by the opening up of a transcontinental route to the Far East by the emperors of the Han dynasty in China, who facilitated the passage of caravans from the Yellow Sea to the borders of Parthia, and more especially by the enterprise of a Greek skipper named Hippalus (perhaps *c.* 100 B.C.), who discovered the proper seasons of monsoon navigation on the Indian Ocean and laid the foundations of a brisk trade with western India. Chinese silk, Indian jewels, and spices were now regularly exchanged for Mediterranean wine and glass, and the gold and silver coins of the Roman emperors. But this eastern trade, together with the by no means insignificant traffic with Germany and Scandinavia, was not nearly equal in volume to that which developed within the four corners of the Roman Empire, and not only linked the provinces with Italy but brought them into direct connexion with one another. The papyrus of Alexandria, the bronze ware of Capua, and the pottery of Gaul now found a market as wide as the Roman dominions. While the city of Rome imported foodstuffs from Egypt and Spain and North Africa, Spanish oil also travelled to the Rhineland and the wine of Bordeaux to Britain. For the wine and ceramic ware which they imported from Gaul the Britons paid with the produce of their lead mines, which also supplied the material for the water-pipes of Rome.

In the third and fourth centuries A.D. the chronic insecurity resulting from the barbarian invasions and the reversion to self-contained economy reduced the volume of trade in the western provinces to a thin and inconstant trickle. The eastern half of the Roman Empire stood the shock of the invasions more firmly, and under its Byzantine rulers it recovered much of its former trade.

The commonest medium of exchange among the Greeks and Romans was coined money. Primitive methods of barter never died out in the ancient world, and trade with the backward peoples on the outskirts of the Mediterranean lands was largely conducted on this basis. Carthaginian merchants bargained with trinkets and gaudy-coloured cloths for Cornish tin and West African gold; the Greek slave-traders in the Black Sea region reckoned the value of their purchases in terms of wine casks. The use of cattle as currency survived in some archaic Greek and Roman laws which prescribed the payment of fines in terms of sheep or oxen, and in the Latin word 'pecunia', which literally meant 'cattle goods';[1] but this form of money became obsolete in the early days of Greek and Roman history. Payment with lumps of metal weighed in the balance was the general practice in the early monarchies of the Near East, and it prevailed in Greece and Italy until the invention of coinage, by which it was eventually superseded in all Mediterranean lands.

Coinage originated in the eighth century among the Lydians of Asia Minor. Its handiness and greater capacity for circulation was soon realized by their neighbours, the Asiatic Greeks, and from these its use spread over the Greek world and beyond. By 500 B.C. only the more backward Greek communities were without a currency of their own, and it has been estimated that at one time or other at least 1500 mints were at work in the Greek world. From Greece the use of coins was diffused, albeit in a more gradual fashion, among the peoples of the western Mediterranean. The Romans did not set up a mint until c. 300 B.C.; as their dominions grew they became the chief providers of money in the ancient world, but until the third century A.D. many Greek cities continued to strike concurrently with the Roman emperors.

The principal metal for currency in the ancient world was silver, with bronze for small change. In Rome, where copper from the Etruscan mines was abundant, the earliest coins were struck in bronze, but these were soon replaced for all major transactions by silver pieces. In the early days of coinage the only state which issued gold regularly was the Persian Empire. The emission of gold by Greek cities was quite exceptional; Philip and Alexander of Macedon struck large quantities of gold, but the Hellenistic kings made but sparing use of this metal. The Roman Republic also remained faithful to silver, but Caesar instituted a gold coinage which eventually (under Diocletian and Constantine) superseded silver as the main form of currency.

The principal Greek denominations were the *drachma*, a silver

[1] The use of cattle-money in early medieval Europe is attested by English 'fee' and Dutch 'vee'.

piece roughly equal in weight to the 1914 franc, and the *obol*, a bronze coin of which six went to the drachma. For the computation of large sums of money the Greeks reckoned in *minae* (100 drachmas) and *talents* (6000 drachmas); but these units, like the medieval *librae*, were nothing but convenient abstract terms. The chief Roman coins were the *aureus*, a gold piece roughly equivalent to the sovereign; the *denarius*, corresponding to the Greek drachma, of which twenty-five went to the aureus; the *sestertius*, which was made of silver under the republic, and of brass under the emperors, and the bronze *as*. The denarius was exchanged for four sesterces or sixteen as-pieces.

The Greek city-states at first issued their coins on a variety of standards which impeded the free interchange of their currencies. Eventually three weight-systems, the Attic, Aeginetan, and Rhodian, shared out the Greek world amongst themselves. In the western countries the question of standards solved itself by the gradual disappearance of the municipal and tribal mints, the last of which were closed down soon after the time of Augustus.

But a new element of confusion was introduced by the failure of some states to maintain the weight or the purity of their coins at face value. Since the bronze pieces were, or soon became, mere token money, their metal content was of less importance; but the lightening or debasing of gold and silver coins was bound sooner or later to have a disturbing effect. Among the Greek city-states Athens maintained an exemplary standard of honesty, and the other towns were constrained by competition among their mints to avoid any gross depreciation. The Hellenistic monarchies and the Roman Republic also issued good money, except in an occasional emergency, and the coinage of the first Roman emperors was above reproach. But from the time of Nero the Roman denarius was progressively reduced in weight, and during the war-crises of the third century it was transformed into a bronze coin with a mere surface wash of silver; and at the same time the weight of the aureus was lowered. The result was a sharp rise in prices, and a partial reversion to weighing money instead of counting it, or even to exchange by barter. A partial restoration of the Roman currency was effected by

Diocletian and Constantine; the aureus was stabilized, and its Byzantine successor, the 'bezant', set a much-needed standard of purity to the medieval world.

Greek traders in the fourth and third centuries B.C. devised methods of payment by paper money in place of cash transfers. They failed to invent the bank note and the bill of exchange, but they made use of cheques, bankers' orders, and letters of credit. Surviving fragments of paper money from Egypt show that under Roman rule at any rate both the Greek and the native populations were familiar with this form of currency; but we do not know to what extent it was employed in the other countries of the Roman Empire. In any case it never displaced coinage as the chief medium of exchange.

The use of coins and paper money brought into existence a special class of dealers in money. Professional money-changers throve on the multiplicity of mints and standards among the Greek city-states, and although increasing uniformity of standards eventually diminished the need for their services, they still found employment under the Roman emperors, because of the concurrent use of Roman and local coinages in the eastern provinces.

The business of banking, which was of old standing in the eastern monarchies, does not appear to have been practised in Greece before the fifth century; and there is no evidence of Greek temples ever engaging in large financial operations, like those of the Oriental countries. The first Greek banking houses that we hear of were established at Athens about the time of the Peloponnesian War. In the Hellenistic age similar firms sprang up all over the Greek world; by the third century they had established themselves at Rome, and under the emperors they were probably to be found in every province.

Greek and Roman bankers took the money of customers on deposit and arranged for them the payments by paper currency described above. They settled debts between their own customers by transferring credits from one to another in the bank's books; and they devised rudimentary clearing systems for payment between customers of different banks, or between banks in different towns. Their other main function was to lend out funds, whether their own capital or the deposit money of their customers. Their rate of interest ranged from four to ten per cent for mortgages and other well-secured loans; for risky advances without adequate cover they charged up to forty-eight per cent.

The scale of ancient banking operations, however, always remained very limited. Governments had occasional recourse to bankers, or kept balances on current account with them. But they usually maintained the greater part of their funds in their own treasuries, and they did not as a rule borrow large sums. Under the later republic Roman money-lenders did a considerable business with eastern kings and Greek cities which had fallen into financial embarrassment—largely as a result of the Roman conquests. In these highly speculative transactions they demanded such heavy rates of interest as sometimes to precipitate the borrower into bankruptcy; but with the assistance of the provincial governors they often obtained repayment and realized handsome profits. But opportunities for this shady kind of deal were sadly diminished under the rule of the Roman emperors. Certain kinds of mercantile loans, and especially those made to shipping venturers on the security of their vessels or cargoes, played an important part in ancient economic life. But the general lack of machinery and other costly plant in commerce and industry rendered it unnecessary to raise large amounts of working capital, and many firms financed themselves regularly out of their private funds. Similarly we hear little of advances to landowners for improvements; and the small peasantry struggling against bad seasons was usually left to the tender mercies of petty usurers, whose operations sometimes gave rise to a cry for the abolition of all debts.

The commerce of the Greeks and Romans was almost as individualistic as their industry. Partnerships were formed in speculative branches of business such as shipping and banking, but the only instance of an ancient joint-stock corporation is afforded by the societies of tax-farmers at Rome, which issued negotiable shares in their enterprises to the general public. The gilds of the merchants resembled those of the craftsmen in being mainly social. For wholesale business large warehouses were built at the Piraeus and Alexandria, at Rome and Ostia. But retail trade was conducted only in small shops, or at stalls in the market-places and at the seasonal fairs, or by kerb-side pedlars.

The interest of governments in commerce was somewhat wider and more continuous than in manufactures. At a very early date in the history of coinage the emission of metallic currency was made a state monopoly. In order to protect the public against exploitation by private traders in the necessities of life, Hellenistic monarchies and city-states not infrequently bought supplies of grain and resold them at wholesale prices or at artificially low rates. From the time of Gaius Gracchus the needs of the population of Rome were in large measure supplied by a similar system of state purchase of corn, followed by gratis distributions or sales below market price. The Ptolemies owned fleets of merchantman on the Mediterranean and Red Seas and on the Nile, but they did not operate these directly.

Greek and Roman governments made a regular practice of levying tolls upon commerce; but these, with rare exceptions, were imposed at a flat rate, and they usually did not exceed the ratio of two to five per cent *ad valorem*. States that did not enter directly into the corn trade sometimes sought to control it by legislation. At Athens shippers bringing grain were forbidden to re-export more than one-third of their cargo, and to prevent the engrossing of supplies corn-dealers were not allowed to hold more than a prescribed number of sacks. In a desperate attempt to check the rise of prices consequent upon the depreciation of coinage in the Roman Empire, Diocletian issued a general schedule of maximum prices and wages; but this tariff was soon withdrawn. The same emperor endeavoured to assure the corn-supply of Rome by forbidding the grain-importers to change their occupation. But as a rule, once a Greek or Roman merchant had paid his tolls and market fees, he was free to buy and sell as he pleased.

8. SERFDOM AND SLAVERY

The feature which most distinguished Greek and Roman economy from that of the present day was its dependence on unfree labour.

In the earliest days of Greek history the northern invaders

reduced the natives of some districts—notably the Helots of Laconia (p. 33)—to a condition of serfdom. In the age of colonization the Greek settlers extended the same treatment to some of the indigenous peoples (e.g. at Syracuse). In the Near East serfdom was an old-established institution, and here the Greek conquerors of Alexander's day merely carried on the practice of the previous rulers.

Serf labour was not employed in early Italy, save perhaps in Etruria. Under Roman rule, and possibly under Roman influence, it disappeared in the Greek lands and was greatly circumscribed in the Near East. But in the third and fourth centuries A.D. the Roman emperors, confronted with the task of arresting the general breakdown of the economic machine, reintroduced compulsory labour on a large scale. They created a species of industrial and commercial serfdom (pp. 121, 128), and they authorized the larger landowners to tie down to the soil their remaining free tenants. The 'predial slavery' of the Middle Ages was a legacy of the declining Roman Empire.

But serfdom played a small part in Greek and Roman history as compared with slavery. Although slaves were kept by all ancient peoples who had the force to catch them or the means to buy them, they were especially numerous in the world of Greece and Rome.

The origin of the slaves was various. In the early days of Greek and Roman history insolvent debtors forfeited their persons to their creditors, whether by judicial sentence or by self-help on the creditors' part. The law-courts punished some serious offences by loss of liberty, and this form of penalty was often inflicted, as an alternative to a death sentence, under the Roman emperors. But a far more prolific source of servitude was warfare and kidnapping. Prisoners in battle who could not find their ransom were sold off by auction, and the entire populations of towns taken by storm were liable to the same fate. Slave traders by profession abducted unwary adults and picked up exposed infants, or bought the unwanted children of certain barbarian tribes. Finally, the supply was kept up by breeding. Under the Roman emperors, when other sources were being cut off by increased public security and the lesser frequency of wars, the home-bred slaves probably outnumbered the rest. The price of slaves varied greatly according to the value of the individual and the general state of the market. The average price for an unskilled man ranged from £4 to £10; for skilled slaves fancy sums, running into hundreds of pounds, were sometimes given.

The proportion of slaves to free persons in Greek and Roman society is difficult to determine. It was higher in the more urbanized and industrialized regions; but even at Athens and Rome the servile population probably remained at all times inferior to that of the free residents. In the smaller Greek cities, in the Near East, and in the western provinces of the Roman Empire, it was in a distinct minority. But in the Greek and Roman world as a whole the servile element was present in sufficient numbers to exercise a far-reaching influence upon the life of the free population.

The uses to which slaves were put were manifold. The women were employed almost exclusively in domestic service (which included the spinning and weaving of wool). In the larger households male domestics were also kept, and in addition to ordinary menial offices they performed the work of secretaries, physicians, and tutors. Trained slaves also served in government offices as clerks, accountants, and messengers; in Athens, strangely enough, they did duty as policemen. But the majority of the servile population was probably engaged in economic pursuits

Agrarian slavery existed sporadically at all times. It never attained great dimensions in the Greek lands, but from the second century B.C. it came to play a large part in Italy. In this country the men who had been enriched by foreign conquest, and had invested their winnings in landed estates, utilized the stream of war captives that was now flowing to Rome to cultivate their domains. These 'familiae rusticae' never wholly ousted the free farm workers, and under the Roman emperors, when the supply of servile labour became less abundant, they were partly replaced by 'coloni', or free tenants cultivating parcels of land under a lease. But rustic slavery never died out completely. The slaves engaged in industry performed most of the heavy and unskilled labour, but were also occupied in skilled crafts of every description.

In commerce they served as salesmen and accountants, and sometimes even as general agents.

The effects of slavery were as various as its forms. That it brought much suffering upon the slaves need hardly be mentioned. Slaves were liable to be overworked and underfed, insulted and flogged, and (in the earlier days) even put to death, at their masters' discretion. They might spend a lifetime in compulsory celibacy, or they might be allowed to found a family, only to be separated from it at their owners' convenience. A curious regulation of Greek and Roman law-courts prescribed that the evidence of slaves might be taken under torture. Domestic servants were exposed to every passing caprice of a master or mistress. Many rural slaves never left the estate; those who were suspected of planning escape were kept in chains and housed by night in an underground dormitory. Slave workers in some mines or quarries died off rapidly under insanitary conditions or through sheer overwork. Servile rebellions were crushed without mercy: insurgents who had surrendered were sometimes crucified *en masse*.

Such ill treatment, it is true, was not by any means the normal lot of slaves in the Greek and Roman world. The more exhausting and deleterious forms of labour were reserved for slaves under sentence from a court of law, or for brutish men from the more backward tribes. Though Greek and Roman lawyers never accepted the full logic of their confessions, they admitted that evidence extorted on the rack was of doubtful value, and they refrained from calling slaves to witness where the testimony of free men was available. Owners of country estates presently discovered that it paid better to treat their staffs humanely. In the first century B.C. they began to play on the hopes of reward rather than on the fear of punishment; in the following century they promoted the best workers to live in married quarters. Domestic workers were usually well fed and clothed and tolerably housed, if only because a sleek and well-groomed staff gave its master a better reputation. Since custom required that wealthy persons should maintain a large household establishment, the daily ration of work for each domestic was far from heavy. Genuine good feeling and even affection sprang up between free and servile housemates. Servants of proved value were taken freely into their owners' confidence; the children of free and unfree played together; in times of civil war slaves gave up their lives on behalf of their masters. Slaves engaged in commerce and industry might rise to the position of foremen or managers. In some cases they took full charge of the business and lived as and where they pleased, subject only to their paying to their masters an agreed sum out of the profits. The public slaves enjoyed similar conditions of life and hardly differed from free workers, save in that they could not change their occupation.

In the course of time public opinion became more considerate towards the servile population. The Athenian democracy withdrew from masters the right of killing their slaves; at Rome the owners' power of life and death was curtailed by Sulla and abolished by Hadrian. Custom demanded that slaves should not be sold away from their families except under sheer necessity. Social enjoyments were not denied to slaves. They were admitted to theatres and circuses and other places of entertainment, and they could found clubs of their own or share membership with free persons. Lastly, Greek and Roman slaves, provided that they were of good character and not too uncivilized, had a tolerable chance of gaining eventual freedom. It was customary to make them an allowance of pocket-money for good behaviour, and when they had saved up a specified sum they were entitled to buy themselves free with it. The statement of Cicero, that slaves had only six years to wait for their freedom,[1] should not be applied indiscriminately to all unfree persons; but undoubtedly large numbers were emancipated, and at Rome in particular masters were liberal with the gift of freedom. The liberated slaves could be indentured to perform specified services for their former owners. On the other hand they were often equipped with a parting gift or loan of business capital, and it was nothing unusual for freedmen to prosper in commerce or industry. Under the early Roman emperors a notable proportion of the *nouveaux riches* consisted of former slaves.

For the masters the possession of slaves meant, first of all,

[1] *Philippics*, viii. § 32.

greater personal leisure. At certain periods of Greek and Roman history, when general economic conditions favoured a rapid increase of production, slaves provided the necessary additional labour. The economic development of Greece in the days of the colonial movement, and of Italy in the last three centuries B.C., would have been retarded, but for the importation of unfree workers. The relative facility with which servile labour could be organized made it, under certain conditions, more economical than that of wage-earners. On some of the large Italian estates the work of the slaves was regulated with minute care: the muscular but stolid men were told off to the plough-land, while the quick-witted ones were sent to the vineyard; each grade of labour was made up into squads under a special foreman; and the time-table of the estate was so arranged as to provide continuous profitable employment for the whole staff.

But in a servile establishment good management was indispensable, if any profits at all were to be realized. The upkeep of the staff constituted a permanent overhead cost, and gave rise to a dead loss whenever the work in hand was not sufficient to go round. Though individual slaves might respond to good treatment and to the hope of promotion or emancipation, the unfree labourers in general were indifferent, if not disaffected. They worked at a slow stroke, they handled the master's property carelessly, or pilfered it. When the foremen and the manager were also unfree, as was often the case, the entire staff might engage in a tacit conspiracy to defraud the master. Unless the owner understood his business, and was prepared to give much personal attention to it, he was apt to find his profits unaccountably leaking away. On the whole, slaves were cheap in terms of wages, but expensive in terms of labour costs.

The effect of slavery upon the free labourers was not so much to deprive willing workers of a livelihood as to create a 'mean white' population, which was too proud to set its hands to 'niggers' jobs' and preferred to live penuriously on small allotments, or to depend on public or private patronage. For the remainder, who were willing to render service for wages, there was probably no dearth of work in normal times, but little opportunity of making a good bargain with employers, for these could, temporarily at least, reduce the demand for free workers by importing slaves. Consequently the wage-earners never rose far above subsistence level.

The same aversion to labour as such, which the presence of servile workers engendered in the free proletariat, also affected the slave-owning class. Though some used their leisure to work all the harder in the service of state or city, or to cultivate the Muses, others became 'gentlemen' in the worst sense of that term, giving the whole of their energy to sport or to a laborious and insipid ritual of social functions. As in the modern slave-owning communities, the questionable blessing of cheap labour reduced mechanical inventiveness and organizing efficiency. If the Greek and Romans made fewer practical discoveries in a thousand years than the medieval world achieved between A.D. 1000 and 1500, the reason is to be sought, not in any lack of inventive ability, but in the absence of any adequate spur to its exercise.

Lastly, slavery furnished an ever-present temptation to those lacking in personal self-control (p. 147); and even in the strong-minded it instilled a latent fear of reprisals which found an outlet now and then in the unpitying repression of mutiny. In the long run, servitude perhaps did more harm to the masters than to the slaves.

9. TRAVEL

The principal connecting link of the Greek and Roman world was the Mediterranean Sea. The geographical factors that favour and impede navigation on its waters have already been described (pp. 2-3). The cities of the Mediterranean coast were hardly ever situated at the mouth of a river. They were sometimes built on an open beach, but more commonly they lay recessed in a natural inlet of the sea, or under the lee of an offshore island. A few of the most favourably located towns, such as the Piraeus and Corcyra, were built on the neck of a promontory jutting into the sea, so as to afford a harbourage on either side of the isthmus. The natural advantages of harbour-sites were supplemented by the building of breakwaters. At Alexandria the Ptolemies constructed a mole to connect the mainland with the adjacent island of Pharos, thus forming a double port of the Corcyraean type. The Roman emperor Claudius made a new cut for the Tiber estuary, so as to avoid a dangerous mud-bank at its natural mouth, and scooped out a huge basin, which he protected with gigantic sea-walls of concrete. The Ptolemies also set the example of lighting up harbour entrances by night. They erected on the island of Pharos a lofty tower, from the top of which a flare of blazing pine-wood was projected, it is said, to a distance of thirty miles. 'Phari' of lesser proportions were built at many other points, e.g. at the Straits of Messina, and on either side of the Straits of Dover.[1]

Greek and Roman ships were of relatively small size, seldom exceeding 250 tons. A few 'leviathans' of 2000 tons and over were constructed for special purposes; but these, being built with a wooden keel, were liable to have their backs broken in a rough sea,[2] and they could not have found sufficient merchandise to fill their holds in ordinary commercial ventures. A more serious defect of ancient ships was their unhandiness. They usually had a single mast and carried one mainsail, which was sometimes supplemented by a topsail and a bowsprit-sail. The mainsail, being cut square, was unsuitable for travelling close to the wind. Ships encountering a head-wind were therefore obliged to make very wide tacks, or to wait for a change in the wind. If caught in a storm, they might not be able to keep their head to the wind, and would remain exposed to heavy seas on their broadside.[3] In place of a rudder they carried a pair of linked paddles at the stern, which required greater skill in the handling. Moreover, ancient seamen had no compass to guide their course.

Under such conditions navigation was to a large extent

[1] The stump of the Roman lighthouse at Dover may still be seen inside the Castle grounds.

[2] This point is illustrated by chapter xxvii of the Acts of the Apostles. —A vessel, not of outstanding size, has to be braced with cables to prevent the keel from breaking.

[3] See again Acts xxvii.—The captain endeavours to set the ship 'eye to eye' with a wind of gale force, but cannot keep her sufficiently close-hauled for safety.

Merchant vessels sometimes carried a complement of oars to row them round a headland or into a harbour.

suspended during the boisterous months of winter, and the more timid seafarers did not creep out again before May. With the growth of geographical knowledge a number of open-sea routes was brought into operation (Rhodes-Alexandria, Ostia-Carthage, and from Corunna to Cornwall); but seamen in unfamiliar waters seldom ventured out of sight of land. Ships ran to regular time-tables on frequented tracks such as the passage between Corcyra and Brundisium, or on seas under the influence of trade-winds; but nearly all merchantmen belonged to the 'tramp' class.

On the other hand the ancient square-rigged vessels could make fair speed with a favouring wind. They reckoned to cover about fifty nautical miles under average conditions in a daylight period, or ninety miles in twenty-four hours—a rate of sailing that was hardly improved upon until the eighteenth century. The expenses of operation were small, and passenger fares were low. Freight-rates stood higher, because of the labour costs of handling cargoes, but they compared favourably with those of land transport. In the summer season, accordingly, the Mediterranean Sea was alive with traffic. Until the day of the Roman road it was the general highway, and it probably carried at all times the greater part of the merchandise.

The Greeks and Romans made good use of their opportunities for inland travel, but these opportunities were not extensive. In Egypt under Greek and Roman rule the Nile remained as before the main artery of communications. Small sea-going vessels ascended the Tiber as far as Rome; the cargoes of the larger ships were hauled up from Ostia in lighters tugged by teams of oxen. Merchantmen sailed up the Rhine to Nijmegen and Cologne, and the prosperity of Roman London was mainly based on its river-trade. Under Roman rule the river system of France was more thoroughly exploited than at the present day. The Rhône, which has now been quite superseded by the railway, was a main line of communications; the trade of Arelate (Arles) outgrew that of Massilia (Marseille), and Lugdunum (Lyon) became the St. Louis of the ancient world. On a more modest scale, Lutetia (Paris) took advantage of its parallel situation as a river-fork city. But in the Mediterranean countries the rivers lend themselves ill to navigation. They carry too little water in summer, and break into spates in winter, and their mouths are often obstructed with mud-bars. In the Greek homeland river-navigation was practically non-existent.

Navigation by canal was even more restricted. The Romans cut a number of fosses in level stretches of land: from Forum Appii to Tarracina in the Latin plain; from Massilia to the apex of the Rhône delta; from the Zuyder Lake (as it then was) to the North Sea; from Peterborough to Lincoln and the Trent. But ancient engineers could not overcome the difficulties of construction and maintenance in less favourable territory. Ptolemy the Second and Trajan in turn repaired an old Pharaonic canal connecting the apex of the Delta with the Red Sea, but this waterway always relapsed into disuse, presumably for lack of adequate dredging. The Corinthian tyrant Periander (c. 600 B.C.) made a first attempt to perforate the Isthmus of Corinth, and Nero carried on the good work. But in either case the cost of breaking through a ledge of hard limestone without the aid of blasting materials proved to be prohibitive.

In Greece the natural difficulties of land travel intensified the need for good roads. The beginnings of a road system were made by the prehistoric rulers of Cnossus and Mycenae, who built paved streets across Crete and Argolis; but the subsequent disunity of the Greek city-states was a bar to road-making on any large scale. In the neighbourhood of great religious centres like Delphi 'Sacred Ways' were constructed for the benefit of pilgrims and processions, and the building of carriage-ways in Attica was begun in the days of the Athenian tyrants. But Athens was not connected with Corinth by an all-weather road until the reign of the emperor Hadrian. In many parts of Greece the only aids to travel were grooves cut for carriage wheels in outcrops of rock. Vehicular traffic was therefore rarely possible for long distances: travellers by land went almost exclusively on foot, or on the back of a mule or donkey. The successors of Alexander maintained the highways which the former kings of Persia had constructed along their main lines of communication, but they do not appear to have been active road-builders.

The great improvement which the Romans introduced into ancient travel by land was, in the first instance, an incidental result of their far-flung conquests. Their earliest trunk roads, the Via Latina and the Via Appia, were constructed between 350 and 300 B.C. to secure their military hold on Latium and Campania. In the next two centuries they completed a network of highways radiating from the capital to all parts of Italy. During the republican period they were slow to extend the system to the provinces, but from the time of Augustus to the end of the third century they built new roads almost without intermission. It is estimated that by A.D. 300 the Roman Empire was covered with a grid of considerably more than 50,000 miles of paved roads.[1]

Roman roads did not as a rule exceed twenty feet in width, and in broken country their gradients were severe. But their course was carefully traced. In regions which offered no natural difficulties they held an uncompromisingly straight direction. In land liable to be waterlogged they avoided the valley-bottoms, and where necessary they were carried on artificial banks with deep ditches. In mountain country they took the line that was least endangered by avalanches. They were laid on foundations of heavy stones, with one or more intermediate layers of chips or pounded brick, and were surfaced with the hardest available material—flat blocks of lava in Rome; rammed gravel, not unlike that of a modern macadam road, in Britain. The main roads were furnished with bridges on stone piers, some of which are still in use; the lesser roads had trestle bridges or paved fords. Distances were marked by milestones.

The Roman Empire was provided with more roads and better roads than most countries of moderm Europe before 1850. They were designed primarily for the use of pedestrians and pack-animals, and their stiff gradients rendered them unsuitable for the haulage of heavy merchandise.[2] But they were fit to carry light springless carriages in every season of the year, and

[1] Roman Britain is reckoned to have possessed some 5000 miles of good road.

[2] Further handicaps to road haulage were the lack of horseshoes and collars. Horseshoes appear to have come slowly into use under the Roman emperors; collars were quite unknown.

the couriers of the 'cursus publicus' (p. 87), using relays of carriages or mounts, could make fifty miles a day on them. Private travellers who could not afford a coach of their own could hire conveyances from jobmasters, and outside the gates of Pompeii there was a 'taxi-stand'. The roadside inns had none too high a reputation; well-to-do voyagers kept private rest-houses, or relied on the hospitality of friends. But for those who were not fastidious accommodation at 'The Elephant' or 'The Three Camels' was at any rate cheap. The Roman roads accordingly carried every kind of wayfarer: soldiers and traders; pilgrims and holiday-makers; teachers and students, and tourists 'doing' the classical sites (p. 164).

APPENDIX

WEIGHTS AND MEASURES

The weights and measures of the Greek and Roman world need not be described in detail. They were based on the usual principles of metrology. Linear measures were multiples or sub-multiples of the foot; their squares and cubes provided the measures of surface and capacity. Measures of area were also expressed in units of field-work; the Roman *iugerum* (five-eighths of an acre) was the amount of ground which a standard plough would cover in a day. Small weights were denoted in terms of grains of corn, large weights in terms of a man's carrying capacity. Originally there was a great variety of local systems of reckoning, and this was never reduced to complete uniformity. But the political and commercial ascendancy of Athens led to a wide diffusion of Attic weights and measures in the Greek lands, and the Roman conquests achieved a similar result for the Roman systems in the western countries. The Attic *stadium* was a distance of 600 feet; the Roman *mille passus* or mile measured 1000 paces or 5000 feet.[1] The Attic *talent* was a weight approximately equal to 56 lb. av.;

[1] The Greek and the Roman foot were smaller than the English one. The Roman mile was 4880 English feet.

the Roman *libra* and *uncia* were a shade lighter than our pound and ounce troy, which are derived from them.

In early Greece and Rome a corresponding diversity of methods obtained in regard to time-reckoning. All Greek and Italian cities originally observed a lunar calendar, but the systems on which they inserted 'leap months' in order to bring their year back into line with the solar seasons varied from place to place. Their subdivisions of the months also followed different rules, and their years had their beginnings at diverse seasons. The Athenians divided their months into three periods of nine or ten days each. The official Roman calendar observed a strangely unsymmetrical system. The first division of each month was reckoned from the *Kalends* to the *Nones*, the second from the Nones to the *Ides*, the third from the Ides to the next Kalends; but the Nones fell in some months on the fifth day, in others on the seventh, and similarly the Ides fluctuated between the thirteenth and the fifteenth day. The Romans, however, also used an unofficial and much simpler system of continuous reckoning by *nundina* or stretches of eight days, in accordance with the general Italian custom of holding a market on every ninth day. At Athens, New Year's Day came with the summer solstice; at Rome it fell originally on the first of March, but in 153 B.C. it was transferred for administrative convenience to the first of January. In 45 B.C. Caesar introduced an improved calendar based on Egyptian and Hellenistic observations of the solar year, of which our present 'Gregorian' calendar (established in Britain in 1752) is a slight modification. But the new Roman calendar did not drive out all the local systems of time-reckoning.

Another source of confusion was the lack of a universally accepted system for measuring the flow of years. The Greek and Italian city-states dated by the names of their annual chief magistrates. The Athenians would say that Salamis was fought in the year 'when Calliades was archon'; for the Romans the Second Punic War began 'when Publius Cornelius Scipio and Tiberius Sempronius Longus were consuls'. About 300 B.C. the Greeks began to use the reputed year of the first athletic festival at Olympia (776 B.C.) as a starting-point for numbering the years;

and in the last two centuries B.C. the Romans adopted the conventional date of the founding of their city (753 B.C.) for the same purpose. But in spite of their manifest convenience these eras were not adopted universally.

It was left to the Church to standardize time-reckoning by adopting Caesar's calendar, by enforcing observance of the week with its seventh day of rest, and by introduciug the Christian era.

IV

Social Life

1. FAMILY LIFE, AND THE POSITION OF WOMEN

THE GREEKS and Romans, like most of the peoples of ancient Europe and the Near East, were originally organized in families of the patriarchal type. These families were miniature states in themselves, and they were held together by a rigid code under the authority of the *pater familias* (usually the eldest male member). The paterfamilias exercised over his household a power similar to the *imperium* of an early Roman consul (p. 55). He could sell his housemates into slavery and even put them to death. The only check upon his sovereignty was an unwritten law that required him to convene a family council to assist in trying the more serious offences against the family code.

At the death of the paterfamilias all the adult male members obtained their personal freedom; after marriage they became 'fireside despots' in their turn. But the women never escaped the bond of tutelage. So long as a woman remained unmarried, she stood under the authority of her father or some other male relative. A married woman passed into the power (Lat. *manus*) of her husband; a widow might 'belong' to her son. The match was arranged over her head between her father or guardian and the bridegroom (or his parent), and in consideration of a sum paid to her family to compensate for the loss of her services, she was conveyed from one household to another. She owned no property save her strictly personal outfit; and if she was furnished with a dowry, this passed into her husband's keeping. If she did not satisfy her husband, she might be returned to her family, or transferred to another husband.

The history of the Greek and Roman family is mainly that of a progression from patriarchy to a more modern condition. The patriarchal code was broken down under the pressure of several forces. The dispersion of the members of a family by commerce, colonization, or foreign warfare caused the authority of the paterfamilias to lapse through disuse. The rise of the city-states brought him under the overriding control of rulers who would not brook a 'state within a state' and used their legislative and judicial powers to curtail the family 'imperium'. But the principal solvent of the patriarchial family was the growth of an enlightened public opinion, which demanded greater freedom for the individual and no longer approved the complete subjection of women.[1]

But the evolution of the Greek and Roman family was necessarily a slow one. Long-established traditions could not be abandoned in a hurry, and legislators would not venture to interfere in matters of private life where public opinion was not ripe for reforms. Besides, the transition did not proceed everywhere on uniform lines. Among the Greeks the tyranny of the old over the young was soon abated, but the inequality of the sexes was long maintained; the Romans preserved parental authority while they improved the status of women.

In Greece the authority of fathers over their sons was legally terminated when these were enrolled as citizens (usually at the age of twenty). The right of fathers to kill or enslave their kin was abolished or severely curtailed by legislation; at Athens the sale of children was prohibited in the code of Solon. At Rome the *patria potestas* suffered little statutory diminution before the time of Constantine: as late as 63 B.C. a Roman nobleman carried out a death sentence upon an adult son without interference by a magistrate; but such a harsh procedure had by then become highly unusual in Roman society.

In one respect Greek family law remained more primitive than that of Rome. In most Greek states the right of the father to expose unwanted children was not restricted by legislation. In actual practice infanticide was probably uncommon before 200 B.C., indeed the necessity for it was to a large extent removed by a high rate of infant mortality. But after that date it seems to have become frequent enough to keep the Greek population at a stationary level, and even to induce a sharp regression in some cities. At Rome the exposure of sons (other than cripples),

---

[1] Greek opinion was largely influenced by the Homeric poems, in which women played an important and honourable part.

and of the first-born daughter, was forbidden by custom, if not by law, from the earliest times; and it is probable that the Romans, like the other peoples of western Europe, habitually reared all their healthy offspring.

The patriarchal family organization survived for a long time in the Greek and Roman marriage customs. Though the daughters of the family soon ceased to be objects of sale, for a long time they were literally 'given away' to husbands not of their own choosing. While the men as a rule did not enter matrimony until they were well in their 'twenties', or even had passed their thirtieth year, the girls were usually wedded between the ages of fourteen and sixteen. But by the end of the republic the marriage customs of the Roman world had so far been reformed that in current practice, if not in strict law, the bride's consent was required, and in the Christian era it became a common usage for the future husband and wife to arrange their match on their own initiative, subject to the veto of the parents.

In one respect the patriarchal law of marriage underwent an important change. In Greek cities the right of divorce was conceded to wives, probably not later than the fifth century B.C., on the ground of ill-treatment or adultery. At Rome a woman who had once passed into the hand of her husband could not release herself; but as early as 450 B.C. a new type of marriage contract had been invented, by which the bride remained under the authority of her father or guardian. On the death of her parent (or at age twenty-five, if she had a guardian) she became independent and acquired the right of terminating her marriage on the same terms as her husband, i.e. on a simple declaration of her intention to divorce. By the third or second century B.C. the custom of 'free' marriage had become common.

The financial status of women was somewhat improved by the usage which sprang up in quite early times, among the well-to-do families, of providing their daughters with dowries. Although the husband was entitled to the usufruct of the dowry, he did not acquire rights of property in it, but was bound to return it to his wife if he divorced her. In the Greek world women long remained incapable of inheriting property in their own name— curiously enough, Sparta was one of the few states to break with this rule before the time of Alexander; but in the Hellenistic period the ban on bequests to women was removed. According to Greek law women were never entitled to transact business without the authorization of a male guarantor, but in some cases the guarantor was a man of straw, and the functions which he performed were purely formal. At Rome the practice of making bequests to women had become so common in the age of the Punic Wars (during which no doubt many daughters became sole heiresses), that it was legalized in 169 B.C., and the restrictions which the statute of 169 imposed soon became dead letters. By the end of the republican era a considerable amount of property had accumulated in the hands of women. Roman law still required that women should be represented by male 'tutores' in commercial transactions, but this tutorial supervision was soon reduced to a matter of form.

The freedom of movement enjoyed by women naturally differed according to their economic status. In the poorer households they were tied down, not by any social convention, but by the never-ending round of domestic work. In well-to-do families the code that controlled them was of varying degrees of severity. In Greece down to the time of Alexander women lived a comparatively secluded life. Even in households where sufficient slaves were kept to perform the menial tasks, the wife and daughters were expected to spend much of their time in spinning and weaving and miscellaneous indoor work. They took no part in the reception of guests, and when strangers entered the house they retired to their special quarters. They were free to leave the house on shopping expeditions, on visits to their lady friends, or to witness religious spectacles; but they were expected to take a chaperon (perhaps an elderly slave) with them. At Athens, and probably elsewhere in Greece, they were not admitted to the theatre. The freedom or licence which women enjoyed at Sparta, because their menfolk were too busy drilling to look after them, aroused the scandalized envy of their sisters at Athens.[1] In the Hellenistic age Greek women obtained

---

[1] It is sometimes stated that the Dorian Greeks allowed their women more freedom of movement than the Ionians. But there is no adequate evidence for this.

more liberty. The example of some masterful Hellenistic queens no doubt contributed to raise their status, and the rapid movements of population during this period disturbed the sedentary habits to which the women of the classical age had been trained. It is significant that at this time opportunities for a higher education were no longer withheld from women. Nevertheless it is doubtful whether women in the Greek world ever exercised their due influence.

At Rome the patriarchal attitude to women still found occasional expression under the later republic, e.g. in the epitaph of a lady whose crowning achievement was to have 'minded the house and done work in wool'. But Roman women at all times enjoyed a relatively large amount of freedom. In a Roman house there was no separate quarter for the women; the Roman housewife met her husband's guests and dined out with him.[1] Custom required that Roman ladies should have an escort out-of-doors, but with this safeguard it permitted them to move at their ease in public. At the theatre and amphitheatre special blocks were reserved for women, but it was left to their own good taste to decide which entertainments they should attend or avoid.

From the second century B.C. onward the education of Roman women was often carried beyond the elementary stage. Though their early marriage would prevent them from attendance at higher schools, Roman ladies were given opportunities of further study at home. In the Roman world, no less than among the Greeks, the learned professions were always reserved for men, and those Roman women who studied with more zeal than discretion were marked down as bluestockings; but educated Roman ladies were freely admitted to the literary circles of their day. The intellectual accomplishments of Cornelia, the mother of Tiberius and Gaius Cracchus, and of Iulia Domna, the consort of the Emperor Septimius Severus (c. A.D. 200), whose salons were the headquarters of 'high-brow' society, were no doubt exceptional. But before the end of the republican era intellectual companionship between men and women had ceased to be a matter for wonder or scandal.

---

[1] See the comment of Cornelius Nepos (Preface, §§ 6 and 7) on the restrictions placed upon women in Greece.

The growth of material civilization brought with it certain temptations that left their mark on the Greek and Roman family. Among the wealthier inhabitants of the larger cities 'fast sets' were formed which no doubt merited the strictures of contemporary moralists and satirists, and the chief centres of traffic contained the usual underworld population. A particularly insidious danger grew up out of the institution of slavery, which offered innumerable opportunities to those lacking in self-control, and served to perpetuate laxities in the moral code. A considerable number of female slaves in the Greek and Roman world were prostitutes, and no stigma was attached to celibates or widowers who kept a concubine.[1] In the last days of the Roman Republic and under the early emperors freedom of divorce was grossly abused both by men and by women in high society. The worst offenders were men of political ambitions, who made and unmade marriages with a single eye to their political career. Caesar, who had four wives, and Sulla, who had five, were regarded as somewhat unconventional; but Pompey, who also married five times, was considered a model of respectability.

Yet it would be a sad mistake to generalize too freely from individual instances of notorious evil living among the Greeks and Romans.[2] The general conditions of life in Mediterranean lands make for temperate habits; and there is abundant evidence in Greek and Latin literature that the sense of family loyalty which was the most precious legacy of the patriarchal age to later times retained its hold upon the Greek and Roman peoples in general. It was no mere accident that the *Odyssey*, an epic of conjugal fidelity, was the 'best seller' of the ancient world.[3] Even more eloquent are the not infrequent epitaphs of slaves, petty craftsmen, and bourgeois in the cities of the Roman Empire which commemorate in simple but fervent language the felicity of a married couple who lived thirty or forty years 'without a

[1] One result of the comparative segregation of men and women among the Greeks was that homosexual practices gained a wide vogue and attained a measure of respectability.

[2] An entirely misleading view of ancient society is given in modern novels and popular histories which merely reproduce scenes from Juvenal or Petronius. This is a dangerous economy of truth.

[3] Homer says outright that life can offer nothing better than a happy marriage (*Od*. vi. 183).

single complaint', or the deep distress of parents at the untimely loss of a darling child (pp. 175–6). In a word, the evolution of the Greek and Roman family brought it to a stage equivalent to the modern European household.

The ritual attending the great family events in the Greek and Roman world did not differ materially from that of the present day. The place of infant baptism was taken by a formal ceremony at which the new-born child received its name and (at Rome) underwent a ritual purification. Birthdays were kept as they are now, and were the occasion of an exchange of presents among friends. Under the Roman emperors, when astrology came into vogue, the remembrance of their natal day bceame an obsession with many persons. Wedding ceremonies began with an exchange of contract deeds and a sacrifice and prayer at the house of the bride, and ended at nightfall with a joyous procession, in which the bride was conveyed to her new home.

In the disposal of their dead the Greeks and Romans practised inhumation and cremation side by side; in the Christian era burial became the general usage. This diversity of custom sprang originally from a difference of race, for the early inhabitants of the Mediterranean bestowed their dead in the ground, whereas the northern immigrants burnt them. But in historic times the prevalent usage was largely a matter of convenience or of fashion. Greek and Roman funerals were often made an occasion for pomp and circumstance. The wailings of the professional mourners who attended the obsequies of wealthy persons, and the provocative luxury of the undertakers' outfit, were carried to such lengths in some towns as to give rise to sumptuary legislation. A more pleasing feature of the ancient funeral customs was the observance of an All Souls' Day, at which the survivors poured libations on the graves of the departed and (in Italy) bedecked them with flowers.

2. INDOOR ENTERTAINMENTS

Among the principal social functions of the more well-to-do Greeks and Romans was the dinner-party. To some these gatherings merely offered an opportunity for repletion. Among the Romans the over-elaboration of the menu, and the unashamed gluttony of some diners who gorged to the point of falling sick and then began all over again, was sufficiently frequent to provide a broad and easy target for satirists; and Greek young men as well as Roman sometimes drank more than they could hold and fell to brawling and 'ragging'. But these lapses from good taste were by no means characteristic of Greek and Roman conviviality. The real test of success in these functions lay not so much in the table fare as in the entertainment. To facilitate the free exchange of talk the number of diners was usually limited to nine, and the couches were arranged to make three sides of a square, so that all members of the company were within earshot. Professional musicians or dancers or jugglers were sometimes hired to keep a party going. In Greece, however, the company usually provided their own entertainment, by singing ballads or catches,[1] or with the game of 'kottabos', which was played by flicking a jet of wine out of a saucer at a mark.

At Rome it was the custom for men of high station to hold a morning reception in the atrium of their house. This practice was a survival from earlier times, when patricians kept a morning hour for clients who called for assistance or advice. Under the emperors this function lingered on in a degenerate form. The visitors now were mostly office-seekers and hangers-on, and their patrons were more concerned to cut a figure than to render service.

The Greeks and Romans had their 'parlour games' for whiling away time within the home circle. Playing-cards were unknown to them, but they had various games of hazard, such as tossing coins and throwing dice or knuckle-bones. The lure of gambling of course proved too strong for some enthusiasts who played away their whole fortune, and a law at Rome which made dicing into a punishable offence except at certain holidays remained a dead letter.[2] Those who preferred to match their skill rather

---

[1] The singing of ballads to commemorate the exploits of famous ancestors was a custom of the early Romans. But it seems to have died out by the time of the Punic Wars.

[2] A surviving letter of the Emperor Augustus describes a dicing-party at which his stepson Drusus 'broke into loud shouts over the fun of the game' (Suetonius, *Augustus*, lxxi. § 3).

than their luck played games resembling modern draughts or backgammon. The 'draught-board of King Minos' was recovered in the excavations at Cnossus, and a similar table was brought back to Rome by Pompey, as part of the spoil from the palace of King Mithridates. The most difficult of these board games was probably the one named 'latrunculi', in which the different pieces had diverse values, as in chess.

Greek and Roman children amused themselves with the same playthings as we see in present-day nurseries. From rattles they passed on to dolls and marionettes, or to figures of animals and small go-carts: many of the terra-cotta toys which have been recovered from children's coffins might have come straight out of a modern children's bazaar. They rode hobby-horses, they played pick-a-back, hide and seek, and blind-man's-buff. Among household pets dogs naturally held the chief place, but several varieties of birds, including even geese and quails, were kept in the house. The domestic cat was a comparative rarity (except in Egypt).

On the whole, the Greek and Roman home did not play an important part as a social centre. Like the modern inhabitants of Mediterranean lands, the Greeks and Romans did not readily admit strangers to the intimacy of their homes and did not confide family affairs to the ears of outsiders. The Greek house in particular lost much of its social value because of the comparative seclusion of women. Besides, the Mediterranean climate lures men abroad: the house is a place for eating and sleeping, and sometimes for working, but men commonly meet their friends and take their pleasure in the open. The Greeks and Romans accordingly sought most of their entertainment out-of-doors.

3. THE TOWN AS A SOCIAL CENTRE

The cities of the Greek and Roman world offered such a variety of pastimes as has not been surpassed until recent times. Every such town was in itself a club, and not the least advantage of urban life in Greek and Roman eyes was that it brought men into daily contact with congenial company. The chief rendezvous of the city was the market-place, and the baths, porticoes, and colonnades, where the townsfolk forgathered, in their leisure hours and conversed on the topics of the day with the easy affability of Mediterranean people. The taverns drew the poorer folk together for a chat over their drinks, and the barbers' shops were recognized resorts for the exchange of gossip among the more well-to-do.

For those who preferred a more limited circle of companions there was an abundance of clubs in the proper sense, with a regular membership and fixed articles of association. The earliest of these societies were the gilds of craftsmen and merchants, whose object was largely, or even mainly, convivial (p. 120). As industry became more specialized and trade expanded, these gilds multiplied and spread over all the Greek and Roman lands. Similar clubs were subsequently founded by actors, athletes, and other groups whose members were bound together by a common occupation, and the religious conventicles which were formed for the communal worship of deities not on the state calendar (p. 307) also served as social centres. In the Greek lands club life did not reach its full development until the Hellenistic period, and in Italy it did not become widespread until the last days of the republican era. Its growth was hampered here and there by official regulations which were primarily aimed at treason dens and conclaves of the underworld, but sometimes hit a broader target. From the time of Caesar and Augustus the right of meeting was, strictly speaking, limited to associations that had received a special permit. But in actual practice the Roman government was inclined to be tolerant, and even encouraged the formation of clubs among the poorer classes. In the first two centuries of the Christian era accordingly the number of such associations was remarkably great—particularly in Italy and in Asia Minor—and the club habit had spread to the humblest social classes. Even the slaves had their gilds, and in some societies membership was open alike to those of free and of servile status. A special attraction of some clubs to the poorer folk was that they made provision for the decent burial of their members on payment of a small annual premium. Such clubs frequently maintained their own *columbaria*, or underground chambers, in which the bones or ashes of departed members were disposed in separate niches with a commemorative epitaph.

The principal social events of the Greek and Roman clubs were the dinner-parties which were held on Founder's Day, on the birthdays of generous patrons, and at intermediate dates. Orderly behaviour was the general rule of these reunions, and fines were exacted from offenders against club etiquette.

Among the organized entertainments in Greek and Roman cities one of the commonest was a display of pageantry. The ceremonial at the festivals of the city-gods often included a procession of priests and their attendants, together with chosen representatives of the citizen-body. A progress of this kind has been preserved for our gaze on the frieze of the Parthenon (part of which is still in situ, part in the British Museum). Here we can still see the flower of the Athenian population as they defile to the Acropolis on the occasion of Athena's birthday. The Hellenistic monarchs now and then feasted the eyes of their townsfolk with grand military parades; but these exhibitions were not of such regular occurrence as the triumphs with which the Roman generals celebrated their interminable victories.

The Roman triumphs were originally ceremonies of thanksgiving and purification, in which the home-coming imperator placed his laurel wreath on the lap of Jupiter's statue on the Capitol. Eventually this ceremony was made subordinate to the preliminary pageant, which became continually more elaborate until the time of Pompey and Caesar, who kept their processions on the move for several successive days. The triumphator was conveyed to the Capitol in a gilded chariot attended by picked detachments of his army. In front of him went the captive chiefs in chains, a choice selection of the spoils of battle, pictures of war scenes and models of captured cities, and posters on which the results of the campaign were set forth as in a modern advertisement.[1]

The lesser cities of course could not stage such a dazzling

[1] The spoil from the Temple of Jerusalem is depicted on the Arch of Titus. War-scenes like those sculptured on Trajan's Column were exhibited on painted panels. Among the posters carried at one of Caesar's triumphs was one which bore the famous words 'Veni, vidi, vici' (Suetonius, *Iulius*, xxxvii. § 2).

display, but they made as brave a show as their means permitted. Small Greek towns that had no material wealth to exhibit, and no victories to celebrate, would make up for this deficiency by organizing a parade of their school-children.

4. DRAMATIC PERFORMANCES

The Greek and Latin drama, regarded as a branch of literature, will be described in a later chapter (VIII. 3, 5). As a means of entertainment, its performances bore a closer similarity to the theatrical presentations of the Middle Ages than to those of the present day. They formed part of the festivals of the city-gods —the Athenian drama was consecrated to Dionysus, that of Rome to Apollo and other deities. They were accordingly limited to a few days in the year, but on these occasions each festival-day witnessed a succession of plays from morn to eve. The prices of admission were low, and in some cities entry was free; and the audiences resembled a town meeting in numbers and in liveliness. The habit of playgoing established itself in Greece in the fifth and fourth centuries, and at Rome in the second century. In the Hellenistic age the Greek colonists in the eastern countries set up theatres wherever they went: even a small town like Ptolemais in Upper Egypt kept a complete troupe of performers; and under the Roman emperors theatres sprang up in all the western provinces. The deterioration in the character of the plays that eventually set in by no means abated the popularity of the drama. The auditoria of the theatres were designed to accommodate anything up to 30,000 spectators; at first they were run up for the occasion in trestle-work, but eventually permanent stone buildings took the place of these temporary structures.[1] The Romans sometimes erected their theatres in tiers of solid masonry, but the more usual procedure was to scoop the auditorium out of a convenient hill-side and to line it with stone seats.

Dancing, apart from the simple steps of the country folk

[1] The first stone theatres were built in Greece in the fourth century. The earliest permanent playhouse at Rome was dedicated by Pompey in 55 B.C.

(p. 163), reached a high degree of elaboration in the Greek and Roman world. Like the modern ballet, it brought into play the whole body, and it called for dramatic ability, for the dancer's motions were intended to imitate physical actions or to convey mental impressions. Among the Greeks and (to a less extent) in Italy dancing attained an early vogue as part of religious ritual, and young men and women of good family would undertake the necessary training for the honour of 'dancing before the Lord'. But eventually the dance became more and more secularized, and often vulgarized, and it tended to become a professional occupation. In Italy dancing by amateurs was never more than a passing fashion, for it offended against the Roman ideal of 'gravitas'. But troupes of Greek performers were hired to give displays at public holidays, and under the emperors the 'pantomime' or dancing opera became the most popular of theatrical entertainments.

5. MUSIC

The music of the Greeks and Romans is not easy for us to appreciate, for while we possess several Greek treatises on musical theory, and the remaining scores (which were expressed in letters and numbers) have been successfully transcribed to the modern cinque-stave, the number of the surviving pieces is too small to provide an adequate idea of the composers' technique and range of expression. The Greeks had, in theory at least, a wider variety of melodies than modern Europeans, for they recognized a larger number of scales, and they made use of quarter-tones. But their attempts at harmony seemingly did not extend beyond a simple accompaniment of a vocal score by an instrument; vocalists sang in unison or at intervals of an octave. They possessed a considerable variety of string and wind instruments, and they invented a miniature organ with a water-blast; but they did not use a bow to their string instruments, and their trumpets and horns served for signalling only. The commonest instruments were the lyre and the *aulos* (Lat. *tibia*). The lyre was a miniature harp which could be played by twanging the chords or by tapping them with a light hammer.

It had an efficient sounding-board and produced a louder note than the harp; but the number of the strings—seven in the earlier and fifteen or a few more in the more developed instruments—was not sufficient to allow of a wide range of execution. The aulos was a wood-wind instrument, which in its most usual form consisted of two convergent tubes. The sound was produced by a reed in the mouthpiece, and according to the type of reed employed it bore some resemblance to the modern oboe or clarinet. The aulos in its double form commanded at least twenty notes, and so had a wider compass than the lyre, but it was more difficult to play.

Whatever the quality of their music, there can be no doubt about the part which it played in the life of the Greeks. It was valued not only as a means of entertainment, but as an instrument of education, and it was commonly taught in the higher schools. In polite Greek society every guest was expected to be able to sing a solo part and to accompany himself on the lyre. The singing of hymns formed a regular part of religious services, and oratorios in which voices and instruments supported or followed each other were performed at some of the festivals. At Delphi and other religious centres virtuosos in vocal and instrumental music assembled from all the Greek lands and gave displays of their prowess. The principal performers ranked only below the athletic stars in popular esteem, and they received official votes of thanks from cities where they had afforded more than ordinary delight to their audiences.

The abundant musical talent of the Italian people remained strangely latent in ancient times. The Romans never regarded music as anything more than an entertainment; they borrowed most of their instruments from the Greeks, and although a few gentlemen and ladies from the time of Augustus took up singing and playing on the lyre as elegant accomplishments, they mostly remained content to listen to the performances of Greek professionals. Some men of wealth maintained small private orchestras to entertain their guests. The general public developed a taste for music as an accessory at the popular festivals, but it had no ear for 'classical' Greek compositions and preferred a jolly noise by massed bands.

6. PHYSICAL RECREATIONS—ATHLETICS

The open-air games of Greek and Roman children were as modern as their indoor amusements. They rocked themselves on swings and see-saws; they trundled hoops, set tops spinning, and flew kites; they played with marbles and stuffed balls.

Ball games were also popular with older players. Special courts for ball exercise were attached to gymnasia and to baths, and to the private mansions of some wealthy Romans. But the use of bats and rackets to propel the ball seems to have been hardly known.[1] The games mostly consisted of simple catching bouts, or of a rudimentary form of net-ball or fives. We may suspect that when distinguished Romans kept up their ball-play into middle age (as Cato the Younger and the emperors Augustus and Marcus Aurelius are said to have done), they did so mainly in order to keep down their weight.[2]

The Mediterranean Sea was naturally the chief swimming school of the Greeks and Romans; in the hot season it drew numerous holiday-makers to its shores (p. 164). At Rome the younger men took their daily plunge in the Tiber. In addition, baths were attached to the gymnasia in Greek cities, and under the Roman emperors the towns of Italy and the western provinces provided themselves with a veritable profusion of such establishments. Rome in the fourth century A.D. is said to have had 850 bathing places, and in the largest of these, the Bath of Caracalla and of Diocletian, the swimming-tanks were as large as in the monster modern pools. Pompeii, with its 20,000–30,000 inhabitants, possessed at least three public baths, and even in a mining village of Portugal a properly equipped bath was to be found. These establishments usually contained a suite of air-conditioned chambers for Turkish bathing. Great as was the number of baths, it appears to have been no larger than was needed to satisfy the bathing mania of the townsfolk. The amount of time which the people of Rome spent in the baths was so

[1] A fifth-century relief at Athens shows some youths armed with instruments like hockey sticks. But the rules of their game are unknown.

[2] An amusing account of such eupeptic ball-play will be found in the *Letters of Sidonius Appollinaris* (v. 17), where a middle-aged gentleman 'fluffs his catches', but sets his circulation going.

extravagant that the Emperor Hadrian reduced the hours of opening.

Despite the fondness of the Greeks and Romans for water, they took little interest in aquatic sports or boat-races. Regattas were held at the Panathenaea and a few other Greek festivals, but they apparently found no favour with the youth of Italy.[1]

Among the Greeks the most important form of physical recreation consisted of athletics. The origin of Greek athletics goes back to prehistoric Crete, where boxers and acrobats performed at the Court of King Minos, and 'toreadors' of both sexes, after literally taking an onrushing bull by the horns, turned a somersault on to his back. But these virtuosos were probably professional entertainers. Unlike them, the Achaean chieftains took a personal part in boxing and wrestling competitions and foot-races.

As soon as the Greek cities emerged from the Dark Ages they took to athletics as a national sport. In the eighth and following centuries one town after another set up a gymnasium and organized local competitions. These festivals subsequently enjoyed the patronage of the city-tyrants, and the most important of them were raised to the status of Panhellenic gatherings.[2] A further stimulus to the cult of athletics was given by the Persian Wars; in the period that followed these wars the Greek athletic spirit was at its best.

Among the festivals of this period there was a group of four which attained a special pre-eminence: the Olympian, Pythian, Isthmian, and Nemean games. The first of these was held once in four years at Olympia in western Peloponnesus; the second, also a quadrennial contest, took place at Delphi; the Isthmia were celebrated every second year near Corinth, and the Nemea, another biennial event, at Cleonae, near Argos. The Panathenaea, which were celebrated at Athens in every fourth year,

[1] Virgil's account of a Trojan boat-race (*Aeneid*, v. 114 ff.) should not be taken as a description of an actual Roman regatta.

[2] According to the generally accepted Greek tradition the Olympian festival was founded in 776 B.C. This date may be roughly correct; but the games probably did not become Panhellenic until the seventh century.

also included an athletic competition which ranked but little below the 'Big Four'.

The character of these festivals may be best illustrated by describing in outline the one at Olympia. This site lay in a somewhat out-of-the-way part of Greece which never took a prominent part in politics or commerce. For a long time it contained no permanent buildings except a few temples and store-houses, and it was not until the fourth century that porticoes and other concessions to material comfort began to be provided. As the games were held in the hottest season of the year, they must have taxed severely the physical endurance both of the performers and of the onlookers. But the high authority of Zeus, the patron god of the festival, the unquestioned probity of the stewards and judges (who were drawn from the nobility of the neighbouring city of Elis), and the zest of the Greeks for a supreme 'blue ribbon' competition, raised the prestige of Olympia above that of the other athletic gatherings. To ensure a representative attendance, the stewards sent out heralds to proclaim a 'sacred truce' among all the cities of the Greek world, and to request a safe-conduct for all travellers to Olympia through their territory; and their demand was scrupulously obeyed. The passion for athletics was the one force which could, for a moment at least, quench the mutual animosities of the Greek states.

The programme of events at Olympia included a group of five events, known as the 'pentathlon', in which the best all-round performer gained the first prize. The first event in the pentathlon was a flat race of one stadium (600 feet). The second was the long jump, which the Greeks held in greater esteem than the high jump, although the obstacles to travel in their country were walls rather than ditches. The competitors carried weights like dumb-bells, which they shot forward to arm's length as they made their landing, as a means of adding a few inches to their leap. The third event was the casting of the discus, a plate of stone or bronze, with an average weight of five pounds, which was lobbed with a long underhand swing. The fourth was the hurling of the javelin. To impart a steady flight to their missile, the athletes gave it a spin, like that of a rifle bullet, by pulling with their fingers at the moment of discharge on a string wound round the javelin-shaft. Last came a wrestling bout, in which, if we may judge by surviving illustrations, only body-grips were allowed.

The events outside the pentathlon included races of various lengths up to twenty-four stadia (*c.* 2½ miles).[1] The most exacting of these was probably a race of two stadia, out and home, in which the competitors wore part of their military armour and carried a shield. Another important event was boxing. Greek pugilists used a considerable number of leads and understood the value of a good stance. But they ruined their sport when they reinforced the soft leather strips which they had originally worn to protect their knuckles with thongs of crude leather, so as to increase the weight of the blow.[2] Allied to wrestling was a contest known as the 'pancratium', in which the combatants strove to put one another into chancery by means of a wrestling grip or a jujitsu twist, and the successful competitor pummelled the loser until the latter gave the signal of defeat. Lastly, men of wealth competed in horse and chariot races; but the entrants in these usually provided professional jockeys or drivers.

Little is heard of team events at the Greek athletic festivals. At the Panathenaea a relay race was run in which the members of each company passed a torch from hand to hand, but at Olympia all competitions were between individuals.

The prizes awarded at the major festivals were of small or of merely nominal value:[3] at Olympia they consisted of simple wreaths of wild olive. But Greek cities, intent on attracting 'star' performers to their local competitions, began to offer substantial sums of money to the winners. In so doing they paved the way for the professional athlete, who specialized in some particular branch of the sport and went round from meeting to meeting

[1] There was no Marathon Race at Olympia or any other Greek festival. This is a purely modern invention.

[2] Professional boxers of the Roman period weighted their gloves with knobs of iron or lead, thus reducing the 'noble art' to a mere Red Indian contest of endurance.

[3] At the Panathenaea the prizes were large vases filled with olive oil and decorated with athletic scenes. (See the surviving specimens in the British Museum.)

to carry off the prizes. In the fourth and following centuries the amateur performers were gradually driven out of the field by itinerant professionals; but they continued none the less to frequent their local training schools. In the lands conquered by Alexander the Greek colonists everywhere built themselves gymnasia in the same way as they set up theatres: in Egypt membership of a gymnasium was made the official test of Greek nationality. The Olympic games endured until A.D. 394, when the Emperor Theodosius I suppressed them as a relic of paganism. Greek athletics had their faults and their deficiencies, but they inspired some of the noblest works of classical literature, and some of the choicest ancient statues and vase-paintings, and they established that cult of physical fitness which is one of the best legacies of Greece to the modern world.

7. PHYSICAL RECREATIONS—ROMAN SPORTS

The men of Rome from early days raced and boxed and wrestled in an informal fashion on the Campus Martius, and horse-races formed part of their early religious ritual. But when they became acquainted with the organized sports of Greece they showed no eagerness to imitate them, for Greek athletics had by then become over-specialized and had ceased to serve as a concomitant to military training. The Roman aristocracy, however, realized the entertainment value of athletic performances by professionals. From the second century, therefore, they hired Greek gymnasts and jockeys to perform at the Roman popular festivals, and these aroused at Rome such an interest in one branch of their sport, chariot-racing, as they had never been able to stimulate in their own country. Under the later republic the charioteers conceived the happy idea of organizing themselves into teams with distinctive colours; the Roman proletariat now 'followed' the White or the Red, the Green or the Blue party, and worked themselves up to a frenzy on behalf of their favourites.[1] Under the emperors the Circus Maximus

[1] See the description of the Circus crowd at Constantinople in Gibbon's *Decline and fall*, ch. 40.

Betting at the circus is mentioned by Latin writers. But there is no evidence of organized and universal gambling.

between the Palatine and Aventine hills had to be enlarged so as to accommodate anything up to 250,000 spectators. The circus races lasted the entire day, and by the fourth century A.D. sixty-four days in the year had been set apart for them. The leading charioteers not only were popular heroes but amassed considerable fortunes. But perhaps their fees were not excessive, in view of the great risks run by four-in-hands hurtling round the sharp bends of a Roman race-course.

Another alien sport, which the Roman nobility imported for the amusement of the populace, consisted in the gladiatorial games. These were possibly a survival of the primitive custom by which servants or war captives were slain at the funeral of a departed chieftain. Among the early Etruscans this antiquated ritual was revived as a form of entertainment at which the retainers, instead of being helplessly massacred, dispatched one another in duels. From the time of the Punic Wars similar displays were provided from time to time by the noble houses at Rome on the occasion of a death within their family; but by the end of the republican era the gladiatorial shows were fast losing their connexion with funeral ceremonial, and the performers now consisted of prisoners of war, condemned criminals, and a few volunteers who risked their lives for their livelihood or to acquire notoriety. Under the emperors the gladiatorial games were organized as a regular part of the calendar of amusements.

The gladiatorial contests had at least the merit of being real trials of skill and nerve. The performers were men of first-rate physique who received a careful preliminary training in the use of their weapons. They were pitted against antagonists who usually carried a different but equivalent armament, so that the chances of the duellists were even at the start. A fencer who had survived some thirty or forty assaults-at-arms was comfortably pensioned off; and even a defeated combatant might live to draw his allowance, for the etiquette of the arena required that the winner should not administer the *coup de grâce* until the spectators had given him the signal, and the onlookers not infrequently chose to spare the life of a plucky loser. Even so, it is difficult to understand the popularity of these contests, which was inferior only to that of the circus races. The largest of the 'amphitheatres' or circular arenas in which these displays were given, the so-called 'Colosseum', was built to accommodate at least 60,000 spectators, and the most accomplished duellists acquired a reputation similar to that of the principal jockeys. The vogue of the gladiatorial games also extended to all the western provinces: even in distant Britain at least six towns had their arena.

A variant of the gladiatorial contests was the 'naumachia', a mimic naval battle in which criminals or other undesirables were condemned to sink each other in imitation battleships on some improvised pool of water. The Emperor Claudius staged a veritable Salamis on a mountain tarn in the Apennines, where 19,000 men are said to have fought.

Finally, beast-baiting played its part in the underworld of ancient sport. The Greeks satisfied their blood-lust with fights between cocks or quails. At Rome big game (tigers, leopards, and even elephants) from all the wilder regions of the empire shared the arena with the gladiators. The animals were pitted against one another, or against armed combatants who had every chance of winning their match, or against unarmed men and women (condemned criminals) who had no chance at all.

The Greeks and Romans nowhere showed a greater contrast than in the character of their public amusements. In this respect the Romans failed to learn many of the lessons which the Greeks had to offer them, and their taste in amusements consequently remained undeveloped.[1]

8. COUNTRY SPORTS—TRAVEL

For the Mediterranean peasantry the breaks in the daily routine of work are fewer than in more northerly countries, because field operations do not suffer any long interruption in the winter season. For Greek and Roman rustics holiday-time was reduced to the usual seasonal festivals that mark the completion of the chief agricultural processes: sowing, harvest, and vintage. The merry-makings on these occasions included chain

---

[1] It is fair to add that educated Romans took little delight in the blood-sports of the arena, and that Seneca expressly protested against them.

dances, processions with impromptu patter, improvised dramatic performances, and rough-and-tumble sports. (The ancient equivalent of climbing the greasy pole was for tipsy yokels to dance a breakdown on oiled wineskins.) These amusements endured for centuries, regardless of the march of culture in the neighbouring towns.

For the gentlefolk residing on the countryside the chief pastime was the chase. So long as big game was to be found, they took their sport dangerously. But the shrinkage of tall forest under the axe of the woodcutter gradually reduced the preserves of the more formidable quarries. The lion, which was still to be encountered in Greek lands in the age of Homer, disappeared soon after, and the wild boar retreated into the mountain zones of Greece and Italy. As the suburban coverts were reduced to brushwood, Greek and Roman sportsmen had to be content to follow lesser game such as hares. In the absence of quick-firing weapons, the pursuit of hares was not much more than a ride behind the hounds. For the purpose of the hunt hounds were specially bred as questers or coursers. For bringing down the larger quarries the powerful brutes that still sometimes endanger travellers in Epirus, and British animals with some resemblance to the bull-dog, were in special request. Fox-hunting and hawking were practised in Gaul, but do not appear to have been pursued as a sport in Greece or Italy, where the foxes were valued only for their skins, and birds for their feathers. Among the less strenuous forms of the hunt, fishing with hook and rod had its attractions for elderly men who preferred to combine their sport with a rest cure.

During the hot season Greek and Roman families in easy circumstances used to leave the sweltering towns for the cooler air of the mountains or seaside. Athenian holiday-makers would retire, as they do now, to the woods and springs of Cephissia; these summer outings, we are told, were especially welcome to the women and children. By the end of the republican era the habit of *villeggiatura* had become firmly established among the wealthier Italian households. The exodus from Rome in particular was heavy, for the capital had the reputation of being noisy and nerve-racking at all times, and of becoming oppressive during the dog-days; except in times of crisis, the Senate suspended its sessions during August. The pleasant foot-hills of the Apennines were favourite holiday haunts, and the western shore of Italy from Pisa to Sorrento was studded with the villas of summer residents. The queen of Italian holiday resorts was Baiae on the bay of Naples. The special attractions of this bay were the brisk breeze of the summer afternoons and the holiday atmosphere of the Neapolitans, who still preserved their Greek tongue and Greek gaiety. At Baiae fashionable society celebrated a 'high season', in which the stiff social etiquette of the capital was set aside for the time being, and built itself villas whose provocative luxury aroused the wrath of Roman moralists.

Increased security and ease of travel under the shelter of the Pax Romana give rise to the sight-seeing holiday. This usually took the form of a tour to places of artistic or historical interest in Sicily, in the Greek lands, or in Egypt. Athens, Delphi and Olympia, Troy and Pergamum, the Pyramids and the temples of Karnak, were the favourite resorts of the tourist, and the city of Rome held ever-increasing attractions for visitors from the provinces. While the Greeks and Romans had a keen appreciation of serene and smiling landscapes, they seem to have had no eye for the sterner scenery of mountain lands. The Alps were for them (as they remained until the nineteenth century) mere 'protuberances' and obstructions to traffic, and their peaks never tempted the ancient explorer. But Mount Etna drew so many visitors that the town of like name at its base came to wear the aspect of an ancient Zermatt or Grindelwald; and an inn was erected near the summit for those who, like the Emperor Hadrian, made the ascent for the sake of the sunrise.

V

The Written and the Spoken Word

I. THE GREEK AND LATIN ALPHABETS

MAN HAS always asked for signs. On stone or metal, skin or bark,[1] he has made scratches[2] in his attempt to impale the flying word and to leave significant marks so as to preserve for the future his acts or his thoughts. The art of writing was therefore much older than Greek or Roman history, but the Greeks and Romans did much to perfect and diffuse it.

In Greece the prehellenic 'Minoan' script, which had been adapted by the Achaean invaders (pp. 15–16) to the needs of an Hellenic tongue, was replaced at a date not later than 700 B.C., and perhaps as early as 1000 B.C., by an alphabetic system of writing derived from the Phoenicians. The Greeks acknowledged their debt to the Phoenicians in a legend which related that a Phoenician prince, Cadmus, had brought the alphabet to their country, and 'Cadmean' letters (not unlike the Ionic Greek script of his own time) were shown to Herodotus at Thebes. Indeed, the derivation of the Greek alphabet from the Phoenician is demonstrated beyond doubt by the fact that the serial order of its letters was the same as that of the Phoenician alphabet, and that the names by which the Greeks designated their individual letters were not Greek but Phoenician. Thus *alpha* is a Greek form of the Phoenician word *aleph*, which means 'ox' (the shape of this letter roughly resembling the horns of an ox); *beta* and *gamma* are Greek versions of Phoenician *beth* ('house') and *gimel* ('camel'). A further proof of the Phoenician origin of the Greek alphabet is that in the earliest Greek inscriptions the letters ran from right to left, as in Phoenician and other Oriental scripts.

It was a fortunate accident for the Greeks—and for the many people who were ultimately their pupils—that it was the

---

[1] *Liber* in Latin meant 'bark', and the German *Buch* is derived from 'Buche', i.e. beech.

[2] Both *graphein* in Greek and *scribere* in Latin mean 'to make grooves.'

Phoenician system of writing that was first brought to their notice and therefore served as a prototype for them. The Phoenician alphabet had the merit of great simplicity, for it contained no more than twenty-two symbols, and the completed Greek alphabet had only twenty-four. Unlike the 'cuneiform' scripts of Mesopotamia and Asia Minor, which never contained less than one hundred symbols, and could therefore be memorized only by professional scribes in the service of temples and business firms, the Greek alphabet was easy to learn, and the art of reading and writing was thus brought within the reach of everybody.

The Greeks, however, did not copy the Phoenician alphabet in a blind and mechanical manner, but adapted it to the special requirements of their own tongue. They invented some additional letters, they discarded some Phoenician signs and gave to others a different sound-value. Their most important contribution to the world's alphabets was the provision of vowel-signs, the Greek tongue being as rich in vowels as the Semitic languages were poor. (In Phoenician the vowels were not indicated at all, and in Hebrew they were represented, after the eighth century B.C., by mere dots or strokes, above or below the consonants.[1]) They also introduced the practice of doubling consonants when they were pronounced double, and of distinguishing between long and short vowels.

The Greeks, in addition, gave more symmetrical shapes to their letter-symbols, and they abandoned the inconvenient Oriental method of writing from right to left. By way of an early experiment they wrote in alternate directions (*boustrophēdon*, like an ox that turns at each furrow-head), but after 500 B.C. their script ran invariably from left to right. Originally many varieties of local alphabets were current in Greece, but a big step towards unification was taken in 403 B.C., when the Athenians adopted the 'Ionic' alphabet from the Greeks of Asia Minor, which presently became standard throughout the Greek lands.

From Greece the alphabet passed to Italy. Here it was first introduced among the Etruscans, who used Greek letters derived

[1] Hence the perplexity of a contemporary Afrikaans translator of the Old Testament over a vowel point, which was solved by the remark of the native boy who brought in his coffee! 'But, Baas, that is where a fly has sat'.

probably from the town of Cumae, near Naples. Other Italic dialects, like Oscan and Umbrian, seem to have borrowed their letter-system from a later form of the Etruscan alphabet, and the Latins are now believed to have drawn their alphabet from the same source. It was probably during the seventh century, when the Etruscans were predominant in Central Italy, that writing was introduced into Rome. Our earliest Latin inscription, written on metal with letters still running from right to left, dates from about 600 B.C.; the earliest text on stone, written in the 'ox-winding' fashion, belongs to about 500.

The Romans had no need to make extensive alterations in the Greek alphabet to suit the requirements of Latin, which was far closer phonetically to Greek than Greek was to Phoenician. But they made experiments with new letters and improved letter-forms, and even indulged in spelling controversies. The modifications which they finally incorporated into their alphabet made for simplification and legibility, and produced the 'fair Roman hand' that Shakespeare refers to (in contrast to the pointed and complicated 'Gothic', which is nothing but a deviation from Latin script). Above all, it is through them that the script has spread over the greater part of Europe. In recent years the Turks have adopted the Latin alphabet, and its further extension in Asia may safely be predicted.

2. WRITING MATERIALS

The material on which man writes necessarily has some influence on the forms of his symbols. Thus on stone angular letters are more natural than rounded ones; curves develop with the use of brush or pen; but again, on wax the cursive hand is difficult and tends to become a series of straight strokes.

For writing of a casual nature the ancients largely used scraps of pottery, and these *ostraka* (specimens of which may be seen in the British Museum) formed the waste paper of the Greeks. Tablets of wood with a wax coating were also used for taking notes, for school exercises,[1] and even for business transactions.

---

[1] A famous Greek vase, signed by the artist Duris, and now in the Berlin Museum, shows tablets suspended on the walls of a school.

At Rome accounts were rendered on wax tablets (whence the phrase *novae tabulae* for the abolition of debts); legal documents, particularly wills, were written on them. The tablets had a raised rim and were fastened together in sets of two or more.

In Mesopotamia and Asia Minor the earliest writing material was clay, and the Minoan script of prehistoric Crete was also engraved on clay tablets. But the Phoenicians soon abandoned the use of clay for papyrus, which the Egyptians had always used for writing. They introduced this material into Greece, together with the alphabet, and by the sixth century at latest papyrus had come into general use in the Greek world.

Papyrus sheets were prepared from the pith of the papyrus reed which used to grow plentifully in the Nile Delta. It has now disappeared from Egypt, though it is still plentiful in the Sudan and may be seen round Syracuse. The full-grown reed was about an inch and a half in thickness. It was cut vertically into very thin slices, which were laid side by side and were then overlaid crosswise with a second set of strips. When pressed, the strips were made to adhere by the natural gum in the plant, and thus a sheet of papyrus was formed. After careful smoothing, the sheets were stuck together into a long strip which was rolled up on a stick. The memory of these rolls is still preserved in our word 'volume' (*volvere*, to roll). The inner side of the roll, on which the fibres run horizontally, was called the *recto*; the outer, on which they run vertically, the *verso*. Normally only the *recto* was used.

The writing was done with a reed pen and carbon ink (vegetable gum mixed with soot and water). The roll was held in the left hand and unrolled with the right, and the writing was in vertical columns, the lines running parallel to the long edge of the roll. As the reader finished the columns on the left, he would roll up that part of the papyrus again. The average length of the literary roll in Greece and Rome has been estimated at twenty to thirty feet, and its width as eight or nine inches.

To picture a Greek or Roman in his library, we must imagine, as the archæological finds have taught us, a series of pigeon-holes in which the rolls were placed, while a label (*titulus*) attached to the cover announced the name and the author. Thus a *titulus* recently found in Egypt reads: 'Sophron: Mimes about Women'.

Though the word *papyrus* (also called *bublos* or *biblos*, whence 'Bible' and its derivatives) gives us our word 'paper', paper, as we know it, was first made from rags by the Arabs in the early medieval times and was manufactured in China before it came to Europe.

Nowhere in the ancient world was there so large a collection of papyrus books as at the great library of Alexandria, and it is said that one of the Ptolemies, in his zeal for Alexandria and his jealousy of her rival Pergamum, forbade the export of papyrus. Whether this is true or not, Pergamum began, in the early centuries of the Christian era, to prepare skins for writing, and the word 'parchment' (*pergamena*) to-day recalls the city of its origin. The typical form of parchment was the codex, the sewn book, though rolls were also found; just as the typical form of papyrus was the roll, though it sometimes appeared as a codex. Martial mentions a codex as early as the first century A.D., and with the advance of the Christian era vellum codices supplanted papyrus rolls altogether.[1] Vellum is more durable, and papyrus may have been dying out. Lastly, for monumental inscriptions and public records, the Greeks and Romans often used panels of whited wood (λευκώματα, *alba*), or comparatively indestructible materials such as bronze and stone. The great majority of surviving Greek and Latin inscriptions are engraved on stone.

3. WRITTEN RECORDS IN PUBLIC LIFE

The vested interests of the early city-governments, which endeavoured to maintain a monopoly of legal knowledge within their own social class, delayed for some time the commitment of Greek and Roman laws to writing. The Homeric *themistes* (royal judgments) were handed down by word of mouth; at Sparta the so-called 'Laws of Lycurgus' were not recorded in writing—indeed it was supposed that one of these laws set a ban on written statutes. But eventually popular insistence broke

[1] The convenience of the codex for looking up a particular chapter in reading the lesson is obvious.

the aristocratic barriers, so that laws emerged into the light of day and were set up on tablets for all to read. The first written code was that of Zaleucus at Locri in Southern Italy, dating from the seventh century; the first Athenian code was compiled by Draco about 620 B.C. The laws of Solon were still on view in the Prytaneum or town hall of Athens about 200 B.C., and fragments survived as late as Plutarch (after A.D. 100).

At Rome the same conflict between official conservatism and popular demand was experienced, and ended in like manner. A credible Roman tradition records that about 450 B.C., at the time when Athens was in the full blaze of Periclean democracy, the farmer-town on the Tiber sent commissioners to study the Athenian laws. What they formulated and published, however— the code of the Twelve Tables—was so characteristically Roman that it appears to have derived little inspiration from the Greek legislators.

In Homeric Greece voting in the popular assembly was by clamour, and this rudimentary method of testing popular opinion survived in Sparta until the fourth century. Political voting at Athens was generally determined by show of hands; but when a ballot was taken in the Ecclesia to decide whether a political leader should be sent into exile, each voter inscribed the name of his intended victim on a potsherd (*ostrakon*—hence the name of 'ostracism' for this procedure).

In early Rome the voters at the Comitia merely shouted assent or dissent to the question put by the magistrate; but by the time of the Punic Wars they entered an enclosure in the Campus Martius and declared their choice to an official, who picked it off on a wax tablet. Hence the Horatian phrase:

Omne tulit punctum [*qui miscuit utile dulci*].

('He carries all the points (i.e. votes) [who blends utility with beauty].')

After 139 B.C., when voting by ballot was introduced, each elector received a blank tablet on which he personally wrote the names of the candidates whom he favoured. When a law was voted on, each citizen received two tablets, one marked V.R. (*uti rogas*, 'be it as you ask'), and the other A. (*antiqua probo*,

'I prefer the old state of things'). Hence *antiquare legem* came to mean to reject a law.

State archives were kept at Athens in the *Metrōon* (the temple of the Mother of the Gods). At Rome public records were housed until the later days of the republic in the temple of Saturn in the Forum or in the temple of Ceres on the Aventine; after 78 B.C. they were lodged in the Tabularium on the SE. slope of the Capitoline Hill. Copies of treaties with foreign states were engraved on bronze tablets and deposited in the temple of Jupiter Capitolinus.

Elaborate records of all manner of official transactions were kept by the Hellenistic kings. The magistrates of the Roman Republic began to accumulate similar dossiers of *acta*, and the bureaucracy of the emperors carried the 'culte de la paperasse' to a still further point. Besides the *acta forensia* there were also the *acta militaria*, drawn up by registrars, who collected the particulars of every soldier.

In 59 B.C. Julius Caesar enacted that the proceedings of the Senate should be officially compiled and published. Augustus stopped publication, but provided for their redaction by a regular editor, styled *ab actis senatus*. Verbatim reports of senatorial speeches were usually not made, but in the year of his consulship (63 B.C.) Cicero arranged for important debates to be taken down in shorthand and subsequently published. In 59 B.C. Caesar issued an official journal containing information of general public interest. These *acta diurna* corresponded in some sense to our newspapers. They were put up on whited boards (*alba*), and copies might be made for persons absent from Rome. In Petronius' novel (p. 271) the clerk at the banquet of Trimalchio reads to him a parody of the public gazette: 'July 26th: Thirty boys and forty girls were born on Trimalchio's estate at Cumae. Five hundred thousand pecks of wheat were taken up from the threshing floor to the barn. Five hundred oxen were broken in. . . .'

Official calendars, which were of importance for the timely observance of the religious festivals of the state, were commonly kept in the Greek cities; but especial care was given to their construction by the Romans, whose sense of order and meticulous regard for religious ritual combined to make them into careful time-keepers. The regulation of their state calendar, which was ascribed by tradition to their second king, Pompilius Numa, was certainly of very early date. At first, it is true, the calendar was not made public, and the *pontifices* who had charge of it contented themselves with making seasonal announcements of the festival days, court days, and so on. But in 304 B.C. a certain Cn. Flavius transcribed and published the year's calendar, and henceforth the setting up of official time-tables in public places became not uncommon in Italian towns.

Pieces of some twenty Roman calendars (*fasti*) have been preserved. A special feature of these *fasti* was the placing of letter-marks against those days of the month on which public business might be transacted. Thus F stood for 'dies fastus', i.e. a court day.[1] A somewhat different type of calendar, for the guidance of the Italian husbandman, is preserved in the Naples Museum. It is cut on four sides of a cube, each face being divided into three columns and each column containing a month. At the top of the column is carved the appropriate sign of the zodiac, followed by a list of days, the length of day and night, the various agricultural operations to be performed, a list of the chief festivals, and other details.

At an early date the *pontifices* began the practice of entering on the calendar the lists of annual magistrates at Rome and events of public importance such as triumphs. These entries were eventually disgested into separate catalogues which also received the name of 'fasti' (*fasti consulares, triumphales*). In the days of Augustus the fasti consulares and triumphales were revised and transcribed on to marble panels on the walls of the Regia (the residence of the Pontifex Maximus). Visitors to Rome may now admire this spacious record in the Museo Mussolini.

4. LETTERS AND PRIVATE DOCUMENTS

Letters were originally written on wood, potsherds, or lead; then wax tablets and papyrus were used, but hardly ever

[1] Some days were *fasti* only in part. Thus 15th June was marked QSDF, 'quando stercus delatum, fastus'. This was the annual day for cleaning the temple of Vesta, when legal business could be transacted only after the rubbish had been swept out.

parchment. The papyrus letter was folded or rolled, with the address written on the outside, left and right of the sealed string that secured the consignment.

In the absence of newspapers—other than the Acta Diurna at Rome—letters were important for keeping residents outside the capital city informed of current events. At Rome there was a kind of gentlemen's agreement that friends in the city should send news to those abroad. Thus Cicero writes to his friend Trebonius, asking him urgently to write much and often, on the understanding that he will do likewise (*Ad Fam.* xv. 20). To Atticus he writes: 'There never was a day when I was at Antium but I was better up in the news of the capital than those who were living there. The fact is, your letters used to put me *au fait* not only with the city news, but with all the political events; not only what was happening, but what was going to happen' (*Ad Att.* ii. 11). Important letters were sometimes multiplied and sent to various friends, thus taking the shape of political pamphlets. A good example of this type is Cicero's apologia to Lentulus for his political changes of front (*Ad Fam.* i. 9).

Though state posts were not unknown in the ancient world— the Ptolemies maintained a regular postal service in Egypt, and Augustus instituted a *cursus publicus* for the Roman Empire— these transmitted only official dispatches. Private correspondents therefore depended on trusty slaves to act as couriers, and the absence of such might cause delay in transmission. Messengers might let confidences leak out, and sometimes they were waylaid: letters were exposed to the same sort of insecurity as a modern telephone conversation. Cicero sometimes tried to lessen the danger of 'tapping' by writing in Greek, or gave the courier a message for oral transmission. Letters were also sent in duplicate. Falsifications of letters were not unknown. In 296 B.C. the consul Volumnius, greeting his colleague Appius, says that he has come in accordance with Appius' own letter; but if the letter is a forgery, he will go back at once (Livy, x. 18).

5. INSCRIPTIONS

Inscriptions on stone and other durable material have become increasingly important to the student of the Greek and Roman world. It is estimated that we now possess more than 75,000 Greek inscriptions; the Corpus Inscriptionum Latinarum comprises more than forty huge volumes—the North African section alone has more than 30,000 numbers—and the archæologists are almost daily adding to the score. These texts throw light on every side of Greek and Roman life. In the field of politics they provide us with the actual words of resolutions passed by the popular assemblies of Athens and other Greek towns, and by the Roman Comitia and Senate, of ordinances from the chanceries of Hellenistic kings and Roman emperors, of treaties and alliances. They furnish us with most of our knowledge of Greek inter-city arbitration, of the organization of the Roman imperial executive, and of Roman municipal administration.

Athenian imperialism is illustrated by the 'tribute lists' which set forth the relations between Athens and her dependants in the Delian League from 454 to 415 B.C. One of our chief documents of Greek law is a long inscription containing the code of the Cretan city of Gortyn (450–350 B.C.). The first penetration of Egypt by the Greeks is brought into relief by a text, carved on the leg of a colossal statue at Abu-Simbel in Nubia by some Greek mercenaries in the service of a sixth-century Pharaoh. Their later ascendancy in that country is made evident by the 'Rosetta Stone' (now in the British Museum), which records in Greek and in Egyptian hieroglyphs the (strictly official) devotion of the native Egyptian priesthood to the Ptolemaic dynasty.

The most important of Roman political inscriptions is undoubtedly the 'Monumentum Ancyranum', a brief autobiography of Augustus which was engraved on his tomb and reproduced in various towns of the Roman Empire. Our principal surviving copy is at Ancyra (Ankara) in Asia Minor. Scarcely inferior in interest are an inscription recording the actual words of a speech by the Emperor Claudius, in which he advocated the extension of the Roman franchise to the provinces, and the surviving fragments of Diocletian's tariff of prices and wages (p. 128). A series of documents of high value for the history of the Roman army is preserved in the *diplomata* issued to soldiers on their discharge. These were bronze tablets setting forth the past records of the soldiers and their future privileges.

For our knowledge of Greek economic conditions we are in no small measure indebted to the elaborate accounts of expenditure on materials and wages in connexion with the construction of temples at Athens, Delphi, and elsewhere, which were drawn up and exhibited on stone slabs by the building commissioners. Still more instructive is a series of texts, ranging from 314 to 166 B.C., which preserve the annual budget of the priests of Apollo at Delos. In the light of these inscriptions it has been possible to construct price and wage curves for a century or more of Hellenistic history. The principal economic achievement of the Romans, the opening up of undeveloped provincial lands by intensive cultivation, is illustrated by several texts from North Africa, showing the organization of the great imperial estates in that country.

For the understanding of ancient family life we cannot afford to neglect the evidence of the numerous surviving epitaphs (mostly Latin). A particular showpiece of this class is the *Laudatio Turiae* (Dessau 8393), in which a Roman husband relates how he was saved during the reign of terror after the death of Caesar by the heroic exertions of his wife; but hardly less important are the short and plain texts in which the ordinary folk of the Roman Empire speak out their minds to us. The following artless (and ungrammatical) outpouring may serve as an example: 'To the sainted soul of Mevia Sophe, C. Maevius Cimber has erected this memorial to my most revered wife and preserver, my heart's desire, who lived with me for 19 years, 3 months, and 13 days, because I lived with her without a quarrel [a not uncommon boast on Latin tombstones]. For now I importune Dis [the god of the underworld] that he restore my wife, or else do you give me back to her [by death], who lived so happily with me until her last day. Mervia Sophe, if there are Powers below, bring it to pass that I no longer suffer this wicked separation' (Dessau 8190). In general, the epitaphs offer a valuable corrective to the sweeping generalizations by

Tacitus, Juvenal, and others on the degeneracy of Roman family life.

Other epitaphs strike an endless variety of notes, now sceptical, now jocular, now matter-of-fact, now rhetorical, now stricken with inarticulate misery. An actor remarks: 'Several times ere now have I been dead (on the stage), but never quite like this.' Another man adjures the election agent: 'Mr. Bill-poster, please pass this tombstone by. I trust that any candidate whose name is written on this tomb may lose his election.' Another utters the not infrequent curse that the tomb-violator may find no place in the underworld.

The relations between masters and slaves are illustrated in many intimate details by the surviving manumission records. The social life of the bourgeoisie and the common people is revealed to us in many inscriptions, both Greek and Latin, containing extracts from the rules and the minutes of their clubs. A Latin text sets forth the rules of a club which included slaves (Dessau 7212). It stipulates that if a member should die at a distance, the club shall arrange for the funeral, and makes provision for travelling expenses and subsistence allowance for the club representatives. In case the deceased is a slave and the master refuses to surrender the body, there is to be a symbolical funeral. The president, who was appointed in rotation and might therefore be a slave, was bound to stand the club a dinner on his appointment: if he failed them, he was fined 100 sesterces (about £1).

A pleasing sidelight on ancient social life is thrown by the large number of texts which commemorate some conspicuous act of generosity by men or women of wealth—the provision of a bath-house, the endowment of a school, the institution of a fund for poor relief, and so forth. These inscriptions show that the faulty distribution of wealth in the Greek and Roman world was to some extent mitigated by a healthy tradition of public munificence.

Inscriptions also provide much material for the study of the Greek and Latin languages. They enable us to trace in fuller detail the evolution of letter-forms, of grammar and orthography. In particular, they give us a better insight into the popular tongue, with its peculiar idioms and spellings, and allow us to gauge its influence on literary Greek and Latin.

Again, inscriptions have contributed greatly to our knowledge of Greek and Roman religion. In some texts we may study the ceremonial of the great state festivals (e.g. the order of proceedings at the Ludi Saeculares in 17 B.C., at which the *Carmen Saeculare* of Horace was sung—Dessau 5050); the words of the hymns (such as the recently discovered hymn to Isis at Andros), and the musical scores to which they were set (as at Delphi); the questions submitted by consultants to the Greek oracles (as at Dodona). In other texts we can make acquaintance with the numerous unofficial cults of the Greeks and Romans, and may penetrate to the underworld of magic and superstition (as revealed, for instance, in a considerable number of leaden tablets—*defixiones*—in which spiteful men and women 'pin down' their personal enemies with more or less elaborate curses). In the light of inscriptions we can also trace more closely the diffusion of the vigorous and propagandist religions—the worships of Isis and Mithras, Judaism and Christianity.

Among the shorter inscriptions we may instance Athenian tickets for admission to jury-service; Roman vouchers for a ration of free corn or seats at the games; stamps on weights and measures and wine-jars (like the amphora that was born with Horace in the consulship of Manlius—*Odes* iii. 21); and slave-badges ('Hold me, lest I escape, and bring me back to my master Viventius').

Finally, we may close this list with some specimens of 'graffiti', i.e. scrawls made by uneducated men on any handy material. These include the hard-hitting messages which Roman soldiers posted to the enemy on sling-stones; the laconic SATIS ('I've done my whack!'), which an operative at Silchester scratched on a tile as he knocked off work; the philosophy of a street-artist at Timgad in N. Africa: ''unting (i.e. watching beast-fights), bathing, gaming, them is life' (Dessau 8826). But by far the largest collection of graffiti was found on the walls of Pompeii. Some hundreds of these relate to the annual municipal elections. The praises of the candidate, the jeers of his opponents, the stealth of the agent who puts up his 'poster' by night, his curses on the man who comes to smudge his work, all find a place in these vibrant fragments of ancient election propaganda. One inscription invites support for a candidate because he is a *probus iuvenis* ('a nice young man'), another because *hic aerarium conservabit* ('he will look after the ratepayers' money'). Two sarcastic messages, which demand that So-and-so be put in charge of police affairs, purport to come from the *seribibi* ('midnight revellers') and from the *furunculi* ('sneak thieves').

A modern note is also struck by the following advertisement: 'To let, from July next, the Arriana Pollia *insula* [block of flats] . . . containing shops with rooms over them, apartments *de luxe*, and a dwelling-house. Intending lessees should apply to Primus, the slave of Cn. Nigidius Maius' (Dessau 6035). The daily work of the town is illustrated by a piece of advice from a slave to a donkey who was to relieve him at the corn-mill: 'Work, Neddy, work, just as I used to work, and it will be the better for you!' Its favourite amusement is revealed by notices (equivalent to our handbills) of gladiatorial games and beast-hunts, some with awnings against the powerful Italian sun, and *sparsiones* (free gifts to be scrambled for) thrown in. From Christian times comes a note of moral indignation against a town whose patron saint was Venus: SODOMA GOMORA (in large letters).

6. PAPYRI

The vast masses of papyri (many of them still undeciphered) that have been recovered from the soil of Egypt are mostly written in Greek, and they have made large contributions to our knowledge of Greek life and literature. The administration of Egypt by its Ptolemaic and Roman overlords is illustrated by countless pieces of 'government paper'—land registers, taxation lists, police orders, petitions. These introduce us to the daily routine of an ancient administration, and bring into relief the manifold points of contact between rulers and ruled, as no other order of document does. The most important single specimens are a roll of some 600 lines, the 'Revenue Law of Ptolemy Philadelphus', which sets forth in full detail the regulations for the production of oil and wine in Egypt and the farming of the taxes on these commodities; a copy of a speech by the Emperor

Claudius in answer to a deputation of Alexandrian Greeks, in which he warns them to cease quarrelling with their Jewish neighbours; and part of the *Constitutio Antoniniana*, by which the Emperor Caracalla extended the Roman franchise to all the free population of the empire (A.D. 212).

The economic life of Egypt under Greek and Roman rule is presented to us in the departmental literature of the *architectones* (Commissioners of Works), who were responsible for the up-keep of the dikes and canals controlling the Nile waters; in contracts, bank papers, and household accounts. The intensive exploitation of the country's agricultural resources is copiously illustrated in the 'Zenon Papyri', a bundle of letters which the bailiff of a large estate belonging to Ptolemy the Second's minister Apollonius had kept on his file.

A peculiarly intimate insight into the daily round of life among the resident Greek bourgeoisie of Egypt is afforded by the plentiful remains of their correspondence. The schoolboy letters show how little human nature has changed.

So writes the Bad Boy in the third or second century B.C.:

'Theon to Theon, his father, greeting! That was a fine trick, not to take me to the city with you! If you don't take me to Alexandria, I won't write to you, I won't speak to you, I won't say good morning to you! If you do go to Alexandria, I won't hold your hand or have anything more to say to you! That's what will happen if you don't take me. . . . And you did a fine thing! What a present to send to me, those beans! [This seems to refer to some child's game.] They kept me in the dark at home on the 12th when you sailed. So please send for me. If you don't, I won't eat, I won't drink! So there! Good-bye.'

And now enters the Good Boy:

'To my revered father Arion from Thonis, greeting. Before all else I make supplication for you daily, praying also before the ancestral gods of this place in which I am living, that I may find you and all our relations in good health. See now, this is the fifth time that I have written to you, and you have not written to me except once, not even about your health. . . . No, you didn't come to see if my teacher was looking after me or not.

And he himself, too, inquires about you almost daily. . . . Come quickly, then, before he leaves. May you fare well, my revered father, you and my brothers, in all prosperity, unharmed by the evil eye, I pray, for many years.' There is a charming postscript, written between the lines: 'Don't forget our pigeons.'

Other papyri reveal to us the contacts between the Greek and the native religions and their partial fusion. The survival of superstition, and its renewed extension under the Roman emperors, find expression in numerous collections of magical formulae.

But the most distinctive contribution of papyri to our knowledge of Greece and Rome lies in the field of literature. Though nothing remains of the contents of the great library at Alexandria, numerous copies of works by Greek authors have been recovered on the sites of up-country towns (notably at Oxyrhynchus in the Fayum, where the Oxford scholars, Grenfell and Hunt, made their right royal hauls). These literary papyri have provided us with earlier and usually more authoritative texts of works previously known (e.g. the greater part of *Iliad XXIV* in the Bankes Homer, now in the British Museum); and they have made us acquainted with many hitherto unknown compositions or fragments. The new discoveries, include lyric pieces by Bacchylides, Corinna, Pindar, Sappho, and Timotheus (whose *Persae* can now be read in a manuscript assigned to the fourth century B.C., and said to be the oldest in existence); parts of Sophocles' satyric drama, *The Trackers*, and of several comedies by Menander; the mimes of Herodas; speeches of Hypereides; fragments of apocryphal Christian gospels, such as the *Logia*, or Sayings of Jesus. The most notable single find was Aristotle's *Constitution of Athens* (written on the back of a set of farm accounts belonging to a bailiff of Hermopolis).

7. THE GREEK LANGUAGE

Suppleness and a capacity for expansion have always characterized the Indo-European languages, whereas Turkish, for example, in spite of its territorial extension in the wake of a conquering army, has remained rigid, preserved from change by an iron schematization. The Indo-European tongues are always sending off new offshoots, forming new groups, assimilating what they found useful from other languages; in a word, they reflect the mobility of life itself. The Greek and Latin tongues, which belonged to the Indo-European group, shared to the full its capacity for growth and change, and therefore had a long and varied history of their own.

Of the two languages, Greek was nearer to the parent Indo-European tongue, as may be seen by many of its grammar forms, such as the Middle Voice, the Optative Mood, the Aorist Tense as distinct from the Perfect, and by its retention of the tonic accent, whereby a syllable is pronounced on a higher or lower musical note, according as the form or meaning of the word varies. These features, of which traces survive in conservative modern languages like Lithuanian, were typical of the other stages of Indo-European.[1]

Greek was an isolated language-group within the Balkan peninsula, the result of a northern thrust into a Mediterranean land, and it remained virtually intact as a northern language. Some borrowed elements from the language which the invading northerners found in Greece, like the proper names whose stem ends in -nth and -ss (*Korinthos, Mykalessos*), and names of plants and animals (especially fish), affected the Greek tongue only to a slight extent.

Greek was at first divided into three main dialects, Aeolic, Ionic, and Doric, which in turn fell into smaller groups. Thessalian and Lesbian formed distinct sub-forms of the Aeolic dialect, while Arcadian and Cyprian may be classed as a separate group; and different varieties of Ionic Greek were spoken in Euboea, in the Cyclades, and in Asia Minor. The most important and most delicate of the sub-dialects, Attic, in which most of our extant Greek literature is written, was classified separately by Strabo, but it is now generally attached to the Ionic group.

Diversity of speech was favoured in Greece by geographical barriers, and by the multiplicity of autonomous city-states; but

---

[1] Similar features are found in modern Bantu. By the end of the second century A.D. Greek had shed almost all traces of its tonic accent; at the present day it is characterized by a strong stress accent which has largely affected the ancient vowel quantities.

the unifying forces eventually prevailed. The Greeks of the historical age had the immense advantage of starting with the common heritage of Homer. His language, a blend of Ionic and Aeolic elements which was, however, based on a living and spoken tongue, came to be accepted in all parts of Greece as the appropriate vehicle for certain kinds of literature. Writers of epic and didactic poetry, of elegy, of oracles, and dedicatory inscriptions used the Homeric language. The amazing persistence of the Homeric language is realized when we come to Quintus Smyrnaeus, who attempted after twelve hundred years to continue the *Iliad* in a tongue remarkably like that of Homer: only something like sacred tradition could explain such a continuity. Ionic Greek also obtained general currency as the language of science: it was used by the physician Hippocrates, who came from the Dorian island of Cos. On the other hand Doric Greek, in a more or less modified form, came to be associated with choral lyrics, even when these were written by Ionians like Bacchylides or Aeolic-speaking Boeotians like Pindar. Similarly Bion, from Ionian Smyrna, who imitated the pastorals of Theocritus, also adopted his Dorian dialect.

The tendency towards unification of language was reinforced in the fifth century by the political and intellectual ascendancy of Athens, and in the fourth century by a growing sentiment of Panhellenism. Under these influences attempts were made to set up Attic Greek as the standard language of educated men, and Atticism as the test of culture. This movement was so far effective, that Alexander and his successors composed their official documents in the dialect which Demosthenes had used to heap invectives on the Macedonian king's father. Indeed the Macedonians, whom the Athenians had long regarded as a semi-barbarous folk, proved to be the greatest upholders of the Attic language and culture.

A further impetus in the same direction was given when Alexander conquered and sought to hellenize the East. It was then that the *Koine* came into being, the common speech of the whole Greek world. Inscriptions show that after the fourth century B.C. the local dialects gradually disappeared: by the first century A.D. attempts to use Doric in documents to give them a venerable appearance went no further than the substitution of $\bar{a}$ for $\bar{e}$. Even Attic, the accepted test of refinement, and the chief constituent element in the Koine, began to lose ground. It is true that in the first and second centuries A.D. Attic again became fashionable with men of letters and was used by Plutarch and Lucian; but so far had it diverged from the speech of ordinary folk that Attic dictionaries had to be composed, some of which, like those of Moeris and Phrynichus, are still extant. By the fourth century Attic had been relegated to the schoolmaster and the professor. A papyrus of this period mentions a teacher of Berytus (Beyrout), who was specially praised because he knew Attic.

It was customary at one time for scholars to describe the Koine as bad Greek. Influenced by a static conception of grammar and by the predominance of Attic before the Macedonian conquest, they condemned the Common Speech as corrupt and artificial. But latterly most scholars have realized that language is an organism subject to growth and change—a truth that Horace understood when he said that Custom was the arbiter of speech. The Koine is now recognized as the normal development of spoken Greek; its emergence, in fact, was part of the same phenomenon that we have seen with the rise of Afrikaans in South Africa—the upward thrust of the speech of ordinary folk into literary usage. Something similar happened when Old English, ignoring the refined Norman French of Court circles, developed into literary English, and when Vulgar Latin, using the diminutives and uninflected forms of popular idiom, grew into the Romance languages. So again the Greek of the present day, which has regained the rank of a literary language, abounds in diminutives and other usages of the common people.

8. THE LATIN LANGUAGE

Latin was originally one of a group of Italic dialects which resembled Greek in being northern insertions into a Mediterranean world. Despite the close association of the early Romans with the Etruscans, it had no connexion with the non-Aryan Etruscan tongue. Its affinity to Greek in vocabulary and grammar is obvious; but it represented a later development from the parent Indo-European language, as may be seen in the comparative simplicity of its structure, and especially by its use of accent by stress instead of pitch. The 'Saturnian' metre of early Latin[1] was based on stress rather than on syllable-length; and although the Romans came to adopt the Greek system of versification by syllable-length, and probably also to impart a tonic quality to their accent, it is significant that, when Greek influence declined, Latin verse reverted to stress accent.

In the early days of Roman history Latin was nothing more than a local dialect and had no currency outside the boundaries of Latium. It had therefore to compete with other dialects, such as Umbrian in the northern and Oscan in the southern Apennine regions, and with cultural languages such as Etruscan in the north and Greek in the south of the peninsula. Yet it had established itself as the *Koine* of Italy before the end of the republican period. The main reason of its supremacy lay of course in the Roman conquest of Italy; but it would be a mistake to think that the other Italian languages were simply wiped out by violence or stifled by law. The Romans never legislated against a language. The other Italian tongues therefore lived on so long as they retained their innate vitality; in the first century B.C., Oscan was still spoken at Pompeii, and Greek lingered on in the south even later. But Latin spread everywhere in Italy as the Roman dominion extended and was consolidated with the founding of colonies and the building of roads, and it was diffused still further with the increase of commerce and education. Nay more, it throve on the very principle of Roman statesmanship which allowed the conquered to retain the use of their native tongue. Had the Romans tried to suppress Oscan, for instance, they might have ensured its survival by engaging the pride and resentment of the Oscan peoples in its behalf. Lastly, allowance must be made for the natural vitality of Latin, which maintained its individuality among all the other

---

[1] This metre is exemplified in the line: 'dábunt málum Metélli Naévio poétae'.

Macaulay's English equivalent! 'The quéen was ín her párlour, éating bréad and hóney', is probably less accurate than: 'Máry tídied the párlour, áll was in a múddle' (five beats instead of six).

languages with which the Roman expansion brought it into contact, and at the end of the Roman Empire was still strong enough to serve as the basis for the Romance languages of the present day.

There was one foreign tongue which the Romans not merely tolerated but deliberately fostered, the Greek language. Feared at first in the days of Naevius, welcomed with enthusiasm by Ennius, and looked at askance once more by Cato, Greek gradually found a permanent and uncontested place in the Roman world. It influenced Latin in spelling, vocabulary, accent, rhythm, and made it into an instrument of refined literature. In the fourth and fifth centuries A.D., when Greek influence died out, cultured Church Fathers like Augustine shuddered at the 'rusticitas' of contemporary Latin. The splendour of Latin at its best was due to the concurrence of two elements, its native sonorousness and dignity, and the artistic refinement of Greek. This does not mean, however, that 'post-classical' Latin has no cultural value, that we must throw a spot-light on the language of Cicero and the Augustans and admire only that. The later literature of Rome has been unduly neglected, largely because of the common idea that Latin 'degenerated'. But language grows as much as it decays, and every age has its linguistic virtues. We must admit that Cicero's heights of eloquence were not reached again, and that Vergil's fineness of texture was unique; but we need not on that account ignore the freshness of many passages in Apuleius or Augustine or the Medieval Latin lyric.

The chronological development of Latin may be broadly summarized as follows. From the seventh century B.C. until the age of the Punic Wars it was the speech of a farmer-soldier community, not insensible to the linguistic influences around it, but sturdily maintaining its native vigour. It was still in the main the speech of a slow-moving and hard-working folk which had little time or taste for art and letters.

About 240 B.C. came the first attempt to make Latin into a literary language on the Greek model. Cultured Romans modified their pronunciation of Latin; men of letters closely and sometimes slavishly followed Greek authors, to the extent of replacing good Latin words by Greek (e.g. *Camena* by *Musa*);

soldiers and traders too brought home Greek phrases from their expeditions overseas, and the comedian Plautus gave them back to his audiences.

But the partnership of Greek and Latin was not completed until the Ciceronian-Augustan period (approximately 80 B.C. to A.D. 14). The language was now thoroughly adapted to Greek metres—we can trace the long process from Ennius to Vergil—and became more refined in rhythm. Cicero used Greek words as natural allies in his letters, and not as a *tour de force*. At the same time Latin began to spread beyond Italy to the more civilized regions of the western Mediterranean, and even obtained a temporary footing in the East.

In the ensuing Silver Age a certain artificiality crept into literary Latin. This was largely due to a growing divergence between the written and the spoken language. Men of letters now formed a class apart and took refuge in tricks of style that emphasized their isolation. It is true that Seneca adopted some popular idioms into his writings, but the tendency was rather for prose writers to incorporate poetic expressions, and Tacitus was full of Vergilian phrases. During this period Latin also established itself as the language of educated people in all the western half of the Roman Empire and in the Danube lands.

Between A.D. 150 and the ninth century Latin passed through its last stage. The provinces, which had entered the field of Latin literature in the age of Augustus, now came to dominate it more and more: Spain took the lead in the first century, Africa in the second, and Gaul in the fourth century. At the same time popular speech re-entered into literature with the help of the Church, which led a reaction against formal rhetoric and showed favour to 'rusticitas'. A struggle ensued between the more cultured Church Fathers and the ignorant brethren who in their opposition to paganism wanted to go too far in the direction of formlessness.[1] But although Augustine and Jerome secured at least the partial acceptance of Vergil and Plato in the schools, and Christian bishops modelled their sermons to some extent on the old pagan rhetoric, the rise of Vulgar Latin was assured, and

[1] Haarhoff, *Schools of Gaul*, p. 166 ff.

its progress was facilitated by the Germanic invasions. But the invaders who made an end of the Roman Empire did not disown its heritage. Just as Greece had formerly captivated her captor, so Latin, refined and moulded by Greek, converted its Germanic conquerors to Christianity; and since Christianity stood for education, it thereby secured its survival as the language of all the cultivated classes in the West until the seventeenth century.

9. THE GENIUS OF THE GREEK AND LATIN LANGUAGES

How do the Classical languages strike a modern reader who is able to understand more than their mere grammatical structure? In the words of Virginia Woolf,[1] 'Greek is the language that has us most in bondage; the desire for which perpetually lures us back. First there is the compactness of expression. . . . Every ounce of fat had been pared off, leaving the flesh firm. Then, spare and bare as it is, no language can move more quickly, dancing, shaking, all alive, and yet controlled. Then there are the words themselves, which we have made expressive to us in our own emotions, *thalassa*, *thanatos*, *anthos*, *astēr*, *selēnē*, to take the first that come to hand; so clear, so hard, so intense, that to speak plainly yet fittingly, without blurring the outline and clouding the depths, Greek is the only expression.'

The economy of Greek, and equally of Latin, their concentration and sharpness of outline, which disdain adornment like the sculptures of the Aegina Pediments, is with difficulty understood by a 'romantic' age, and it defies translation. Imitated in the modern idiom, it becomes bare and jejune. The reason is partly that we have largely become insensitive to the sound of words, whereas in ancient times sound played a vital part; partly that in Greek and Latin the system of inflexions gave great variety to the word-forms; partly that the order of the words was extremely significant and permitted shades of meaning that we cannot indicate with equal compactness. Hence the impression that the Classical languages are cold and dry. It is not until we realize the significance of the word-order that we can feel the vibrant life of Cicero's speeches, so tame and dull in literal

[1] *The Common Reader*, p. 55.

translations; and in a sensitive artist like Horace the arrangement of the words is of supreme importance.

Most modern readers are struck by the melodiousness of Greek and Latin, especially if they do not nationalize the pronunciation and make 'nice-eye' of *nĭsĭ* and 'jam' of *iam*.[1] There are more open and sonorous vowel sounds in Greek and Latin than in most languages, and fewer consonants to impede them. Anyone who has tried to imitate the Classical hexameter in modern verse has become aware of this. Take for example a line at random from the *Iliad*:

> *eu gar ego tode oida/kata phrena kai kata thumon,*

and compare Matthew Arnold's version in the same metre:

> 'For that day will come/my soul is assured of its coming.'

Two things strike us at once. Firstly, in the English, there are at most only four open syllables, i.e. syllables ending in vowels, and there are twenty-five consonants (not counting aspirates). as against seventeen in the Greek, which is a measure of the far freer flow of the Greek. Secondly, if the ambiguous last foot be omitted, the English line has three would-be spondees ($\perp$ -), and the Greek has none at all—an indication of the lighter movement of the Greek. It is one of the inevitable difficulties in our modern use of the dactylic hexameter that there are comparatively few natural dactyls (- ◡ ◡) in English.[2] Much the same difficulty would arise in translating Latin, for although the Latin epic hexameter had more spondaic feet, its open syllables give it a freedom of movement that most modern languages fail to imitate.

A well-marked quality of Greek is its capacity for forming compounds—*iostephanos*, 'violet-crowned', *arguropeza*, 'silver-footed', *poluphloisboio thalasses*, 'the heaving, plashing sea'. Every modern science has discovered this, even in such un-Greek

---

[1] Some, however, will no doubt continue to anglicize the pronunciation, in defiance of the ascertained facts of Greek and Latin speech, on the ground expressed by a correspondent in *The Times*, that 'if the reformed pronunciation were accepted, Latin would sink to the level of a Dago language'.

[2] Haarhoff and van den Heever, *The Achievement of Afrikaans*, p. 68 ff.

things as 'cinematographic technical science', which is Greek in two words and Latin in one. The Greek poets naturally made full use of this happy endowment of their language; the multiplicity of their coinage is the despair of every beginner in Greek.

The attempts of the early Roman poets to imitate Greek compounds in Latin met with doubtful success. Pacuvius' *repandirostrum incurvicervicum pecus*, 'the splay-snouted, sinuous-necked herd', produces too cumbrous an effect (especially when *incurvicervicum* is set by the side of its Greek equivalent, *kurtauchena*). In the first century B.C., Lucretius and Catullus coined double words that were resonant without being ponderous, as in the line:

> *ubi cerva silvicultrix, ubi aper nemorivagus.*
> 'where the woodland-haunting hind, and the forest-roaming boar.'

But the Augustans seem to have thought this practice contrary to the genius of their language and discouraged it, just as the French frowned on the attempt of their Pleiad to naturalize the compound: even Horace and Vergil exercised great economy in its use. Of some seventy new compounds only a few survived the Augustan censorship: not even such choice specimens as *velivolus, frondiferas, montivagae* were spared. Similarly the occasional experiments of Ausonius and other poets of the fourth century A.D. failed to set a new fashion.

On the other hand Latin fell naturally into alliteration, and the early poets such as Ennius used it as naturally and heavily as the Germanic bards (*O Tite tute Tati, tibi tanta, tyranne, tulisti*). In later writers it is rarer, perhaps because of Greek influence, for Greek authors were little inclined to alliterative effects. A language with a tonic accent and a quantitative basis finds alliteration less natural than one in which stress accent predominates.

Latin shows a tendency for words to flow together, which has been called 'liaison'. Thus, if we have a final consonant followed by a word beginning with a vowel, the consonant tends in pronunciation to go with the subsequent word: *amat equos* in speech becomes *amatequos*. In verse this led to the practice of elision or, as Cicero put it more positively, of 'joining vowels,' so that a syllable ending in a vowel or -m (equivalent to a nasalized vowel) was run on to a syllable beginning with a vowel or aspirate. But whereas in Greek elision was clean-cut and the elided syllable actually disappeared, as in *hekont' einai*, in Latin the elided syllable had some effect on pronunciation, though for metrical purposes it did not count. In this respect Greek might be compared to a perfect liquid, Latin to a slightly viscous fluid. Similarly the Frenchman has the Latin flow when he says 'un âne'; the Englishman to a lesser extent; the average South African not at all—he inserts a glottal stop: 'an . ass'.

Apart from the phenomenon of elision, the syllables of Greek and Latin give the impression of precise blocks of marble, in contrast with the lumps of wax which we manipulate in our modern languages. This is due to the fixity of their quantitative system. The essential difference between ancient and modern metres is simply this, that whereas our syllables are freely altered in length by the incidence of the stress accent, in Classical Greek and Latin the quantity normally remained fixed and had to be respected. Thus in English we find the same word changing its length in the same line because of the accent:

'Fárewell, home of the proud, farewéll thou castle accursed',

whereas in the Latin line,

Fáto Deucalion, fato servatus Ulixes,

the change of stress does not carry with it a change of quantity.

Precision is generally recognized as a mark of the Classical languages. Indeed this belief is often carried to excess. The notion, for example, that Latin is consciously built up of logical constructions is a fallacy. If it was logical, the reason was that the people who spoke it were logical on particular occasions. Under a similar misapprehension Grillparzer is reported to have said that he could not imagine a girl speaking Latin to her lover. That was because he was thinking of school Latin, stiffly presented. If he could have heard Catullus read his lyrics, or Plautus' characters arguing, or Petronius declaiming his 'Cockney' Latin, or even Cicero, letting himself go about Antony, if he could have given the emphasis to word-order that we so often neglect, he would have changed his opinion. We may be sure that Horace's Pyrrha—the golden-haired Italian that we observe in Titian's pictures and may still admire to-day—found a natural tone to adopt to her 'slender boy' in the rose-bower. The ancient poet, it is true, spoke a language that was a refinement of the refined speech of the educated. Greek and Roman men of letters would have agreed with Coleridge's definition of poetry as 'the best words in the best order', interpreting 'best' as 'aristocratic', and allowing the poet an order that was different from the order of prose. The plebeian word, especially at Rome, was excluded; for the most part a new word was regarded with the same jealous conservatism as the 'novus homo' in politics. Yet this insistence on form did not necessarily involve the crushing of spontaneous life. Even the Augustans, in their desire to standardize an admittedly beautiful form, could not check the growth of Latin. In order to appreciate the Greek and Latin languages, we must understand them as a whole and follow the various stages of their development.

The surviving specimens of Minoan script, most of which have been found in the palace archives of Cnossus and Pylos (home of the Homeric hero Nestor in Peloponnesus), have recently been deciphered by M. Ventris and J. Chadwick (*Journal of Hellenic Studies*, 1953, pp. 84ff.). They contained a system of linear signs which had been developed at Cnossus from an earlier pictographic script ('Minoan Linear B'). Unlike those of the historic Greek alphabet, its signs stood, not for single letters, but for syllables. But its component words were modified by inflexions like those of the Indo-European languages; and several of the personal names among them are those of Homeric heroes (Achilles, Hector, Aeneas) or gods (Pallas, Poseidon). The general picture of the society which they portray is that of a warrior aristocracy of Homeric type.

VI

Philosophy and Science

I. THE GENERAL LINE OF DEVELOPMENT

WONDER, IN Plato's much-quoted phrase, is the beginning of philosophy; and in the wonder that led to voyaging through strange seas of thought the Greeks were the world's foremost pioneers. But wonder was not enough: it needed courage to defy established taboos and to break the 'cake of custom' that constricted the fear-ridden mind of early man. The right to think things out and to live according to reason was vindicated for western man first of all by the Greeks. 'The unexamined life', said Socrates, 'is no life for man'; and the Greek in the course of his examination, faced with a mysterious universe, upheld no dogmatic exclusiveness, but was willing to investigate every form of experience. He thus evolved not only various sciences but the scientific attitude of mind, the attitude that envisages the facts without the bias of sentiment or preconceived theory, and is careful to avoid premature generalization.

The Greeks made thought free and emancipated discussion from the domination of priestcraft that lay heavy upon it in the older countries of the East. They brought knowledge from the confinement of esoteric coteries into the open air of the market-place. In the clear light of reason all manner of superstitions wilted away. 'It seems to me', said a writer in the Hippocratic Collection, in discussing epilepsy, which was called 'sacred', 'that this disease is no more divine than any other. It has a natural cause just as other diseases have. Men think it supernatural because they do not understand it. But if they called everything supernatural which they do not understand, why, there would be no end of such things!' Similarly, the Greeks detached the quest for knowledge from the pursuit of material profit or immediate practical results. In Oriental countries measurements were made for more or less utilitarian purposes; the Greeks measured the section of a cone for the sheer love of knowledge.

It is equally true that in the modern world many of the most useful inventions (the telegraph, telephone, radio, X-rays, etc.) are owed by us to disinterested seekers after truth.

We may broadly trace the general course of Greek science and philosophy as follows:

(1) Greek colonial expansion brought to the Greeks a mass of new facts about the world which they, being Greeks, proceeded to compare and reduce to order. Significantly, the first essays in natural science were made among the Ionian Greeks of Asia Minor, and especially at the city of Miletus, which was one of the chief pioneers of commerce and colonization. The Ionian Greeks, whose chief contribution to science was made in the sixth and fifth centuries, took a special interest in geography, astronomy, and physics, in biology and medicine. Their interest in physics and medicine was communicated by them to the Greek colonists in the western Mediterranean. But the particular field of the Italiote and Siceliote Greeks was mathematics.

(2) In the fifth century, as the frontiers of the Greek world became fixed, the impetus to scientific exploration was spent, and interest was transferred from the world of Nature to that of Man. Already in the sixth century the diverse and fruitful experiments of the Greek city-states in forms of government had given rise to political theory. In the fifth century the more general problem of the relation of Mind to Matter forced itself upon the Greeks as a result of their studies in natural science. These researches inevitably raised the questions, how far were the senses to be trusted, and what was the ultimate test of truth? These problems became a challenge when an Italiote Greek named Zeno (not to be confused with the later founder of Stoicism) formulated paradoxes like those of Achilles and the tortoise which he could never overtake in a race, thus emphasizing in abstract argument the incapacity of the senses to perceive infinitely small quantities and intervals. Under these new influences Greek thinkers came to decide that 'man is the measure of all things', and that therefore 'the proper study of mankind is Man'.

This 'humanistic' tendency had its origin in various parts of Greece, and its early exponents, the so-called 'Sophists' (a word that originally meant 'one who puts you wise', and carried no invidious meaning), were mostly travelling teachers who did not reflect any special local characteristic. But in the later fifth and fourth centuries the new school of thought fixed its headquarters at Athens. In this city interest in politics naturally went hand-in-hand with its absorbing problems of practical statecraft. Wider problems of general ethics were raised by the Attic dramatists (p. 246), and these, together with the questions of logic and psychology broached by the Sophists, claimed the attention of Socrates, the greatest teacher of his age, who abandoned a youthful interest in natural science to devote himself to the study of Man. The same bent towards humanistic studies characterized Socrates' greatest pupil, Plato, who was incidentally a distinguished mathematician, but concentrated on the same problems as had previously engrossed Socrates. It was chiefly through the influence of Socrates and Plato that Athens became the chosen home of mental and moral philosophy.

(3) On the other hand, Plato's greatest pupil, Aristotle, while not forsaking his master's attachment to the humanities, created a renewed interest in the study of Nature, and especially in the organic and biological branches thereof, as befitted the son of a medical practitioner. Though Aristotle's range was not encyclopædic—mathematics, for instance, were neglected by him—he was deservedly called by Dante 'the master of them that know'. More important, he asserted, as Plato had already done, the interrelation of all knowledge, and he exemplified this truth in his own writings.

(4) In the third and following centuries the division between philosophy and natural science again became more sharply drawn. The Academy (as the school of Plato came to be called) became absorbed in abstract problems of logic. On the other hand, the Peripatetics (the name given to the disciples of Aristotle) specialized not only in natural science, but in the several branches of that science. A further impetus to scientific study was also provided when Alexander of Macedon, himself a pupil of Aristotle who shared his teacher's interests, opened up a new world for the Greeks, and gave a stimulus to scientific research like that which had resulted from early Greek colonization. Between 300

and 150 B.C. the Greeks made contributions to natural science which remained unsurpassed until the sixteenth and seventeenth centuries A.D. But over-specialization eventually sterilized natural science and dried up the wells of mental and moral science.

(5) The Roman contribution to knowledge was to harness the brilliant theories of the Greeks—sometimes brilliant and unclouded by a single fact—to the uses of the everyday world, and with their aid to improve upon land-surveying, road-construction, water-conservation, calendar-making, and other practical devices. The Roman point of view was accurately described in the following self-satisfied words of Cicero: 'The Greeks held the geometer in the highest honour, and in their esteem no one came before the mathematicians. But we Romans have established, as the limit of this art, its usefulness in measuring and reckoning. The Romans have always shown more wisdom than the Greeks in all their inventions, or else improved what they took over from them, such things at least as they thought worthy of serious attention.' The Greek tended to leave mechanical crafts unexplored; and Archimedes, in spite of his remarkable engines, preferred to be remembered by his contributions to scientific theory. The Roman tended to look down upon abstract theory and wanted 'to get on with the job'. Though Aristotle appreciated the importance of practical sagacity, he still thought that the highest life was that of contemplation. Cicero, who could write imaginatively about the after-life and voyage among the stars, yet considered that the citizen should limit speculation to what is useful for the state.

2. THE PIONEERS OF NATURAL SCIENCE

The influence of the Greek colonial movement upon Greek science was nowhere more apparent than in the field of geography. In the days of Homer (c. 850 B.C.) the geographical horizon of the Greeks did not extend beyond the eastern Mediterranean—the adjacent continents and the seas beyond Sicily remained to them a land of fable. By 500 B.C. the Greeks had explored the entire Mediterranean and had peeped into the Atlantic; on the mainland Greek pioneers had adventured themselves some distance up the rivers of Europe (especially the Rhône and the Danube), they had ascended the Nile to the First Cataract, and had perhaps penetrated with the Persian armies as far as India. Many of these pioneers kept their discoveries to themselves, in the interests of trade monopoly; but the Greek desire for knowledge could not be denied, and in due course the new facts were divulged and tidily arranged.

About 500 B.C. a Milesian traveller named Hecataeus published a 'Circuit of the Earth', under which ambitious title he actually described the whole circuit of the Mediterranean. Some fifty years before him another Milesian, Anaximander, had constructed the first map which was more than a local survey, yet was based in some measure on data of observation. The early Greek map-makers, it is true, evolved the continents to a large extent out of their inner consciousness, and their native sense of symmetry betrayed them into depicting the land-masses to north and south of the Mediterranean as similar in size and structure. But critics were not lacking who insisted on keeping fact free from fancy. Herodotus (himself an experienced traveller) rejected the story of a Phoenician circumnavigation of Africa (which modern geographers regard as quite feasible), and doubted the existence of the Tin Islands (really a generic name for the tin lands of the North Atlantic).

Not content to describe the earth's surface, the Greeks sought to understand the forces that had carved it into shape. When Herodotus suggested that the Vale of Tempe had been caused by an earthquake fissure in the sea-wall of eastern Thessaly, he made a bad guess, for this valley was formed by erosion. But he showed true appreciation of the formative force of water when he described the Egyptian Delta as 'a gift of the Nile', and estimated that the silting process must have lasted some tens of thousands of years. His time-scale was here more correct than the modern one, found in Shakespeare ('The poor world is almost six thousand years old'—*As You Like It*), and still current in the nineteenth century, that the world began in 4004 B.C. Still more remarkable was the achievement of an Ionic thinker named Xenophanes who correctly explained the shell-fossils in the mountains of Asia Minor as deposits from a prehistoric flood. In thus discarding the crude cosmogonies, replete with miracles, which their early compatriots had shared with the people of the Near East, the Ionic Greeks took a premature trip into the nineteenth century; in emphasizing the formative action of water they adopted a view that did not finally prevail among geologists till *c.* A.D. 1850.

The Greeks derived from Babylon the division of the day into hours, together with shadow-sticks and sundials to measure the flow of hours, and a formula for predicting eclipses, which enabled a Milesian named Thales to forecast a total obscuration of the sun in 585 or 557 B.C. The early Greeks were discriminating in their choice of gifts from Babylon, for they kept clear of astrological theories: once they had discarded the primitive idea that the stars were gods, they refused to allow them any influence on human affairs, and studied them in the dry light of a purely material science. Anaximander, rejecting the early Greek view that the earth was a disk floating on a bed of water, declared that it was a solid body, like the drum of a column, and freely poised in space. A notable advance in astronomical theory was made by an erratic genius named Pythagoras, half a mystic and half a man of science, who migrated from Samos and founded a school in South Italy (*c.* 530 B.C.). He (or one of his early disciples) gave out that the sun,[1] not the earth, was the centre of the planetary system, and that the moon (perhaps even the sun) shone by a reflected light. This was mere guesswork, but it raised issues of fundamental importance. A century later another Asiatic Greek, Anaxagoras, combining Babylonian knowledge with Greek imagination, explained as well as forecast eclipses.

The Greeks were the first to give sustained attention to the ultimate problems of chemistry and physics, the composition and structure of the material world. The Egyptians, watching the Nile build the land in the Delta, believed that the ultimate element of matter was water, and Thales, who had travelled in Egypt, accepted this view. But other Greeks declared in favour of air (the most pervasive substance), or fire (the chief transforming agency), and they presently abandoned the search for a single

[1] The Pythagoreans spoke of a 'central fire'. Some scholars think that this was not our sun.

constituent element for a closer study of the structure of matter
A Sicilian Greek named Empedocles suggested that the elements
were brought together and pulled asunder by 'love' and 'strife',
thus foreshadowing the modern doctrine of 'affinities' and
'repulsions'. Anaxagoras gave out that the agency by which
the primeval chaos of matter was sorted out was a rotating
motion—a theory which recent astronomers have again taken
up. Lastly, two contemporaries of Anaxagoras, Leucippus of
Miletus and Democritus of Abdēra, divining that matter is dis-
continuous, envisaged it as consisting of exceedingly small but
indivisible and indestructible 'atoms', which floated freely in
space until they were made coherent by some (unexplained)
motion. This 'atomic' theory was taken over by the Epicurean
philosophers and expounded with missionary fervour by the
Latin poet Lucretius (p. 262). It was brought back to life in
the nineteenth century, when Dalton verified it with the aid of
the chemical balance; and although the physicists of the present
day have proved each atom to be a complicated microcosm, with
varying numbers of constituent parts, they have confirmed the
essential part of the ancient Greek doctrine, that matter is an
aggregate of separate particles grouped amid an intervening
space.

In maintaining that motion was a formative force among the
elements, Anaxagoras and the atomists contradicted the view
held by some Greek physicists, that the material world was
essentially static. Previous to them Heracleitus of Ephesus had
made the sweeping (but correct) generalization, that *panta rei*
('all is in flux'). This recognition of the eternally changing
character of Nature has been one of the most fruitful ideas of
modern science, indeed it has been the starting-point of biology
since the days of Wallace and Darwin.

Geometry was an art in which the Egyptians had attained
a considerable empirical proficiency. The Greeks converted it
into a science, and with their keen visualizing faculty they made
quick progress in it. This branch of studies was pursued with
special zeal by Pythagoras and his school, who solved in advance
many if not all of the problems contained in the first book of
Euclid. Pythagoras also laid the foundations of acoustics and

musical analysis, when he discovered that the sections of a string which produce the octave and the fifth of its fundamental note are simple aliquot parts of the string in regard to length. But his most notable contribution to science was his unbounded faith in mathematics. His dictum that 'all is number' sounds naïve, but given a slightly different wording, 'all is numerable (and measurable)', it reveals itself as an important truth. In proclaiming mathematics as the master-key of scientific research, Pythagoras was a forerunner of Galileo and the giants of the seventeenth century.

The Greeks at an early date became inquisitive about the origin of life and found the answer, like most unsophisticated peoples, in a special act of creation. In the sixth century, however, Anaximander approached this problem in the manner of nineteenth-century biology. Realizing the severity of the early struggle for existence, he surmised that the earlier animal species lived in the shock-proof water, and that when they first adventured on the dry land they wore protective carapaces.

By 500 B.C. the Greeks had acquired an empiric knowledge of medicine comparable with that of the Egyptians and Babylonians; but where their experience failed them they fell back, like the Orientals, on invoking the aid of the gods. About 500 B.C., it is true, an Italiote physician named Alcmaeon made a beginning of medical research by dissecting animals, and by this method he first revealed the true function of the brain and the nervous system; but the importance of his discovery was not realized at the time. Strangely enough, it was near one of the temples frequented by patients in hope of a miraculous cure, the sanctuary of Asclepius at Cos, that medicine was first proclaimed to be a science. About 425 B.C. Hippocrates founded at Cos a school which studied disease in the firm belief that it was wholly due to natural causes (p. 192). In assuming that health is controlled by four internal 'humours' (blood, bile, etc.), the Hippocratics adopted too simple an explanation; but they laid the foundations for a more scientific diagnosis by their careful observation and recording of the symptoms of disease. Hippocrates is generally acknowledged as the 'Father of Medicine'. Indeed medicine has gradually been returning to the Hippocratic principle that

Nature is the healer as well as the bringer of illness, whereas for some sixteen intervening centuries the civilized world put its faith in periodic potions and bleedings.

3. SOCRATES AND PLATO

Between 425 and 350 B.C. the main channel of Greek thought was moulded by Socrates (469–399 B.C.) and Plato (428 or 427–348 B.C.). Socrates, as we have seen (p. 194), shared in the movement of Greek scientific interest from Nature to the Humanites. 'Socrates', said Cicero, 'was the first to call philosophy down from the heavens and to set her in the cities of men, bringing her into their homes and compelling her to ask questions about life and morality and things good and evil.'

Herein he shared the general tendency of the Sophists who were his contemporaries. But he also led a reaction against the Sophists, from whom he differentiated himself sharply. The speculations of the Sophists on the nature of truth had induced a sceptical trend of thought among them, and one of their leaders, the Sicilian Gorgias, had come to the devastating conclusion that 'there is no truth, and if there were, it could not be known'. Against this intellectual nihilism Socrates contended that truth lies hidden at the bottom of every man's mind, and he showed the way to evoke if from this recess. He is now probably best remembered as an eccentric who buttonholed passers-by, questioned them on topics of general interest, such as 'What is Courage?', 'What is Justice?', and invariably revealed some flaw in their reasoning. In thus showing up the easy dogmatism of the ordinary 'practical' man, Socrates might appear at first sight to be himself a missionary of scepticism. But in his own words he was performing the function of a midwife and assisting the birth of correct ideas. His dialogues, in fact, were lessons in careful definition and logical thinking, Believing that 'the greatest power on earth is the power of reflection', he helped to provide in logic an unerring instrument of reflection.

The Sophists, surveying the diversities and discrepancies of established laws and usages, had come to the conclusion that morality was merely conventional, and some of them inclined to moral anarchy. Socrates was even more resolute in opposing this tendency.[1] In spite of his interest in argument and definition, his aim was essentially practical. "I have no other business', he says in the 'Apology', 'than to go about persuading you all, both old and young, to care less for your wealth than for the perfection of your souls, and telling you that goodness does not come from wealth, but it is goodness that makes wealth or anything else, in public or private life, a good thing for men.' If by 'soul' we mean our moral personality, we might say that Socrates discovered the soul. Moreover, if he emphasized the soul's self-determining power, he also professed belief in a beneficent Providence that guided men's choice of what was best. Indeed, with all his practical sense, Socrates was a mystic. In his prayer at the end of Plato's *Phaedrus* he said: 'O beloved Pan and all ye other gods of this place, grant that I may grow to beauty in the things within, and that outward possessions may not disturb the harmony of the inner man. The wise man only may I consider rich; and of wealth may I have so much as only the wise man can bear.'

The teaching of Socrates was purely informal and made no pretence of system. His loose threads were gathered up by Plato, but Plato's doctrine likewise was not woven into a definite pattern. He stands not so much for a logical system as for an attitude of mind; he is one of those spirits whose inspiration transcends the objective validity of their opinions. But in his teaching we may discern three main objects.

In the first place Plato inherited Socrates' interest in logic. To him too truth was better, more beautiful, than self-interest, and therefore worth pursuing with the utmost patience and in a disinterested scientific spirit. But in his quest for a valid test of truth he became deeply convinced of the imperfection of the senses, so that instead of appealing from first to later sense impressions, he decided that the eternal verities must be sought in a supra-sensual world. Sense-perception, being temporal, could give us, at best, opinions; true knowledge must be derived from the timeless 'ideas' (i.e. forms, patterns) that are not of this earth.

---

[1] It is the Greek principle that scientific and ethical law are *universal* that has been challenged by the Nazi philosophy.

Secondly, he developed Socrates' ethical doctrine. All desire happiness, but most people miss it, because they confuse it with something external like wealth or health or power or fame. Actually, happiness depends on inner harmony, which we cannot attain unless we are able to distinguish the real from the apparent good, the eternal from the transient. This doctrine of harmony, moreover, was applied by Plato to human societies as well as to individuals. In his treaties on the *Republic* (or better, the Ideal State), he began with the ordinary Greek conception of justice as the bond of society, but went on to show that justice in this case meant the proper relation between the constituent classes of a state—in his Ideal State he provided for three classes, the Guardians, the Combatants, and the Wealth-producers—and the inner harmony of the Guardian class, for the attainment of which he prescribed for its members an almost forbiddingly severe course of training. The Utopian state of Plato embodied some features, such as communism of property and of wives for the Guardian class, which his readers, ancient and modern, have generally rejected as too advanced, and others, like slavery and warfare (at any rate against barbarians), which betray a residue of conservatism in him. Yet in its analysis of the ultimate controlling forces in politics, and as a means of clarifying our political thinking, the *Republic* of Plato remains unsurpassed.

Thirdly, Plato transformed Socrates' mysticism into a reasoned theology. God governs the Universe on moral principles, and to man is vouchsafed some measure of free-will. Before his birth his soul is allowed to choose from the lots given him by Fate, and 'the responsibility rests with the chooser: God is not to blame'. In a world used to expiation by sacrifice, Plato proclaimed that a man could not buy divine favour: each must bear the consequences of his deeds. For the soul is immortal and passes from one body to another in the lapse of cycles; and on earth, imprisoned in the body, it remembers in rare flashes the beauty it once knew in heaven: 'For in Heaven, perchance, is laid up a pattern for him who wishes to see it, and seeing, to shape his life in accordance therewith' (*Republic*, 592 B).

The influence of Plato on the world's thought has been immense. The *Academy* which he founded to carry on his teaching lasted 916 years—longer than any university up to the present day—and his voice penetrated far beyond the walls of his school. Cicero was full of Plato, and through his philosophical works (especially the *De Senectute* and the *Tusculan Disputations*) he introduced Plato to the Latin Church Fathers. The greatest of these, Augustine, said that the only fundamental Christian truth not contained in Plato was the Incarnation. Broadly speaking, the Church derived its ethical theory from the Stoics, and its metaphysics from Plato. The *Logos* (the 'Word', or better, 'Reason') of St. John's Gospel was derived from Plato through Philo of Alexandria. Dr. Inge has said: 'Plato and Augustine have been the intellectual sources of Anglican theology at its best'. The Christian schools admitted Plato (with Vergil) into their scheme of studies, and popular medieval thought imbibed Platonism in Boethius' *Consolation of Philosophy*. On the other hand the doctrine of Plato was also mobilized by the last champions of expiring paganism against the Church, by Plotinus, the founder of the 'Neo-Platonist' school (p. 215), by his pupil Porphyry (the ablest of the polemists against Christianity), and by the Emperor Julian. In the twelfth century he was supplanted in western Europe by Aristotle, whose more formal teaching appealed to an age of scholasticism. But the Platonic tradition was revived in the Renaissance; it has since been continuously cherished at Cambridge and Oxford, and it colours modern thought in many ways. In the words of A. E. Taylor, 'whenever, in the subsequent centuries, men are concerned to plead the cause of a real and living God and a genuine moral government of the world against scepticism, pessimism, or indifferentism, we find them looking to Plato as the chief source of their inspiration and their arguments'.[1]

The literature of Europe is full of Platonism—that personal Platonism of Wordsworth and Coleridge, 'the mood of one who

[1] E. Eyre, *European Civilization*, iii, p. 775. The influence of Plato also extends to modern mathematics and science. 'In his most recent attempt to construct an adequate philosophy of Nature, Whitehead has found himself led to take as his starting-point the general view of Nature put by Plato into the mouth of Timaeus. It certainly looks as if the *Timaeus* may again become the standing background for the educated man's vision of Nature.'

has a curious eye for the endless variety of this visible and temporal world and a fine sense of its beauties, and yet is ever haunted by the presence of an invisible and eternal world beyond'. When Goethe writes: 'Alles Vergängliche ist nur ein Gleichniss', or Shelley:

> The One remains, the Many change and pass!
> Heaven's light forever shines, earth's shadows flee;

or Wordsworth:

> Heaven-born, the soul a heavenward course must hold;
> Beyond the visible world she soars to seek—
> For what delights the sense is false and weak—
> Ideal Form, the Universal Mould,

they are keeping company with Plato, as many other English poets, such as Spenser, Sidney, Keats, and many writers in Holland or Germany or elsewhere in Europe have done.

4. ARISTOTLE

Aristotle (384–322 B.C.) was a native of a small town on the Macedonian coast, but he spent much of his life at Athens. He was for twenty years a pupil of Plato, and his master's influence on him shows through in all his work on Mental and Moral Science. But after Plato's death he not only diverged from him in this branch of studies, but he broke away into the field of Natural Science which Socrates and Plato had avoided. He shared out his interest between Man and Nature, and refused to admit a sharp dividing-line between the worlds of Sense and of Reason. He exemplified better than any other the Greek capacity to 'see life steadily, see it whole'. In the words of Roger Bacon, 'he set in order all parts of philosophy'.

His proficiency in the whole of his vast range of subjects was of course not equally profound. He did not share Plato's talent for mathematics, and his treatise on Physics was of lesser merit. On the other hand, he had a natural bent for the organic sciences, and he could read lessons and discover beauty in the lowliest manifestations of Nature, as well as among Nature's aristocrats. His descriptions of animals (especially of marine animals) showed true scientific accuracy; in some cases they were condemned by modern zoologists, only to be rehabilitated by later researchers with better miscroscopes. But the breadth of his vision was as remarkable as its minuteness. He took the entire field of Nature within his purview and traced in it a continuous gradation from the lowest to the highest forms of life. This discovery of a 'Scala Naturae' was one of the most valuable legacies of ancient science to the modern world. Another important contribution of Aristotle to scientific thought was his doctrine that every structure and function are related to a final purpose, and that this must be perceived in order to understand the organism at various stages of its growth.[1] Darwin freely acknowledged how deeply Aristotle had influenced him.

In his treatises on mental science Aristotle aimed at building a new bridge between the world of Reason and the world of Fact. He shared Plato's intuition that beyond the world of Sense there might lie an invisible and imperishable world, for which the human heart might well yearn. But instead of regarding the objects of Sense as inferior reflections of a reality which dwelt apart in the heavens, and incapable of imparting true knowledge, he saw in them the beginning of truth and part of the structure of reality. The task for the seeker after knowledge was to apprehend the 'form' or the universal; but these forms (unlike Plato's 'Ideas' or 'Forms') were not stored away, disembodied and self-sufficient, in a world of their own, but were immanent in the visible world of matter: pure form, like pure matter, was a mere abstraction, without any independent reality. In addition, Aristotle elaborated and as it were consummated the work of Socrates and Plato by writing a systematic treatise of deductive logic, in which the method of correct reasoning was set forth, not in sweeping outline, but step for step.

In his *Politics* Aristotle accepted Plato's general ideal of government by a highly educated aristocracy; but he tempered Plato's idealism by numerous concessions to the actual exigencies of political life, as revealed by the record of history, of which he possessed a wide knowledge. He criticized Plato's communism, trusting to education rather than to institutions to achieve

[1] On the importance of this conception, see A. W. Pickard-Cambridge, *Proceedings of the Classical Association*, 1939. Aristotelian 'teleology', i.e. belief in the end or purpose inherent in natural phenomena, recurs in eminent modern scientists like Dr. Robert Broom.

social justice, and acknowledged the broad good sense of the common people in political matters, remarking that in actual practice the moderáte democracies had the best record among the Greek city-states. He followed current Greek thought in accepting slavery, albeit with misgivings, and in drawing a sharp line between Greeks and barbarians. He even advised his pupil, Alexander of Macedon, to 'treat the Greeks as friends and the barbarians as enemies'—a counsel which Alexander, himself half a barbarian, naturally and wisely ignored.[1]

Aristotle again followed Socrates and Plato in accepting the contemplative life as the ultimate ideal; but recognizing that a life of action must remain the lot of most, he sought for a general working principle to guide men through their daily round, and found it in the dictum that 'virtue lies in the middle', and consists of avoiding excess in either direction. In this he systematized and justified an old Greek rule, which the oracle of Delphi had formulated in the saying: 'nothing overmuch'! Here too Aristotle sided with the 'man in the street' against Plato, who took a more ascetic view of life and tended to regard pleasure as an evil, rather than as a good of which, as of all good things, there could be too much. His attitude to the emotions was also illustrated in his treatise on poetry, in which he defended against Plato the educative value of drama and contended that, far from indulging the emotions and making them unmanageable, it gave them a healthy outlet (*katharsis*), implying that you will better control your feelings when you must, if you open the safety-valve while you may. Here Aristotle is in touch with the latest psychology of the emotions, as expressed in Freud's doctrine of repressive complexes and the need for their release.

Lastly, while Aristotle accepted the theology of Plato in main outline, he was entirely devoid of Socrates' mystic fervour, and less acutely troubled than Plato by a sense of human imperfection. A close and interested student of life, he nevertheless maintained towards it an attitude of scientific detachment.

Though Aristotle followed the example of Plato in founding a school at Athens (the *Lyceum*, or the school of the Peripatetics), and thereby gave a fresh stimulus to scientific research, his

[1] On this whole subject see Haarhoff, *The Stranger at the Gate*.

immediate influence was not comparable with that of his master. Not long after his death his manuscripts were lost, and although they were recovered and published in the first century B.C., they were little studied until the rise of the Neoplatonists (third century A.D.; p. 215). The Neoplatonists, intent on conserving the tradition of Greek philosophy and science against the Dark Ages which they foresaw, went beyond Plato to Aristotle for those branches of knowledge on which Plato had been reticent, and thus ensured his survival in the Byzantine Empire. From Byzantium the study of Aristotle passed to the seats of learning in the world of Islam, and from these (more especially from Cordova) to western Europe. In the thirteenth century the Church lent its authority to his writings, until he became almost an incubus to the further advancement of knowledge. This Aristotelean 'fundamentalism' was overthrown by the scholars of the Renaissance, and so long as modern men of science were mainly concerned with its mathematical and physical branches, Aristotle remained in the background. But with the rise of the biological sciences, and the application of scientific methods to social problems, he stands forth once more as one of the two master-minds of ancient Greece.

5. HELLENISTIC PHILOSOPHY AND SCIENCE

Of the many branches of natural science which flourished in the Hellenistic period, geography experienced an inevitable revival. The conquests of Alexander carried the Greeks far beyond the Mediterranean border and gave them a considerable knowledge of the Asiatic continent. His forcible discoveries were followed by two peaceful but abortive explorations. About 300 B.C. a Massiliote captain named Pytheas ventured out into the Atlantic, circumnavigated Britain, and skirted the coast of western Europe as far as the Elbe estuary. Modern geographers are agreed in recognizing the scientific value of Pytheas' cruise, but some of his own compatriots denounced him as an impostor, and no other Greek followed in his wake. The effective discovery of Atlantic Europe was therefore left over to the Romans. Towards the end of the second century B.C. a still bolder navigator, Eudoxus of Cyzicus, made two return journeys between Egypt and India, and discovered the right seasons for sailing out with the monsoon, and home with the counter-monsoon. He next embarked on a yet greater enterprise, the circumnavigation of Africa; but he never came home from this voyage. Alexander's conquests, however, definitely opened up the Asiatic continent, and the Greeks' range of geographical knowledge was in consequence doubled.

With these explorations went the discovery of new means to plot them on the map. During the fourth century unknown Greek observers drew the right inference from the circular shape of the earth's shadow in a lunar eclipse, that the earth was a globe (a fact known to Aristotle). About 225 B.C. an Alexandrian savant, Eratosthenes, applied his knowledge of Euclid (p. 209) to the measurement of the earth's circumference, and obtained a result which some modern scholars believe to have been correct within 200 miles. The same investigator also planned to construct a network of meridians and lines of latitude to assist in map-making. This plan, it is true, was never realized. Although a practical demonstration of the value of taking latitudes (by means of a shadow-stick) had been given by Pytheas, no systematic attempt to obtain other such data was made, and the lack of reliable time-pieces prevented the Greeks from fixing longitudes with any degree of accuracy. Nevertheless the map of the world which Eratosthenes drew was considerably more accurate, besides being far more extensive, than anything previously attempted.

In the field of astronomy the Hellenistic Greeks harnessed their native gift of imagination to a new faculty of patient investigation (after the manner of Aristotle). Once the Greeks had abandoned the notion that the earth is a flat disk, their original belief that day and night were caused by the sun 'looping the loop' round it became difficult to uphold. The correct explanation was at last offered by a pupil of Plato named Heracleides, who suggested that the earth turned round its axis, and in so doing started a scientific revolution. The same scholar observed the orbits of Venus and Mercury, and inferred that these planets were satellites of the sun. A more general study of the planetary paths by Hellenistic Greeks led up to the theory (first formulated by Apollonius of Perga) that the planets moved in epicycles, i.e. in small circles which were being carried round (in an opposite direction) on the circumference of a wider orbit— a theory which held the field till the day of Kepler.

In the second century an Alexandrian astronomer, Hipparchus, utilized the data of Greek and Babylonian observers to fix the length of the solar year and the lunar month, and applied trigonometrical methods to measure the distance of sun and moon. His estimates of distance were but moderately accurate, but his computation of the solar year was correct within five minutes, and that of the lunar month within one second. Hipparchus also computed the rate of precession of the equinoxes, thus confirming a notable Babylonian discovery. Lastly, he made the first comprehensive star-chart for the guidance of future astronomers.[1]

When Heracleides declared that the sun had satellites, and that the earth was in motion, he implicitly confirmed the theory of the Pythagoreans, that the earth moved round the sun (p. 197, note). About 300 B.C. Aristarchus of Samos reaffirmed this opinion in a more authoritative manner. Herein he found few supporters— indeed it required much telescopic observation before the heliocentric theory was raised above doubt; but his speculations became known to Copernicus (through Ptolemy—p. 214), and thus gave an impetus to a momentous modern discovery.

About 300 B.C. an Alexandrian mathematician, Eucleides, collected the results of past Greek research in geometry in a treatise (the *Elements*), which was almost ideal in the orderly progression of its propositions and the economy and neatness of its demonstrations. Sir Thomas Heath predicts that Euclid will yet dispossess the variegated modern substitutes for him. Two new branches of plane geometry were created when Hipparchus introduced trigonometric measurements and Apollonius wrote the first treatise (still extant) on Conic Sections.

[1] In making contact with Babylonian mathematics the Greeks also made acquaintance with astrology, which indeed was the main object for which the Babylonians observed the heavens. Astrological practices gradually invaded the Greek and Roman world, and even men of education (including some emperors) had their horoscopes taken.

Solid geometry, which had engaged the attention of Greek mathematicians in the fourth century, was greatly advanced by Archimedes of Syracuse (*c.* 250 B.C.), who regarded his discoveries in this field as his highest achievement.

The study of physics and chemistry was not resumed on any large scale by the Hellenistic Greeks, but Archimedes created a new branch of these sciences by discovering the fundamental laws of hydrostatics. The incidental study which Archimedes made of mechanics led to great improvements in the construction of cranes, pulley-systems, and suction-screws for hoisting water. Two Alexandrian engineers of uncertain date, Ctesibius and Hero, invented various ingenious toys, mostly actuated by wind or water power, e.g. a penny-in-the-slot machine, a taximeter, and a miniature steam-engine. But these inventions did not lead on to a 'machine age'. The scarcity of coal, the lack of cheap hard iron, and above all, the institution of slavery (p. 134) prevented any such development.

The impetus given to zoological studies by Aristotle was, strangely enough, of short duration. But in the neighbouring field of botany his pupil Theophrastus broke new ground in two treatises, of which one, the *History of Plants* (really a description of all the species then known), has earned the praise of modern botanists on the score of its accuracy.

In no sphere of studies did the intensified methods of observation introduced by the Hellenistic Greeks yield better results than in medicine. About 300 B.C. two physicians, Herophilus and Erasistratus, practised dissection of the human body at the schools of Alexandria. This enabled them to trace the nervous system in main outline, and to confirm the discovery of Alcmaeon (p. 199) that the brain, not the heart, was the centre of consciousness. For the heart they found alternative employment by proving its connexion with the pulse and the arteries, thus preparing the way for the modern discovery of the circulation of the blood.

The discovery of many new plant species in the newly opened districts of Asia gave a stimulus to pharmacology. Among the drugs now brought into use were opium and atropin, and these sedatives, coupled with the new knowledge of human anatomy, led to the establishment of surgery as an independent branch of medicine. Major operations (e.g. for hernia) could now be undertaken with a reasonable prospect of success.[1]

The mental sciences, now again dissociated from natural science, made little progress after the death of Aristotle. Political science lost its keen edge with the decline of the city-state and republican institutions. But individual ethics were studied more intensively, because the conventional codes of conduct which each Greek city had set up for itself broke down in the general confusion of population that followed Alexander's conquest and colonization of the East, and a universally valid rule of behaviour (which Socrates and Plato had already postulated) was now in demand among all thinking men.

In answer to this quest two new schools, the Epicureans and the Stoics, came into being, with headquarters at Athens and branches in many other cities. The Epicureans, recognizing that all men are alike in the pursuit of pleasure, boldly gave out that this was the right object of moral endeavour. Their study of pleasure soon convinced them that physical enjoyments were inferior (i.e. less pleasurable) to those of a social and intellectual order. But they underrated the pleasures that attend effort and achievement; consequently they favoured the life of the recluse, and thereby diminished their influence. Yet the *ataraxia* or serenity which distinguished the Epicureans made a strong appeal to gentle minds which recoiled from the storm and stress of Greek politics and Roman republicanism in its declining days.

By way of contrast, the Stoic gloried in man's strength: to live good lives, men need but follow unflinchingly the dictates of Reason and Will, so as to command their fate, or if fate were obstinately adverse, to meet its slings and arrows calmly and without fluster. This doctrine, which reminds us of Kant's 'categorical imperative', proved too strong meat for the general, and the idealized picture of the perfect Stoic sage excited mild ridicule by reason of its dummy-like impassivity. Yet Stoicism inspired many of the best characters of Hellenistic and especially of Roman history, and it was largely incorporated into the

[1] Contrast the lack of anæsthetics in medieval times.

ethical teaching of the Christian Church. One further consequence of the Stoics' exaltation of mankind was that they minimized the importance of the divisions which happen to obtain between different human groups, and assumed a cosmopolitan outlook. This cosmopolitan influence was not without effect upon Roman statesmanship, and facilitated the conversion of the Roman Empire into a commonwealth of equal partners.

6. PHILOSOPHY AND SCIENCE IN THE ROMAN EMPIRE

The Roman attitude to intellectual studies, as we have seen (p. 195), was mainly utilitarian. Even educated Romans refused to think ahead of necessity; they curbed their imagination and seldom gave full play to their critical faculties. Their lack of scientific imagination is well illustrated by the *Natural History* of the Elder Pliny (A.D. 23–79), which is a vast repertory of facts (or fictions) amassed from various sciences, and thrown together with hardly any method of classification and without explanatory comment.

In the application of science to practical needs, however, the Romans were more thorough and methodical than the Greeks. They borrowed Greek inventions and utilized them on a scale hitherto unknown. They absorbed enough of the elements of Greek geometry and trigonometry to become expert surveyors, road-constructors and hydraulic engineers, and they measured land (for their colonies), built roads and aqueducts, and carried out irrigation schemes with un-Greek pertinacity. The barrages and cisterns with which they captured the winter rains of North Africa for their wheatfields and olive-yards were hardly improved upon until the last fifty years. Their roads, as we have seen (p. 138), remained unsurpassed until the time of Telford and Macadam. The Greek sites of Delos and Olympia had to wait till the days of Roman rule for an adequate supply of water, and the first metalled road between Athens and Corinth was completed by Hadrian.

Similarly the Romans studied mechanics to the point of being able to hoist and balance heavy weights, and in the Colosseum and Pantheon (p. 223) they proved their practical mastery in the calculation and absorption of architectural stresses. They were slow to achieve proficiency in medical practice, which they left largely in the hands of the Greeks; but they were the first to construct rudimentary hospitals (in their camps and on their large estates). Finally, it was left to Caesar to enlist an Alexandrian astronomer (Sosigenes) to devise a satisfactory calendar, and to introduce order into the chaos of overlapping local years (p. 140).

In 155 B.C. an Academic philosopher named Carneades gave an exhibition of logic-chopping at Rome, and stood in danger of being dismissed the city for his pains. This incident illustrates the attitude of the Romans (before they came to feel at home with Hellenism) to the more abstract branches of Greek philosophy, which they tended to regard as laborious trifling. A century later Cicero undertook to explain the Platonic theory of knowledge to his countrymen; his philosophical treatises became the chief means by which the study of Plato was kept alive in medieval western Europe, but they did not go far to popularize Platonic doctrine in Rome itself.

Greek political science had apparently something more substantial to offer to the Romans, and in the days when republican government was breaking down Cicero turned in all seriousness to it for political counsel. But his treatise *De Republica*, though ostensibly a counterpart to Plato's *Republic*, derived its inspiration much less from Greek philosophy than from the past history of Rome, and Cicero's ideal state, far from being a Utopia, bore a family resemblance to the earlier Roman Republic and showed a greater tolerance of human limitations.

The only branch of Greek philosophy that exerted any serious influence upon Roman thought was ethics, which alone seemed to have any obvious bearing on the art of life. Educated Romans took up Greek ethics all the more readily, as they realized that their native 'mos maiorum', however well adapted to the needs of a self-contained agrarian state, was not an adequate guide to the problems of an imperial people. Of the two main Greek systems, Epicureanism exercised a passing attraction in the last days of the republic, when sensitive men sought a refuge therein from the turmoil of Roman politics. Lucretius became its inspired

15

prophet; Vergil and Horace embraced it in their younger days. But most of its Roman students merely toyed with it. On the other hand the Stoic philosophy made many converts in Rome and captivated some of its best minds. The call which it made upon men's powers of endurance met a willing response among a people who naturally 'fought back' when hard pressed, and its cosmopolitanism was congenial to the enlightened rulers of a world-state. But in adopting Stoicism the Romans tempered it with a dose of common sense. They did not aspire to the complete impassivity of the ideal Stoic sage, and they sought to control rather than to stifle their emotions.

The first effect of the Roman dominion upon Greek philosophy and science, and upon Greek culture in general, was to arrest its further development. Numbed by the shock of conquest, the Greeks fell into a state of inertia. But when the Pax Romana became firmly established under the Roman emperors they again gave freer play to their minds, though they never fully recovered their former enterprise.

In one branch of science the Romans provided new material for the Greeks to work upon. The advancing Roman armies opened up large tracts of continental and Atlantic Europe, and of the North African interior, which had been very imperfectly known to the Greeks. Moreover, while the Roman soldier was extending the frontiers of knowledge in the West, Greek sea-captains, following a pioneer named Hippalus (probably in the first century B.C.), laid open the Indian Ocean as far as Cape Comorin, or even to Singapore: a few adventurers in the second century A.D. found their way to Southern China.[1] In the light of the information thus acquired an Alexandrian scholar named Ptolemy (Claudius Ptolemaeus, c. A.D. 150) wrote a comprehensive geographical treatise which remained definitive until the modern age of discovery. Ptolemy's maps, for which he devised a good system of projection, contained some glaring faults, but they are comparable to those of the present day.

Ptolemy was also the author of an astronomical manual which contained little that was new, but summed up the achievement of the Hellenistic Greeks in a convenient form. This work was

[1] E. H. Warmington, in Cary and Warmington, *The Ancient Explorers.*

much studied by Islamic scholars, and it was declared by the Medieval Church to be the last word on the subject.

Mathematical studies showed considerable vitality among the Greeks of the later Roman Empire, and the researches of the Hellenistic period were rounded off in different directions. A discovery of great potential importance was made when an Alexandrian named Diophantus (probably of the third century A.D.) devised a rudimentary system of algebraic notation. But Diophantus lived too late or too early; his work was slightly extended by the Saracens, but not systematically developed until modern times.

Of the organic sciences, medicine alone produced another notable research student, Claudius Galenus or Galen, who lived in the later second century A.D. Galen carried physiology and anatomy to the point where the physicians of the Renaissance took them up again. He is, however, best known by his medical encyclopædia, which summed up the work of his predecessors and found no successor until the Renaissance, since it was invested by the Church with canonical authority. A minor work which also remained standard until the sixteenth century was the *Pharmacology* of Dioscorides (c. A.D. 60).

Greek philosophy took a final meteoric flight in the middle and later third century A.D., when the 'Neoplatonists' established their school at Alexandria. Its chief figure, Plotinus, revived the robust belief of Socrates and Plato, that human salvation lay in sheer hard thinking. In this faith he created a spacious new abstract world, through which he proposed to guide mankind away from the illusory world of Sense, through a hierarchy of intermediate realities, to the ultimate reality of an absolute and wholly discarnate 'One'. Plotinus' construction was a veritable *tour de force*, and it gave cold comfort to an age that craved for a quick release from the disasters that beset it. Neoplatonism therefore soon dissolved into a facile mysticism. But before it became a spent force it had imparted to the Christian Church some of its saving faith in intellectual effort and integrity.

VII

Greek and Roman Art

I. GENERAL CHARACTERISTICS

THE REMAINING monuments of Greek and Roman art form but a small proportion of the numberless temples, statues, paintings, and so forth, which were produced in the world of Greece and Rome. Of this scanty remnant, again, much is of inferior quality. We possess comparatively few Greek works of sculpture; the greater part of our surviving specimens consists of copies made in Roman times, and much of our statuary, whether good or bad, has come down to us in a fragmentary condition. ('If that's Victory', said the working-man of the defaced Nike of Paeonius, 'I'd like to see the chap wot lost!') Furthermore, most of us make our acquaintance with these survivals through plaster casts or book illustrations which are generally misleading. We must go to the Acropolis Museum at Athens to realize in full the vividness of Greek art in the sixth century B.C., to take in the fresh vigour of those 'Maidens', whose vitality still radiates through the stone and makes mock of our ideas of 'genteel' Attic grace.

In addition to these inevitable obstacles, our appreciation of Greek and Roman art is apt to be marred by an inherited prejudice which condemns 'classical' work as being necessarily lifeless and dull. As in the case of Egyptian art, which is commonly dubbed stiff and conventional because some of its products in certain periods or genres had this fault, we are apt to affix general labels to Greek and Roman art, as if it were all of one piece. But if we study this art with open minds we shall realize its various stages of growth, its all-round excellence, and the vital part which it played in Greek and Roman culture.

Of all ancient arts, that of the Greeks most repays study. 'In Greek civilization at its height', says Roger Fry, 'sculpture and painting were cultivated with an intensity and a vigour that have rarely been equalled. The artist of this period became fully conscious of his role as an interpreter of the spiritual life of man. . . . Such a recognition of the high purposes of art, when the artist is regarded as the equal of the poet and the philosopher, has only occurred at rare intervals' (e.g. in China in T'ang times, in Italy during the Renaissance, in France since the reign of Louis XIV). . . . 'We may note that these periods have always occurred in times of free intellectual speculation.' But if the Greek artist received due recognition, he was not 'lionized' or exposed to the idol-worship of small coteries. He was a *demiurgus*, a public worker, and his reward was a candid and not uncritical appreciation by the Greek nation in general.

A special feature of Greek art was its devotion to the human figure, which the artist had unique opportunities of studying in free and graceful motion at the gymnasia. Though all men tend to make their gods in their own image, none have been so anthropomorphic as the Greeks; captivated by the beauty of the human form, the Greeks saw it everywhere. This tendency perhaps made them unduly neglectful of other forms, e.g. of animals, in the representation of which Eastern art excelled. But the human emphasis of Greek art at least kept it sane and prevented such extravagances as the Central American bird-wings that play over into fish, or the Scythian deer that mix their metaphors and change their antlers into birds' necks. It also provided them with a standard of beauty that has endured amid changing tastes and varying fancies, the healthy human body.

Greek art, like so much else of Greek civilization, had its roots in earlier cultures. Its debt to Egypt is revealed by the remains of early Greek statuary, the predominant type of which is a young man or an Apollo, standing very straight in Egyptian fashion, with one foot advanced, the knees bearing the weight of the body equally, and the arms close to the sides; and the avenue of seated statues that lined the approach to the temple of Apollo at Didyma (near Miletus) plainly recalls the monumental alleys of Karnak. The influence of Minoan Crete upon Greek art is not so easy to determine, for the latter appears as a renaissance rather than a survival from the prehistoric age. But it may be no mere accident that Minoan art was characterized by a liking for objects in free and vigorous motion, such as we find again among the historic Greeks. A hidden link of transmission perhaps connects the prehistoric and the historic arts of Greece. But whatever Greek art may have borrowed from elsewhere, it became the most individual of ancient arts. It soon emancipated itself from its teachers by developing its own technical processes and striving to express its own ideals.

Residents in uni-racial or uni-lingual countries sometimes find it hard to understand how, as in ancient Italy and modern South Africa, two languages and two cultures can live together and maintain their individuality. For this reason the relation of Roman to Greek art has often been misunderstood. The former has often been mistaken for a mere copy, and a bad copy, of Greek art; a statue, once recognized as Roman, is put down as second-rate and blinked at with delicate aversion. Yet the Elder Pliny assures us that ancient Italy produced an art of its own, and archæological discoveries in early Italic and Etruscan cemeteries have amply confirmed this statement. The pottery and bronze work of the prehistoric Italic peoples showed considerable technical proficiency and a nascent sense of form; and their art traditions were not destroyed by the Etruscan conquest, but lived on independently. Etruscan art, though manifestly indebted to that of Greece, developed on original lines. It acquired a special proficiency in the use of terra-cotta (for statuary and the revetment of temple walls), and in goldsmiths' work, and it displayed a tendency to grim realism that was anything but Hellenic. Moreover, the researches of the past forty years have made it plain that Rome produced an art which, for all its borrowed elements, was distinctive and appropriate to Roman culture.

It is true that Roman art was late in coming to birth. The early Romans lacked the desire and the leisure to cultivate art, and contented themselves with the importation of Etruscan or (more rarely) Greek craftsmen to build their temples, and to execute an occasional statue or fresco for them. In the last three centuries B.C. Rome became well stocked with Greek objects of art, which were acquired by the plunder of Greek cities or by purchase on the part of connoisseurs among the Roman aristocracy. But the very profusion of their importation seems at first to have stifled rather than stimulated the native sense of art. It was therefore not till the end of the republic and the age of

Augustus that an independent Roman art came into being; but in the first two centuries A.D. the new-born Roman art surpassed the senescent art of Greece.

2. GREEK ARCHITECTURE

In prehistoric Greece stone architecture (with large, un-cemented blocks, usually polygonal) had come into use for large buildings such as palaces. The early Greeks, however, fell back upon more primitive materials, timber and sun-dried brick. For private houses the use of mud-brick continued to the time of Plutarch (c A.D. 100), and it survives to the present day. Athens in the fifth and following centuries was a strange mixture of splendid and solid public buildings and flimsy private dwellings. Hence burglars were called 'wall-diggers': instead of picking locks, they cut holes in house walls. The construction of early public buildings may be exemplified from the seventh-century temple of Hera at Olympia, which had half-timbered walls with fillings of crude brick, and wooden columns. The use of stone was resumed in the eighth century, but did not become common until the sixth century. It is not unlikely that the Greeks learnt the art of stone-construction in Egypt.

Like the Egyptians, the Greeks made almost exclusive use of the post and lintel type of construction. As in Egypt, the supporting posts were usually columns. But the Greeks made no attempt to imitate the vast dimensions or the complex plans of Egyptian architecture. Their temples and public buildings were nearly always of plain rectangular, though occasionally of circular, shape; they were strictly functional, each column being proportioned to the weight which it would bear, and the orna-mentation being no more than sufficient to relieve the monotony of blank surfaces; and the modesty of their dimensions may be gathered from the fact that the Parthenon, which measured 225 by 100 feet, was a relatively large temple.

Greek architecture was therefore characterized by simplicity; but simplicity went hand in hand with beauty. Its detail was carefully thought out, so that the proportions of the entire building, the ratio of plain to ornamented surface, the spacing of the columns, should be singly and collectively pleasing to the eye. The 'refinements' of the Parthenon—the subtle curves of its outlines, which were nicely calculated to correct a mass of small optical illusions—are sufficient to fill a book; nevertheless (or because of this) the temple as a whole is easily grasped by the eye, as the plot of a Greek tragedy is readily seized by the mind.

The principal surviving specimens of Greek architecture are temples, and its development may best be traced in reference to these. These temples always had a pillared portico, and were frequently surrounded by a colonnade. The arrangement and style of their columns were therefore the distinctive features of each temple. Greek architecture made use of three 'orders' of columns, the Doric, Ionic, and Corinthian. The Doric column was probably indigenous: indeed the Doric temple of historic times probably grew out of the *megăron* or hall of the Mycenaean palace (like the one that survives at Tiryns), with its columned porch, which was also imitated in private Greek houses (as at Priene). The leading feature of the Doric column was its plain bevelled capital. The Ionic column, whose capital ended in two symmetrical, snail-like curves, was probably borrowed from Egypt, but it had become a standard component of Greek architecture by the sixth century. The Corinthian column, with its richly floriated capital, was a development from the palm-capitals of Egypt; it made its first appearance in the later fifth century B.C.

Until 500 B.C. the Doric and the Ionic styles were equally in favour. The early Doric style is best represented by the majestic temples at Paestum in South Italy; the finest early specimens of Ionic architecture are some of the small 'treasuries' or store-houses at Delphi. In the fifth century the Doric style obtained a decided preponderance. The great Sicilian temples of that century and the temple of Zeus at Olympia were in the Doric style. At Athens the Erechtheum was a masterpiece of Ionic architecture, but the Parthenon and the Propylaea (the entrance gate to the Acropolis) were Doric. In the fourth century Ionic in turn eclipsed Doric—the new temples of Artemis at Ephesus and of Apollo at Didyma, and the Mausoleum or tomb of King Mausolus at Halicarnassus, were in the Ionic style—and it remained prevalent in the Hellenistic age. But in the Roman period the Corinthian column obtained an ascendancy which it has resumed in the modern 'classical' style: though sometimes denounced as too ornate, it provides in effect the most satisfying join between the column-shaft and the architrave. The temple of Zeus Olympius at Athens, begun by Peisistratus in the Ionic style, was completed by the Emperor Hadrian with Corinthian columns.

The only type of Greek building that imposed by its size alone was the open-air theatre, with a seating capacity rising to 20,000 (as at Athens) and even 30,000 (at Ephesus). The stage was small and had a simple background; below it was the *orchestra*, or dancing place of the chorus, of circular shape, or approximately so, and round this the seats rose on three sides in long and continuous flights. The fourth-century theatre at Epidaurus exhibits the symmetry of a Greek auditorium at its best, and its acoustics are perfect.

3. ROMAN ARCHITECTURE

Architecture, like art, made a late entry into Rome. Until the days of the great conquests the Romans could not afford ambitious schemes of building. The last Roman king, it is true, erected a temple of Jupiter Capitolinus, whose still visible foundations prove it to have been of exceptional size; but all the other early temples of Rome were of modest dimensions. In style they conformed to the Italic and Etruscan rather than to the Greek plan. They had deeply recessed porticoes with front pillars, but no encircling colonnade; they stood on a high basement and had a comparatively steep pitch to their roofs. In general, they accentuated the vertical rather than the horizontal lines. This style of temple architecture persisted in Rome until the third century, as the remains of some recent discoveries of that date have shown.

After 200 B.C. wealth from the foreign wars began to accumulate in Rome, and much of this was applied to building. But in the first instance the Romans devoted their spare money to utilitarian enterprises like paving and draining. The chief architectural innovation of the second century was the construction of *basilicæ*, or covered halls for the use of officials or traders[1]—a type of building which reached Rome from the Hellenistic East or from Sicily.[2] Roman temple architecture now drew closer to the Greek type, with columns of the Doric or Ionic order.

From the time of Sulla (80 B.C.) a tradition of decorative architecture became firmly established among the Romans, and their activity in building reached its height between A.D. 50 and 150, when not only the capital city but many of the Italian and western municipalities freely devoted their funds to architectural purposes. After A.D. 200 the progressive impoverishment of the Roman world put a general stop to new construction, but some emperors still found means to embellish Rome and a few other towns that enjoyed their favour. Among the most notable remains of Roman architecture are the baths of Caracalla (A.D. 215) and Diocletian (A.D. 300) at Rome; the amphitheatre of Diocletian at Verona; the palaces of Diocletian at Spalatum and of Constantine at Trier.

The materials of the earliest Roman buildings were timber and mud-brick, which were sometimes revetted in Etruscan fashion with terra-cotta plaques. Under the republic stone came into extensive use; after 400 B.C. quarries were opened at some distance from Rome, and the crumbling and unsightly local tufa was replaced by hard-wearing freestone. In the second century B.C. the Romans acquired the art of mixing concrete, which henceforth became their ordinary material for the cores of buildings. Until the first century A.D. the concrete walls were usually lined with stone, and sometimes finished with plaster or stucco. But from the time of Nero baked bricks (of rather flat shape), laid in lime mortar, were brought into general use for the facing

---

[1] The basilica in due course served as a prototype for Christian churches. One feature of church architecture, the division of the roof into a central higher section and two lower wings, with 'clerestory' windows in the walls supporting the higher roof, was a very ancient Egyptian device. It was occasionally copied by the Greeks (e.g. at Delos in the third century), and passed from Greece to Rome.

[2] The influence of the Sicilian Greeks upon early Roman architecture is visible in the new ring-wall which was built round the city about 380 B.C. It has recently been shown that masons from Syracuse worked on this wall.

of walls. The Romans also took early advantage of the invention of a cheap glass-blowing process (p. 116) for the making of window-panes (which went out of use again in the early Middle Ages, except for churches).

In the assemblage of their materials the Romans were the first to exploit to the full the possibilities of arch-construction, which the Orientals, the Greeks, and the Etruscans had used only for substructures, or to span a narrow interval (e.g. in a city gate). In 179 B.C. they supplemented the old trestle bridge across the Tiber with the first of many structures resting on stone arches. In 78 B.C. they flanked the new Record Office on the Capitol with a continuous arcade. From arches they went on to vaults and domes, which were not unknown in Eastern architecture, but only of small dimensions. The advantages of vaulting on a larger scale were probably realized at first in the building of theatres and amphitheatres (which the Romans as a rule did not excavate out of hill-sides, but built up from a level piece of ground). The substructures of the Colosseum show that by A.D. 70–80 the Romans had learnt to bind intersecting barrel vaults with stone or concrete groins—a device which later became an essential feature of Romanesque and Gothic architecture. Lastly, Roman architects mastered the art of spanning roof-spaces of 100 feet and over with vaults or domes. The vaults of some of the imperial palaces and public baths, and of the Basilica of Maxentius and Constantine in the Forum, have spans far wider than those of St. Peter's; and the concrete dome of the Pantheon (which in its present form belongs to the reign of Hadrian) remains unsurpassed in boldness of construction.

In the development of building technique at Rome the most creative periods were the late republic and the century from A.D. 50 to 150. The Augustan age was more conservative and devoted itself rather to perfection of detail, after the manner of the Greeks.

Roman methods of construction facilitated the erection of buildings of imposing size; and the need of such buildings arose when Rome became a monster city, requiring tall dwelling-houses, large public halls, theatres and baths for the general population, and roomy palaces for the emperors. But even where gigantic edifices were not strictly requisite, the Roman architects strove for large effects. In the Forum of Trajan they almost wasted space in order to provide long vistas, and in moderate-sized towns of North Africa they reared up theatres and amphitheatres on a monumental scale. Similarly they abandoned the simplicity of plan which characterized Greek architecture. The palaces and baths at Rome, and the country villas of the plutocracy, were laid out elaborately with long suites of apartments; but in these a straggling effect was avoided by the symmetrical disposition of the various pieces.

The Romans also showed greater boldness than the Greeks in the matter of decoration. From the first century B.C. they made extensive use of coloured marble for columns and revetments; they replaced the Doric and Ionic by the more ornate Corinthian column; under the emperors they also employed columns and pilasters in order to break up blank spaces rather than to sustain weights.

The larger scale and more profuse ornamentation of Roman buildings may suggest that Roman architects worked in a spirit of vulgar ostentation, and that at best they achieved something like the baroque style of the seventeenth century. It is true that their surviving early temples were ill-proportioned, and that some of their later giant edifices look gaunt and clumsy in their present ruinous state. Yet if Roman constructions did not attain Greek perfection of detail, they did not lack harmony, and their decoration showed up rather than obscured their outlines. Whether we consider the little Augustan temple at Nîmes (the 'Maison Carrée'), or the Colosseum, we find in Roman architecture the Greek combination of strength with grace; and in its larger works we observe a structural inventiveness and a grandeur of appearance that is specifically Roman. The influence of Greek architecture upon that of modern times has been great; but Roman architecture has exerted a continuous effect upon the builders of Europe, and has been their principal storehouse of models.

4. GREEK SCULPTURE

In the history of Greek sculpture the following periods may be distinguished:—

(1) *The Archaic Period* (600 B.C., or earlier, to 480 B.C.).

This was the period of apprenticeship, in which the Greek sculptors learnt the use of their tools. By the end of the sixth century they had become proficient in technique. They now produced figures that retained no more than a trace of archaic stiffness; they had begun to solve the difficulties of facial expression, and if their efforts to present a pleasing countenance sometimes resulted in a screwed-up face and a smirk, they eventually succeeded in producing a natural and thoughtful cast of features. Their output consisted mainly of single figures (deities or votive statues of youths and maidens); but they also tried their hand at group composition, whether in relief (on friezes) or in the round (on temple pediments). Certain surviving archaisms in the sixth-century statues, the patterning of the costume and the hair and the 'frontality' of the figure, which is intended to be viewed from one point only, should be regarded as conventions in deference to a passing fashion, rather than as signs of imperfect craftsmanship. The lack of individualism in the portrait-statues was certainly deliberate: indeed it long remained a tradition in Greek portraiture to idealize the subject slightly, so as to represent a type rather than a particular person.

(2) *The Fifth Century* (from 480 B.C.).

This age is characterized by a further mastery of technique, which shows up particularly in the increased proficiency of bronze-casting, and by a studied naturalism, in which the patterns and conventions of the previous century are discarded. Its austerity was no doubt a result of the grim struggle of the Persian Wars. An extreme instance of this severe style may be seen in the pediment sculptures (now at Munich) of a temple raised at Aegina soon after 480, showing a battle-scene. Here the figures are stripped and taut, without any superfluous detail or ornament. Another battle-scene is the theme of the gable-sculptures on the temple of Zeus at Olympia (*c.* 460 B.C.). Here the combatants seem made of flesh rather than wood, but the battle is stern and no mere stage-effect, and the whole composition is skilfully grouped round the majestic central figure of Apollo, the arbiter of the struggle. These sculptures are now generally regarded as the masterpieces of the 'hard' Greek style. Next to them ranks the 'Delphi Charioteer', a bronze statue commemorating a victory by a member of one of the Sicilian tyrant families—a triumphant erect figure, but with many subtle irregularities in the drapery and the details of the face which suggest 'the uneven tremor of life' and redeem the charioteer from stolidity.

As the memory of the Persian Wars faded, sculptors specialized more on athletic types. An Attic master named Myron (c. 460 B.C.), availing himself of the facilities which bronze-casting affords for the rendering of freely poised limbs, produced figures in vigorous but rhythmical motion, as in the 'Discus-thrower', whose balanced swing will be appreciated by any modern bat or racquet player. Myron's younger contemporary, the Argive artist, Polycleitus, a careful student of the proportions of the human body, showed his mastery in slow-motion figures such as the 'Spear-bearer', who strides along with perfect poise and combines the stability of manhood with youthful grace. The freedom of the Spear-bearer's legs, the weight resting on the right while the left takes off from the toes, should be compared with the uniform tenseness of the archaic male figures.

Fifth-century sculpture culminated in the work of Pheidias and his school (c. 440 B.C.). Though his greatest masterpieces, the gold-and-ivory statues of Zeus at Olympia and of Athena in the Parthenon, have perished, and are not well represented in copies, the art of this school may be studied in the 'Elgin Marbles' at the British Museum and the sculptures still in situ on the Parthenon. These faithfully reflect the spirit of the Periclean age, in which the strain of the Persian War period had made way for calm exultation in the past achievement of Athens, unclouded confidence in its future, and an urgent desire to glorify the patron goddess Athena.

> In an old land of heaven upholden,
> A proud land untrodden of war,
> They are hungered, and lo! their desire
> With wisdom is fed, as with meat.
> In their skies is a shining of fire,
> A joy in the fall of their feet.

One main *motif* of the Parthenon sculptures was the festival of the Panathenaea: the frieze represents the procession of the city's choicest delegates (maidens and old men, as well as smart cavalry troopers), and the eastern end displays the principal gods of the Greek pantheon assembled as guests of Athena. The mastery of technique in Pheidias' school is betrayed by many small touches, by the rich and flowing folds of the goddesses' drapery, by the quivering muzzles of the sun-god's steeds, by the figures of gods and men, which convey a glow of health but no longer suggest intense physical training.

(3) *The Fourth Century* (to 323 B.C.).

After 400 B.C. Greek sculptors maintained but did not materially improve existing standards of technique. In keeping with the tendency of the age, which suffered from political disillusionment and turned from the problems of society to those of the individual, they sought to express the personal features of their subjects rather than abstract types of beauty, and to emphasize more strongly the play of emotion in the features; and they regained an interest in feminine figures which had not been alien to the early sculptors but had waned in the strenuous fifth century. Of the three great masters of this period, Scopas of Paros is the most difficult to assess, because we possess no undisputed specimens of his work; but the subjects of his compositions, Love, Yearning, Desire, the Raging Maenad, are significant. The Athenian Praxiteles may be studied in copies of his 'Aphrodite' and in his 'Hermes', the original of which probably survives at Olympia. These reveal sinuous forms with soft flesh and glossy skins (in the rendering of these two features the 'Hermes' is unsurpassed), and a pensive expression. In his 'Demeter' a follower of Praxiteles created a Sorrowing Mother, with features ennobled by grief. The third master, a North Peloponnesian named Lysippus, remained true to the athletic tradition; his 'Apoxyomenus' (a figure of a youth scraping off the lubricant oil after exercise—is as perfect as the work of Polycleitus and Myron—it looks well from whatever angle it is viewed—but it shows a lighter and more 'springy' physique than the fifth-century stalwarts. Moreover, by his own confession

Lysippus strove to express 'men as they appeared to the eye', not general types. Herein no doubt lay an element of danger. The sculptor who reproduces natural details without selecting what suits his design may end by becoming a waxwork artist. But the fourth-century masters at any rate contrived to combine realism with beauty, and often with fine feeling.

(4) *The Hellenistic Age* (323–*c*. 100 B.C.).

In this period Greek art remained truer to itself than the closer contact between Greeks and Orientals might have led us to expect. The main tendency was to emphasize still more the characteristics of the fourth century. The portrayal of passion was carried a degree further in the sculptures of the Great Altar at Pergamum (commemorating a victory of King Attalus I over the Galatians), where the old theme of a battle between gods and giants was reproduced with a riot of vigour recalling Hindu sculpture, and in the Laocoon group, in which the main figure is almost distorted with anguish. The tenderness of the Praxitelean school became more pronounced, as in the swan-like neck of the 'Aphrodite of Melos', and the rather flabby 'Apollo Belvedere'. The interest of this school now extended to children, who had hitherto been rendered somewhat perfunctorily as undersized adults, but were now portrayed with loving accuracy of detail. Realism found scope in worthy themes like that of the 'Dying Gladiator', really a Galatian chieftain, whose Celtic physique has been reproduced by a Pergamene sculptor with observant and sympathetic precision, in trivial scenes from daily life, or in positively repulsive subjects, such as battered pugilists and drunken old women. But the technique of Hellenistic sculptors remained as skilful and conscientious as ever. In one direction they broke new ground, in the suggestion of depth and space on work in relief. This development, suggested by pictorial art, eventually had a notable influence on Roman sculpture.

(5) *The Roman Period* (after *c*. 100 B.C.).

Greek sculpture did not die from internal decay, but from an external cause, the Roman conquest, which entailed in the first instance an impoverishment of the country and an extensive spoliation of its accumulated works of art. Roman connoisseurs, it is true, now gave scope to a new school of copyists who reproduced with varying skill the works of the 'Old Masters'. It is by such copies as these that many of the most famous Greek statues are known to us. In the later first century B.C. an ephemeral school of 'archaizing' sculptors endeavoured to recapture the style of the sixth century. But this reactionary movement, like that of the Pre-Raphaelites in the nineteenth century (to say nothing of present-day 'neo-Gothic' and negroid art), did not last long. Greek sculpture had lost its inspiration beyond recovery. Greece henceforth ceased to be a land of artists and became a land of antiquarians.

5. ROMAN SCULPTURE

In Italy one branch of plastic art was indigenous. The prehistoric Italic peoples carved rough portrait-heads on the lids of their terra-cotta burial urns, and death-masks of wax were in use among the Etruscans and in early Rome. Realistic portraiture, which outlasted all other forms of sculpture in Rome, was also the earliest Italian art.

The first Italian people to acquire from the Greeks the technique of chiselling stone and casting bronze were the Etruscans, who also developed a technique of their own in making entire statues of terra-cotta. Two outstanding examples of this style are the 'Apollo of Veii', who has the pose of an archaic Greek statue, but instead of the archaic Greek smile wears an uncanny and almost forbidding look; and the representation of an old man and his wife on a cinerary chest at Volaterrae. 'The man's wrinkles and rugged face, his stupefied look and tired sunken body contrast with the alert expression of his shrewish wife. . . . This head scarcely has its match among the many Roman portraits of ageing female autocrats' (Eugeni Strong).

In the fifth and fourth centuries the political eclipse of Etruria carried with it the gradual extinction of a specific Etruscan civilization and art. In the meantime some of the peoples of South Italy were learning to apply Greek technique to their native art of portraiture: one of the finest pre-Roman heads in bronze (characteristically Italian in its live realism) comes from Bovianum Vetus, an out-of-the-way town in Samnium. But it was the Romans who at a later date filled the gap left by the Etruscans.

The Romans naturally obtained their first pieces of sculpture from Etruria. But the Elder Pliny preserves a tradition that two Greek artists were employed to decorate a Roman temple in the early fifth century; and we may probably assign to a Greek rather than to an Etruscan artist a masterly bronze statue of a she-wolf (the legendary foster-mother of Romulus), which was set up on the Capitol *c.* 500 B.C. In the age of the great conquests many choice specimens of Greek statuary were brought to Rome by victorious generals, the largest hauls being made at Syracuse and Tarentum in the Second Punic War, and at Corinth in 146 B.C. But the immediate influence of this treasure-trove on the development of Roman art was small. Down to the time of Sulla the Roman contribution to sculpture consisted of little more than grave-stone heads (mostly of old men, and still somewhat archaic in technique).

After 80 B.C. the future promise of Roman sculpture was revealed in two surviving heads of Pompey[1] (at Copenhagen) and of Cicero (at Apsley House). The native tradition of realism is manifest in these works: the portraitist of Cicero, naturally enough, reproduced, line for line, the mobile and intensely intellectual features of the orator; but the Copenhagen artist did not spare Pompey's undistinguished and rather yokelish lineaments—his snub nose, pig-eyes and tumbled hair are all there, like the wart on a famous portrait of Cromwell. At the same time these two heads reveal a technique comparable to that of Greek work of the fifth century. But the Roman sculptors did not 'find themselves' till the days of Augustus. Now at last they had acquired high technical proficiency, and had made a definite choice of the native and the Greek elements which were to go into Roman art. They made no attempt to follow the Greeks

[1] Some long-accepted indentifications of Roman portrait-heads with personages of the late Republic have now been discredited. The head of Julius Caesar, which used to stand in the Roman gallery at the British Museum (but has now been discreetly removed), has been proved a modern work.

into all the fields which these had entered, but confined themselves to two special genres, portraiture and historical reliefs.

Of the large number of portrait-statues and heads that survive from the time of Augustus and onward, those of the emperors themselves would fill a long gallery. First and foremost is the Vatican statue of Augustus. Though lacking in the easy poise of Greek figures, it shows Greek influence in the delicate workmanship of the head and the somewhat idealized features, which are of almost divine serenity; yet this serenity expressed a real and outstanding trait in Augustus' character. The portraits of Augustus' successors are rendered with an almost uniformly high standard of technique down to Gallienus (A.D. 260), but they break away from Greek idealism and render the imperial likenesses with unflattering fidelity: the flabby cheeks and myopic frown of Nero, the hard eyes and tight lips of Domitian, the weak chin of Marcus Aurelius, the vicious scowl of Caracalla, none of these are glozed over. The same individualism reappears in the numerous portraits of other personages, ranging from the *grandes dames* with haughty mien of the imperial court to the coarse-featured Pompeian banker Caecilius Iucundus, whose beady eyes and jug-handle ears betray and almost advertise the upstart bourgeois. This pervasive realism should not be explained away as mere philistinism, which requires works of art to be facsimiles; it was rather an expression of that Italian frankness and downrightness which was also the making of Roman satire. But behind all the individual differences of Roman portrait-sculpture we may detect a common feature, the national Roman (rather than Italian) *gravitas*: the countenances are composed, the mouths firmly set, the ladies never seem to forget that they are the mistresses of their household.

Relief sculptures recording historical scenes (usually of battles and campaign incidents) were a characteristic form of Assyrian art. In Greece they were replaced by renderings of combats between gods and giants, Lapiths and Centaurs, and the like, which served to symbolize rather than to reproduce the actual events. In the days of Augustus the historical relief again became the principal type of group sculpture. Its first notable specimen was a composition which showed a thanksgiving procession on the occasion of Augustus' return from a long journey through the empire and the dedication of the Altar of Peace (13 B.C.). The figures on this relief are uncomfortably crowded, and the procession in consequence seems to be standing rather than progressing. These faults of technique have been overcome in the reliefs on the Arch of Titus, commemorating his triumph over the Jews in A.D. 71: here there is freedom of movement, and even stir and bustle, as befits a holiday scene. On these panels the sculptor made an experiment in perspective, after the manner of Hellenistic reliefs, and succeeded in giving an impression of depth and distance. The largest of ancient historical reliefs was the spiral band that ran from base to top of Trajan's Column in the Forum Traiani, and chronicled the entire series of this emperor's campaigns against the Dacians. This monster composition, containing some 2500 figures, was naturally lacking in high finish. But the technique, if rough-and-ready, was well adapted to the special conditions of visibility of the column, and the variety and arrangement of the scenes effectively mitigate the monotony of their mere number.

For all their diversity of detail, the sculptures on Trajan's Column insist to the point of wearisomeness on the emperor's prowess in arms. Such self-congratulation was perhaps inevitable in a people with a military record like that of the Romans. But a more pleasing and also a more fundamental trait in the Roman character was expressed in the Ara Pacis sculptures. The most beautiful panel in this composition shows Terra Mater holding two children, with farm animals at her feet, and surrounded by the fruits of the earth. Closeness to the earth and exultation in its riches were typically Italian: their literary counterpart is seen in Vergil's *Georgics*. In Greece, where Nature is niggard, men gave little thought to her; in Italy, where she is more bountiful, they gladly acknowledged her gifts; and the difference is reflected in the art of the two peoples.

6. PAINTING AND MINOR ARTS

(a) *Painting*.—Remains of this branch of ancient art are naturally scanty. Minoan frescoes, showing a fine sense of colour, have been found at Cnossus and other prehistoric sites; but our knowledge of Greek painting is mostly derived from literary descriptions, or from a comparison with contemporary survivals in Italy.

Compared with sculpture, Greek painting made a late start. Its first notable master, Polygnotus, lived about 460 B.C. Like most of the great Greek painters, Polygnotus chiefly worked in fresco on wet stuccoed walls; but he also painted on wooden panels by the 'encaustic' method, which involved the use of melted wax (in a process not clearly understood nowadays), and probably approximated to our easel painting in oils. His pictures perhaps included a Battle of Marathon, but they were mostly mythological. He rid Greek painting of its archaic stiffness and contrived to make some play with facial expression; but his colouring was flat and uniform, and his perspective quite rudimentary.

Later in the fifth century Apollodorus introduced shading, and another great master, Zeuxis, worked with high lights, so as to produce a deceptive realism—it is said that the birds pecked at his grapes. The prince of Greek painters, however, was Apelles, best known by his 'Aphrodite rising out of the Sea' and by his portrait of Alexander the Great. Little is known of his style, but the 'charm' of his pictures suggests that he could produce subtle tones as well as pleasing outlines. Hellenistic painting, which had its centre at Pergamum, probably showed an advance in perspective, if we may judge by its imitators at Pompeii. It seems to have specialized in landscapes and still-lifes, rather than in the old heroic themes, but it is not known to have produced any outstanding master. Greek portrait-paintings of Roman date have been recovered in Egypt, but these make no pretension to high artistic merit.

In Italy pictorial art found favour at an early date. In Rome temples and public buildings were decorated with frescoes (mainly historical scenes) from the early days of the republic. Considerable remains of frescoes, mostly of the fifth and fourth centuries, have been found in the rock tombs of Etruria. These represent scenes from Etruscan history and high life, and of the Etruscan hell. They were no doubt in imitation of contemporary

Greek work, but not being visible in a good light they were rough in execution. A few pictures, from the time of the late republic or early emperors, have been recovered from the house-walls of Rome, and a large gallery of similar works, ranging from c. 200 B.C. to A.D. 75, from those of Pompeii. The subjects of the Roman and Pompeian paintings included portraits, scenes from daily life, landscapes in considerable number, but especially episodes from Greek mythology. Some of them were copies of famous Greek pieces, and taken as a whole they illustrate Hellenistic as well as Italian art.

The earliest pictorial work at Pompeii was merely intended to pick out the architectural scheme of the walls by adding colour to the pilasters, plinths, and dados, or to divide the walls into separate panels. Towards the end of the second century B.C. some of the wall-panels began to be filled with object-pictures, and in some houses large surfaces were covered by them. Though naturally lacking in high finish, the Pompeian house-paintings reveal a remarkably good technique: the colours are bright but not garish, and are toned in various degrees of light and shade. Most striking is their boldness of perspective (especially in the later specimens), which succeeds well in conveying an illusion of a vista into distant space. But with the destruction of Pompeii in A.D. 79 the record of ancient painting is virtually closed for us.

(b) *Vase-decoration.*—The technique of pottery among the Greeks and Romans has already been described (pp. 115–16). It will here suffice to repeat that the finer grades of Greek and Italian ceramic ware had pleasing shapes and colours, and to add that their surfaces, whether glazed or merely burnished, were smooth enough to take on colouring.

The art of vase-painting, already carried to a high standard in prehistoric Crete, survived through the Dark Ages of early Greece, but its technique again became more primitive. In the 'geometric' pottery of the eighth and seventh centuries the field was mainly taken up with panellings and hatchings, more in the style of marqueterie than of clay-ware, and the figure-drawings were crude. After 700 B.C. Greek vase-decorators began to imitate the metal and tapestry ware of the Phoenicians, filling the space with figures of animals (real and imaginary) in superimposed bands. But by 600 B.C. the 'orientalizing' style had made way for a more typical Greek ornamentation, in which human figures prevailed, and the usual subjects were scenes from daily life and episodes from mythology. The new style was developed in different parts of Greece, but its principal centre was Corinth.[1] The figures on the Corinthian vases were drawn with a precision of outline which became the most characteristic feature of Greek vase-painting; but they often overcrowded the field, and their colouring did not stand out well against the matt buff fabric. During the sixth and fifth centuries, accordingly, Corinthian ware was almost driven out by Attic, which in its best products has never been surpassed.

In the sixth century the Attic potters applied their figures in a glossy black glaze on a warm red background, limiting severely the number of the figures, and making but sparing use of additional colours. About 525 B.C. they inverted their procedure, first outlining their figures on the fabric, then covering all the rest of the vase with black glaze, so that the figures showed in red silhouette against a dark frame, and finally picking out the figures with inner markings, which they drew in black paint with a very fine brush.[2] This Attic 'black-figure' and 'red-figure' ware, whose development can be closely studied with the help of the painters' signatures, had an immense vogue in the fifth century; but after 400 it succumbed to a turn of fashion, which brought plates and cups of metal ware (especially of silver) into general use among the well-to-do. In the fourth century Attic red-figure pottery was freely imitated at Tarentum and other towns of South Italy, but without the exquisite delicacy of outline that distinguished the Athenian products.

In the Hellenistic period painted pottery virtually disappeared from the Greek market and was replaced by vases with linear ornaments in relief, after the manner of embossed metal goods.

[1] The place of origin of some wares, such as the so-called 'Chalcidian', 'Milesian', and 'Naucratite', is under dispute. But it is now made out that 'proto-Corinthian' pottery, which used to be referred by some scholars to Argos or Sicyon, really came from Corinth.

[2] Attic pottery is well represented in the British Museum. One of its most noted specimens, the 'François Vase', an early but large and handsome mixing-bowl with numerous scenes from Greek mythology, is at Florence.

These vases were shaped in moulds, into which the patterns had been previously carved.

Apart from the 'red-figure' ware of the fourth century, painted pottery was scarcely produced in Italy. The Etruscans, who did not lack skill in the making of fine ceramic fabrics, satisfied their desire for painted ware by mass importations from Greece. The Romans never manufactured any but ordinary pottery, and imported but little Greek ware. About the time of Augustus an improved type of embossed pottery was produced at the Etruscan town of Arretium, in which the pattern-decoration was replaced by figures, after the manner of painted ware. The best Arretine vases were real works of art; but their fineness and consequent costliness handicapped them in competition with the factory-made *terra sigillata* from Gaul (p. 119), which soon drove the Italian ware out of the field. The Gallic ware was never more than competent craft-work, and it soon reverted to pattern ornamentation.

(c) *Metal-work.*—Our knowledge of Greek and Italian work in precious metals is derived from sporadic finds in graves which happened to escape the attentions of the professional tomb-rifler. Our main source of information for Greek work in this medium comes from the burial-mounds of the Scythian chieftains of South Russia, who commanded a supply of gold and silver (the former from the Urals or Siberia), and employed Greek craftsmen to make the gold into articles of personal adornment, and the silver into table-ware. These Russian finds, the finest of which date from the later fourth century, show that the Greek smiths were masters of many processes (engraving, embossing, beating, and filigree-work), and exhibited the same delicate sense of shape and design as the Greek potters and vase-painters. Of the Alexandrian silver ware, which commanded a large market in Hellenistic times, it is difficult to form an idea, except from some stray finds of Roman date. The most notable of these, from Boscoreale near Pompeii, is typically Roman in its choice of subjects—scenes from the life of the emperor Tiberius; but its technique of embossing in high relief, with delicately engraved inner markings, was probably of Greek origin.

The closest rivals of the Greeks were the Etruscan goldsmiths, who produced 'granulation-work'—the affixing of minute granular beads or plaques to thin strips of gold, by a process not yet recovered—of unsurpassed precision and fineness. Though the city of Rome had an entire 'jewellers' quarter' in the days of the emperors, and wealthy Romans paid fabulous prices for pieces of rare merit or reputation, the remains are insufficient to indicate the special features of Roman smith-craft.

One special branch of ancient metal-work, the striking of coins and medallions, is represented by countless surviving pieces. The early Greek coins had archaically stiff designs and were of very rough workmanship, and in the fifth century the technique of the coiner lagged behind that of other Greek artists. But in the fourth century the Greek die-cutters executed complicated naturalistic designs (e.g. teams of horses in full gallop, and raised in higher relief than on modern coins) with a clarity of outline comparable to that of the best vase-painters, and the Hellenistic coiners excelled in their portrait-heads. There is nothing to surpass the equestrian types of Syracuse and Tarentum, or the head of Alexander on some coins of King Lysimachus.

The coinage of the Roman Republic was carelessly executed, and the work of the imperial mints was merely that of good craftsmen. An obstacle to good design in the coins of the Roman emperors was that they overcrowded the field with lettering, in contrast with the Greeks, whose coin-legends were tantalizingly brief. But the big brass pieces from the senatorial mint included some real works of art. Among these were a few idealizing portraits in the Greek tradition (e.g. the effigy of Tiberius' mother Livia); but the finest specimens from the senatorial mint were ruthlessly Roman in their realism. With the coin-head of Galba in front of us, we can almost see the living emperor.

(d) *Work in precious stones.*—Seals were in common use in the ancient world, and jewellery for personal adornment was in great request, especially under the early Roman emperors, when the importation of costly stones from India into Rome assumed alarming proportions. The Emperor Elagabalus (*c.* A.D. 220) even bedizened his footgear with gems engraved by the foremost artists. Gem-cutting reached its climax in the fifth and fourth centuries among the Greeks who excelled as usual in the rendering of the human figure; in the Hellenistic period they carved the best portrait-heads. The art continued at a high level in Rome under the late republic and the early emperors. Under the emperors some fine cameo-work was also executed. The chief show-piece in this genre (now at Vienna) portrays Augustus and his family in a light-coloured stone against a luminous dark background.

Mosaics in the houses of the wealthier Greeks and Romans played a decorative part not unlike that of carpets and tapestry at the present day. They were mostly pattern-work, but naturalistic and even realistic designs were produced: a mosaic at Pompeii depicts an episode from one of Alexander's battles; and one or two Greek mosaic artists attained a reputation comparable to that of the great Greek painters. The use of costly and translucent stones in this type of art was Oriental and Byzantine rather than classical.

VIII

Greek and Roman Literature

I. GENERAL CONSIDERATIONS

OUR UNDERSTANDING of Greek and Roman literature is impeded by some of the obstacles which also hinder our appreciation of Greek and Roman art. The remains of that literature constitute but a small fraction of the total output of Greek and Roman men of letters. Not only are the works of particular authors missing —we have but 7 out of 90 plays by Aeschylus, 7 out of 123 by Sophocles, 18 out of 90 by Euripides, and other authors of repute survive in nothing but a few quotations and references—but entire periods, such as the Hellenistic age in Greek, and the Gracchan and Sullan era in Latin literature, are very poorly represented.

Other obstacles arise out of our modern habits and preconceptions. Greek and Roman literature from earliest days was wedded to sound. The earliest epic was chanted to the notes of a lyre, and lyric poetry of necessity implied a musical accompaniment. Where music did not give support to the words, as in the later epic, in drama, and in prose, the text was written not merely to be read but for recital. Herodotus composed his *History* not for book-readers, but for listeners at public recitals, and Cicero, following a general custom, kept a trained slave to read out to him the works which he was studying. In the fifth and fourth centuries the recitation of Greek literature became an object of exact study, and teachers of rhetoric set up meticulous standards of *prosodia*, i.e. reading with the right accent, quantity, and expression. Henceforward *prosodia* remained a cardinal point in education and always engaged the attention of writers. In a letter to Philip of Macedon Isocrates laments that Philip's secretary will read it unfeelingly and miss all the author's persuasiveness. But at the present day authors have mostly ceased to write for the ear. Consequently we have come to regard the classical texts as jigsaw-puzzles to be solved by the eye alone;

we fail to appreciate the sound of the ancient tongues (p. 187), and so remain obtuse to one of the essential beauties of Greek and Roman literature.

Our appreciation of classical authors is also apt to be blunted by the romantic and sometimes sensational writing of the present day. A general characteristic of classical literature was its economy of materials, its preference for simplicity and directness of expression. The Greek writers in particular resembled the Greek artists in their liking for clear, strong lines and firm rhythm, and expressed themselves in taut and balanced language. For this reason they may seem dry and bare, like the Greek landscape, to readers whose perceptive faculties have been trained in a less searching atmosphere.

Nevertheless classical literature commands the attention of the modern world. In mere quantity of output Greek and Latin literature hold a high place. The list of Greek writers extends in time from c. 850 B.C. (some three centuries after the Trojan War) to the end of the Roman Empire: indeed it might be prolonged to A.D. 1450, for the writers of the Byzantine Empire stood in the ancient classical tradition. Similarly Roman literature, which had its beginnings in the Punic Wars, outlived the Roman Empire and did not cease to grow until the seventeenth century A.D. In the variety of their production the classical authors have been equalled but scarcely surpassed in modern literature. Their works include epic, lyric, dramatic, and satiric poetry, history, oratory, and philosophy, the essay, the sermon, and a rudimentary form of novel. Moreover, the remains of Greek and Latin literature, though small in relation to its entire output, are fairly representative of the whole field and cover every one of the above branches. Greek or Latin authors have served as models for almost every class of modern literature, and their influence upon present-day thought and style is by no means exhausted.

2. GREEK LITERATURE TO 480 B.C.

A unique feature of our extant Greek literature is that it begins with two of the world's masterpieces, the *Iliad* and *Odyssey* of

Homer. These did not of course emerge ready-made, like Athena from the head of Zeus, but had a long ancestry. At the courts of the Achaean chieftains minstrels sang lays of the deeds of contemporary or recent heroes, and Achilles himself 'sang the famous deeds of men' in his hut before Troy. After the Dorian Invasion emigrants of Achaean and kindred stock who found new homes in Asia Minor preserved the best of these lays, and especially those relating to the Trojan War and its sequel. Regular schools of poets here worked over the old pieces in a bardic language, which, however, was not far removed from the speech of the people. About 850 B.C. a supreme genius, Homer, summed up their work in the *Iliad* and *Odyssey*. These two poems, therefore, in spite of their early date, were by no means primitive. They were composed in a poetic mixture of Aeolic and Ionic Greek, in a fairly elaborate metre (the hexameter), and contained many conventional phrases, and some apparent false joins in their story. These incongruities, and the great length of the two poems (the *Iliad* has about 15,000 verses and the *Odyssey* some 12,000), gave rise to the idea, which F. A. Wolf put forward in 1795, that they were a more or less mechanical assemblage of shorter lays, and the battle between 'Pluralists' and 'Unitarians' was thus set. In recent years the 'Unitarian' theory has come back into favour, and it is now generally agreed that the component parts of the *Iliad* and *Odyssey* were fused together in the brain of one master-poet.[1]

The mastery of Homer in Greece was promptly acknowledged and never challenged: his songs rose 'above the reach of envy'. At first they were diffused over the Greek world by *rhapsodoi*, or professional reciters.[2] From the time of Peisistratus they were read out in Athens at the public festival of the Panathenaea, and it was probably under his direction that the text received approximately fixed form. It was cast into final shape by learned editors and commentators at Alexandria. Literary

[1] W. J. Woodhouse, *The Composition of the Odyssey*. C. M. Bowra, *Tradition and Design in the Iliad*.

[2] The transmission of Homer by the rhapsodes was mainly oral, as is still the case with local epics. J. T. Bent found a poet-blacksmith on a Greek island whose business it was to preserve the island epics by oral tradition.

critics, such as Aristotle and Horace in ancient times, and Goethe and Arnold among moderns (to mention but two poets), have analysed the essence of the Homeric epic. They have found it in the dignity of the subject, the rapidity and unity of the action, and in the simplicity of speech and thought that carry the action along.

The sovereignty which Homer exercised over Greek epic poetry was almost tyrannical. All his successors imitated his language and metre and sought to reproduce his tricks of style. But epic inspiration almost died out with him. Of the considerable epic literature that was produced after Homer it will suffice to mention the 'Homeric Hymns', miniature epics which were recited at the festivals of Apollo, Hermes, and other gods since the seventh and sixth centuries, and retold their adventures with occasional real pathos or humour; and the works of Hesiod.

Under the name of Hesiod a poem known as the *Theogony* has come down to us, which is an attempt to systematize the principal myths of Greek religion. Though cast in epic form, it has but a glimmer of epic fire. The real Hesiod lives in another epic, the *Works and Days*. In contrast with Homer, who sang of lords and ladies, and for them, and introduced a common man like Thersites into his *Iliad* merely to show how such persons should be kept in their place, Hesiod was the Greek Langland, a yeoman farmer on the bleak and unfertile uplands of Boeotia in Central Greece, who had no love for the 'gift-devouring' lords. In his *Works and Days* he composed what was primarily a farmer's manual; but like his successor Vergil he illumined his technical dissertations with the flashes of a poet's fancy, for he had an intimate and loving knowledge of Nature, and could tell delightful stories, like those of Pandora and the Five Ages of Man. He was roughly a contemporary of Homer.

The main reason for the decay of epic poetry may be sought in the altered conditions of Greece after 800 B.C. The world of Homer was Greece in its Dark Age, when men's thoughts turned from a cheerless present to a glorious past. But in the eighth and following centuries the growth of the city-state and the colonial movement gave a new direction to Greek thought. The exciting and exacting world in which the Greeks now lived absorbed their attention, and in their literature they voiced the passions and the problems of their own day. After 700 B.C., therefore, the Greek epic was replaced by new genres, the elegiac, iambic, and lyric. These three branches of poetry had one feature in common, their brevity as compared with Homer. Life was now too full for epic breadth of treatment, and poets had to put under contribution the natural terseness of the Greek tongue. But each class of poem had its peculiar form and content.

Elegiac came nearest in outward form to epic, for it still employed the hexameter, in alternation with pentameters. But its language was nearer to that of daily life, and its stock of subjects was drawn from the actual present. Callinus and Tyrtaeus wrote war-songs; Solon expounded his political principles; Mimnermus expressed the sensations of the 'ordinary sensual man'; others discussed their experience in a pensive or mournful note. A sub-species of elegiac, the epigram or short dedicatory poem, acquired a special distinction through the epitaphs written by Simonides on the dead of the Persian Wars. Simonides' distich on the Spartans that fell at Thermopylae has been a challenge and a source of despair to countless translators.

Iambic poetry, which specialized in satire and invective, reflected the storm and stress of the age that produced it. It revealed some ugly sides of Greek life; but in Archilochus and Hipponax (who from his tomb warned passers-by to beware of his 'fiery words') it produced two virtuosos in the use of the tongue as a weapon; and it adapted to its use a tripping, pattering metre which subsequently gave force and tang to Greek drama.

Lyric poetry covered a similar field to that of elegy, but it reverted to the pre-Homeric usage of setting words to music. It developed a large variety of metres to suit the singing voice, and it struck a more highly emotional tone. Of the two greatest lyricists (both from the island of Lesbos), Alcaeus was a 'he-man' who played men's games—war, politics, high life—and sang of them, with equal zest. Sappho expressed a woman's most intimate passions with complete frankness—'Byzantium burnt her poems', says Gilbert Murray, 'as being too much for the shaky morals of the time'; but she ennobled them with superb imagery. The erotic songs of Anacreon gained fame, not so much by their thought, as by their melodiousness.

In the late seventh and sixth centuries the increasing prosperity of Greece was reflected in the growth of pageantry. In the leading Greek cities, and at religious centres like Delphi and Delos, an elaborate musical liturgy was now being introduced at the public festivals; youths and especially maidens were trained to sing choral odes, and a new branch of lyric poetry, choral lyric, sprang up. The earliest of the choric poets, Alcmaeon, or Alcman, was an Asiatic; but he composed his hymns at Sparta (which was as yet unmilitarized), and the Dorian dialect which he used for the Spartan festivals coloured the language of his successors. He lives on in the poem of Goethe, 'Über allen Gipfeln ist Ruh', which one of his odes inspired. We still possess complete choric odes by Bacchylides, a sixth-century writer, some of whose compositions were recovered on a papyrus in 1897, and by Pindar, the acknowledged master of this style. Himself a member of a noble Theban family, Pindar gave his services to the aristocrats of the Greek mainland, and especially to the tyrant families of Sicily and the kings of Cyrene, who had carried off prizes in the great athletic festivals and wished to commemorate the occasion with a special *epinikion* or song of triumph. The odes of Pindar were written in a complex metre; the rapidity of his thought and the 'eagle flight' of his imagery put a strain on his readers: indeed in translation, and divorced from their music, they may seem almost grotesque. But those who have patience to follow out the gorgeous and intricate device of his tapestry will have their reward. Pindar took strangely little notice of the Persian Wars, of which he was a contemporary; but he gave classic form to some of the old legends, notably to the tale of Jason and the Golden Fleece.

3. GREEK LITERATURE IN THE FIFTH AND FOURTH CENTURIES

Though choric lyrics continued to be produced after Pindar, they lost their place in the public regard to the drama. Rudimentary dramatic performances were produced in Greece, as part of a religious ritual, from early times; but the principal element out of which the Greek literary drama was evolved was probably a song and dance in honour of Dionysus, at which men are said to have dressed up as goats (*tragikos choros*; hence the name *tragoidia*, 'goat song', which later became the name of the fully developed drama).[1] The decisive step towards the creation of literary drama was taken at Athens. Here the tyrant Peisistratus instituted a contest between rival poets; and a poet named Thespis had the happy idea of supplementing the song with a spoken dialogue between the chorus-leader and a separate personage, the *hupokrites* or 'answerer', which was written in the iambic metre, as being the most suitable for a rapid interchange of speech. This dialogue developed in the next thirty years into a dramatic action, which was sustained by several *hypokritai* or actors, as they had now become. The subject of the action was disconnected from the legend-cycle of Dionysus, and the chorus, which had laid aside its animal trappings, was relegated to an accessory part. By 450 B.C. the programme of representations at Athens had been standardized. At the chief festival of Dionysus three poets competed with four plays apiece, of which three were 'tragedies' (dramas in the developed sense), and one a 'satyric drama' (which retained more of the original Dionysiac element). The performances lasted all day, and were presented to a crowd of some 20,000 spectators, who followed the plays with rapt but critical attention (p. 153).

Even in its developed form Greek tragedy retained some of its archaic simplicity. The number of actors (all of whom were men) did not usually exceed three, and though each actor might change his dress and mask and so take several parts, the total number of roles remained small. The plays were short, seldom exceeding 1500 lines, and the stage-property was scarcely more elaborate than that of Shakespeare's Globe. Yet with these limited means the Attic dramatists of the fifth century constructed plays which can hold even a blasé modern audience.

[1] Some say it was because a goat was originally given as a prize, or because a goat, the enemy of the vine, was sacrificed to Dionysus; or, more fantastically, because the drama was an initiation ceremony, and the young men had incipient goatees. The vase-paintings afford little evidence for the goat dress in early tragedy.

17

The subjects of the Attic tragedies were sometimes drawn from actual history, as when Aeschylus dramatized the battle of Salamis in his *Persae*, but were more usually derived from the Greek legends, especially from those which harboured a conflict of moral principles and so presented a problem. The plots were carefully constructed—in some, as in Sophocles' *Oedipus Tyrannus*, the train of events moves on with inexorable directness to the appointed end; their dialogue was brisk and pointed; their choral odes served to provide reflective interludes between the acts.

Each of the master-dramatists, Aeschylus, Sophocles, and Euripides, was truly representative of his generation. Aeschylus, who had fought at Marathon, saw life as a conflict, but not without a purpose: out of the mysterious ways of Providence good comes in the end, wickedness reaps its reward, wisdom comes to men through suffering. Sophocles, who lived in the spacious days of Pericles, a Victorian era of prosperity and bouyancy, in which all problems seemed solved in the general well-being, looked for no explanations. He was content to state the facts and to show that they are glorified by human heroism, by beauty, and devotion to truth: terror and misery there may be, but there is also splendour. Then came the Peloponnesian War, and the harmony of normal opinion at Athens was shattered. Euripides, a sensitive intellectual, could neither believe like Aeschylus, nor be content like Sophocles. He brooded over many of the problems that still agitate us: false patriotism, unjust suffering in war, the handicaps of womanhood, superstition and dogmatism in religion, the conflict between mysticism and reason. Yet in a dark and distracted world he saw one beacon, charity and helpfulness among mankind. His plays fell short of the Sophoclean standard of technique, but they gained in pathos; hence to Aristotle he was 'certainly the most tragic of the poets'.

In the fourth century the annual competition between tragedians went on, but the new plays hardly ever survived their first production. Interest in the great problems of life which the fifth-century tragedians had treated was by no means dead at Athens, but these problems had now been transferred to the field of philosophy.

Greek comedy also had its roots in various parts of the Greek world, but reached its full development at Athens. Here it originated out of the merry-makings at vintage-tide, when rustics mummed up and went in procession (*kōmoi*), singing odes to Dionysus (*kōmoidiai*), and exchanging ribaldries as they strolled along. By 450 this primitive 'comedy' had come to town and had been organized as part of the state worship of Dionysus. At one of these holidays, the Lenaea, three comic poets competed with one play each. Comedies sometimes took the form of burlesques on legendary themes; but at Athens they were drawn from actual life, and in the fifth century they turned mostly on the political events of the day—a sure index of the universal interest which politics evoked at Athens.

The plays of Aristophanes, which alone have survived from the older Attic comedy, are not easy to appreciate by a modern reader. They are full of topical allusions and parodies, the full meaning of which is lost to us, and they betray their rustic and Dionysiac origin in their frequent and seemingly gratuitous coarseness. Himself a political partisan (an enemy of the extreme and 'jingo' demagogues of the Peloponnesian War), Aristophanes hit out lustily at his victims, but always with saving good humour; and he carried off every situation with his inexhaustible play of fancy, which now broke into a riotously funny scene for his actors, now into an exquisitely beautiful ode for his chorus. His nearest modern parallel is Gilbert and Sullivan in their most abandoned mood. The disillusionment which came over Athens after the Peloponnesian War was fatal to the older comedy. It was replaced by a 'comedy of manners', of which hardly anything survives: certainly it was less hard-hitting and altogether tamer.

In the fifth century prose established itself alongside of poetry, and in another hundred years became the leading branch of Greek literature. Before 500 B.C. reading and writing was not yet common enough, and writing material was still too dear, to give rise to book-production on any large scale. Knowledge was therefore preserved by oral tradition, or by literature in poetic form (in which metre or music would assist the memory). But by the end of the sixth century authors could reach their public by means of books, and prose literature came into being. Men of science, from Hecataeus onwards, wrote in the new medium; but the prose of the fifth century may now be best judged by its survivals in the field of history.

The birth of Greek historiography, took place significantly enough, in the age of the Persian Wars. This conflict provided an absorbingly interesting topic, and also furnished a central theme round which the scattered histories of the Greek cities could be grouped. The 'Father of History' was an Asiatic Greek named Herodotus (c. 484–424 B.C.) who travelled widely in the mid-fifth century and so came to realize the importance of the Persian Wars as a clash, not only of armed forces, but of civilizations. As a pioneer of historiography, Herodotus was naturally imperfect in his technique. He was casual in the collection and the sifting of his information, and his attitude to his subject was rather one of epic admiration than of scientific detachment. Moreover the studiously discursive character of his narrative (which was written in Ionic Greek), though entirely suitable to an audience at a recital, is at times disconcerting to a reader. But he is a perfect mine of knowledge about the fifth-century world—his excursuses on the 'barbarian' neighbours of Greece, whether civilized, like the Persians and Egyptians, or truly barbarous, like the Scythians, are of fundamental importance for the study of those peoples; his information has again and again been proved correct by modern research; and the broad-minded appreciation which he expressed for the gallant deeds of the Persians showed up the Greek achievement in its full value.

Compared with the Persian Wars, the Peloponnesian War was a dismal theme for a historian, yet it produced the greatest of ancient historical writers, Thucydides (c. 454–400 B.C.). Though Thucydides, as an Athenian, stood on the losing side, and suffered personal ruin through the war, he wrote of it in the dispassionate tone of a man of science. He had worked out for himself the principal rules of historical technique and applied them resolutely to his own work. He rigorously sifted his materials (which included archæological as well as oral and literary information), discarding false or doubtful facts, though they might amuse his readers or flatter their prejudices; and he arranged them tidily in an austere but lucid narrative, in which the sequence of events was measured by a precise chronology, while the play of cause and effect was brought out clearly, and the motives of his personages were mercilessly probed. In the strict sense of the word *historia* (sure knowledge, based on methodical inquiry), Thucydides was the first master of this science.

The standards of Thucydides proved too exacting for most ancient historians—his chief pupils have been the pioneers of scientific historiography in the nineteenth century. Of the fourth-century historians, Xenophon was little more than an agreeable memoirist, writing in a placid and disarming Attic Greek. He was at his best in his *Anabasis of Cyrus*, the record of a military foray in the heart of the Persian Empire, in which he had taken a leading part (*c.* 400 B.C.). The chief historian of fourth-century date, Ephorus, wrote the first universal history of Greece, which appears to have been wholly lacking in Thucydides' insight into fundamental factors and underlying causes. Theopompus, who composed a history of the times of Philip of Macedon, has been called the 'Greek Macaulay' on account of his vigour and descriptive power; but he seems to have let his prejudices run away with him.

The art of public speaking was practised in Greece from early days: in Homer the Achaean warriors are equally ready with their weapons and with their tongues. With the advent of democracy it became a mainspring of power in politics, and recognition of this fact in the later fifth century led to the formal study of rhetoric in all its refinements. The influence of this study first appears in Thucydides, who recast into his own words the speeches actually delivered by his personages, in conformity with the rules set up by the rhetorical schools. In the fourth century it showed through in the law-courts and popular assemblies of the Greek cities, and especially at Athens, where Lysias (*c.* 445–365) and Demosthenes (384–323) achieved the highest excellence in practical oratory. Lysias wrote speeches for pleaders in the dicasteries which are models of clear and straightforward statement. Demosthenes commanded a variety of styles to suit the changing moods of his audience, but he was at his best in making an appeal on some great issue to the elemental passions of his hearers, and especially in playing upon their honest if somewhat narrow city-patriotism.

For sheer technical ability in the selection and arrangement of words another Athenian, Isocrates, held the first place. His 'speeches', not being intended for delivery, were rather in the nature of pamphlets. As a publicist Isocrates was an enlightened thinker who deplored inter-city animosities and called upon Philip of Macedon to save Greece in spite of itself. The extent of his practical influence is debatable, but his effect upon Greek prose admits of no doubt. In particular, Isocrates fixed the rules of prose rhythm which, in contrast with verse, demanded avoidance of hiatus and of any regular metrical progression.

The writings of Plato have already been discussed from the standpoint of their philosophic content (p. 201 ff.). As a master of style, Plato was also outstanding: he was essentially a poet, though he wrote little verse. His treatises were usually cast in the form of dialogue, which he, as a disciple of Socrates, regarded as the best means of eliciting truth, and also valued for its dramatic tension. His prose moved with an easy rhythm, and was lighted up with a poetic imagery which gave distinction even to his more abstract reasonings. Plato has influenced prose style more than any other Greek writer.

Aristotle's works in their present form are devoid of style, yet he was an acute literary critic (p. 206). His pupil Theophrastus also exerted some effect on later literature (e.g. on the French essayist La Bruyère) through one of his minor writings, the *Characters*, in which he threw out rapid but shrewd sketches of various human types (e.g. the Vain Man, the Country Cousin).

4. GREEK LITERATURE IN HELLENISTIC AND ROMAN TIMES

In the Hellenistic age men of letters enjoyed abundant patronage at the royal courts (especially at Alexandria and Pergamum); they possessed in the *koine*, or standard Greek, an instrument by which they could make themselves easily understood to the entire Greek world; and they had a better educated public. In sheer bulk of output they far surpassed their predecessors, but in quality they fell notably short. The Hellenistic poets wrote in almost every genre from the epic to the epigram; in craftsmanship they were conscientious to the point of meticulousness; but they could not recapture the emotional tension or the play of imagination of earlier Greek writers. The huge zest for life and sense of adventure which had carried Alexander from conquest to conquest did not communicate itself to the Hellenistic world of literature. A partial explanation of the tameness of Hellenistic poetry may be found in the excessive seclusion in which men of letters lived at the royal courts.

The two outstanding figures in Hellenistic poetry were Theocritus and Menander. Theocritus, a protégé of Ptolemy II and of Hiero of Syracuse, wrote pastoral idylls in epic metre, in which real goatherds and dairymaids bantered and made love in the glowing Mediterranean summer. The animation and naturalness of Theocritus have captivated his readers in ancient and modern times, and the list of his imitators, direct and indirect, is endless: it includes Vergil; Milton, Pope, Sidney, Spenser, Shelley, Tennyson, Matthew Arnold in England; Hooft, Huygens, Cats, Vondel (to mention only a few of the 'herderdichters') in Holland, and many other modern poets. Menander was an Athenian who carried on an established tradition by writing comedies of manners (c. 300 B.C.). His plays usually turned on conventional subjects such as the long-lost heiress, but by skilful plot-construction and delineation of character they gave a constant illusion of freshness; they lacked the uproarious vivacity of Aristophanes, but they were better suited to a cosmopolitan public and therefore found more imitators. Menander served as a model to Plautus and Terence, and through them to Molière, Congreve, and Sheridan.

Other poets who influenced Roman literature were Apollonius Rhodius, whose epic on the Argonauts was utilized by Vergil; and Aratus, the author of an astronomical epic, the *Phaenomena*, whose practical usefulness seems to have been the reason of its strange popularity among the Romans—it was imitated by Vergil (in the *Georgics*), and was several times translated into Latin. On the other hand an Alexandrian named Callimachus (c. 250), who was the most versatile and finished poet of his age, had a strangely limited influence.

Of the innumerable Hellenistic works in prose, those on science and philosophy made no pretence to literary style. With the decline of the city-state oratory lost its practical importance and evaporated into mere style without substance. Historical studies, on the other hand, received a new impetus from the stirring events of Alexander's day, and brought forth a literature that ranged from local histories and biographies resting on documentary research, to ambitious and imaginative works like that of Cleitarchus (*c.* 300 B.C.) on Alexander, which nowadays would perhaps be discribed as historical novels. Almost the only survival out of this extensive literature, which suffered in the estimation of later scholars because it was written in the *Koine* tongue (p. 182), was a large and authoritative work by an Arcadian Greek named Polybius, who was deported to Rome in 167 B.C., but there won the friendship of Scipio Aemilianus and obtained through him a wide insight into Roman institutions. The knowledge thus acquired by Polybius was put to good use by him in a general history of the Mediterranean world from 264 to 146 B.C., the central part of which was occupied by Rome's conquests at the expense of Carthage and the Greek Powers. In accuracy of technique Polybius fell but little below Thucydides; in his grasp of the fundamental causes and the lasting significance of the Roman conquests he displayed an acumen which not even Thucydides surpassed.

A by-product of Alexander's conquests was the tale of fictitious adventures, cast in historical form and held together by a plot. Herein we may find the prototype of the modern novel.

After 150 B.C., under the Roman conquest, the Greek became less productive in literature, as in art and science. Significantly enough, their chief activity in the last century B.C. was to continue the work of Polybius in co-ordinating Greek with Roman history. One result of this effort was an attempt at a universal history in the full sense, by a Sicilian named Diodorus (*c.* 50 B.C.). But this work, which has had the undeserved fortune to survive in large part, was a wholly uncritical compilation. In the age of Augustus the history of early Rome (to 264 B.C.) was presented to the Greeks by Dionysius of Halicarnassus, but without Polybius' understanding of the distinctive features in Roman civilization.

Dionysius achieved greater success in a literary study of the Greek prose classics; but in this field he was surpassed by an unknown author (conveniently misnamed 'Longinus'), who wrote discerningly 'On the Sublime' (i.e. elevation in style), and quoted among other examples of fine writing the beginning of Genesis (from the Septuagint version). The most notable Greek work of the Augustan age, however, was a geographical description of the whole Roman Empire by Strabo, a scholar from the east end of Asia Minor. Though mostly based on second-hand information, this was a highly competent treatise, giving a panoramic view of the Roman Empire as it was settling down under the Pax Augusta, and it is our main source of knowledge about ancient geography.

After a pause of some hundred years Greece again produced a writer of enduring importance in Plutarch (c. A.D. 45–125). Unlike most of the later Greek authors, Plutarch was not a professional scholar, but a country gentleman from a quiet corner of Boeotia,[1] who lived the great days of Greece over again in his fancy, but also had a high regard for the achievement of Rome. His *Moralia* (better, Miscellaneous Essays) were a curious medley of serious research and impromptus on trivial subjects, e.g. 'Why do women kiss their kinsmen on the mouth?' His fame rests on the *Parallel Lives* of Greek and Roman worthies, written in an engagingly artless style and without any sustained erudition, but with a fine eye for the high light and shade in his personages. His appeal in modern Europe has been especially to his own counterpart, the cultured amateur of the classics.

In the second century A.D. the return of material prosperity to the eastern Mediterranean, and the favour which Hadrian (nick-named 'Graeculus') bestowed upon Greek intellectuals, gave a fresh impetus to Greek literature. Renewed interest in the niceties of Greek style was revealed in the vogue of the 'Later Sophists', who revived the rhetorical exercises of the Hellenistic

[1] Rather like some cultured parson living with his library in the depths of the country.

age and declaimed in correct Attic, but entirely without conviction, on a wide range of topics. By the delicate application of all the complex rules of their craft in regard to words as well as voice and gesture, to which their audiences were peculiarly sensitive, they achieved an astonishing and enduring success. A certain Polemon charged £2400 for a private lesson, and when Herodes Atticus, the Andrew Carnegie of his day, sent him £6000 for attending one of his lectures, he sent it back, but agreed to accept £10,000! A more sincere note was struck by a rhetorician named Aelius Aristeides, who spoke with genuine appreciation of the Roman Peace: 'The cities have abandoned their old quarrels and are occupied with a single rivalry, each ambitious to be most pleasant and beautiful. . . . To-day Greek or foreigner may travel freely where he will . . ., as though he was passing from homeland to homeland.' The New Sophistic had a long lease of life. In the fourth century it produced a considerable crop of rhetoricians (Libanius, Themistius, and others), who at least had the merit of maintaining the traditions of fine style in an age of growing barbarism.

A partial antidote to the New Sophistic was a Syrian Greek named Lucian (c. A.D. 150), who made a stand for the old Attic sobriety and applied the weapons of irony and parody against the fashionable superstitions of his day. His pretty wit and alluringly simple style won him many readers in the modern Age of Illumination, and his *Vera Historia*, a skit on Herodotus' tall tales of travel, has had a copious progeny, including *Gulliver's Travels*. The most serious but also the most humane Greek work of the second century was the *Meditations* of Marcus Aurelius. The fact that a Roman emperor should have used Greek as a vehicle for his inmost thoughts shows that educated Romans were now completely bilingual, and that Roman literature had acquired familiar ease in two media of expression.

Plutarch's efforts to recall the glories of earlier Greece were continued by Arrian (c. A.D. 140) and Pausanias (A.D. 175). Pausanias, the 'Baedeker' of ancient Greece, wrote a comprehensive if matter-of-fact account of the antiquities and works of art which the Greek homeland still harboured in his day, thus putting modern students of Greek art, and also of Greek religion, under obligation to him. Arrian was a Bithynian Greek who combined the active life of a high official in the Roman imperial service with varied literary activities. His *Anabasis of Alexander*, a plain unvarnished record of Alexander's military exploits, is the best surviving account of the Macedonian world-conquest. A century after Arrian another Bithynian Greek, who had held the highest posts under the Emperor Alexander Severus, Dio Cassius, sought to satisfy the growing Greek interest in Roman affairs by composing a general history of Rome on a scale only inferior to that of Livy. Though Dio lacked the sure touch of Polybius, he made some attempt to explain as well as to chronicle the course of events, and he remains one of our chief sources of knowledge of the Roman emperors.

In one branch of prose, the novel, the Greek writers of the third century A.D. made a new departure. It was through them that the erotic motive of two lovers finding one another after sundry trials and adventures became the main theme in this class of literature.

The intellectual revival of the Greek world under the Roman emperors may also be seen in the great scientific encyclopædias of Galen and Ptolemy (pp. 214–15), and, lastly, in the 'neo-Platonic' after-bloom of philosophy (p. 215).

In the Hellenistic age Greek had become an international language which every person in the Near East who desired an official position or high social standing was bound to acquire. Its use became widespread among the Jews of the Dispersion: the large Jewish colony at Alexandria spoke nothing but Greek, and used a Greek version of the Old Testament, the 'Septuagint'. Eventually Jewish writers entered the field of Greek literature. About A.D. 70 a Palestinian Jew named Josephus, who had joined the rebellion against the Emperors Nero and Vespasian, but soon came to terms with the Romans, composed for the benefit of Gentile readers a general history of the Jews (the earlier part of which was an excerpt from the Old Testament), and a special treatise on the recent rebellion, which was first written in Aramaic and then in Greek.

But the chief of the hellenizing Jews was the missionary Paul, who carried the Christian message to the Greek or

Greek-speaking peoples, and to this end not only spoke Greek but studied the Greek philosophers. Thanks to the lead which he thus gave, Greek became the language of the Church throughout the Near East, and a reconciliation between the Christian religion and Greek culture was effected. About A.D. 70 the Gospel of St. Mark was written in Greek, and by 200 the entire New Testament had been completed in the same tongue. Between 175 and 225 the Alexandrian Church Fathers Clement and Origen incorporated part of the Platonic and Stoic philosophies into Christian theology. Early in the fourth century a Palestinian bishop, Eusebius, wrote in Greek a standard history of the Church, and composed a comprehensive set of chronological tables, by which Jewish and Christian dates were securely keyed into the general chronology of the ancient civilized peoples.

5. EARLY ROMAN LITERATURE. THE MEETING OF ROMAN AND GREEK TRADITION

The rudiments of Latin literature may be sought in the ceremonial incantations (*carmina*) of the Roman state religion, in the Laws of the Twelve Tables, and in the ballads that were sung at early Roman banquets. The *carmina* and the Twelve Tables gave the Romans their earliest training in terse and accurate diction, and their national pride of achievement first found expression in the ballads. But it was not until the time of the Punic Wars that the Romans became fully articulate.

Their almost unbroken run of military conquests between 250 and 150 B.C. increased their national consciousness and self-confidence, and brought them into closer contact with the world of Greece; in particular, educated Greek slaves who found their way into the wealthier Roman households in the third and second centuries contributed in large measure to the training of their masters. The essential story of Roman literature is its gradual accommodation to the Greek tradition.

The peaceful Greek invasion of this period, it is true, did not pass without protest, and occasional Roman authors from the time of Naevius and Cato to that of Juvenal attempted a reaction against it. Nay more, in literature no less than in art, the

Romans maintained their independence, and adapted their models rather than copied them mechanically. They asserted their individuality, not only in the matter of their writing but in its form. They gave additional stability to the hexameter by introducing more spondees into it (especially in the fourth foot): and in the lyric metres they set up more stringent rules: as Martial said, *musas qui colimus severiores*, 'we Romans, who cultivate a stricter Muse'. But Roman capacity to learn from other peoples is nowhere better exemplified than in the realm of literature. From the time of the Punic Wars to that of Augustus, when their mastery in most forms of literature was well established, Roman men of letters were diligent in the study of their Greek exemplars, and it was by dint of striving to emulate the expressiveness and melodiousness of Greek that they raised their own language to the level of a classic.

Significantly enough, the earliest figure in Latin literature, an ex-slave from Tarentum named Livius Andronicus (fl. 240 B.C.), devoted himself to translating Greek tragedies and the Odyssey of Homer, which no doubt made a special appeal to the Romans after their naval ventures in the First Punic War. Andronicus, however, omitted some of Homer's nautical detail (which his Latin readers would hardly have understood), and he rendered Homer's galloping hexameters into the hobbling Saturnian verse of Italy.

Livius' younger contemporary, Naevius, first tried his hand at adapting Greek tragedies and comedies; but by way of asserting the independence of Latin literature he went on to compose plays on episodes of Roman history, and an epic on the First Punic War. To judge by the remaining fragments of the epic, Naevius went too far in his reaction from Greek influence: his narrative was as bald as a bulletin, and his Saturnian metre limped rather than marched along.

But in the early second century B.C. a poet from Apulia in the far south of Italy, Ennius, produced another epic which was an earnest of Rome's future achievement in literature. As a soldier of Rome and a client of the Scipios, Ennius shared the born Roman's pride in the city's achievement; but the Scipios were frank admirers of Greek culture, and Ennius became an enthusiastic phil-Hellene. Like his predecessor, he proceeded from translations and adaptations of Greek originals to an epic of Roman history, the *Annales*, in which he told the story of Rome from its beginnings; but in his work he always kept Homer in view, and he discarded Saturnian verse for the hexameter. Ennius himself declared that he had three hearts, Oscan, Greek, and Roman. Broadly we may say that the Italian element contributed liveliness and colour, the Greek element technique, and the Roman stateliness and dignity. But his most remarkable triumph was the adaptation of the hexameter to the Latin tongue. His verse was more massive than Homer's, yet it moved with a steady swing, and it revealed for the first time the sonority of the Latin tongue.

The most important of the early Roman poems, as was to be expected, was in the epic style. But the most prolific branch of early Latin literature was the drama. The rudiments of an Italian drama were to be found within the peninsula itself. In Etruria 'Fescennine verses' were bandied, as in the Greek *kōmos*, between the members of a holiday crowd, or between them and a leader in improvised patter. At Rome itself the *satura* or 'medley' seems to have combined impromptu dialogue by merry-makers with music and dancing. But Italian tragedy and comedy were in the main derivative from Greek drama. In South Italy the Oscan-speaking peoples had by the fourth century followed the Greeks in producing comic burlesques, with stock characters, and masks, the rudiments of a plot, and an iambic metre (*fabulae Atellanae*). At Rome dramatic representations were organized *c.* 200 B.C., as in Greek towns, in connexion with the public festivals; and the two principal playwrights, Plautus (254–184 B.C.) and Terence (195–159 B.C.), took their plots from the Attic New Comedy, and adopted the Greek iambic for their metre. This metre was not ill suited to Latin, but the transference of Greek plots to a Roman stage was attended with danger. In the plays of Plautus Greek and Italian elements were artlessly jumbled together, and if Terence steered clear of such incongruities, he did so only by keeping too close to the Greek original and thus making the action somewhat unreal to his Italian audiences. But the Italian element in

Plautus' comedies, the boisterous fun and the 'Italian vinegar' of mordant but good-humoured raillery, can carry even a modern reader along and make him forgetful of Plautus' faults of arrangement; and the careful plot-construction and character-delineation which Terence derived from Menander explain the influence which he exercised upon the Comedy of Early Modern Europe. The good craftsmanship of Terence, who was a swarthy (but not negro) native of Africa, and first came to Italy as a slave, is no doubt to be explained by the influence of the Scipionic circle, to which he had access.

Of the other early Roman dramatists some (e.g. Pacuvius) wrote tragedies based on actual Roman history, and others (e.g. Afranius) took Italian life and manners as the subject of their plays; yet these had no such enduring hold on the Roman public as the mongrel production of Plautus. Moreover, after the second century the Roman drama ceased to be productive. A partial explanation of this sterility may be found in the competition of a new form of entertainment, the mime, which was a variety show with more or less lascivious dancing and smart quips but no real plot. This kind of performance no doubt made a greater appeal to the fibreless and spineless proletariat of the later Roman republic.

A partial substitute for comedy at Rome was the satiric poem, which was truly racy of the soil, in that it developed out of the native Italian spirit of raillery. The homely wit that found expression in such Roman cognomina as Cocles ('Squint-eye'), Plancus ('Splay-foot'), and Caesar ('Curly-head') was first sharpened into a keen-cutting weapon by Lucilius (c. 180–100 B.C.), a member of the Scipionic circle who used his art to pillory political opponents and the vulgar New Rich, and thus created one of the most characteristic branches of Latin literature.

Prose literature at Rome came into being during the Second Punic War, and naturally enough its first production was in the field of history. It is more surprising that the father of Roman historiography, Fabius Pictor, wrote his work, a general history of Rome, in the Greek tongue—presumably he was seeking to satisfy the nascent Greek interest in Roman affairs and to justify Roman imperialism in answer to the Greek writers on the

Carthaginian side. Despite this propagandist aim, Fabius' history seems to have been a colourless and generally honest piece of writing. The use of Latin in Roman historiography was not established until Cato the Elder (234–149 B.C.) composed another general history of Rome in his native tongue. From the second century onward a continuous stream of authors wrote on this same theme (or occasionally on some selected topic like the Second Punic War), on an ever-increasing scale, but with little change in their methods. Although many of the early Roman historians had practical experience of public life, they seldom made any attempt to probe the inner meaning of events after the manner of the best Greek historians.

At Rome the art of public speaking was cultivated from the time when the Popular Assemblies acquired political importance, and c. 300 B.C. a senator named Appius Claudius became famous by his oratory. But this art remained on a purely empiric basis until Gaius Gracchus supplemented his practical apprenticeship in the Forum by studying the Greek technique of rhetoric. Although little is now preserved of his speeches, their immediate effect was so great that he gave an impetus to the systematic study of rhetoric at Rome, the fruits of which were gathered in the later days of the republic.

6. THE GOLDEN AGE OF LATIN LITERATURE. THE HARMONIZATION OF ROMAN AND GREEK TRADITION

After 150 B.C. the great age of Roman conquest came to an end, and carried away with it the first creative impulse of Latin literature which it had engendered. The period extending from 150 to 80 produced no author of the first rank, and it is no mere accident that the two early dramatists of whom we possess complete works, Plautus and Terence, as well as Ennius (of whom we still have considerable fragments), belonged to the early part of the second century. Yet in these seventy years Roman men of letters were by no means inactive. Within the Roman governing class enlightened men were not wanting, who realized that Rome had a civilizing as well as a conquering mission, and by their patronage of conscientious if uninspired authors they established a high tradition of literary craftsmanship at Rome. Though the poets and dramatists of this period wrote no work of enduring importance, they prepared for the Golden Age of Latin literature by their assiduous filing and polishing of the Latin language. By many experiments they prepared the way for the final harmonization of their literature with Greek tradition. In the next generation Lucretius could still complain of the *patrii sermonis egestas*, the inadequate range of the Latin vocabulary, as compared with Greek; yet by 80 B.C. the Latin tongue had been rendered capable of almost any form of literary expression.

The Golden Age of Latin literature falls into two divisions, the Ciceronian and the Augustan periods, either of which roughly coincided with an era of relative stability and prosperity after civil wars and reigns of terror. In the third and second centuries Latin writers had turned to Homer and classical Greek literature; in the Ciceronian period there was a school that cultivated the Hellenistic authors; in the Augustan age Roman men of letters returned in the main to the earlier models. The contemporaries of Cicero strove with considerable success to acquire the technical dexterity and the high finish of their Alexandrian models, but unlike these they had substance as well as form: they had a message to convey, and they were on the whole the most individual and least conventional of Roman writers.

The personality of a Roman author is nowhere revealed more vividly than in the poems of Catullus, a young man-about-town of the sixties and fifties. After the usual preliminary course of translation from Greek writers (mostly from the Hellenistic poets), which gave him proficiency in the use of Greek lyric metres, Catullus applied his art to the composition of short pieces in which he reflected each passing mood of his impressionable mind with exuberant spontaneity. We may catch him now and then in a playful frame of mind, but more often he gave expression to the elementary passions of love and hate, and none of his poems are more characteristic than those in which he avowed his infatuation for a fashionable beauty named Clodia, and vented his disillusionment on discovering that Clodia was merely trifling with him. The *abandon* of Catullus was so far removed from Roman 'gravitas' that we may perhaps attribute it to the Celtic blood in his veins—he was a native of Cisalpine Gaul. But he was a thorough Roman in the discipline which he applied to himself in regard to form, and the melody of his metres showed that Latin, no less than Greek, could be a singing language.

The other notable poet of the Ciceronian period, Lucretius, was as solid as Catullus was unstable—in him Roman 'gravitas' was reinforced by the intellectual stamina of a Greek and the absorbing ethical interest of a Hebrew—and his poem *De Rerum Natura* was a long didactic epic in hexameters. But Lucretius was as individual in his outlook as Catullus: his consuming passion was to liberate mankind from its false gods, and from the pervasive atmosphere of fear which those gods induced. With this end in view he proclaimed to the Roman world the ethical doctrine of Epicurus (p. 211), which banished the gods to another world and left man free to pursue his own pleasure, and he linked Epicurus' hedonism with the 'atomic theory' of Democritus (p. 198), which explained the physical world in a purely mechanical fashion and seemingly left no room for a divine creator. In consonance with this general theme he also combated the popular view of a 'Fall of Man' from a primitive Age of Gold to the present Age of Iron, and set up the opposite theory of continuous human progress and (in anticipation of Darwin) the natural survival of the fittest. In the last resort Lucretius was unable to dispense altogether with a guiding Providence, which appears now and then amid his 'fortuitous concourse of atoms' and helps to establish an ordered universe. But no other Roman ever made a like effort of sustained scientific imagination, and his artistry in language and metre gave attractive form to his severe reasoning.

In the Ciceronian period historiography continued to be the principal form of prose literature, though little survives of it except two minor works of Sallust, and the short sketches of the Gallic and Civil Wars by Caesar. The writing of history at this stage was perverted by a general habit of embroidering upon the facts, for purposes of patriotic or party propaganda, or merely of 'bright' writing. Of the two historians whose work we still have, Caesar was as versatile in the field of literature as in those of war and politics. He dabbled in poetry and grammar and astronomy, and wrote a depreciatory memoir of his political opponent Cato the Younger. His war sketches, which he modestly described as *Commentarii* or memoranda, were not intended by him to form part of the permanent stock of Roman literature, but they survive as the best ancient work of military history. Though not free from propagandist touches, they have been proved on the whole remarkably accurate, and their studiously simple style, which Caesar based on that of the severest and most economical Greek prose writers, revealed that Latin could be no whit inferior to Greek in clearness of expression.

In contrast with Caesar, Sallust was an ambitious writer who tried to measure himself against Thucydides. The comparison was damaging to him, for he was infected with the carelessness about facts that characterized the Roman historians of his age, and in point of accuracy he fell far behind his model. But he learnt from the Greek writers to look for the underlying causes of historical events, and sought to explain as well as to chronicle the 'decline and fall' of the Roman republic. Like Caesar, he cultivated a Greek terseness of style, but he introduced a fashion, which had a long vogue in Rome, of seasoning his narrative with epigrams and speeches in imitation of Thucydides.

Among the prose writers of the Golden Age the dominant figure is that of Cicero (106–43 B.C.). Of all Roman personages he is known to us most intimately, both by the great quantity of his literary works and by the remains of his private correspondence, of which about 900 pieces survive. His letters and speeches cast a searching light upon his foibles. By nature an unstable and 'touchy' intellectual, he was never really at ease in the rough-and-tumble of politics under the late republic, and the mishaps which virtually closed his political career after the year of his consulship tended to undermine his self-confidence and to make his temper more brittle. Yet Cicero stands out as one of the most completely formed personalities of the ancient world. He realized in great measure the ideal Roman in whom (to use his own words) Roman 'gravitas' is united with Greek 'humanitas' or refinement of taste and manners, and 'Greek training in theory is applied to a lofty and brilliant character'; and in his range of interests and appreciation of the inter-relation of all knowledge he invites comparison with Plato.

Cicero is remembered chiefly as the supreme master of Roman oratory. Since the time of Gaius Gracchus the study of oratory had been assiduously pursued at Rome (p. 260), and some of Cicero's contemporaries, including Caesar, attained a considerable reputation by their gifts of speech; but Cicero by common consent outstripped them all. 'Learning in law and literature, knowledge of men, skill in argument, gift of clear statement, telling gesture, control of voice, mastery of the subtle cadences of the Latin language when declaimed, and an infallible instinct for the right rhythm in the structure and at the close of a sentence, all combined to make Cicero the greatest of the orators of Rome.'[1]

Cicero used the leisure of his later years in writing philosophical works, which ranged from light and serene essays, like that on Old Age, to systematic expositions of the Academic and Stoic doctrines. Like a true Roman he adapted his models to the needs of his own countrymen: he tempered the austerity of the Stoics with Roman common sense, and in his treatise on the Ideal State he did not imagine a Platonic Utopia, but merely gave a modified version of the time-honoured constitution of Rome (p. 213). Yet in basing his ideals on the actual methods of Roman government, with their hospitable traditions, and refraining from Greek dogmas about Barbarians and a Chosen Race, he envisaged a community of nations under Roman leadership.

The vocabulary and the prosody of Latin prose were firmly established by Cicero: his influence on later Latin writers was such that he sometimes cramped their stylistic development. Through him the Latin language became almost as versatile as Greek, and it was due to him more than to any other Roman author that it was adopted throughout western Europe as the vehicle of cultured intercourse.

[1] J. Wight Duff, *The Writers of Rome*, p. 40.

In the period of turmoil and civil war which marked the downfall of the Roman Republic literary production was not wholly arrested; and it received a powerful new stimulus from the political and cultural Renaissance which Augustus brought about. The world of letters also profited by the liberal and enlightened patronage of the emperor himself, and of various *grands seigneurs* of his day, chief among them his ministers Maecenas and Asinius Pollio. The authors who enjoyed their favour were allowed a wide freedom of thought and expression —neither Horace nor Vergil could fairly be described as 'court poets'—but they were held to an exacting standard of workmanship. The poetry of the Augustan age surpassed that of all other periods in its high finish, indeed in the lesser composers we may now discern an incipient tendency to overvalue form as compared with substance.

The minor Augustans stood particularly under the influence of the Hellenistic poets, whom they followed not only in their careful craftsmanship, but in the choice of their subjects. Erotic poetry in elegiac metre formed the main theme of Tibullus and Propertius. The latter of these had native force and fire, but he cramped himself with an involved and allusive style. Another Hellenistic genre, the miniature epic, was cultivated with conspicuous success by Ovid (43 B.C.–*c* 18 A.D.). Like Catullus, Ovid was a member of a 'fast set', and he thereby incurred the displeasure of Augustus, who virtually ended his literary career by banishing him from Italy. He was entirely lacking in passion; but he displayed great skill in arranging a story or setting forth an argument, or in describing the scenery of Italy, for which he had a genuine feeling. His hexameters and elegiacs had a mellifluously easy if somewhat monotonous flow: as in the case of Pope, the 'numbers came', and in the right order. His *Metamorphoses* were one of the principal channels by which Greek and Roman mythology were transmitted to the modern world of letters and art.

The two major Augustan poets, Horace (65–8 B.C.) and Vergil (70–19 B.C.), were personal friends and followed similar careers. Both were caught in the storm of the civil wars, but were rescued by Pollio and Maecenas and introduced by them to Augustus.

Horace first made his mark as a writer of satire. But his natural *bonhomie*, and the sense of balance which he developed, like most of the Augustans, in reaction to the excesses of the civil wars, took the sting out of his shafts, and his own countrymen thought of him as the poet who teased rather than rasped their heartstrings (*circum praecordia lusit*). His fame now rests mainly on his Odes, through which he acclimatized in Rome the lyric poets of early Greece. In the Odes he touched upon a large variety of themes: he flirted and trolled the drinking-bowl, he soliloquized on human frailty and made appeals to Roman patriotism; but on the whole, the Odes mark a progression from the philosophy of a refined *bon viveur* to a serious concern in the regeneration of Rome after the recent disorders. But the Odes are less remarkable by their content than by their perfection of form. Horace smoothed and planed their verses and rearranged their words until language and metre were in perfect harmony; the chiselled delicacy of the Odes had been the despair of countless imitators. The fine finish of Horace's poems, together with his cultured man-of-the-world outlook, explain his hold on the ordinary educated person of modern times.

The work that first brought Vergil into notice was his *Eclogues*, pastoral idylls after the manner of Theocritus. These were plainly apprentice work; but they foreshadowed the poet's future in the deep love of country life which they breathed; and the Fourth Eclogue, which hailed the coming of a new Golden Age after the horrors of the civil wars, contained the germ of his *Aeneid*, an epic of delivery after trial and sorrow. Vergil's *Georgics*, or 'Farmer's Manual', were in outward form a Latin counterpart to Hesiod's *Works and Days* (p. 242). But their interest lies, not in their technical instruction, but in the philosophy which they embody. The ancient Italian love of the land was one of Vergil's dominant passions. He saw in the land not only the source of our livelihood, but the giver of that peace of mind for which his post-war generation was craving: creative work on the soil, and contemplation of the wonders of Nature, were the true prizes of life.

In his later years, Vergil, like Horace, felt a quickened interest in Augustus' work of reconstruction, and gave it support by composing a national Roman epic. His *Aeneid*, which was acclaimed in advance as something 'bigger than the *Iliad*', was outwardly a counterpart to Homer's poem, with the same metre and a similar arrangement of episodes. But speculations as to which was the 'bigger' epic fall beside the mark, for the Homeric and Augustan ages exclude comparison, and Vergil's outlook was intensely Roman and Augustan. His hero, *pius Aeneas* ('Aeneas the faithful'), lacked the Homeric heroes' elemental vigour, but his patience and fortitude were precisely the qualities which the Augustans, living in an age of stabilization, held in most esteem. Nay more, the *Aeneid*, unlike the *Iliad*, had a dramatic purpose: in it all roads lead to Rome, and its episodes of disaster are but incidents that prepare for the foundation of the city, just as the civil wars were the prelude to the reign of Augustus.

As a national epic, the *Aeneid* was a triumphant success. The ever-changing rhythm of its hexameters, and the subtle allusions and 'overtones' in Vergil's language, were calculated to keep its readers constantly on the alert; but above all, it appealed to the national pride of the Romans, and fortified their belief that Rome had been built to last for ever. But if Vergil spoke with the authentic voice of Augustan Rome, he also had a message for all mankind. His Roman pride was completely purged of the arrogance of a conquering people: for him the mission of Rome lay not only in the exercise of fortitude and justice, but also of pity. Compassion for suffering was never far from Vergil's mind, and it shines through his verse at countless points. Though the false assumption that his fourth Eclogue was a prophecy of the coming of Christ contributed powerfully to his survival in the Middle Ages, the fascination that he exercised upon the best minds of that period (as upon Dante, who would fain have plucked him out of the Inferno) was largely based on a recognition that his was an 'anima naturaliter Christiana'; and the secret of the unabated force of his appeal to modern readers is that he was not only the proudest but also the kindliest of Roman writers.

While the Augustan period marks the climax of Roman poetry, its output of prose literature would have lacked distinction but for the work of Livy. The history of the civil wars was recorded in a seemingly competent work by Pollio, but this treatise was obliterated by the new general history of Livy, which superseded the whole output of previous Roman annalists. The history of Livy (59 B.C.–A.D. 17) may be regarded as the prose counterpart of the *Aeneid*. It was composed with an epic breadth of narrative, so as to comprise 142 books (of which 35 survive), and it was less concerned to analyse the deep-seated causes of events than to commemorate the achievement of Rome. Livy had no practical experience of politics, and he not only lacked the scientific outlook of Thucydides, but fell below his standards of technique. He made no systematic attempt to sift the work of the earlier annalists upon whom he drew, and consequently incorporated in his story much material which modern critics have rejected. But his story, for all its false detail, gave the right general impression of Rome's conquests, and presented them in the light of an intelligent patriotism which took as much pride in Roman justice and generosity as in prowess of arms. Livy's power of vivid description, and the skill with which he made his speeches sound real and impressive, more than atoned for the excessive length of his work. He therefore established himself as the standard historian of the republic, and ranked with Vergil as the most effective defender of Roman imperialism.

7. THE SILVER AGE OF LATIN LITERATURE

The Silver Age of Latin literature is the period extending from the death of Augustus to that of Hadrian (A.D. 14–138). This was a time of general political stability and economic prosperity. Men of letters no longer enjoyed the unstinting patronage of the Augustan age; yet the emperors on the whole were friendly to them, and they did not curtail freedom of speech, except against political propagandists. Literary circles were never more numerous at Rome, and it became a fashion to attend the recitals of new composers, as it is now to go to lectures. Roman education (which included Greek studies—p. 290) was becoming more common in the western provinces, and it was no mere accident that four of the principal writers of the first century, Lucan, Martial, Quintilian, and Seneca, were natives of Spain. As we have seen (p. 253), this period also witnessed a revival of Greek literature.

But in comparison with the spacious days of Augustus, the world now seemed cramped and without wide scope, and the prevailing spirit of the Silver Age were therefore critical and negative. At this time, moreover, Roman education developed on wrong lines. It gave a one-sided preference to rhetorical studies, and organized these in such a way as to encourage superficial smartness rather than sincere feeling and ripe reflection.

The flow of epic poetry was stimulated rather than stanched by the *Aeneid*. But only one of Vergil's successors, a writer named Lucan (A.D. 39–65), achieved more than a momentary success. Lucan called his poem the *Pharsalia*, i.e. the civil war between Caesar and Pompey; he produced an atmosphere of epic tension and drew a compelling picture of Caesar as a daemonic and destructive force. But, like a true child of the rhetorical schools, he sought to dazzle rather than to enlighten, and his over-coloured descriptions of war-episodes give us a foretaste of the modern sensational Press.

Under the Roman emperors the theatre continued to attract the urban multitudes at holiday-time. But the performances now consisted predominantly of mimes (p. 259) and pantomimes (the prototypes of the modern ballet), and were little more than showpieces. Literary drama, which had already become almost extinct, was temporarily revived by Seneca (*c.* A.D. 4–65), whose plays had a considerable influence on early modern tragedy. But Seneca's dramas (which took for their subject the more gruesome themes of Greek mythology) were mere exercises in rhetoric, and were meant to be declaimed rather than acted. Their immense influence on western Europe is one of the ironies of literary history.

The most congenial form of poetry to the Silver Age Romans was satire. In Persius (A.D. 34–62) Roman satire produced an honest reformer who wrote with Stoic earnestness. ('Give me a sense of duty to man and God blended in my mind . . . and I shall make acceptable sacrifice with but a handful of meal.') But Persius could not resist the verbal trickery of the rhetorical schools, and in his attempts at clever writing he often achieved obscurity. His successor Martial (*c.* 40–100) was a trifler who threw off short epigrammatic poems with a ready sense of fun; but in the hammer-strokes of his concluding lines he exploited the full clean-hitting vigour of the Latin language. The greatest of the Roman satirists, Juvenal (*c.* 47–127), differed from his predecessors in being a man with a personal grievance. An Italian of old stock, he bitterly resented the invasion of Rome by parvenu adventurers (especially by newcomers from the Greek East), and reintroduced into Roman satire the note of malice of which it had been purged by Horace and Persius. But his honest anger gave purpose and concentration to his rhetorical craft, and his tense epigrammatic phrases are often cast in such perfect form as to defy translation. Juvenal's influence on English letters may be traced through Chaucer and Swift to Dr. Johnson, whose *London* is based on the Third Satire (where the Frenchman is Juvenal's supple Greek).

> 'All sciences a fasting Monsieur knows;
> And bid him go to Hell, to Hell he goes.'

At this day persons who have never heard of Juvenal keep tags of him on their lips ('rara avis', 'mens sana in corpore sano').

The prose writers of the Silver Age did not hold all the ground captured in the Ciceronian period, but they broke new ground in several directions. With the fall of the republic the scope of oratory was so far reduced that its study, though carried on with unabated zeal, was no longer directed to practical ends, but became an academic exercise. The rhetoricians abandoned Cicero's ideal of wide knowledge, sound morality, and practical experience, and endeavoured to disguise the lack of content in their speeches by the pyrotechnics of *sententiae* or pointed sayings. It is true that the greatest of the teachers of oratory, Quintilian (*c.* 35–100), endeavoured to revert to the sounder traditions of republican times. In his authoritative book *On the Training of the Orator* he emphasized the need of a sound general education, a wide reading in the Greek and Latin classics (which he surveyed with acute but sympathetic criticism), and a special study of Cicero. But he failed to carry his contemporaries with him.

Cicero's attempt to interpret Greek philosophy to the Roman

world was repeated, albeit on a more popular plane, by Seneca, whose main work in prose consisted of essays and letters, mostly on ethical subjects. The general trend of his moral teaching, which commended the simple life and the gentler virtues, was sufficiently near to that of the early Christians to create a tradition (now wholly discredited) that Seneca had held converse with St. Paul. Though himself a man of great wealth, and for many years a minister of Nero, he no doubt gave honest expression to his ideals in his philosophical works. Seneca adopted the epigrammatic style of his day, which indeed was well suited to a popularizing treatise, and salted his Latin with words drawn from popular speech.

The satirical tendency of the age found expression in prose no less than in poetry. Seneca (here acting in opposition to his own principles) indited a very malicious if clever skit on the defunct Emperor Claudius. Another minister of Nero, Petronius, wrote a story, in a novel that was loosely constructed but superior in characterization to the Greek novels, in which he poked broad fun at the rhetoricians of his day, and described the over-rich fare and the inept talk at the dinner-party of a parvenu in a small Italian town. His satires revealed Italian skill in portraiture, and they gained in realism by their profusion of vernacular language.

The great work of Livy diverted rather than dammed the stream of historical treatises at Rome. Historians now turned to contemporary or recent history, and covered shorter periods in greater detail. But just as Livy eclipsed the historical writers of the republican period, so the remaining annalists of the Silver Age were put into the shade by Tacitus (c. A.D. 54–117). This author was drawn on by his success in a short biography of his father-in-law Agricola (governor of Britain in A.D. 77–84), and in a study of the peoples of Germany (whose future importance he dimly foresaw), to the writing of a general history of the emperors from A.D. 14 to 96. Of its two constituent portions, the greater part of the *Annals* (A.D. 14–68), but only a small fraction of the *Histories* (A.D. 68–96) survives. Tacitus came nearer than any extant Roman historian to scientific composition. He possessed the necessary industry in collecting information, and critical power in sifting it, and he made some attempt, like Sallust, to understand the underlying causes of events. But he was influenced by a subconscious bias against some of the Caesars and their environment. His romantic yearning for the good old republic did not make him hostile to the régime of the emperors as such—he had passed through a distinguished career in the imperial service—but he lost patience with the intrigues and suspicions that played about the Imperial Court, and his ancient Roman 'gravitas' revolted against the undignified bearing of some emperors, and the servility of their place-men. It is probable that he also allowed his *flair* for dramatic scenes to warp his sober judgment, and he abused his art in throwing out subtle innuendoes. His estimate of the Caesars has often been challenged, and it is now generally admitted that he did scant justice to Augustus' successor Tiberius. But his portraits stand out from their background like those of no other ancient author, and his artistry in the 'pointed' style of Latin was not surpassed, save perhaps by Juvenal. His highly charged epigrams are like stinging hail on the face, and his terseness conveys an impression of great reserves of power.

Roman history in the days of the Republic is the record of a great people rather than of great individuals; but from the time of Caesar outstanding or at least intriguing personalities filled the Roman scene, and the interest of Tacitus in portraiture is a sign that a special field for historical biography had now opened. This field was assiduously cultivated by Suetonius, a secretary to the Emperor Hadrian, who wrote biographies (now mostly lost) of men of letters, and the extant *Lives of the Caesars* (from Julius Caesar to Domitian). Suetonius was an indefatigable worker who amassed materials with indiscriminate zeal, but made hardly any attempt to sift them, or to combine them into a harmonious picture. His neat arrangement and his unpretentious style make his *Lives* attractive to read, and he embodies much valuable information; but his readiness to pass on mere gossip makes him an untrustworthy guide, and it set a bad example to others.

Though Cicero wrote his letters without any intention of publishing them, a large collection of them was subsequently put together and found such a ready market that the epistle became established as a special branch of Latin literature. A rival collection was issued by Pliny the Younger (62–114; a nephew of the encyclopædist—p. 212), which included his official correspondence with the Emperor Trajan. The prosperous career and placid temperament of Pliny precluded him from writing anything to match the correspondence of Cicero; but the simple and cultivated style of his letters makes them pleasant reading, and the description which he gave as an eye-witness of the destruction of Pompeii (vi. 16, 20) can still arrest the modern reader. The writings of Pliny and Quintilian introduce us to two authors whose kindly disposition stands in contrast to the general acidity of the literature of their period, and may serve as a warning against hasty generalizations from the diatribes of Tacitus or Juvenal.

8. LATER LATIN LITERATURE. THE DECLINE OF THE GREEK TRADITION

After the death of Hadrian the flow of Latin literature became less abundant. Henceforward Italy in particular brought forth scarcely any writer of importance. But the failure of the Italian supply was partly compensated by the increasing productivity of the provinces. Gaul and Spain and Africa furnished a full quota of Latin writers—the pioneers of Christian literature in the West came mostly from Spain and Africa—and even the Greek East made its contribution. The reasons for the weakening of the stream and the diversion of its channels are not easy to discover, but a partial explanation may be found in the divorce of Latin education from real life (which offers ever-new problems and points of interest), and its absorption in academic exercises that became stale by repetition. In this case it is not strange that Italy, which had the longest tradition of rhetorical teaching, first showed signs of exhaustion.

The barbarian invasions gave a severe check to literary activities in the third century, but could not prevent a partial revival in the fourth and fifth. Their worst effect was to impede communications between the western and the eastern Mediterranean, and thus to bring about a decline of Greek studies in the West: after A.D. 300 competent teachers of Greek became sadly to seek in the western countries. But Latin authors at this stage no longer needed the guidance of Greek models, though they might still benefit from the play of Greek thought. The impoverishment of the Roman Empire also entailed a decline in patronage of letters, but education in general was not neglected (p. 283). On the other hand, not even the barbarian invasions could jerk the majority of Latin writers out of the grooves which they had cut for themselves.

The most important new factor in the history of later Latin literature was the advent of Christianity in the West and its spread among the educated classes, who put their literary training at the service of their new religion. The educated Christians, it is true, had to face opposition from 'isolationist' members of the Church, whose aversion from pagan polytheism, from the flaws in pagan morals, and the unreality of rhetorical education, impelled them to renounce pagan culture altogether. But the Church as a whole adhered to the old Roman principle of critical and selective imitation; it made pagan culture serviceable to its own ends, and in so doing gave it a new lease of life.

In the later second century an African writer named Fronto gave a new turn to Latin prose by introducing archaic phrases and imitating the artless abrupt sentences of the early republican authors. His paternally benevolent letters to his former pupil, the Emperor Marcus Aurelius, are a museum of this *elocutio novella*. The same style was used with considerable vividness and artistry by another African, Apuleius, in his *Metamorphoses*. Apart from its adventurous Latin, this work was remarkable for its contents. It was a novel, in which stories of black magic and scenes from the human underworld were mingled with the charming romance of Cupid and Psyche, whose opening words, *erant in quadam civitate rex et regina* ('once upon a time a king and a queen lived in a certain city') introduced the fairy-tale into Latin literature.

A similar archaizing is noticeable in a remarkable poem of uncertain date, the *Pervigilium Veneris*. This reverts to a trochaic metre (- ⌣), which had been occasionally used by the early

comedians and suited Latin rhythm well. This metre imparted a
fine swing to the haunting refrain

cras amet qui nunquam amavit, quique amavit cras amet
('who never loved shall love to-morrow, to-morrow love who loved
before').

Though the poem ends on a note of disillusion, its chorus of
praise for the Bountiful Giver of Life recalls the old Italian
gladness in the exuberance of Nature.

The *Pervigilium Veneris* foreshadowed a later development in
Latin verse, in which accent replaced length in fixing the metre.
But the classical metres died hard, and the principal poets of
the fourth and fifth centuries retained the use of hexameters and
elegiacs. On the score of their literary merit mention may be
made of Ausonius, a Gaul from Burdigala (Bordeaux), who
composed clever *vers d'occasion* and in a descriptive poem, the
Mosella, showed genuine appreciation of the sunny landscapes
of the Moselle valley; and of Claudian, a native of Alexandria,
who partly wasted his talent on panegyrics of distinguished
contemporaries, but came nearest to the poets of the classical age
in artistic sense and depth of feeling. Claudian's most notable
work is a valedictory poem on the greatness of Rome, 'the mother
that took all peoples to her bosom'.

Among the later prose authors the historians are singularly
ill represented. The only extant writer of any merit was a Syrian
named Ammianus Marcellinus (*c.* A.D. 330–400), who wrote a
continuation of Tacitus. The only surviving part of his work,
covering the period 353–378, shows that he was a poor stylist,
but a competent reporter and a close observer. Another work
of slightly earlier date, the *Historia Augusta*, carried on Suetonius'
biographies of the emperors down to Diocletian. Its author or
authors added to Suetonius' fault of gossip-mongering that of
wholesale forgery, and had the distinction of producing the worst
historical work in the Latin language.

The list of notable Latin orators closes with Aurelius Symmachus (*c.* A.D. 340–400), who delivered laboured panegyrics on
the emperors of his day, and the series of letter writers with a
Gallic grandee named Sidonius Apollinaris (A.D. 430–483), whose
descriptions of country life in Gaul are not without interest.

Latin Christian literature dates back to *c.* A.D. 200, at which time the chief concern of the Church was to state its case to the world. The earliest surviving Christian apology is the *Octavius* of Minucius Felix, an African convert who presented his argument in the form of dialogue, after the manner of some of Cicero's philosophical works, and wrote with Ciceronian urbanity. His compatriot Tertullian (*c.* A.D. 160–230) employed the distorted African style and hit out with more zeal than discretion. But the most authoritative and comprehensive statement of the Christian position was the treatise *De Civitate Dei* by another African, Augustine (A.D. 354–430), who stood in the true Ciceronian tradition, writing in a measured cultivated style and reviewing the past history of Rome in the spirit of a philosopher. Though Augustine set the 'City of God' above any secular power, he described it in words that might have been applied to pagan Rome: 'a City that calls her citizens out of all nations and gathers together a great society of all races and languages, not caring for differences of character, laws, or customs.'

But from the time of Constantine, when the Church had won its battle, its literature turned mainly into other channels. The general rules for a Christian education were laid down in the *Institutiones Divinae* of Lactantius, a tutor of Constantine's son. Lactantius not only wrote good Ciceronian Latin, but advocated a grounding in the Latin classics. Hieronymus (or Jerome, A.D. 340–420) prepared the 'Vulgate' or standard Latin translation of the Bible, and not only translated but extended the chronological tables of Eusebius (p. 256). A famous bishop, Ambrose of Milan (*c.* A.D. 337–397), laid the foundations of Christian Church music and was the pioneer of an important branch of Latin literature, the Christian hymn. Another hymn-writer, Prudentius (*c.* A.D. 348–410), produced the finest examples of early Christian poetry.

Latin remained a medium of literature, both sacred and profane, throughout the Middle Ages and the Renaissance. In the seventeenth and eighteenth centuries poets like Milton and Johnson still found expression for some of their verse in this language.

IX

Education and Scholarship

1. GENERAL TYPES OF EDUCATION

THE GREEK word for education, *Paideia*, means merely the art that has to do with children; the Latin word *Educatio* is more interesting. It does not imply 'eliciting thoughts from the child's mind', as many text-books say, for it is not derived directly from *edūcere* but from *edŭcare*, which means 'to nourish', 'to bring up', and may be connected with an old Italian goddess of infant nutrition, Educa. 'Educatio', then, like 'opvoeding' in Dutch, implies supplying the right food for the child's development, and is linked with the Roman principle of growth.

If we attempt a survey of Greek and Roman education—and it must be remembered that there are many gaps in our knowledge—the following types might be distinguished:—

1. The 'Heroic' Age, as pictured by Homer (thirteenth century B.C.), in which a man was trained to be a good speaker and an effective member of the state. 'Peleus sent me forth', says Phoenix to Achilles. 'to teach you all this' (military science and political institutions), 'to be a speaker of words and a doer of deeds' (*Iliad*, ix. 443).

2. The education of certain Dorian states, like Crete and Sparta, which emphasized rigid discipline and war-training, with a strong tendency, as in Sparta after Lycurgus, to neglect art and science. (The records of Dorian educational systems are some centuries later than the entry of the Dorians into Greece.)

3. Ionian education, more elastic and humane, with a lively interest in art, science, and philosophy, aimed, in its best days, at the education of the whole man. This type of training is found first in Ionic Asia Minor and then, from the sixth century B.C., at Athens, where the Sophists develop the rhetorical tradition, imported from Sicily in the fifth century, and introduce specialist study for professional purposes.

4. The Hellenistic schools (after Alexander's conquest of the East), which emphasize the intellectual side of education, continue the tendency to specialization, particularly in Rhetoric, and inaugurate an age of universal scientific learning (mainly third to first centuries B.C.).

5. Meantime Rome practised her own home-made system of education from the seventh century to the middle of the third, emphasizing personal and political behaviour in accordance with the customs of their ancestors.

6. With the advent of Greek letters came intellectual interests. The Ciceronian ideal of 'humanitas' envisaged the man who combined abstract learning with sound character and avoided undue specialization. The educated Roman was now bilingual.

7. This ideal passed into the imperial period and is found in Quintilian, though Rhetoric showed signs of artificiality, due to specialization in form and style as opposed to content. This tendency was seen, too, in the Greek world, where rhetoric became fashionable. But the emphasis on the moral aspect of education continued, as in the treatise on education ascribed to Plutarch.

8. From the fourth century A.D. two significant changes took place: the gradual disappearance of Greek from the West, which made an end to the bilingual tradition of Roman schools, and the rise of Christian education, which largely took over the framework and, to some extent, the substance of the pagan system. Quintilian reappeared in the precepts of Jerome.

9. Graeco-Roman education passed into the Middle Ages and beyond. The Seven Liberal Arts of Martianus Capella (fifth or, according to some, third century A.D.), based ultimately on Varro's lost *Disciplinae*, formed the two parts of the medieval curriculum; the *Trivium* (Grammar, which, as the Art of Letters, might include Literature, Rhetoric, and Dialectic, the last ranging from bare Logic to the combination of pagan and Christian philosophy that led to Scholasticism), and the *Quadrivium* (Geometry, including some Geography, Arithmetic, Astronomy, and Music). As late as the seventeenth century the school exercises contained in the *Rhetores Graeci* were used in the schools of Europe.

2. EDUCATION AND THE GREEK STATE

In the Dorian states of Greece and Crete, and in Rome, agricultural communities interested in state organization, laws, and conventions played an important part in early training. As society develops, the motive of mere safety merges into the conception of well-being, and the educational pattern acquires a cultural interest and a tinge of morality. Technical training as we know it, with its advantages and its danger of producing skilled barbarians, was strictly no part of ancient education, but handed down privately in families. Thus Socrates was a stone-cutter, and at Rome crafts were taught by gilds.

The Dorians seem, for the most part, to have shown a rigidity, reminiscent of the Iron Age, in their state-patterns of education. Strabo says that the institutions of Sparta were really Cretan customs, elaborated by the Spartans, and there seems to have been state-controlled education of a kind in post-Dorian Crete. There were meals in common, paid for by the state, and the youth was organized in troops, controlled by the father or the group-leader. They tempered knowledge with art, by learning the laws of the state, set to music, as well as hymns and the praises of national heroes. Their favourite metre, the cretic ($-\,\cup\,-$), was supposed to inculcate restraint by its 'severity'. There was keen competition between the troops, whose aim it was to excel in courage, endurance, and military efficiency.

Before the sixth century Sparta had shown an interest in culture, as archæologists have testified and as the lyric poetry of Alcmaeon (p. 244) proves. But when it was decided to transform the Spartan state into a military machine, culture died and education became narrowly vocational. The educated man was the fighter and, to produce him of a sufficiently martial hardness and cunning, athletics, savage physical punishments, and practice in undetected stealing were pressed into service.

From birth the state laid a heavy hand upon the child; if weakly, it was exposed on Mount Taÿgĕtus. At the age of seven a meticulous and inflexible organization began its work of repression. Boys were taken from home, submitted to severe discipline on a sparse and unpalatable diet—a visitor at a Spartan meal remarked that he now understood why the Spartans did not fear death!—and enrolled in troops under military leaders. The leisure enjoyed under a system that freed the individual from cares of business and money-making was devoted, not to developing the personality, but to acquiring an efficient and healthy body for the service of the state in war.

There is evidence that schools existed both in the Ionian cities of Asia Minor and in early Athens. We hear of regulations prescribed for schools by Solon in the sixth century B.C.—though it must be admitted that the references of Aeschines to the subject are not above suspicion—and Herodotus tells of a school in Chios, the roof of which collapsed and killed nearly all of the one hundred and twenty pupils in the building. The philosopher Anaxagoras (500–428 B.C.) stipulated in a legacy to Clazomenae, his native town in Asia Minor, that the anniversary of his death should be celebrated as a school-holiday. We first hear of a state contribution to education in 480 B.C., when the Athenians were forced to abandon their homes before the Persian War was over and the Troezenians, who gave them shelter, resolved that the refugee children should be educated at the public cost. The earliest record of regular endowment belongs to the third century, when a certain Eudemus left a large sum for the perpetual endowment of a school for the sons of the free citizens of Miletus. The salaries are not impressive: thirty drachmas a month for gymnastic, and forty for elementary teachers—the former being approximately the pay of sailors under Pericles at Athens. A Hellenistic inscription of Teos, a town on the Ionian coast, gives a higher rate, ranging from 600 to 500 drachmas a year. By the second century B.C. endowment of schools in the Greek islands seems to have been fairly common; thus in 162 B.C. Rhodes accepted a large donation of corn from Eumĕnes of Pergamum, 'that its value might be invested and the interest devoted to pay the fees of the tutors and schoolmasters of their sons'. The 'Museum' or School of Research was lavishly endowed by the Ptolemies (possibly with a view to combating anti-monarchical opinion like that of Athens).

But at Athens we do not hear of endowment; although Plato

says that the laws required parents to train their children in music and gymnastic, the schools seem to have depended on private enterprise. The social status of the teacher was low; he eked out an existence from the monthly fees of the pupils. Yet it is interesting to note that while schooling was not rigidly organized, it was nevertheless very widespread; and Plato has described the intense interest aroused by the Sophists—young Hippocrates banging before daybreak in breathless excitement on the door of Socrates to announce the arrival of Protagoras—and the willingness of Athenians to spend relatively large sums on the lectures of these itinerant professors. Hippias made about £600 during a short visit to Sicily, receiving about £80 from an insignificant town; on the other hand, he frequently lectured to the Spartans without wringing an obol from their dour temperaments. Euenus of Paros charged £20 for a course in citizenship, Prodicus £2 for a lecture on correct speaking, though he seems to have envisaged many grades of audience, for there was a version of this lecture that cost 10 pence and in some cases he came down to 5 pence! The gains of the fifth-century Sophists were not great; Isocrates mentions that Gorgias, the richest of them, left only about £800 at his death. Plato charged no fees at the Academy but accepted presents; the tyrant Dionysius gave him some 80 talents (±£19,200). We have already referred to the vast sums that the rhetoricians of the New Sophistic Movement in the second century A.D. and later collected for teaching an art that was the gateway to political and social distinction (p. 254). Finally we may note that the only military training required by the state at Athens extended over two years, while at Sparta it lasted a lifetime.

3. EDUCATION AND THE ROMAN STATE

Early Roman education was conducted by the family—*in gremio matris educari* was the regular phrase—but always in relation to the larger family, the Roman state. Cicero says that in his boyhood all children learned the Twelve Tables by heart, and he regrets that this practice was later dropped. As at Sparta, the object was the training of the citizen, but without the exclusive military emphasis of the Spartans. A boy would accompany his father to political gatherings in the Forum or in the Senate House 'sitting near the door and learning both from what he heard and what he saw'. Education was regarded as important from early times. Plutarch's statement that Spurius Carvilius was the first to open a school for pay, about the middle of the third century B.C., probably means that he was the first to charge regular fees as opposed to the older system of voluntary gifts. The gains of schoolmasters, mostly slaves or freedmen and therefore of low social status, were meagre. Orbilius, famous from Horace's reference to his severe discipline, remained poor, and wrote a book on the slackness of parents in paying school-fees.

Ambassadors who supplemented their political work by lecturing on academic subjects at Rome evoked an enthusiasm that alarmed the authorities. The first was Crates of Mallos, who came in 168 B.C. on an embassy from Pergamum, the great rival of Alexandria in letters, and then identified with the theories of language that Crates upheld as against the famous Aristarchus. In 161 B.C. the Senate expelled teachers of philosophy and rhetoric from the city, for fear that foreign customs and intellectual subtleties would corrupt the *mores maiorum*. But such was the popularity of the new teaching that their decree was without effect. Similar enthusiasm attended the visit of the three philosophers from Athens, Carneades, Critolaus, and Diogenes, in 155 B.C., and Cato secured the expulsion of two Epicurean teachers in the following year. But, step by step, conservative fears were laid to rest; Panaetius bridged the gap between abstract Greek Stoicism and Roman ethics, and rhetorical theory was linked to native Roman oratory. In 92 B.C. came a much discussed decree forbidding Latin rhetors to teach; but thereafter the state ceased to interfere on the ground of preserving the Roman tradition. On the other hand, the schools followed the legions and travelled along the Roman roads, as in Gaul, where the difference in culture between the north, with its bad roads, and the south, where roads were good, was noticeable even in the fourth century A.D.

As late as 54 B.C. Cicero could write 'our institutions are

opposed to any system of education which is fixed by law or officially established or uniform in all cases', which throws an interesting light on the Roman principle of elasticity.

Julius Caesar, who wrote a book supporting Crates' theory of language, marked the increasing regard of the state for education by enfranchising teachers of the liberal arts; but Vespasian was the first to institute state appointments of Greek and Latin professors of rhetoric. They received about £1000 a year, as Verrius Flaccus, the tutor of Augustus' grandsons, had done. The later emperors gave teachers at various times exemption from taxes and military service, and Eumenius, one of the fourth-entury panegyrists, considers a salary of £5000 as quite ordinary. The younger Pliny supplied one-third of the revenue of a school at Novum Comum. Trajan provided for the education of 5000 children; Septimius Severus gave class-rooms and scholarships for the poor. But there was no general government provision for elementary education. By the third century A.D. the emperors, for the most part, assumed control of the schools, and Diocletian fixed the rate of pay for the various subjects. The fourth-century panegyrists and the Theodosian Code show how completely the teacher had become dependent on the emperor. In 425 A.D., with the advancing *rigor mortis* of the empire, a decree constituted the government the sole educational authority and made it a penal offence to open schools without permission. For the most part, however, though there is evidence that literacy was widespread, education remained the privilege of the higher social classes.

After the fourth century, the Church came to be recognized more and more as a society distinct from the state; the bishops, using the organization of the empire as a model, developed their own empire and used their own laws (*ius canonicum*). Similarly they controlled the Christian schools far more meticulously than the emperors had controlled the pagan schools, and simplified the problem of finance by using the free services of the monks. The poor benefited by a more widespread provision for elementary education.

4. MORAL AND RELIGIOUS TRAINING

The pattern according to which children were trained in early times implied a certain ethical convention in regard to other human beings and a contract with the gods who preserved, or had power to destroy, the life of the community. Hence knowledge of the law of man (*ius*) and the law of god (*fas*) was important in education. Both at Sparta and at Athens children were initiated into the religious festivals of the state. The Spartans showed how much importance they attached to character-training—according to their lights—by entrusting education, not to hirelings, but to citizens of the highest status under a specially appointed 'paidonomos'; and among the Romans, Cato similarly scorned slaves for the education of his son and personally undertook his instruction.

Even Athens, for all her eager intellectual interest, thought of the chief end of education as ethical. Socrates aimed at moral education and was interested in training that led to right action —to right action rather than to successful action. Plato, himself a poet, regretfully banished poets from his ideal state, largel because he considered their moral injury to the child greater than their aesthetic or intellectual gain. Moral lessons were sometimes drawn from Homer: Circe had made the men of Odysseus into pigs because they had made pigs of themselves. Some, like Prodicus in *The Choice of Herakles*, tried to give a moral turn to old legends. Even music was to be studied for moral profit and too stimulating or too relaxing types of music were to be eschewed. 'Children learn music that they may be more gentle and harmonious and rhythmical, for the life of man throughout has need of harmony and rhythm' (*Protagoras*, 325). Aristotle struck a new note when he said that music should be studied for pleasure and that literature existed 'for enjoyment'.

Prevailing Greek opinion (as we see, for instance, in Xenophon and Aristophanes) stressed good manners. Parents send children to school, says Socrates, and 'charge the master to take far more pains over their good behaviour than over their letters and music'. Modesty of demeanour, good form (*aschemon esti* the Greeks said, the Romans, *deforme est*, of what was not good form), and respect for elders were greatly emphasized. The person of the boy was carefully guarded. A special slave (*paidagogos*) escorted the boy to school and supervised his conduct. He was not allowed to go out at night or to sit up late at parties or to attend performances of comedy at the theatre. Xenophon, in his *Education of Cyrus*, says of his hero: 'As he grew up, he talked less and in gentler tones; he was so bashful that he blushed whenever he came into the presence of his elders.'

Socrates' doctrine that virtue could be taught was widely held, and was turned against him by the Athenians who held him responsible for the excesses of Critias and Alcibiades. Hence the responsibility of the teacher was great. But the low status of *paidagogoi* and teachers at Athens did much to counteract their moral influence. They were, in fact, what the Spartans and the early Romans objected to—hirelings. Children enacted the tale of Mary with her little lamb and brought their pet dogs or cats or leopards to school, playing with them during lessons, while loungers and idlers looked on and interrupted the work.

Isocrates in the fourth century B.C. stood for the unity of moral and intellectual education. 'The greater a man's desire', he says in the *Antidosis*, 'to persuade his audience (by the arts of rhetoric), the more he will train himself in true culture, aesthetic and moral, and in gaining the esteem of his fellow-citizens.' Elsewhere Isocrates set up as his ideal the production of the 'gentleman'. The educated man must have *savoir faire*, a sense of fitness, and a faculty for hitting on the right course. He must know how to behave in society and treat everyone 'with the utmost fairness and gentleness'. He must show self-control both as regards pleasure and as regards pain. He must be balanced and not unduly puffed up by the gifts of fortune, taking pride rather in the results of his own efforts and intelligence. 'Those whose soul is well tuned to play its part in all these ways ... I regard as truly educated' (*Panathenaicus*, 239).

Of Hellenistic educational theories we know little. There was an enormous extension of intellectualism, and possibly there was a tendency to argue about morality rather than to practise it. But we must be careful not to generalize, for philosophy played an important part in Hellenistic times and the key-philosophy was Stoicism.

In early Rome, as we have noticed, the emphasis on moral education was strong; and it was augmented by the solidarity of family feeling such as we find neither in Sparta nor in Athens nor in the Hellenistic cities. Tacitus remarks on the strict and careful house-training that characterized early Rome and especially on the influence of the mother. At a later stage, the father of the family, with the all but unlimited powers legally accorded him, the *patria potestas*, felt responsible for the training of his sons, and Cato even produced a text-book 'written in large letters'. 'Every child had his father for schoolmaster', says Pliny, of this time. Discipline, both in the home and in the school, was severe; Cato said with reason that the roots of learning were bitter, though the fruits were pleasant; but there was a real interest in the child and a real respect for his potentialities. *Maxima debetur puero reverentia* is a Roman sentiment. On festal days the boy joined in the religious ritual or went with his father to banquets and sang ballads in praise of famous ancestors. When he came of age and assumed 'the toga of manhood', at fifteen or sixteen, he was often attached to a distinguished man with whom he lived in close personal contact for a year, as a preparation for public or military life. 'I was taken by my father to Scaevŏla', says Cicero, 'and bidden as far as possible never to leave his side.' But the father's 'potestas' ended only with his life. No wonder that Ennius, in summing up the stability of the Roman state, begins with 'the morals of old'—

Moribus antiquis res stat Romana virisque.

No wonder that Cicero, in reviewing Graeco-Roman civilization, could think in general terms of the Roman contribution as character, and the Greek as intellect.

As intellectual attainments and political power, with wealth in its train, increased, Roman moral standards were relaxed. It is true that Cicero, following the tradition of Isocrates, combined morality and knowledge in his Catonian ideal of the educated man—*vir bonus dicendi peritus*; and that Augustus, teaching the people through the poets' precepts and his own example, attempted a moral restoration, not without success. But, again and again, the imperial writers looked back with wonder to the strength and austere simplicity of the early days, somewhat idealized by the haze of distance. Greek individualism and the solvent effect of sceptical philosophies loosened the ancient solidarity, but never quite swept it away.

By the fourth century A.D. there was a decline in morals that both Julian the Apostate and the Christian schools sought to amend. There can be no doubt that the latter, though they failed to reform society as a whole, advanced ethical standards in regard to slaves, gladiatorial games, the theatre, marriage, and the general status of women. Filled with the inspiration of a great ideal they represented the main source of moral training in the future.

5. INTELLECTUAL TRAINING

It is clear that in the Dorian states and in early Rome there was little stirring of the mind, such was the concentration on supporting and consolidating the traditional pattern of behaviour. It was in the lively cities of Asia Minor, with their bustle of commerce and many races, that the Greek brain began to function (p. 196). This activity must have been reflected in the schools, for which our evidence is extremely fragmentary.

Athens received the torch from Ionia and fostered a general enthusiasm for the things of the mind. School education was divided into two stages: from six to fourteen the boy attended the elementary school; from fourteen to eighteen the secondary school; and then for two years he did his military training. On the intellectual and aesthetic side the teaching was confined to writing, simple arithmetic, weights and measures, reading, and music. Trades and crafts were considered unworthy of inclusion in a 'liberal' education, i.e. the education of a 'liber' or free man. Ancient education was designed for the upper classes: in Latin the word for school is 'ludus', 'play', and in Greek 'scholē', 'leisure'.

In school the poets bulked large, as they did at Rome; for the poet was considered, as Aristophanes says, the teacher of the community, or, less crudely, the spiritual interpreter of the state's ideals. In the old-fashioned education portrayed by Aristophanes, boys were taught 'the fine old national songs'. Homer naturally had a special place of honour; to some he was the source of all wisdom; and Niceratus in Xenophon says that his father, wishing him to grow up a good man, made him learn the whole of Homer by heart. In the *Banqueters* of Aristophanes a father tests his son's diligence at school by asking him the meaning of archaic words in Homer. Recitation of passages included acting, and the Greeks, as Juvenal said, were a nation of actors. The emotion produced by acting seemed morally dangerous to Plato.

The secondary school, attended only by the richer class, busied itself with mathematics and rhetoric and more advanced literary studies. The meaning of the poets was discussed, sometimes with considerable sophistry. Grammar and metre are mentioned and, occasionally, art. The commentary on literature gave rise to ethical and political discussions.

University education was catered for by the schools of philosophy like Plato's Academy, and by the wandering Sophists. The latter, coming chiefly from Asia Minor and southern Italy, regarded both teaching and learning as vocational. They taught virtue, 'aretē', that is, they imparted knowledge on special subjects that were supposed to fit a man for a particular place in the state. As opposed to the philosophers, who followed the road to knowledge, they followed only the road to success. They were sceptical of the claim of philosophy to lead men to truth. Their teaching was literary and scientific and, to a large extent, rhetorical. They performed a great social service in supplying knowledge, but they did not always give a true insight into fundamental principles.

This deeper study was left to the philosophers, who were less mobile, less interested in fees. It was they who worked out the principles of knowledge and of research and set up the ideal of the lover of wisdom, the *philo-sophos*, the man who pursues truth because it is good to know. The emphasis of Plato on mathematics and of Aristotle on the natural sciences lit beacons that shone far into the future. Education was regarded as a process that continued throughout life; Aristotle was Plato's student for twenty years by way of preparation for his own studies. 'We must learn', says Seneca, 'as long as we lack knowledge; and that means, as long as we live.'

In the Hellenistic cities we may suppose that education proceeded after the Athenian fashion, but that with the increase of science and literary technique, higher studies were influenced in this direction. It may be, too, that the interest in practical invention affected education. But we have no direct evidence.

At Rome we may regard the early republican period as negligible for intellectual education, though not necessarily for the development of the mind. But by the middle of the third century, and probably earlier, the pupils of the *litterator* (elementary schoolmaster) learned reading, writing, and simple arithmetic; the last with the help of the *abăcus* used by the Greeks—a calculating-board still found in the East and instrumental in the formation of the modern decimal system. Horace comments on the prominence of arithmetic in the schools of the practical Roman. After the second Punic War came the secondary school —that of the *grammaticus*, who read texts with his pupils and made them learn passages by heart, paying careful attention to their pronunciation and enunciation, and adding a commentary (*enarratio*) on grammatical, metrical, historical, philosophical, or scientific points.

We hear from various sources of a more or less regular list of high-school subjects, called ἐγκύκλιος παιδεία on the model of the Hellenistic schools, or *encyclios disciplina* or *artes liberales*, or simply *artes bonae*. Cicero mentions rhetoric, literature, philosophy, music, and mathematics. Varro includes medicine and astronomy. Vitruvius prescribes for architects literature, drawing, geometry, optics, arithmetic, history, philosophy, music, medicine, law, and astronomy—a truly catholic syllabus. Galen's list for medical students of the second century A.D. includes medicine, rhetoric, music, geometry, arithmetic, dialectics, astronomy, literature, and law. Seneca, perhaps because of his quarrel with the Ciceronianism of the contemporary authority, Quintilian, omits rhetoric altogether (Seneca, *Epist.* lxxxviii. 21 ff.). Experimental science was characteristically absent.

We possess specimens of essays and discussions preliminary to the rhetor's school in the *progymnasmata* of the *Rhetores Graeci*, which were to pave the way to a university training in the school of the rhetor—an institution that dates from the first century B.C. Instead of being asked to write an essay, the student was asked to make a speech, either in the form of a *suasoria*, advocating a certain course of action ('I, too, have counselled Sulla to retire from public life', says Juvenal) or a debate (*controversia*). The situations were often highly artificial and under the early empire this artificiality was increased by the cult of the epigram (*sententia*), in which the student was regularly trained. Sometimes the student had to paraphrase or expand a passage of the poets: 'I was given the task', says St. Augustine, 'of speaking on what Juno said in her anger and grief at not being able to keep Aeneas from Italy' (*Confessions*, i. 17). But usually the speech was entirely imaginary, e.g. the words of Menelaus when he saw Troy burning.

As in Greece, special stress was laid on the poets. 'Eagerly pursue the Muses', Theodosius advises his son at the end of the fourth century A.D., 'while your mind is impressionable';[1] and this emphasis is evident from first to last. 'Musae'—from a root that means 'remember'—are the civilizing agents that remind people of memorable things; it is as such that Horace invokes them and as such they appear in the school studies mentioned by Ausonius in the fourth century A.D.

One of the distinguishing marks of Roman education was bilingualism; the Greeks were conscious monoglots.

From Andronicus onward, Greek was taught in the Roman schools; an inscription tells of a boy of twelve who won a prize for Greek given by Domitian in 94 A.D. Indeed, Greek took precedence; we find authorities like Quintilian advocating that a Roman child should begin with Greek, and we know from Petronius and others that this was the regular custom. Pliny the Younger complained that in legal studies students began with the civil suits of the centumviral court, as in schools boys began with Homer, and he comments that in either case they began with what was most difficult (*Epist.* ii. 14). We know that

[1] Claudian, iv. *cons. Honor.*. 396.

the Latin rhetors were forbidden to teach in 92 B.C. For this there may have been a political reason, as some have supposed; but there was also the idea, based on the prestige of Greek letters, that education was mainly a training in Greek. Cicero was dissuaded in his youth from attending the popular Latin lectures of Plotius, on the ground that practice in Greek declamation was better training. Modern pedagogy, however, stresses the importance of beginning with the mother-tongue, with what is natural to the child, otherwise the memory is developed at the expense of thought.

Greek tutors in Roman homes played an important part from the second century B.C., and must have helped effectively in making the Roman of the upper class bilingual. Many a Greek library found its way to Rome in the wake of a conquering general, and among the lower classes Greek words and phrases were disseminated by soldiers returning from the Eastern Mediterranean.

6. SPECIALIZATION AND VOCATIONAL TRAINING

The problem whether to concentrate immediately on a narrow field and become an expert in that, or whether to start with a more general training, agitated educationists in ancient times no less than to-day. Specialization is inevitable; but need you run your course in blinkers? If a wider training is desirable, is it suitable for all types? Should education include the training of the body? How are intellectual studies related to the world of affairs? What is the connexion between education and the trades and professions? Where does the education of girls come in? Many answers were given to these questions. Sparta so concentrated on education for state purposes that her system took on a vocational colour. It did not embrace the trades and professions, but depended with aristocratic self-sufficiency on the agricultural labour of serfs.

Yet in educating girls it was more liberal than brilliantly intellectual Athens. Girls shared all the physical exercises and the musical drill of the boys, striving after physical perfection so as to be worthy mothers of strong men. In the races they were scantily clad in the Doric chiton, and one tradition represents them as competing naked. Hence Plato's conception in the *Republic* of training girls on an equal footing with men. But in the Athenian schools no girls were allowed and women lived secluded in the women's quarters.

In other respects, however, Athens showed far more elasticity than Sparta and it is to her that we owe the conception of a 'liberal' education. The training of the body was linked with the training of the mind, and to be deficient in either was to be uneducated. Moreover, the athlete did not, as is the tendency to-day, train only one set of muscles, but aimed at all-round development and harmony. This 'wholeness' of outlook is evident in intellectual matters too; the educated man sees the significant links between departments of knowledge. 'The detailed sciences', says Socrates, speaking of the Guardians, 'in which they were educated as children, must be brought into the compass of a single survey to show the connexion that exists between them and the nature of real existence.' 'Certainly', replies Glaucon, 'this is the only kind of instruction which will be found to be abiding.' 'Series iuncturaque pollet', wrote Horace: 'it is continuity and connexion that count.' This ideal passes from Plato to all the great humanist educators, and is evident in modern science. It is opposed to that premature specialization which is to-day threatening the whole structure of our culture, and producing learned barbarians who do not know the roots of their own special study.

The Sophists introduced the idea of specialist or vocational training. But the first and greatest of the Sophists, Protagoras, held that a general education was the best education for public life. The general development, however, was towards specialization, and this is well illustrated by the history of rhetorical studies.[1] The smaller men see the immediate object and want quick results. The big men insist on the value of wide interests. Sterility came of efforts to concentrate on the tricks of speech

[1] Cf. Petronius' vigorous protest (*Sat.* i. 1)! 'It is for ever pirates standing in chains on the beach, tyrants writing edicts . . . verbal honey-balls. . . . That is why I think schools educate children to crass stupidity, because they never let them see or hear anything that belongs to the experience of life.'

to the exclusion of insight and knowledge. Isocrates, Cicero, and Quintilian all stressed the importance of a wide and intelligent concern with all the facts of life; not actual knowledge of everything, which is impossible, but an attitude of mind that is interested in the relations of things and sees them in their context.

But was this type of education suitable for all? The *artes liberales* were meant for those of higher social status and for them the 'banausic' arts, trades by which you made money, were disgraceful.

Athenian educators like Plato aimed at a training that would fit the best men for public life. But in this they were hampered by their besetting sin of abstractness and dogmatic schematization, as the course of Athenian imperialism shows. Here the Romans, starting from the soil, show a different outlook. To them philosophy was to be pursued only in so far as it produced better citizens, and Cicero, as we have seen, adapted Greek theory to the needs of the Roman state but could still move among the stars in 'Scipio's Dream'. The Greek had a natural gift for theory: if you asked him to define an animal, he would think out a formula. The Roman would say, 'An animal is, for instance, the dog over there, or that pig across the way'. His native caution warned him against the pitfalls of premature generalization and made him concrete, if limited, in his thinking. Hence he was a good law-maker and a successful organizer, avoiding the Utopias in which Greek imagination was fertile. And for those reasons his education was closely related to actual life. When Seneca wrote in the later days of rhetoric 'non vitae, sed scholae discimus', it was a reproach and a reminder of a falling away from Roman practice.

Greek athletics were never popular among the Romans, to whom the sight of people lounging about in the *gymnasia* and *palaestrae* seemed strange. The regular exercises in the Campus Martius after lunch to some extent took the place of Greek athletics. Universal military training did not take up most of life as at Sparta, or even two years as at Athens. Nevertheless, closeness to the soil, and life in the open, made the Romans for the most part as physically fit as Spartans or Athenians of the best period; while the Romans of the Republic and the early Empire tended to look down on the contemporary Greeks as weaklings.

Within the sphere of *artes liberales* the problem of specialization, particularly in rhetoric, ran its course, as we have indicated. The Hellenistic centres of learning revealed an interest in special studies side by side with a desire to epitomize all knowledge. This encyclopædic tendency fell in with the predilections of Roman 'gravitas', and Varro, Verrius Flaccus, Pliny the Elder, the codifiers of the law, Celsus, the medical writer, and many others, testify to the Roman liking for solid facts organized and set in order. Roman industry in assimilating facts is symbolized by the schoolboy setting out before dawn with his sooty lantern.

Training for the professions had in Greece been a matter of apprenticeship: it was so that Hippocrates taught his pupils and the method persisted into the Roman Empire. But the Romans organized professional training, drawing, probably, on Hellenistic practice. State-paid doctors—not uncommon in Greek inscriptions[1]—are frequently mentioned with teachers in the Theodosian Code, and we are told that both classes were given exemption from military service and public burdens 'so that they should have leisure to train many pupils in the liberal studies and in their special sciences'. Similarly Vitruvius follows Cicero in trying to train men both in general culture and in specialist knowledge. Like Cicero he believed that all the departments of knowledge were linked together, and he held that every science fell into two parts: practice (*opus*) and theory (*ratiocinatio*), of which the former was confined to specialists, while the latter was common to all men of education; and this 'holistic' outlook was probably general among professional men. They demanded first a liberal and synoptic training, and to this they added the skill of the specialist.   It is questionable whether in departing from this system we have done our professions much good.

Architecture, medicine, teaching, and, probably, land-surveying (the science of the *agrimensores*), though honourable, were

---

[1] And cf. Democedes in Herodotus (iii. 131), to whom the Aeginetans paid a talent 'to be their public physician', for a year. In the next the Athenians hired him for 100 minae and in the next, Polycrates of Samos for two talents.

regarded as inferior to the liberal professions, such as those of the philosopher, the orator, or the lawyer. 'But', says Cicero, voicing a typical Roman sentiment, 'of all the occupations that bring in money' (for these are to that extent 'illiberal') 'none is better than agriculture . . . none more worthy of a free man.' Yet there were no scientific schools of agriculture and it was left for Columella in the first century A.D. to put forward a vigorous plea for agricultural training.

As for the 'liberal' profession of the law, we know from Justinian's preface to the *Digest* that it was apt to be haphazard. The emperor is at pains to reform it, pointing out that the law was the avenue to public office. Lecturing lawyers (*antecessores*) instructed legal aspirants throughout the empire and the course in Justinian's time lasted five years.

7. THE TRAINING OF THE IMAGINATION

We realize more than ever to-day the need for training the imagination. But in ancient times, as now, there was little conscious education in this direction. We may recognize at least two kinds of imagination. There is the imagination of the poet, whose fancy 'bodies forth the shapes of things unknown', and there is the imagination of the ruler and administrator, who has to understand not only facts but feelings and sentiments in people who are different from himself.

In regard to the former kind, Spartan imagination was early crushed by the militarization attributed to Lycurgus; and rigid conformity to pattern, coupled with a policy of isolation, prevented the growth of the second type.

At Athens the poetical imagination, nourished in the soil of Ionian sensibility, bloomed to a brilliant fruition in mythology, art, and literature. But, ethically, it was not an unmixed blessing, and in the sphere of politics it proved a snare, dazzling the Athenians with visions of Sicilian conquest and leaving them at the mercy of fanciful leaders. Lacking the second type of imagination, Athens in the fifth and fourth centuries developed the rigid generalization that the world was divided into Greeks and barbarians, and that against the barbarians there was by the ordinance of Nature a truceless war. Similar generalizations in regard to the members of her empire caused harshness and misunderstanding; and this twice in succession lay at the root of her failure in the imperial task.

The Romans were at first utterly lacking in the poetical type of imagination, but they developed it under Greek and Italian influence. Of the other type they showed signs by the fourth century B.C., when they respected the autonomy of conquered nations and gave them a hope of sharing in the government, whereas Athens normally had never admitted even the Greeks of her empire to her citizenship during the first empire. In politics Rome showed something of the elasticity that the Ionians showed in art and philosophy, and she never consistently thought of non-Romans as a foreign and hostile group. The 'praetor peregrinus' at Rome attended to the cases in which foreigners were involved and the *ius gentium* contained the conception of international law. 'It is our duty', says Cicero, 'to cultivate, protect, and maintain the common bonds of union and fellowship subsisting between all members of the human race.'

In this conception, and in her ability to understand men of different language, customs, and sentiment, Rome was greatly helped by her bilingual education. The Greeks were monoglots, and nothing so promotes insularity as the inability to use a foreign language, which is the key to a host of thoughts and feelings that otherwise seem foolish or inexplicable.

This was one reason why Rome succeeded so largely in her organization of an empire that was of enormous value in preserving the cultural tradition of Europe. whereas Sparta and Athens were unsuccessful. The training of imagination in the citizen was all-important; but he was trained by temperament and circumstances and not by any conscious effort.

It may be added that the Hellenistic Greeks carried on the tradition of Athens in regard to poetical imagination, though limited by bookishness, to the greater glory of mankind, and in the political sphere became less insular through contact with many nations in cities like Alexandria; they discarded, to a large extent, the idea that the world was divided into Greeks and hostile or inferior barbarians; but in their violent seditions they showed that they lacked the basis for the administrator's imagination, the Roman quality of 'gravitas'.

8. EDUCATIONAL IDEALS

The Spartans and the early Romans were intent on education after a pattern of the here and now; the customs of their ancestors had saved the state in the past and the only safety for the future was to inculcate those customs in the growing generation. Reality was found in serving the family and the state, and to protect them one had to keep on good terms with supra-sensual powers by offering traditional sacrifices and prayers.

For Plato and for the Christians the emphasis was different; the pattern was laid up in heaven and the concern of man was to make himself 'as like to God as possible', or, as Aristotle put it, 'to practise immortality'; and a tendency grew up, both in Neoplatonic and in Christian circles, to dispise the body and to be ashamed of it.

We have thus two extreme aims: the one materialistic, stressing objective and concrete facts, with certain safeguards against 'spiritual' powers; the other idealistic, emphasizing the reality of the supra-sensual, tending to abstractions pitched too high for ordinary life.

Between these two poles it was the object of Greek and Roman education in its best periods to effect a harmony. If life was to be seen steadily and as a whole, there must somehow emerge a reconciliation between these two aims; a hard task, in which the ancients, like ourselves, often failed. But the ideal, at any rate, remained, whereas to-day it is openly abandoned in many quarters.

It is in this balance between the things of the earth and the things of heaven that Cicero's 'humanitas' largely consisted; and only so was the Greek ideal of rhythm in the soul and the conception of the *kalos kai agathos*, the man who combined physical and social fitness with moral goodness, to be attained.

The larger minds aim at an intelligent appreciation of life and add thereto the practical and vocational details; the smaller minds seek a short-cut by aiming only at the immediate skill that brings in quick returns. Disinterested pursuit of truth makes way for nicely calculated technical gains. Yet it was the Greek ideal of the single-minded search for truth that inspired students like Faraday or Madame Curie, from whom flow modern electrical comforts and radium. They sought the Kingdom of Truth and the other things were added unto them. And it is in this spirit that Lessing wrote in his *Laocoön*: 'The ultimate aim of the sciences is truth. Truth is necessary to the soul, and in the satisfaction of this essential need it is tyranny to apply even the smallest compulsion.'

'Humanitas' implies elasticity, provision for growth, as against an iron rigidity. It was noted by later Greeks that the Spartans, in spite of their much-admired efficiency, produced many good soldiers but few great leaders. Many writers have commented on their lack of adaptability, amply illustrated during their short period of hegemony. Their methods were mechanical. 'While they attended to their laborious drill', says Aristotle (*Polit.* iv. 4), 'they were superior to all others, but now they are beaten by all others both in war and gymnastics; for their superiority depended not on their method of training the youths, but on the fact that they trained them when others did not.'

Implied in the ideal of 'humanitas' is the choice between regarding man as a machine, or regarding him as a creature filled with the uneven tremor of life and capable of rising to great heights or sinking to great depths. When inner life is strong and abundant and outward circumstances propitious—as in the fifth-century Athens or the Augustan Age—men are given a chance to grow and produce the things that we hold most precious in our cultured heritage. When the inner life burns low and circumstances are oppressive, man turns, as he does to-day, to the low conception that safety and happiness can be attained only by organizing men as if they were machines and producing a mechanical efficiency.

Greek and Roman education lapsed from 'wholeness' at various times in being excessively literary to the detriment of natural and social science, in disregarding the content of literature, in despising the technical arts, in neglecting women and slaves—though it must be remembered that at Rome slaves were often the educators and rose, as freedmen, to high posts. To-day our danger is that we are producing a lopsided society that measures progress only in terms of technical development. That, too, is a sin against 'humanitas'.

Finally, 'humanitas', we have seen, implies a view of a world whose parts are interrelated, and is opposed to the deification of racial or national sentiment at the expense of others. Ionian scientists like Heracleitus seem to have glimpsed the conception of the unity of mankind.[1] Alexander tried to apply it. The Roman Empire represents our nearest approach to it in a world as yet undisturbed by modern nationalism. Not least important in the training of the Roman youth was the idea of the right of different races to their own customs, languages, and sentiments, and the enrichment that could come from a proper understanding of these; the idea that what is different in other people is not to be derided or hated, but may hold a potential contribution to the Whole.

9. GREEK SCHOLARSHIP

'Peisistratus the tyrant is said to have founded the first library of the liberal arts at Athens. The Athenians then worked to increase the collection, bestowing on it greater zeal and care.'

So Aulus Gellius (vi. 17), writing in the second century A.D., when it was hard to prove things that happened in the sixth century B.C. Though it is believed by some scholars that the traditional story according to which Peisistratus had 'gathered together' the works of Homer at Athens really referred to the concentration of the book trade in that city, and Polycrates is said to have collected books at Samos in the sixth century and Nicocrates of Cyprus earlier still, it may be doubted whether books were at all common in Greece until the age of Pericles. But collections of books were necessarily found in schools, and Alexis, the fourth-century comic poet, is quoted by Athenaeus as giving a fairly extensive list. Alcibiades is reported to have beaten a schoolmaster because he did not possess a copy of

---

[1] *Cf.* the saying of Heracleitus: 'All human laws come from one divine source' (Diels, *Vorsokratiker*, i. 114).

Homer. Private collections were rarer; Euripides was satirized for possessing a private library.

Xenophon tells us (*Mem.* iv. 2) that Euthydemus, the friend of Socrates, owned a good library of the poets and Sophists, including many works on medicine, architecture, geometry, and astronomy. Works on specialist subjects, such as the Sophists dealt with, were evidently common. Alcidamas, the fourth-century Sophist, pictures orators sitting round at writing-tables with model passages open in front of them, as material for their speeches (*On Sophists*, iv.). During the fourth century an extensive export trade in books seems to have developed. When the remnant of Xenophon's Ten Thousand arrived at Salmydessus, on the Black Sea, they found among the wrecks of ships that had travelled thither 'many books copied out, such as seamen convey in wooden boxes' (*Anab.* VII. v. 14).

From a passage in Plato's *Apology* (26 D) it appears that books like those of Anaxagoras could be procured for a drachma at most, which suggests that the ordinary price of books was not high.

The relation between teacher and pupil in the fifth-century Athens had largely been a personal one and the instruction was given by word of mouth. Socrates read the poets but never wrote anything himself. On the whole, discussion and meditation bulked larger than the collecting and reading of books.

It was not until Alexander had thrust spear-heads of Hellenism into the East, and the 'common speech' had spread over the Eastern Mediterranean and Egypt, that we find the figure of the scholar and the bibliophile. The production of papyrus, and afterwards parchment, was organized by Hellenistic Greeks, and books were produced and collected on a hitherto unknown scale. The passion of book-collecting appears, and Apellicon of Teos, who found part of Aristotle's library hidden in a cellar, stole what he could not buy. Scholarship became fashionable. Men from the remote parts of the Euphrates came to compete for literary fame at Alexandria; writers enjoyed a degree of power and of royal favour that has hardly ever been their lot since. We know the names of more than 1100 Hellenistic writers, 'litterati' of many kinds, prone to fierce literary quarrels, but for the most part they are the names of shadows, and their battle a battle of the shades.

The means for founding public libraries had hitherto, with a few exceptions, been lacking; now they grew apace. Antioch and Pergamum, Rhodes and Smyrna established state libraries; but the greatest and most famous was the library at Alexandria (containing, if we may trust Aulus Gellius, some 700,000 rolls), founded by Ptolemy I in the third century B.C. and arranged by Ptolemy II, who founded a supplementary library not far away. Equally important was the foundation of the Museum by Ptolemy I, a sort of research university, housing an association of the friends of the Muses. The library was destroyed neither by Caesar nor by the Arabs, as is often believed. What Caesar burnt was probably a stack of rolls on the quay, for which Antony is said to have given Cleopatra 200,000 rolls from the library of Pergamum in compensation. It was Aurelian in A.D. 273 who broke up and partly destroyed the library during his attack on Alexandria.

Athens remained the centre of philosophy, but Alexandria carried on the spirit of Aristotle and organized vast tracts of knowledge. She acquired Athenian treasures like autograph copies of the Attic tragedians and manuscripts of Homer. The coveted post of librarian, equivalent to the headship of a great modern university, was held by men from various parts of the civilized world—Zenodotus of Ephesus, Apollonius, who had been granted the citizenship of Rhodes, Eratosthenes and the great Callimachus of Cyrene, Aristophanes of Byzantium and Aristarchus of Samothrace. Books in other languages, like the Old Testament, were translated. Zenodotus invented textual criticism, Aristophanes conferred on written Greek the doubtful boon of accents. The Alexandrians set Greek literature in order, attending to the text and arranging it in books. Lexicography was founded and literary criticism, commentaries abounded, knowledge was systematized. The enormous catalogue of the whole library made by Callimachus and supplemented by Aristophanes has been lost. It was called 'Pinakes', probably from the tablets affixed to the various presses in which the rolls were kept. The Greek work *bibliothēkē* suggests that chests were used at first in which the rolls stood upright; but in the larger libraries, like that of Philodemus found at Herculaneum, they lay horizontally on shelves.

10. LATIN SCHOLARSHIP

Though literacy came early in Rome, as the first stone inscription ($\pm$ 500 B.C.) in the Forum Romanum shows, books must have been scarce before the middle of the third century B.C. Possibly Andronicus started the book trade at Rome when he opened his school and translated the *Odyssey*. Once the search for knowledge had begun it grew apace, and private collections of books were numerous. Aemilius Paullus in 167 B.C. transported the library of the Macedonian king Perseus. In 82 B.C. Sulla brought to Rome the library of Apellicon, the discoverer of Aristotle's manuscripts, and there they were edited by Tyrannion, who furnished copies to Andronicus of Rhodes for his edition of the philosopher. This Tyrannion, who studied at Rhodes under Dionysius Thrax, author of the first Greek grammar, was taken prisoner by Lucullus and brought to Rome in 72 B.C. There he obtained his freedom and set up as a teacher. He was employed by Sulla and by Cicero to arrange their libraries. He became a rich man and an ardent collector of books; Suidas states that his library contained 30,000 rolls.

Cicero's letters bear ample testimony (*ad Attic.* i. 7, 10; iv. 4; *Q.F.* iii. 4) to their author's enthusiasm for books. Cicero's friend Atticus had a large staff of copyists (*librarii*) and shorthand writers (*notarii*) who were constantly transcribing books, there being no law of copyright; hence the necessity for literary patrons.

The word 'librarius' meant several things: a transcriber of manuscripts; a teacher of book-copying, as distinct from a shorthand or ordinary cursive script; a librarian—*servus a bibliotheca*; and a bookseller, who copied out books and sold them. In front of bookshops (*tabernae litterariae, librariae*) stood pillars (*pilae, columnae*) which advertised their suspended literary ware for purchasers to see. Aulus Gellius tells how he sat in a book-shop in Rome—a common practice, to judge by his writings—looking at a copy of the annalist Fabius Pictor (v. 4). *Nulla taberna meos habeat, neque pila libellos,* is Horace's wish (*Sat.* i. 4, 71). The sale of books took place chiefly in the Potter's Field, Argiletum, near the Forum Romanum, the Vicus Sandalius, and a quarter or street called by Aulus Gellius the Sigillaria, where little images were sold (ii. 3; v. 4). Under Augustus the most famous bookshop was that of the Sosii; under Nero, that of Dorus; under Domitian, that of Tryphon. The cost of books does not seem to have been high; Martial implies that a cheap roll of his poems (probably equivalent to one book) could be acquired for six or ten sestertii—one to two shillings (i. 66); and elsewhere mentions a superior edition 'smoothed with pumice and smart with purple' for five denarii—about three shillings (i. 117).

The first public library at Rome was instituted by Asinius Pollio, one of the most brilliant and versatile of the Augustans (Plin. *N.H.* vii. 30); but he was first only because of the premature death of Julius Caesar who projected a large Greek and Latin library under the superintendence of Varro (Suet. *Jul.* xliv.). Augustus established a public library for Greek and Latin books in the Temple of Apollo on the Palatine, referred to in one of Horace's Odes (i. 31). It was situated in the vicinity of what is now pointed out as the house of Livia on the Palatine. Pliny the Younger speaks of a library that he founded for his fellow-townsmen of Comum (i. 8). Trajan built a famous public library next to the Basilica Ulpia and the Forum that bears his name, with one hall for Latin and another for Greek books. 'One of these halls has very recently been excavated and shows the typical disposition of an ancient library—the podium or narrow platform, three steps above the floor, to support the bookcases in their niches, while a row of columns divided these wallspaces into alcoves. Busts of famous authors must be presumed, and other decorations in keeping with the stateliness of Trajan's Forum.'[1]

Provincial libraries were built on a scale unknown in Greece. To the time of Trajan belongs the library at Ephesus, a rectangular hall that must have been impressive, raised on a podium in Italian fashion, with columns supporting a gallery that contained books, while other books were kept in niches behind the

[1] Moore, *The Roman's World* (1936), p. 246.

columns and stored in adjoining rooms. Excavation has revealed the famous library of Pergamum and that of Hadrian at Athens, close to which, during the recent exploration of the agora, there came to light another library of private foundation from the time of Trajan. The library at Timgad (Thamugadi) in North Africa, occupied some eighty-one feet square. The forecourt was surrounded by a colonnade of white limestone, for the most part restored by modern archæologists. Short flights of steps led up to the colonnade, on each side of which was a large room. The central door of the colonnade gave entrance to a large semicircular and domed hall adorned by twelve columns of white marble behind which were the book-cases. The whole of the interior was decorated with white marble and coloured panels. As at Ephesus, there was a special niche for a statue, probably of Athena. An inscription tells that the library was founded by one Rogatinus, who left 400,000 sestertii for the purpose, a sum to be increased later by his heirs.

Most of the great Thermae, like those of Trajan and Caracalla at Rome, included reading-rooms and libraries. The habit of reading for oneself, as opposed to the aristocratic custom of being read to, must have increased considerably.[1] Hadrian founded at Rome an Athenaeum, where authors read or recited their works, and provincial towns followed his example.

The suppression of undesired books was neither frequent nor efficient. The mob of fanatics that stormed the Serapeum and its library at Alexandria in A.D. 394 probably did make the books their primary objective. The Senate endeavoured to destroy the *Annals* of Cremutius Cordus and Nero the Notebooks of Fabricius Veiento—ineffectually, as usual; for the result was that the former was secretly circulated, while the other acquired an undeserved reputation. Eusebius says that Diocletian decreed the destruction of the Christian Scriptures (*Hist. Eccles.* vii. 2). A subtler circumstance that militated against the survival of books

[1] There is an interesting if incomplete description of a private library in Sidonius Apollinaris (*Epist.* ii. 9). We gather that the walls were lined with high cases (*armaria*), as in the small library discovered at Herculaneum, with shelves on which rolls lay horizontally and higher shelves for *codices*. There were also desks (*plutei*) on which books could be laid when in use.

was the Atticizing movement that took heavy toll of Hellenistic and popular literature, which was considered degenerate and unworthy of preservation in so far as it departed from the Attic standard. Byzantium was infected with the same rigid standard, and in many cases the survival of books was determined by their conforming to that standard and by being used in schools.

X

Greek and Roman Religion

I. GENERAL CHARACTERISTICS

THE WORD 'religio' (for which there is no exact counterpart in Greek) meant originally 'paying regard' to such unseen powers as might influence mankind for good or ill. Religion in this broad sense is an attribute of every human society, and it was almost universally observed in the world of Greece and Rome.

In the fifth century B.C. some Greek Sophists pointed out that religious beliefs are not capable of logical demonstration (p. 200). In the third century a Greek poet named Euhemerus virtually denied the reality of the gods by asserting that all of them were dead men arbitrarily deified. At the same time the Epicurean philosophers openly attacked religion, because in their opinion it was a source of fear and unhappiness among mankind, and although they did not formally repudiate the existence of gods, they denied their intervention in human affairs. But these exceptions merely emphasize the rule that the Greeks and Romans in general were filled with a constant consciousness of dependence on the supernatural element in life. St. Paul found the Athenians 'a most god-fearing people', and the same was said of the Romans by the Greek historian Polybius. Similarly Sallust speaks of the Romans as 'religiosissimi mortales', and Livy makes an old Roman worthy say: 'there is no place in our city that is not filled with religious associations and the presence of the gods'. Horace said to his countrymen: 'it is because you bow before the gods that you are rulers over men'.

The pervasiveness of this religious feeling is plentifully attested in Greek and Roman literature, as also in countless votive inscriptions and dedications. Greek and Roman authors continually imply and frequently emphasize the rule of the gods over mankind. Among the philosophers even the Epicureans admitted the existence of the gods, and the Stoics, for all their insistence on human strength and wisdom, acknowledged an overriding control by Providence. Socrates, the remorseless logician, was anxious before he died about a cock that he owed to Asclepius. Men of science worked out their problems on a strictly rational plane, but (with the exception of the Atomists) they did not assume a purely material or mechanical view of the universe: the 'conflict between science and religion' was not opened in ancient times. Commanders in the field consulted the omens before making an important move, and gave thanks for victory by building new temples or making special offerings. Greek political leaders sometimes referred their problems to an oracle for solution; the outstanding personages in Roman history, Scipio Africanus, Sulla, Caesar, Augustus, all professed, with greater or less insistence, their belief in a divine protector.

Every Greek and Italian city had its patron gods and a highly organized apparatus of state worship. Every public or private club was in outward form at least a religious society, and not a few of them had the cult of some deity as their main object. Every family had its own religious observances: Greek houses commonly contained an altar of Hestia (the goddess of the hearth) and Roman dwellings a shrine of the Lares (protectors of the homestead), and of the Penates (gods of the storeroom). While particular cults might wax and wane, the substitute for one religion was another religion. Under the Roman emperors scepticism almost died out, and the meticulous devoutness of Plutarch was typical of his age.

In the belief of the Greeks and Romans the supreme powers that intervened in the affairs of men were unlimited in number. In addition to the major gods, with a wide range of action, they paid deference to countless minor godheads who were restricted to particular homesteads of fields or woods or springs, and various roving goblins and ghosts. They worshipped some dead men, and some living ones, and even included abstractions in their list of divinities. When the Romans erected a temple to Concord (in a critical phase of the Conflict of the Orders), and of Good Counsel (during the Second Punic War), they were not merely commemorating an important occasion, but were investing a salutary element in their experience with a divine personality.[1]

The Greeks and Romans further shared the belief of many early peoples, that all sorts of objects, though not in themselves sources of supernatural power, might become charged with such power, and serve as the media by which it was brought to bear upon mankind. 'Sacredness' was attributed by them to various inanimate objects. For this reason amulets were commonly worn; fetish-stones were reverently preserved (e.g. the so-called 'Navel of the Earth' at Delphi); altars were not only held to be sacred, but to communicate their potency to those (e.g. suppliants) who touched them. A fortiori, anything endowed with the mysterious quality of life might be regarded as a carrier of divine power. The 'Tree of Life' grew in the Israelite Garden of Eden, and the Persian Garden of Yima, and in Minoan Crete. In Greece worshippers wore garlands and carried branches of olive, whose fertilizing power was intensified by attachments of wool and fruits. Skins of animals were worn as a means of sharing their virtue, as when Heracles clothed himself in the pelt of the Nemean lion, and Mark Antony exhibited himself in a goatskin at the festival of the Lupercalia. Among members of the human race priests were naturally regarded as sacred; but sanctity might also attach to other important personages, such as kings, and the tribunes of the plebs at Rome.

The motives that underlay the religion of the Greeks and Romans were various and to some extent contradictory. According to Lucretius 'it was fear that first fashioned the gods', and this dictum is borne out by many features of Greek and Roman worship. Belief in harmful spirits, which is prevalent among primitive peoples, persisted among the peasantry of Greece and Italy, whose cults were partly 'apotropaic', i.e. calculated to ward off enmity rather than to solicit friendship. Survivals of this atmosphere of fear were also to be found in the state cults. Though human sacrifices were not a usual feature of Greek and Roman religion, they lingered on in odd corners of Greece until the second century A.D., and during the Second Punic War the

[1] These worships, as one would expect in Roman religion, originated in actual experience, not in preconceived abstractions.

Romans were rattled into making similar blood-offerings. In Italy it remained customary to veil the head before invoking a deity. In Greece the view was long upheld by educated men (e.g. by Herodotus, in whom this theme is recurrent) that the gods were jealous of human prosperity, even when this condition was not associated with specific wrongdoing. Similarly it was in order to avert the envy of the gods that when a triumphant general drove to the Capitol, a slave whispered in his ear reminders that he was but a mortal, and that insulting or even obscene ditties from his soldiers were allowed to temper the popular applause.

But among both peoples the view was prevalent that the gods were essentially reasonable, and that if men acquitted themselves of their obligations to them they would enjoy divine favour, or at least escape molestation. The extreme precision and punctiliousness of Roman worship were based on this assumption: religious duties must be discharged as scrupulously as a political compact or a commercial deal, but in return the deity would not fail to honour its reciprocal engagements. The Romans therefore made their sacrifices in a spirit of *pietas*, i.e. of cheerful acceptance of an obligation.

Nay more, in Greece the belief was widely held, even in early times, that the gods were kindly rather than malicious or vindictive. When he invoked a god, a Greek usually stood erect, with unveiled head and hands uplifted, as if to receive a gift, and addressed the deity in words like 'dear Zeus', 'dear Apollo'. The gods were endowed by Greek artists not only with beautiful figures, but with serene or compassionate expressions. At Rome, to the end of the republican period, the conception prevailed that the gods were strictly and merely just; but in the days of the emperors the influence of Greek religion, and also of certain Oriental worships, made itself felt, and the belief gained ground that the gods were prone to help rather than to hinder.

In general, the Greeks and Romans solicited the gods for positive gifts, increase of crops and flocks, victory over enemies, recovery from illness, wise advice on the difficult problems of life. They did not always attribute to the individual deities any sharply defined and unvarying assortment of functions. The

21

provinces of the various gods overlapped at many points, and the field of activities of any particular god often defies exact demarcation. It is therefore misleading to speak bluntly of Zeus and Jupiter as 'sky-gods', and so forth. For the present purpose it is enough to remember that between them the gods covered the whole range of activities by which human life may be influenced.

The ritual by which they sought to win the divine favour was exceedingly varied in detail, for each sanctuary would have its own 'lex sacra' or ceremonial code; but it possessed certain general characteristics. In accordance with the usual custom of early religions, the Greeks and Romans not merely held certain objects sacred, but drew a sharp line between them and what was profane. The place of the god was fenced in and called *temenos, templum,* from *temno,* 'I cut': the Roman *templum* was originally the space marked out and thus cut off from the profane. Altars were not only store-houses of divine power, but served to keep the sacrifice above and away from the common earth. Votive offerings, after their purpose had been fulfilled, were broken up to prevent their returning from the sacred to the profane sphere—hence the surviving heaps of debris. A man who would be in touch with the divine must first undergo a ritual purification from mundane contacts. In particular, a person infected with blood-guilt (whether by murder or accidental homicide) must undergo a ritual cleansing before he could commune again with gods or men. In addition, certain sanctuaries were fenced in with special taboos: they gave no admission to women, or imposed a preliminary period of fasting or a particular mode of attire. Other taboos set a ban on paring the finger-nails during a sacrifice, on putting a ladle across the mixing-bowl, on killing a louse in the sacred precincts on a festival day.

Among the means of securing divine intervention, the primitive device of compelling it by magical actions or incantations was not uncommon in the earlier stages of Greek and Roman religion; many fossilized forms of these remained embedded in the ritual of later periods; and the number of magical papyri that survives from the time of the Roman emperors indicates that witchcraft was again coming into vogue. Yet in general, magical rites played but a minor part in Greek and Roman worship. The usual manner of invoking the gods was by prayer and sacrifice. The sacrifice would consist of a libation of milk or wine, of a cake or an animal immolated as a burnt-offering: it was intended partly as a gift, partly as a means of communion with the deity in a common meal. The advice of the gods was elicited by means of dreams, omens, and oracles.

The place of worship might be any 'templum' or consecrated spot, and an altar was the only essential furniture to a sacrifice. But private houses often had a small shrine for their domestic deities, and it soon became the general custom to house the state gods in temples and to represent them by cult-images. In private dwellings the officiator was usually the paterfamilias; the public worship was mostly conducted *ex officio* by kings or magistrates. In addition, specialists in seercraft, who professed to interpret the will of the gods by intuition or special training, received state appointments or exercised their art for a fee. The ritual of particular temples would naturally be in the keeping of the incumbent priest; but some cities had evolved a general 'ius divinum', of which either a particular family, or a special board of officials, such as the *pontifices* at Rome, would be the repositories. But neither Greece nor Rome knew a clerical order invested with special duties and privileges as a class.

Greek and Roman religion experienced a continuous development which in some cases amounted to a transformation. Like all religions, it tended to be conservative. Its ritual as a rule was firmly fixed; the myths attaching to particular sanctuaries or ceremonies were often embodied in an authorized version which was passed on by oral instruction. A person who openly denied the existence of the state gods was liable to prosecution. The physicist Anaxagoras found it expedient to retire from Athens after asserting that the sun was not a god, but a huge incandescent stone; the Jews and Christians were censured and in some cases persecuted for their supposed 'atheism' (p. 345). Similarly it was a punishable offence to introduce new cults into a city without authorization, because these might disturb the existing cycle of worships: it was one of the charges on which Socrates was put to death at Athens, that he 'introduced new gods'. The Roman emperors forcibly suppressed Druidism in Gaul and Britain, and the cult of Moloch in North Africa, in order to put an end to the human sacrifices which these religions practised. Nevertheless tolerance was the general rule of the Greek and Roman world. Like any polytheistic society, it never presumed to assert that other peoples' gods were 'false' while its own were 'true'; it attached no peculiar sanctity to its own religious opinions and instigated no heresy-hunts. But freedom of thought in religious matters naturally brought with it a development of religious beliefs, and the maturing of Greek and Roman civilization entailed a corresponding change in the character of Greek and Roman worship.

2. GREEK RELIGION

Early Greek religion contained a 'Minoan' and a 'Nordic' element. The former is chiefly known to us from the excavations at Cnossus, and the latter through the Homeric poems. The Minoan pantheon contained a small number of major deities who were conceived in human shape. We may distinguish three goddesses: a warrior-goddess, an earth-goddess, and a Tamer of Wild Animals; and a young male god, standing in a subordinate position to the Lady of Wild Animals (who appears to have been the supreme Minoan deity). Among the major Minoan deities the female element was plainly preponderant. From a recently discovered shrine above a royal tomb we may infer that departed kings also received worship, and there is abundant evidence of an extensive Minoan 'underworld' of demons and goblins. Sacred trees and animals were associated with the deities: snakes twined about the earth-goddess, lions or other jungle beasts were held (often in heraldically opposed couples) by the Lady of Wild Animals. Minoan ritual appears to have been comparatively simple. Though the gods were figured in small statuettes, they had no cult-images, and instead of temples, they had house-chapels dedicated to them, while the demons received their offerings in the caves of the mountainsides. The ritual was largely apotropaic, and the Greek legend of the Minotaur, who devoured men in the labyrinth of Cnossus, has been taken as evidence of human sacrifices to a bull-headed demon. The principal rites were seemingly conducted by the king in person, and there is no evidence of a special class of priests.

The Minoan religion was no doubt indigenous in its main features. But the Lady of Wild Animals and her male attendant have parallels in Asia Minor and may have been imported from there; and many details of the Minoan ceremonial were plainly borrowed from Egypt. The prominence of animals in the cults, the horns on the altars, the 'sistrum' or sacred rattle, are characteristics of Egyptian worship. The symbol of the double axe, which is so ubiquitous at Cnossus and Phaestus that it has been compared with the Crescent of Islam and the Cross of Christendom, is perhaps a derivative from Egypt, though it also has counterparts in Asia Minor.

The gods of the Homeric poems are generally known as the 'Olympians', because the most important of them were imagined as dwelling on the cloud-capped peak of Mount Olympus in Thessaly. But from their distant home they frequently visited the haunts of men, and indeed they were themselves 'men writ large'—undying and more powerful, but of like shape and mind. They were not immune from human foibles, for they intrigued and indulged in amours, they lost their tempers and even fought one another; but they also showed loyalty and compassion, and admiration for the human virtues. The male gods predominated in the Homeric pantheon, and Zeus was figuratively the 'father' of the other deities, i.e. he exercised the authority of a paterfamilias over them. The Homeric religion was not haunted by ghosts and demons; it seems to have been unacquainted with the worship of dead men, and it took little account of sacred trees and animals.

In the Homeric ritual temples and cult-images have begun to make their appearance. The taking of omens (mostly from the flight of birds, and the appearance of the entrails of sacrificial animals) was common, and oracles were consulted on occasion. Human sacrifices were unknown, and the general attitude of the worshipper was one of trust rather than of fear. The performance of the rites was mainly in the hands of the kings and chiefs, but these often had recourse to professional seers for consultation.

The Minoan religion was typical in several ways of an early agricultural community. Fear of the uncanny earth-spirits, worship at graves, and special regard for the female, i.e. the reproductive element, were marks of close attachment to the soil and direct dependence on its produce. The Homeric religion retained vestiges of a nomadic form of life, especially in its unconcern with grave-worship. But its main characteristic was that it reflected the outlook of an aristocratic class which lived in care-free style and fashioned the gods in its own image, because it considered itself not far removed from them. We may therefore speak of a stratification of religion in Greece at the end of the prehistoric period: the Homeric cults were those of the immigrant ruling class, the Minoan worship was that of the earlier and now subordinate population.

The Minoan religion survived the Nordic invasions. The continuity of worship from Minoan to historic times is attested by the *Theogony* of Hesiod, in which many non-Homeric deities are enumerated, and by the finds at various Greek sanctuaries, where an unbroken series of sacrificial vessels or of votive offerings has been recovered: such evidence is forthcoming from the cave of Dicte in Crete, from Delphi, from Eleusis and Acharnae in Attica, and from other sites. To some extent the Minoan cults were taken over by the northern immigrants: it is possible that some of the major deities in the Olympic pantheon, such as Athena, were borrowed from the indigenous population, and not unlikely that the mythology which was current among the Greeks in historic times contained elements from the older religion. But the distinctive features of their worship were derived for the most part from the Homeric religion. While it is not strictly true that Homer 'made' the gods of Greece, his influence was so great, that the cults which figure most prominently in Greek art and literature are mostly of the Homeric type.

Even after the fusion of the older and younger strata of the Greek population, the Greek cults showed great diversity. In religion as in other matters each Greek city was inclined to go its own way and jealously maintained its local worships. But the city-worships had certain features in common, and these on the whole exhibit what was most distinctive in Greek religion. Each

Greek town instituted official worships of a considerable number of deities, but among these a few (perhaps half a dozen) stood out as of higher importance, and most cities paid particular honour to one god whom they regarded as their special patron. At Athens the paramount deity was Athena; Poseidon held a similar position at Corinth, Apollo at Miletus, and so on. The major deities were usually selected from the 'Olympian' circle; but a god whom Homer scarcely noticed, Dionysus, gained a high position in many Greek cities. Contrary to Homeric usage, Greek towns also offered worship to distinguished mortals after their decease; Greek colonies invariably instituted a cult of their 'oecist' or founder, and other towns, strangely enough, paid similar homage to Homeric personalities such as Agamemnon, Menelaus, and Helen. All these were, strictly speaking, worshipped as 'heroes', and the forms of their cult differed somewhat from that of the gods, but the distinction between the two classes was not sharply drawn. Apotropaic rites to fearsome deities played but a small part in the city-state religions; so far as they survived in historic Greece, they were mostly in the hands of private worshippers.

The city-gods were, with rare exceptions, envisaged in human shape, and in the mythologies which set forth their history and their personality they played a part not unlike that of the Homeric gods, though their dignity at least was usually safeguarded. In the seventh and sixth centuries, if not before, they were furnished with cult-statues and temples.

The ritual of the state gods was carefully ordered—the primary object for which the cities kept calendars was to ensure the punctual observance of the prescribed festivities—and it soon reached a far higher degree of elaboration than in the Homeric religion. In addition to prayer and sacrifice, the ceremonies included processions, dancing and music, and a characteristic feature of religious celebrations in Greece was the holding of competitions in which the worshippers glorified their god by exhibiting their prowess as musicians, athletes, dramatists, and so on. The general tone of the Greek festivals was gay, and occasionally it even became ribald. The broad jokes in which the Old Attic Comedy indulged at the expense, not only of men, but of the gods themselves, equalled in audacity the most irreverent passages in the Homeric poems. But, as in the legends and feasts of certain Christian saints, the banter of Aristophanes was no more than the outcome of high spirits and an expression of easy familiarity with the gods, and it was in no way intended to undermine belief in them. In any case, the prevailing tone of the festivals was one of orderliness and sobriety. Deities which required an orgiastic ritual were not as a rule admitted into the state calendar, or else, as in the case of Dionysus, the ceremonial was reduced to comparative quietness and decency.

The ceremonies of the state worship were commonly performed by the higher magistrates, but particular priesthoods were sometimes hereditary in certain noble families, and the receiving and interpreting of omens were largely left in the hands of specially qualified persons. In Greek belief random omens from the flight of birds and other ordinary occurrences were being constantly given by the gods, and their meaning might be divined by any person who witnessed them. In the words of Aristophanes:

> And whene'er you of omen or augury speak,
>   'tis a bird you are always repeating.
> A rumour's a bird and a sneeze is a bird,
>   and so is a word or a meeting;
> A servant's a bird and an ass is a bird.
>   It must therefore assuredly follow
> That the birds are to you (I protest it is true)
>   your prophetic divining Apollo.[1]

But soothsaying in the service of the state was a profession reserved to those who either could see signals and hear voices outside the ken of ordinary folk, or were conversant with the rules of interpretation. At the same time the Greeks usually tempered their regard for omens with robust common sense. In 413 B.C. a general named Nicias brought on the ruin of the Athenian expedition to Sicily (p. 41) by refusing to abandon an untenable position in deference to his seers. But such meticulousness ran counter to the ordinary practice of the Greeks, who treasured up the saying of Hector in the *Iliad*, 'the best of omens is to fight your country's battles'.

[1] *The Birds*, l. 719 ff. (tr. Rogers).

Public worship in Greece was mainly in the care of the particular cities. But the chief gods of the Homeric pantheon, such as Zeus and Apollo, had temples in a great number of towns, and their cult was in some instances organized on a far wider basis than that of the individual *polis*. The festivals of Zeus at Olympia and of Poseidon at the Isthmus were attended by official representatives and by private participants from all parts of Greece. The sanctuaries of Asclepius at Epidaurus and Cos, where cases of miraculous healing of sick men were carefully recorded and published, attracted patients from distant cities. On the island of Delos all Ionian-speaking Greeks forgathered once in a year for the common worship of Apollo, and the same god's oracle at Delphi was the chief bond of union in the early religious institutions of Greece.

Oracular seats were plentiful in Greece: some 250 have been enumerated in all. The most archaic was situated at Dodona in Epirus, where priests 'with unwashed feet, whose bed was the bare floor', interpreted the rustling of the oak leaves in the sacred grove of Zeus, much as 'the sound of marching in the tops of the mulberry-trees' (2 Sam. v. 24) was a sign for Israel to go to war. But Dodona, like most of the other Greek oracles, had only a limited range of consultants, and it was left to Apollo of Delphi to speak to the whole of Greece. Apollo was not the original tenant of Delphi, where oracles had been delivered in prehistoric times, but in the eighth and following centuries he made its reputation. He spoke to his inquirers through a priestess who sat on the sacred tripod in an underground chamber of his temple, and several male *prophetae* ('forthtellers', but not necessarily 'foretellers'). The priestess became 'possessed' in some way not clearly understood—not by 'mephitic vapours', for such did not exist in the temple—and broke into a delirious talk, which the *prophetae* delivered to the consultants in the form of hexameters or (after 400 B.C.) in plain prose. The reputation of the Delphic Apollo was mainly based on sheer common sense. To questions about the future he often made a deliberately ambiguous reply, as when he told King Croesus of Lydia that if he were to invade Persia 'he would destroy a great kingdom'. (Query: whose kingdom?). He announced to Pyrrhus of Epirus 'I declare that you the Romans may conquer'.[1] (Which is subject and which is object in this sentence?) Neither did he resemble the prophets of Israel in being a bold reformer of religion and morals. In general, Apollo was conservative and did not break new ground. But he mostly stood for the more enlightened usage of the day, and his guiding principle of 'nothing overmuch' gave exact expression to the innate Greek sense of balance and harmony. By 600 B.C., accordingly, he had acquired a spiritual dominion that extended over all Greece and even beyond—gifts were poured in to him from the kings of Lydia and Egypt, and from the young Roman republic. He was regularly consulted by intending bands of colonists, and his blessing was regarded by them as conferring a title of possession in the territory which they occupied. He was also an arbiter on moral questions which from time to time vexed the early Greek world, and it was largely under his influence that the Greeks abandoned the blood-feud and substituted for it the ritual purification of the homicide; and he gave authoritative decisions on questions of worship and ritual in other cults. Apollo of Delphi was therefore the most actively Panhellenic god, and the chief standardizing agency amid the welter of city-state worships.

By 500 B.C. the Greek state-worships were well established, and after that date they underwent little outward change. After the conquests of Alexander the new Greek cities of the Near East set up municipal cults which were closely modelled on those of the old country. Apollo became the patron god of Antioch, Dionysus of Alexandria, and so on, and each city organized a calendar of festivals of the usual Hellenic type. The chief innovation in public worship was the deification of kings, living and dead. The ancient Greek practice of paying divine honours to distinguished men after death was naturally revived in the days of Alexander and his successors, who were real giants and often had the opportunity of laying Greek towns under obligation to themselves. But the cities in many cases did not wait for their benefactors to die first, but set up altars or temples to them forthwith. Some of the kings, too, claimed worship for

---

[1] The ambiguity is more evident in the original Greek or in Latin: *aio te Romanos vincere posse.*

themselves *ex officio*, though royal usage in this respect was not uniform. Alexander himself at the end of his reign demanded divine honours from all the Greek cities; but the obviously ironical spirit in which the Greeks complied with his order showed that it was premature. The subsequent rulers of Macedon never received worship, and the Attalids only after death. But the Ptolemies and Seleucids established temples and high-priesthoods in their own name. The importance of Greek king-worship, however, may easily be overrated. It conferred no new political rights, and it argued neither monstrous infatuation in the monarch nor loathsome subservience on the part of his subjects. It was little more than a polite convention, like that by which 'humble petitioners pray and beseech His Sacred Majesty' at the present day.

The contact between Greek and Oriental religions did not produce any immediate visible results, and the cases in which an Oriental cult permeated the Greek world (p. 343) were exceptional. But the general shifting of population that followed the conquests of Alexander, and again in the days of the Roman Peace, necessarily weakened the old parochial spirit which tended to keep the gods of each city distinct and to restrict their sphere of influence, and the inevitable comparisons between the incoming Greek gods and the old-established ones revealed resemblances no less than differences between the various orders of deities. In this manner the Macedonian and Roman conquests prepared the way for monotheism in the Mediterranean lands.

3. ROMAN RELIGION

The origins of Italian religion cannot be studied in the same detail as those of the Greek cults. The intrusion of a Nordic element is proved by the presence in historical times of deities like Jupiter, whose affinity to the Greek Zeus is unmistakable, but little is known about the religion of the indigenous people,[1]

---

[1] In South Italy traces of Minoan cults, e.g. of the Lady of Wild Animals, have been found. Their significance in the development of Italic religion is not yet clear.

and the process by which earlier and later strata became inter-
mingled cannot be followed out. But the general character of
Italian religion in the early days of Rome is clearly discernible.
Our knowledge of it is derived from various Italian towns,
notably from Iguvium in the northern Apennines, which has
provided us with a large fragment of a ritual law reflecting early
usages, and from the 'religion of Numa', the earliest form of
state-worship at Rome (so called from the second Roman king,
who was traditionally believed to have organized the public
worship of the city).

The 'religion of Numa' and kindred Italic cults closely reflected the conditions of an agricultural community whose main
concern lay in its fields and flocks and homesteads. The number
of its deities was very large, for it included not only greater
powers with a far-reaching control over herds and crops, but a
host of lesser spirits that could help or hinder each particular
process in the routine of farm work: sowing, weeding, manuring,
and so forth. In contrast with the religion of early Greece, the
religion of Numa did not endow its deities with human shape
or envisage them clearly—in some cases it was even uncertain
about the sex of the god, and it possessed none of the rich
mythology that attached to the Greek gods. In fact, all that
it professed to know about its 'numina' (the name given by the
Romans to their early deities, as opposed to the anthropo-
morphical 'dei' of their later pantheon) was that they would under
certain circumstances intervene for good or evil in the affairs of
men.

For the worship of such vaguely conceived spirits the early
Italians naturally did not provide cult-images, neither did they
build temples. Apart from prayer and sacrifice, their ritual,
which was, in the main, of great simplicity, occasionally included
a rudimentary dance (whose object was magical rather than
aesthetic), and plain music on the *tibia*. But they attached
great importance to the exact performance of the prescribed
ceremonies. They required that the 'carmina' or formulae of
invocation should be uttered with complete literal accuracy, and
if a mistake was made at any point in the ritual they repeated
that part of it, and sometimes the whole of it; and they insured

themselves against any unnoticed slip in the proceedings by an anticipatory sacrifice of atonement. Yet the scrupulous care with which the rites were performed did not exclude gaiety from the festivals: those which marked the completion of the principal operations of the agricultural season, such as the sowing, the reaping, and the vintage, were celebrated in a frank spirit of merry-making.

In Italy oracles never played a part comparable to that of the Delphic Apollo. In the Latin town of Praeneste, some twenty miles from Rome, the goddess Fortuna gave advice to consultants by the casting of lots; but this was the only native oracular seat to attain more than local importance. On the other hand the taking of omens received as great attention as in Greece.

The early Italic religion underwent changes as city-states grew up, and was overlaid with cults imported from abroad. This development can best be observed in the city of Rome. The Romans included in their public worship a considerable number of rustic deities, which continued to remain embedded in their calendar festivals. But to several of these gods of the countryside they also assigned a political role: Jupiter became the general protector of the Roman state, and Mars the chief giver of victory in Roman wars. For the due observance of the state ritual the Romans made more than usually elaborate arrangements. Though some of the ceremonies were performed in the ordinary manner by the political heads (kings or consuls), a number of permanent priests (*flamines*) was appointed for the cult of particular gods; a special board of *augures* was charged with the ritual of divination; and the college of *pontifices* acted as general adviser on questions pertaining to the *ius divinum*, i.e. the proper procedure in dealing with the gods. But the most peculiar assistants in the service of the state were the six Vestal Virgins, young women of good family, who devoted thirty years of their life to the tending of the sacred fire in the temple of Vesta, the goddess of the hearth (which was the central institution of the city, as of the home).

From the earliest times the Romans came into contact with foreign religious influences. They sought to safeguard their native cults against too close an intrusion of alien deities by ordaining that these should not receive worship within the central area of the city, and in some cases required that the new-comers should take the names of native gods, as when Demeter and Dionysus became transformed into Ceres and Liber. But in religion as in politics the Romans showed themselves hospitable, and they were not too proud to accept the aid of strange gods.

The first foreign religion to affect that of Rome was the Etruscan. This was a strange medley in which Oriental and Greek elements overlaid the native Italic ones. It borrowed from the Greeks the cult-image and the temple; but it differed alike from the Greek and the Italic worships, in that it was demon-haunted to a far greater extent.[1] The Romans were impervious to this most characteristic side of Etruscan religion, and did not allow their native Italic cheerfulness to be affected by it. But they went to school with the Etruscans in order to acquire the *Etrusca disciplina* in seercraft, which was more highly developed than that of the Italic peoples, and extracted omens not only from the behaviour of birds, but from the play of lightning and the appearance of the liver in sacrificial animals. The last of the Roman kings, Tarquin the Proud (*c.* 510 B.C.), also introduced into Rome the worship of a triad of deities, Jupiter, Juno, and Minerva, who were regularly associated in Etruscan worship and were regarded by them as blood-relations. For this trinity he built a temple on the Capitol and set up cult-images in it. The Capitoline triad at Rome was a partnership, not a family, and in it Jupiter was by far the predominant partner. But from this time the major deities in Rome were usually housed in temples and represented by images. These Greek accessories to worship therefore reached the Romans through the medium of the Etruscans. According to a credible tradition, Tarquin also introduced into Rome a code of oracles that had been collected in the Greek town of Cumae. These books were placed in the keeping of a special board of custodians and consulted in times of crisis down to the last days of the republic.

After the expulsion of the Etruscan kings Greek religious influence was exerted more directly upon Rome and gradually

[1] On the gladiatorial games in Etruria and Rome, see p. 161.

ousted that of Etruria. In the early part of the fifth century several Greek deities reached Rome from South Italy or Sicily, though some of these had to assume Latin disguises (p. 322). The subsequent influx of Greek gods was relatively slight, though we may note that in 293 B.C. Asclepius, the god of healing, was lodged in a sanctuary on the Tiber island at Rome. But under Greek influence the ritual of several of the older festivals was brightened so as to comprise music, dancing, horse-racing, and dramatic performances. In the later period of the republic the Roman state religion had, in outward form, many points in common with that of the Greek cities. But the old Italian core of the Roman worship remained unaffected by the accretions from Greece. The Romans became familiarly acquainted with Greek mythology through the study of Greek authors and through their own writers, who adopted the Greek legends about the gods as part of their stock-in-trade; but this mythology had little or no effect on Roman beliefs.

Towards the end of the Second Punic War the Roman government made the strange experiment of introducing from Asia Minor a goddess of fertility named Cybele, or Magna Mater, whose worship was attended by an orgiastic and quite un-Roman ritual. This worship, however, was admitted only under strict safeguards, which debarred Roman citizens from direct participation in it, and for a long time Cybele remained the only Oriental deity in the Roman pantheon.

The immense success of the Roman Republic in the age of the great conquests naturally increased the confidences of the Roman people in its own protecting deities. It also brought about an extension of their worship, for wherever the Romans established a colony they took with them their principal gods and erected a temple in honour of the Capitoline triad. The Roman state cults, indeed, were not ill suited to the needs of the early Roman community, and until the second century B.C. the Senate and the College of Pontiffs showed sagacity in their religious policy. In true Roman fashion, they drew a sharp distinction between *religio*, or 'careful observance', and *superstitio*, i.e. an excessive display of religious emotion. In 186 B.C. they did not hesitate to invoke the 'secular arm' of the consuls in order to suppress a licentious cult of Bacchus which had been introduced into various parts of Italy by unauthorized persons. But while they safeguarded Roman 'gravitas', they by no means sought to repress the natural cheerfulness of Italian festivals. In times of stress and anxiety, such as the Second Punic War, they added to the gaiety of the state ceremonies by introducing Greek ritual into it. To assuage popular alarm or excitement, they promptly ordained a special service of atonement whenever occurrences of 'prodigia' or supernatural happenings were reported.[1]

But the Roman conquests, which undermined the sound structure of Roman politics (p. 70), also exerted a harmful reaction upon the Roman state religion. Under the later Republic Greek scepticism had a transient effect upon educated Romans: Ennius toyed with the doctrines of Euhemerus, and Plautus introduced into his plays an un-Italian note of ribaldry in religious matters. But a more serious break from tradition took place when the Roman governing class began to misuse religion as an instrument for the maintenance of their political ascendancy. Taking advantage of the fact that the cosmopolitan proletariat which now filled Rome had little understanding for the ancient Italic cults of the fields, they neglected these and allowed their sanctuaries to fall into decay. To the worship of the patron gods of Rome they pretended to pay the most meticulous regard. During the Second Punic War two *flamines* lost their priesthoods, the one because he had failed to arrange the sacrifices in the right order on the altar, the other because while sacrificing he had dropped his priestly hat. The practice of *instauratio*, or repetition of rites that had been vitiated (perhaps by a false gesture or intonation), was carried to absurd lengths: in some cases an entire public festival was recommenced three times over. At the same time solicitude for the due observance of omens was carried so far, that public business was sometimes suspended on the mere announcement that an official was about to watch the heavens, or on a manifestly false report (e.g. of lightning in a blue sky). The successive 'instaurations' of

[1] The commonest forms of these 'prodigia' were a rain of milk (i.e. laden with white volcanic dust), or of blood (saturated with particles of sand from the Sahara), or the trembling of spears suspended in the temple of Mars (under the influence of a slight earth tremor).

festivals, it may be safely surmised, were really intended as a means of providing additional amusement for the populace, and the omens were confessedly a means of political obstruction. It would, however, be quite a false inference from these practices that the traditional cults of the Roman household and of the countryside had also ceased to be taken seriously, for these were carried on unbrokenly and in the old-time spirit. But the state religion at the end of the republican period was degenerating into farce.

In the days of Augustus the state worship underwent a reform that was more than a matter of mere appearances. At this time Rome and Italy were stirred by a sense of gratitude for their delivery from the civil wars, and by a heightened national consciousness, in answer to the challenge of the Egyptian queen Cleopatra. When Augustus (himself a man of conservative instincts in religion as well as in politics) set to work to repair the neglected temples, and to revive the antiquated Italian cults, he had a considerable weight of public opinion behind him. The restoration was so far effective that the brotherhood of the Fratres Arvales, to whom was committed the worship of an obsolete rustic deity, the Dea Dia, carried on their duties punctually until far into the third century A.D. But Augustus was an innovator as well as a restorer. In 17 B.C. he revived an old centenary festival, the Ludi Saeculares, but in so doing he transferred the place of honour in it to Apollo, a god who had hitherto played a subordinate part in the Roman pantheon: the hymn of thanksgiving which Horace composed for the occasion was addressed to Apollo and his sister Artemis. To Apollo Augustus also erected an all-marble temple on the Palatine, the costliest of all Roman sanctuaries. The personal preference which the emperor showed for this god was in keeping with the spirit of the age, for Apollo above all gods stood for balance and moderation, and Augustan religion no less than Augustan art and literature was guided by the principle of 'nothing overmuch'.

Still more significant was the introduction of the cult of monarchs into the Roman Empire. In Rome and Italy the worship of men, whether alive or dead, was unknown to the usage of republican times, and it was a new departure when the Second Triumvirate erected a temple to *divus Caesar*, the deified Caesar, in 42 B.C. But the precedent of that year was followed at the death of Augustus, and henceforth it became customary for the Senate to decree divine honours to all defunct emperors, save a few who had incurred its displeasure. But alongside of this worship of dead emperors the cult of living ones was also instituted. In 29 B.C. the Greek subjects of Augustus in Asia Minor, who had previously paid divine honours to the Hellenistic kings (p. 318), built a temple to 'Roma et Augustus', and this worship (to which that of each living emperor in turn was later added) eventually spread over the Roman provinces and was established in Italy and in Rome itself. This new religion was undoubtedly created in a spirit of sincere thankfulness to the man who had rescued the empire from chaos, and it was no more a mark of degraded servility than the robust eulogies of the emperor in the Augustan poets. Augustus himself, however, was not whole-hearted about the new cult. While he favoured its diffusion in the provinces, he received it more coolly in Rome and Italy, and most of his successors viewed it in a similar light. Emperor-worship therefore soon became what the cult of Hellenistic kings had been, a fashionable formality.[1]

A development of far higher importance under Augustus' successors was the spread of certain Oriental religions over the Roman Empire in general. Despite the sympathy of individual emperors for some of the religions of the Near East, these never obtained a secure footing amid the official Roman cults. Nevertheless they penetrated the Roman world by various private channels. The diffusion of these cults, and of the Palestinian religions, will be considered in subsequent sections (§§ 6, 7).

4. THE GROWTH OF MONOTHEISM

The Greek and Roman gods of the home, of the fields, and the city endured for many centuries and eventually died hard. The survival of the traditional cults is plentifully attested in the

[1] Vespasian could joke about his deification on his death-bed: 'Deary me: I do believe I'm turning into a god!'

antiquarian treatises of Plutarch, and in the descriptions of Greek sanctuaries by Pausanias, who found that many archaic rituals were still being practised and hoary old myths kept green in memory. Delphi and other Greek oracles still drew consultants in the second and third centuries A.D. When Christianity issued its challenge to the older religions, both Greek and Latin writers made a vigorous response, and after the establishment of the new faith they still fought as they retreated. In the East the Emperor Julian (A.D. 361–363) made a strenuous if short-lived attempt to undo the work of Constantine, and in the West Aurelius Symmachus (p. 275) rallied the Roman Senate against the encroachments of Christianity. Long after the reign of Constantine, therefore, the Christians had to maintain their polemic against the old Greek and Roman cults. Writing in the early fifth century, Augustine found it necessary to direct his argument alike against the Roman intellectuals of his day, and against the 'pagans' of the country places (*pagi*), where a large part of the peasantry still clung to its time-honoured beliefs and practices.

The persistence of the traditional cults may partly be explained by the natural conservatism of all men in matters of religion, and by the powers of resistance which any established institution possesses. But it was due in no small degree to the genuine hold of the old religion on the Greeks and Romans. It recalled the ancient glories of their national history, and to the Romans it was a symbol of their imperial position. Its ritual was generally attractive, and appealed not only to the masses but also to educated men: like the Medieval Church, the state worship of ancient Greece, and partly also of Rome, was the foster-mother of music, art, and literature. Indeed it was in the cause of classical culture that some of the most stalwart defenders of the old religions, such as the Emperor Julian, made their stand.

But the old religions failed to meet certain needs, the fulfilment of which became increasingly urgent in the Greek and Roman world. They lacked the symmetry and the logical coherence of a monotheistic form of worship; they paid little regard to the problems of after-life; they did not establish a sufficiently intimate connexion between religion and morality; and they tended to become the buttresses of a particular political and social order. In the long run, therefore, they could not prevent the growth of other religions which satisfied some or all of these requirements, and were first supplemented and finally supplanted by newer forms of worship.

The Greeks and Romans, like all polytheists, were prone to add continually to the number of their deities. As the field of their experience widened and the number of their unfulfilled desires increased, they were tempted to invoke more and more supernatural powers. Hence they borrowed gods from other peoples and invented new ones, until their pantheon threatened to become overcrowded and even chaotic. On the other hand the early Greek and Roman religions already contained the germs of monotheism. From the outset Zeus held a predominant position among the Greek gods, and Jupiter among the Roman ones, and either of these tended to assimilate lesser deities. Among the other major gods of Greece Apollo developed a similar absorptive power. It is computed that he was worshipped under some 200 different cult-names, and not a few of these were originally the names of independent deities; e.g. at Sparta Apollo Hyacinthius was a compound of Apollo and an older deity Hyacinthus. With the growth of city-states, the patron gods of each town acquired a unique position therein: to the Athenians Athena was *the* deity, and her cult surpassed all others in its elaborateness.

A further impetus to monotheism came from increase of travel and intercourse, which tended to uproot men's attachment to a host of local deities and inclined them to restrict their devotions to a limited number of gods with a wider range of influence. In the Hellenistic age the belief gained ground that many local deities were but manifestations of a single power, and under the Roman emperors this tendency to amalgamation received a wider impetus. Increasing political union and the substitution of monarchical for republican government were likewise unfavourable to polytheism. Where large masses of men gave their loyalty to one secular ruler, it seemed more natural that they should worship the same god.

These movements of general opinion were accelerated by the speculations of literary men and philosophers, who thought ahead of the masses of mankind. Already in Homer the dim power of Fate appears now and then as a unifying principle behind the Olympian gods. To the early Greek physicists, who postulated an underlying unity of matter behind the variety of things perceived, a single spiritual power was a natural concomitant. In the sixth century one of their number, Xenophanes, professed a faith that was not far removed from pure monotheism:

> One God there is, 'mid gods and man the greatest,
> In form not like to mortals nor in mind;
> He is all eye, all mind, all hearing, He;
> He without toil rules all things by his will;
> Ever unmoved in one place he abideth.'[1]

Among the Attic dramatists Aeschylus, while using the language of polytheism, in his deepest thought conceived of Zeus as lord of the universe and of the other deities as functions or aspects of the one Great Divine. Plato, while outwardly conforming to traditional religion, spoke of '*the* god' when he was expressing his real mind; like the early physicists, he sought to reduce the chaos of sense-perceptions to order and required a single unifying agency. Similarly the Stoics assumed a single directing power behind the world-process; to this authority they sometimes gave the name of Zeus, but since they described it as impersonal, they evidently conceived of it far differently from the Zeus of Homer and the city-states. The Neoplatonist Porphyry quoted oracles of Apollo that asserted the existence of one supreme eternal Being, and regarded the manifold gods of paganism as his angels.

Among the Romans the native vein of speculation was not sufficiently strong to carry them unaided to monotheism; but the more thoughtful among them, in adopting the Stoic system of ethics, also took over the Stoic conception of Providence. Cicero, who derided the ordinary Greek mythology, accepted a Stoic Jupiter. Vergil, who inclined to Stoic philosophy in his maturer days, made profession in his *Georgics* of a belief in

[1] T. R. Glover, *Progress in Religion*, p. 93.

Providence, which he linked with the conception of the father-hood of God. When Tennyson says to Vergil:

> Thou that seest Universal Nature moved by Universal Mind,

it is to his Stoic monotheism that he is mainly referring. With Seneca 'Jupiter' came to mean the supreme ruler of the universe, and his nephew Lucan expressed the same idea forcibly when he wrote:

> Juppiter est, quodcumque sumus, quocumque movemur.
> (Jove is our whole existence and our goal.)

The extent to which monotheism had captured reflective Romans is strikingly revealed in the reply of the scholar Maximus, himself not a Christian, to Augustine: 'Which of us is so mad or blind as to deny the certain truth that there is one supreme God? By many titles do we invoke his virtues, which are spread throughout the universe, because we do not know his name. For "God" is a name that all religions share.' Enlightened pagans never went so far as to deny expressly the existence of more than one deity, and so there remained room for conflict between them and Jews or Christians. Yet their speculations prepared the way for Christian monotheism.

5. RELIGION AND ETHICS

The traditional religions of Greece and Rome were not wholly unconcerned with ethics. It was the general belief that the gods would punish certain forms of wrongdoing. If a man committed perjury, the god whose name he had taken in vain would naturally avenge on him the personal insult thus inflicted; and if a strong man were to kill or ill-treat a weaker person who had invoked the aid of a deity, it might be his turn to suffer at the hands of one more powerful than himself. And the interest of the gods in wrongful human action would not stop short at cases in which their personal honour was engaged. They would intervene in other cases of cheating and double-dealing; they would requite oppression and manifestations of *hubris* or overweening insolence. The primitive Greek belief, that the gods were jealous of human prosperity as such (p. 309), eventually gave way to the view that prosperity commonly turned men's heads, that the resulting *hubris* or infatuation engendered *atē*, and that it was against such displays of arrogance that the gods intervened. This point has been aptly illustrated by a modern parallel. 'I know of nothing', says Mr. Gomme, 'that would have appeared to the Greeks so clearly inevitable, and, in a sense, right, as the disaster to the steamship *Titanic* in 1912. Everything presaged it; her owners loudly proclaimed her the largest and finest vessel afloat; equipped her with every kind of tyrannical luxury; gave her a boastful name; finally, said she was unsinkable. . . . And so, on her first voyage, in a calm sea, with her owners and their friends aboard, she collided with an iceberg and sank'.[1] Among the Greek gods Zeus in particular was held to exert himself on behalf of human truthfulness and modesty and mercy. In the words of Hesiod 'Zeus had thirty thousand watchers', and the oppression of one man by another would not escape him. Along-side of Zeus, the Delphic Apollo ranked as the 'conscience of Greece', and was frequently consulted on problems of human behaviour. As we have seen (p. 318), he stood above all for balance and moderation.

But neither Greek nor Roman religion produced a comprehensive code of ethics or placed consistent emphasis on the need of right living. Their chief concern remained with ritual and outward acts of devotion. The real working code of Greek and Roman morals was rather to be found in the time-honoured precepts of family life and the secular laws of society and the state: the Greek obeyed the *nomos tēs poleōs* (the law and custom of the city), the Roman followed *mos maiorum*, ancestral custom. In the popular philosophy of the Greeks morality was based on other sanctions besides those of religion. If men acted rightly, it was largely because they had *aidōs*, self-respect, or a sense of decency and beauty, or because, in the last resort, they feared to invite the *nemesis* or retribution of irate neighbours upon themselves. Moreover, such improvements as were made from time to time in Greek and Roman standards of morals were not due to religious reformers like the Israelite prophets so much as to lay thinkers whose appeal was to mundane opinion.

[1] In E. Eyre, *European Civilization*, I, p. 580.

The quest for a universally valid rule of ethics underlying the conventional codes of different cities and peoples was opened by the Greek philosophers (p. 211), who succeeded at least in reducing the problem to its simplest terms. Previous to them Sophocles had implicitly raised the same problem in his *Antigone*, where the heroine contravenes the law of the state in order to fulfil the natural duty of giving a kinsman a decent burial. Outstanding anomalies and defects in the ordinary codes were attacked both by the philosophers and by a long succession of literary men. The harshness of early family law, in which women were mere chattels (p. 142), was criticized by them, at any rate by implication. The fine portraits of real personalities among womankind which we find in Homer and the Attic tragedians were an indirect challenge to the traditional family code, and Euripides in particular protested unmistakably against the subjection of women. The ethics of slavery were also thrown open to discussion by Euripides. On this subject the philosophers did not give such a strong lead as might have been expected; but the Stoics, who insisted that even slaves were human personalities, prepared the way for their more considerate treatment. Their influence is plainly visible in Seneca, who vigorously combated the old Roman conception of slaves as *mancipia* or 'articles for sale'.

The cognate question, whether the Greeks should apply the same standard of ethics to foreigners as to themselves, first received a definite answer in the sixth century. The early Greeks were not strongly conscious of their superiority over other peoples. In Homer and other early writers the term 'barbarian' applied to non-Greeks meant merely 'jabberers' or persons of unintelligible speech, and did not convey disparagement. But Heracleitus of Ephesus went further and positively asserted the potential unity of mankind. After their victory in the Persian Wars, it is true, the Greeks adopted a more exclusive and arrogant attitude towards aliens, and 'barbarian' came to mean, as with us, a person of inferior civilization. In the fourth century Aristotle, taking Greek superiority as an axiom, explained it by reasons of climate (pp. 205–6); and he advised his pupil Alexander to treat the Orientals as enemies and slaves by nature.

On the other hand Isocrates declared that the term 'Hellene' stood, not for a particular race or political group, but for a certain standard of culture, and thus implicitly admitted that foreigners might become Hellenes by assimilation. Nay more, Alexander openly reasserted the unity of mankind, and although his attempts to put this belief into practical operation proved abortive, his influence on later Greek thought was profound. To say nothing of various Utopian writers of the third and second centuries, whose influence was local and transient, the Stoics proclaimed the fraternity of the human race (p. 211), and their doctrine reinforced the naturally liberal trend of thought of the Romans in regard to race and nationality. It was partly in deference to Stoic principles that the Roman jurisprudents laid down the doctrine of a 'ius naturae' which should be applicable in all law-courts of the world.

In regard to the ethics of warfare, the general opinion among Greeks and Romans was that it was not a natural right of man, but required justification in each particular case, and that it must be waged subject to certain conventions (pp. 31-2, 51). The Romans in particular disapproved of random violence, as being a mark of *impotentia* or insufficient self-control, a serious sin in the Roman code of morals; and, in theory at least, they maintained the rule that no war should be fought except as a means of redressing grievances. Few went so far as to condemn war as such. The Greek philosophers in general were more reticent on this subject than might have been expected, and various writers from Homer onward spoke of the 'ennobling' influence of battle. Yet Herodotus, who narrated the most glorious of all Greek passages of arms, roundly described war as an evil. Euripides implicitly denounced warfare by showing up the suffering which it caused, and Menander similarly emphasized its seamy side. In Vergil the more enlightened Greek view emerged into Latin literature; to him war was *dirum*, 'accursed', and his battle scenes were protests against it rather than glorifications.

The broad principle of *humanitas*, i.e. our obligation to treat all men humanely at all times, first obtained implicit recognition in the oath which was imposed by the physician Hippocrates upon his students and has recently been reintroduced into the medical faculties of several modern universities. In the terms of this oath, the student swore to honour and obey his teacher and to care for his children if ever they were in need; always to help his parents to the best of his power; never to use or profess to use magic or charms or any supernatural means; never to supply poison or perform illegal operations; never to abuse the intimacy of a house, but to go there only for the benefit of the patient; and 'whatever in my professional practice I see or hear in the lives of men that ought not to be spoken abroad, I will not divulge, deeming that on such matters we should be silent'.[1] The same principle of considerateness to all men also showed through in the plays of Euripides, and it obtained formal recognition among the Stoic philosophers.

The Stoic teaching on the subject of *humanitas* is preserved in a whole series of Latin writers. Among the Romans it makes an unexpected first appearance in the mouth of a republican grandee, Metellus Numidicus, who addressed the people on the occasion of his triumph (*c.* 107 B.C.), and in the spirit of Kipling's *Recessional* proclaimed that 'Good men will rather accept an injury than inflict it on others'. Consciousness of the links between the various parts of the world and a pervasive sympathy with fellow-men were the main ingredients of Cicero's *humanitas* and formed the theme of this ethical works. When modern man behaves in a civilized fashion, it is to this ideal that he returns. The same point of view recurs with unobtrusive insistence in Vergil, to whom quiet service was both a duty and a delight, and in the *Meditations* of Marcus Aurelius: 'It is man's special privilege to love even those who stumble.'

Humanitas was also the keynote of Seneca's philosophy, as exhibited in this passage: 'All this world, in which things human and divine are contained, is a single whole; we are all the members of this great body. Nature has created us akin, forming us of the same elements and to the same end. She has implanted mutual love in our hearts and made us prone to seek out friends. She established fairness and justice, and by her ordinance it is a more

[1] On ethics and Greek religion, see P. Shorey in Sneath, *The Evolution of Ethics*, p. 233.

miserable thing to offer than to suffer injury' (*Epist.* xcv. 52). The Stoic teaching on this subject is also reflected in many small sayings of Seneca whose resemblance to familiar passages of the New Testament will strike every reader: 'The mind, unless it is pure and holy, comprehends not god' (Seneca, *Epist.* lxxxvii. 21)—'Blessed are the pure in heart, for they shall see God. (Matt. v. 8); 'I will be gentle and yielding to my enemies' (Seneca, *De Vita Beata,* xx.)—'But I say unto you, love your enemies' (Matt. v. 44); 'Let us so give as we wish to receive' (Seneca, *De Beneficiis,* ii. 1)—'Whatsoever ye would that men do unto you, do ye so even unto them' (Matt. vii. 12).[1]

That these improvements in ethical theory were not altogether without effect on actual practice may be gathered from what has been said in previous chapters about the political and social condition of the Greek and Roman world. The harshness of early family law was mitigated and the status of women was raised. Slaves received humaner treatment and foreigners were given greater consideration, and the Roman Empire developed into an equal partnership of peoples, the like of which modern Europe seems incapable of realizing. Despite the continued existence of slavery, and of other social iniquities, the second century A.D. was a period of general good will and of freedom from social strain.

But the enlightened men who brought about these ameliorations in moral standards did not use the traditional religion as their instrument of reform. Nay rather, they were more or less outspoken critics of the existing ritual and more especially of the popular mythology. The attack was led by Xenophanes. This bold spirit not only ran a-tilt against the traditional polytheism (p. 329), but he denounced the myths in which the gods 'pilfered, committed adultery, and cheated one another' like bad men. Aeschylus, and still more openly Euripides, used the drama as a means of correcting crude popular conceptions about the gods (e.g. the idea of their vindictiveness). Plato followed in the wake of Xenophanes with a direct attack upon Homer, because of the undignified and sometimes rascally parts which

[1] See further Haarhoff, *Vergil in the Experience of South Africa,* p. 19 ff.

the gods played in his poems, and realizing that most men could not read Homer except in a literal sense, he did not seek to explain away the objectionable passages in him, but demanded that they should be entirely expunged by an official censor. The Stoics attempted to interpret the more demoralizing myths by way of allegory, but in so doing they implicitly criticized the traditional religion. Greek mythology also had its critics among Roman authors: Cicero derided it, and Lucretius fulminated against it on account of its inhumanity.

In a word, such ethical standards as the traditional religion prescribed or implied, failed more and more to satisfy the more thoughtful among the Greeks and Romans, in whose eyes they were insufficient and, at times, downright wrong

6. BELIEF IN AFTER-LIFE

The problem of after-life was not entirely ignored in the traditional religions of Greece and Rome. Some form of belief in such a life is accepted almost instinctively among the great mass of mankind, partly because of dreams and visions in which the departed seem to reappear. In ancient times dreams and other psychic phenomena did not escape scientific investigation.[1] The Atomists put forward a purely material explanation for them, by assuming that the stream of atoms sometimes took the shape of phantoms. Even so, they had to admit that it must depend on the mental condition of the percipient what kind of an impression the phantoms produced; and later philosophers, such as the Stoics, duly laid stress on this fact. Aristotle went a step further and shrewdly pointed out that some dreams are the result of self-suggestion from the subconscious part of the mind. But no ancient thinker could supply any valid test for distinguishing real objects of sensation from imaginary ones, and the view that our dreams and visions have a real source persisted.[1]

The general ancient belief in some form of after-life is illustrated by the common custom of bestowing some of the personal

[1] See E. R. Dodds on 'Telepathy and Clairvoyance in Classical Antiquity', in *Greek Poetry and Life* (ed. Bowra), p. 364.

belongings of the deceased in his coffin, and of placing food or pouring libations on the grave. The tendance of the dead was a deeply rooted habit, and it was widely observed among the Greeks and Romans. But this practice shows that in popular belief the dead remained imprisoned in the grave, or could not move far from it. It is true that some peoples from early times learnt to dissociate man's spirit from his body, and held that at death the spirit slipped out of the body with the last breath (both Greek *psyche* and Latin *anima* meant 'breath') and maintained a separate existence. This was the view set forth in Homer, and it recurs frequently in Greek and Latin literature. Yet the underworld of Hades, to which the spirit migrated, was as dark and dim as the Sheol of the Israelites (Greek *Hades* or *Aides* means 'invisible'). Here the dead flitted about feebly and squeaking like bats (as the ghosts of the South African Bantu do), and lacking in any independent personality. Still less distinct was the conception which the Italians had of after-life: for them the *manes* were a collective mass rather than an aggregate of individuals.

To these speculations of ordinary men the philosophers did little to add precision. The Epicureans stoutly and cheerfully averred that death means annihilation. Caesar, who dabbled in Epicurean philosophy, once asserted this view in the Senate House: the fact that he was head of the college of the *pontifices* was no obstacle to his holding it. The Stoics would not admit that death was the end of all things, but they denied personal survival to all except a chosen few. In the traditional religion, therefore, concern for the after-life hardly went beyond the grave-ritual of the individual families and an occasional All Souls' Day. The ordinary cults of the Greeks and Romans were far more devoted to the affairs of this world than to those of the next.

Nevertheless interest in the next world could not be repressed, and in time it grew stronger. Apart from mere curiosity, several other motives impelled thoughtful men to speculate on the life after death. Upon many Greeks and Romans the transitoriness of our days on earth weighed heavily. In Homer we read: 'As is the race of leaves, so is the race of mankind. The leaves . . .

wind strews some of them on the earth, and others the forest,
when it burgeons, puts forth, when the season of spring is come;
so the race of men now comes into being and now ceases to be.'
Sophocles expressed the same thought in words which Edward
FitzGerald could never read without tears:

> Fair Aegeus' son, only to gods in heaven
> Comes no old age nor death of anything;
> All else is turmoiled by our master, Time.
> The earth's strength fades and manhood's glory fades.'[1]

Again Pindar asks: 'What is man, what is he not? A thing of
a day and the dream of a shade.' Catullus muses: 'After our
brief patch of sunlight one long eternal night must we sleep
through.' The brief span of life was also the burden of many
Greek and Roman epitaphs. Moreover, for the shortness of
human life an eternal hovering round the grave or in Hades
seemed to offer but sorry compensation. In Homer the ghost
of Achilles said to Odysseus on his visit to Hades: 'Don't
bepraise death to me, Odysseus. I would rather be a plowman
to a yeoman farmer on a small holding than lord paramount in
the kingdom of the dead.'[2] It was only the Epicureans that
could derive comfort from a sleep that has no ending.

But an even more insistent motive for concern with an after-
life was the problem of evil. Why should men suffer? This
question vexed thoughtful Greeks and Romans as it puzzled
Job. In Homer the herd Philoetius complains: 'O father Zeus,
thou art most cruel of all gods! Men are thy offspring, but thou
hast no pity for them, making them know pain and tribulation.'
And Zeus grumbles in turn: 'Upon my word, just see how
mortal men always put the blame on us gods! We are ever the
source of evil, so they say, when they have only their madness
to thank if their miseries are worse than they ought to be.'[3]
Aeschylus offered a solution, *pathos mathos*, 'suffering is learning', and Plato concurred. But this explanation gave cold
comfort, and to many thoughtful men the obvious injustices of
this life seemed intolerable unless there was to be a squaring
of accounts in some future existence.

[1] Trans. Gilbert Murray.
[2] W. H. D. Rouse, *The Story of Odysseus*, p. 195.   [3] Trans. Rouse.

From reflections such as these a belief in some sort of a heaven and hell gained strength. In a rudimentary form this belief existed at the beginnings of Greek history. In the Homeric Hades a special corner was reserved as a place of torture for those who had defied or displeased the Olympian gods; and a few eminent personages did not proceed to Hades at all, but to the Elysian fields. This conception of Elysium and Tartarus was probably derived from the Minoan religion: it is significant that in Greek mythology Minos was not merely a king of Crete but a judge in the underworld. It certainly existed among the Etruscans, whose rock-tombs were often adorned with frescoes depicting the after-life. In some of these scenes the departed spirits caroused and held high carnival, more often they were being tormented by hideous demons.

Among the Greeks of historical times, as we have seen, it was a common belief that persons of special distinction survived as 'heroes' and received quasi-divine worship. In Greek litera-ture speculations about heaven and hell are recurrent, though the Attic dramatists were generally reticent on this subject. Hesiod located Elysium in the islands of the western Ocean. Pindar followed suit, but made the important addition that Elysium was the place of those who had lived a consistently just life. Here the view emerges that eternal bliss was not bestowed by the arbitrary favour of the gods, but as a reward of virtue. In Pindar the elect 'pass by the highway of Zeus unto the tower of Cronus, where the ocean breezes blow around the Islands of the Blest and flowers of gold are blazing, some on the shore from radiant trees, while others the water fostereth; and with chaplets thereof they entwine their hands and with crowns'.[1]

An alternative system of retribution was propounded by Pythagoras, according to whom departed spirits migrated into other bodies of men or of animals, and passed through a cycle of existences. This view, however, was reconcilable with a belief in rewards and punishments. In the *Republic* of Plato the 'just' among the dead passed straight to Heaven, the 'unjust' spent a period in Purgatory and then returned to earth, but they

[1] Trans. Sandys.

were left free (in the light of their experience) to choose the form of their next life.

The Romans in general had not enough imagination to speculate insistently on the problems of what lay beyond this life. The first clear description of an after-world by a Roman pen comes from Cicero. On the model of Plato, he introduced a description of the after-world (the 'Dream of Scipio') into his *De Republica*, and his next world was based on that of Plato. But he characteristically reserved his heaven for patriots.

Finally, all the traditions on this subject were gathered together by Vergil: 'Now at length they came to the happy place, the green pleasances and blissful seats of the Fortunate Woodlands. Here an ampler air clothes the meadows in lustrous green, and they know their own sun and a starlight of their own. Some exercise their limbs in tournament on the greensward, contend in games and wrestle on the yellow sand. Some dance with beating footfall and lips that sing; with them is the Thracian priest in sweeping robe and makes music to their measures. . . . Others . . . feast on the sward, and sing in chorus the glad paean-cry, within the scented laurel-grove whence Eridanus river surges upward full-volumed through the wood. Here is the band of them who bore wounds in fighting for their country, and they who made life beautiful by the arts of their invention and who won by service a memory among others, the brows of all girt with the snow-white fillet.'[1]

But interest in after-life was not confined to the world of literature. Among the Greeks and Romans it also gave rise to a considerable number of new cults which are now collectively called the 'mystery religions'. The reason for this name is that participation in these rites was restricted to those who had received initiation (*musterion*, from *muein*, to initiate), and that their doctrines were kept secret. On the other hand initiation was usually placed within reach of all applicants, of foreigners and slaves as well as citizens, though in some cases women were excluded. Essentially, therefore, the mystery religions were democratic, and one reason for the wide appeal which they made was no doubt because their gods were 'no respecters of persons',

[1] Trans. Mackail.

and the cults were in no wise ordained for the special benefit of a privileged class; though men of high rank often underwent initiation, the mystery worships took no account of political or social status. Another characteristic of these religions which attracted many worshippers was that they gave freer play to the emotions than was usually permitted in the state and family cults, for the ceremonial was often 'revivalistic' and sometimes even orgiastic. But their chief distinguishing feature was that they held out a definite hope of a future life of blessedness for those who went through the necessary probation.

The deities of the mystery cults were usually gods of vegetation. As the plants of the earth died in autumn to be reborn in spring, so the vegetation-spirits were assumed to have visited the underworld and to have returned from it, and thus to have become the natural dispensers of immortality among mankind. The most prominent of the mystery gods were the corn-deity, Persephone, and Dionysus, who was both a wine-god and the spirit of plant life in general, representing the principle of the mysterious force and inspiration of the earth.

The mystery rites were to a large extent conducted in private *thiasoi* or conventicles. Collectively, the worshippers in these societies received the name of 'Orphics', from a mythical bard Orpheus, who was believed to have visited the underworld and to have established the first rites of initiation. These conventicles made their first appearance about 600 B.C., and seem to have been particularly common in South Italy Though their ritual was not divulged, their general tenets are known from surviving Orphic hymns, and from works of art, such as the great mural fresco of Polygnotus (described by Pausanias), which reproduced various Orphic features in its underworld scenes. Orphic doctrine may be illustrated from the following fragments: 'They who are righteous beneath the rays of the sun enjoy a gentler lot after death in a fair meadow by deep-flowing Acheron. But they who have worked wrong and insolence beneath the rays of the sun are led down beneath the watery surface of Cocytus into chill Tartarus.' 'There is an ancient eternal degree of the gods . . . when a man stains his hands with murder, and another swears falsely, they become spirits . . . who are doomed to wander thrice ten thousand years far from the blessed; and being born in the course of time into all forms of mortal creatures, they move uncertainly along the hard paths of life. For the might of the air drives them into the sea and the sea spews them on the ground and the land bares them to the rays of the bright sun and the sun throws them in whirls of ether. One receives them from another, but all hate them.' Orphic tablets found in Crete, and the texts written on gold leaves in South Italy and laid into graves as a passport to the next world, picture the joy of the soul that escapes from the wheel of birth: 'I have won freedom from the weary round of sorrow, with eager feet have I entered the desired circle.' Contrary to the usual ancient principles of tolerance, the Orphics sometimes cast unbelievers as well as wrongdoers into their Tartarus. The resemblances of the Orphic tenets to the speculations of Pindar and Plato on after-life are unmistakable.

In some cases a mystery religion was adopted in the official calendar of the state festivals. The most notable instance of this was the cult of Demeter, Persephone, and Dionysus at Eleusis in Attica. Originally an ordinary worship of vegetation-deities, this cult developed into a mystery religion and was included among the festivals of the Athenian state by the tyrant Peisistratus. In this rite the Athenian citizen was symbolically taken through the darkness of death in the process of initiation and came back to renewed life for the service of the state. As befitted an official worship, it was attended with pomp and ceremony, and a costly hall of initiation was built for it. But the essence of the festival consisted of the secret rites, at which the worshippers received the assurance of future immortality. The Eleusinian mysteries attracted large numbers of Athenians, but participants came from all parts of Greece, and not a few Roman grandees received initiation, among them Sulla, Cicero, Antony, Augustus, and Hadrian.

After the first period of diffusion in the sixth century, the mystery religions passed through an age of comparative stagnation. In the fifth century Greek absorption in state politics reached its climax, devotion to the state gods was at its highest, and interest in the secret cults did not grow so rapidly. But in the third and following centuries the decline of the city-state and of local patriotism revived the need for a personal religion, and new mystery worships were introduced from time to time. In the third century the Greeks gained wider acquaintance with the Egyptian cult of Isis (probably a fertility-goddess) and Osiris, the god of the underworld. In the Hellenistic form of this religion Isis became the giver of immortality, and her ritual was assimilated to that of the mystery cults. Her worship was chiefly propagated by merchants and sailors, and it did not stop short at Greece and the Levant, but under the late republic and especially in the first two centuries A.D. it spread over most of the Roman Empire.[1] Though frowned on by Roman magistrates and emperors, who considered its highly emotional cult as 'superstitious', it was admitted by the Emperor Caligula (c. A.D. 40) among the official Roman worships. A surviving inscription attests a cult of Isis at London. Isis was often represented, in Egyptian fashion, as nursing the infant god Horus, and so became a model for the Christian Madonna.

The youngest and most widespread of the mysetry religions. Mithraism, had a somewhat different origin. Originally the Persian sun-god, Mithras, was transformed into the arbiter between the supreme deity of the Persians and mankind, and the agent through whom man obtained immortality. Before the Christian era Mithras-worship was confined to the Near East, but in the second and third centuries A.D. it spread over the Roman dominions and even outranged the cult of Isis. This worship carried with it something of the robust character of the Zoroastrian religion of the Persians, which envisaged life as a perpetual battle between a beneficent god and a power of evil. Its crusading spirit made a special appeal to military men, and its diffusion from the Euphrates to Hadrian's Wall was largely brought about by the soldiers of the Roman army, whose altars to Mithras survive in great numbers. It was also viewed with favour by the Roman emperors and made converts among the members of high Roman society. Of all pagan cults, that of Mithras was the most formidable rival of Christianity, on which

[1] An interesting account of an initiate is to be found in the latter part of Apuleius' *Metamorphoses*.

it exerted a noticeable influence. 'Many of our current Christian practices come from Mithraism. The 25th of December was the birthday of Mithras; the first day of the week, dedicated to the Sun, was his holy day, as opposed to the Jewish Sabbath. The Mithraics also practised baptism (with the blood of a bull) and confirmation, and expected salvation from a eucharistic Last Supper. The Mithraic ethics, like the Christian, were ascetic and pure.'[1]

By promising the largest rewards that man can hope for, and offering these to all comers, and especially to the disinherited among mankind, the mystery religions made an appeal to the Greek and Roman world to which the older cults could furnish no adequate counter-attraction. But for the benefits which they held out they exacted a price: they required not only participation in the prescribed ritual but a certain standard of moral behaviour. Indeed it has been surmised that one reason why the Orphic and Mithraic cults were not diffused even more widely was that their ethical codes were too stiff for the ordinary man. In this respect, as in their tendency to dogmatism and to exclude from salvation all those outside their church, they bore a clear resemblance to the Palestinian religions.

On the other hand it appears that the tests of moral probity were not always applied with strictness. The initiates at Eleusis comprised not only persons of unblemished character, but criminals and notorious evil-livers, and we may surmise that for some persons initiation was merely a matter of fashion. The mystery religions also gave rise to a traffic in 'pardons' which tended to give all such cults a bad repute and drew some severe strictures from Plato. In the long run, their power of gaining and of holding converts proved inferior to that of a religion from Palestine.

7. THE PALESTINIAN RELIGIONS

The Jewish religion enjoyed almost unrestricted toleration under Greek and Roman governments. Among the Hellenistic kings the Ptolemies, who controlled Palestine until 200 B.C., were favourably disposed to the Jews and encouraged large

[1] Gilbert Murray, in Peake's *Commentary on the Bible*, p. 632.

numbers of them to settle in Alexandria. When the Seleucids took possession in Palestine they followed a similar policy in regard to the Jews, until Antiochis IV had the unhappy idea of supplanting the worship of Jehovah at Jerusalem by that of Zeus (c. 165 B.C.). The result was a rebellion, by which the Jews eventually recovered their independence. When Pompey brought the Jews to Palestine under Roman rule (63 B.C.) he gave them complete freedom of worship; and Augustus, in deference to their uncompromising monotheism, exempted them from the newly established cult of the Roman emperors. In the last two centuries B.C. the Jews became widely diffused over the Near East, and from the time of Pompey they formed a considerable colony in Rome. Their religion was thus carried into many Mediterranean countries.

But a strict and unqualified monotheism, such as the Jews professed, usually made an unfavourable impression upon polytheistic peoples on first contact, for it came as a shock to them to be told that their gods were false or ineffective. In a polytheistic world, where 'live and let live' was the general rule in matters of religion, such 'atheism', as it was called, seemed like a gratuitous attack upon its traditional institutions. By reason of their monotheism, moreover, the Jews were compelled to abstain both from public functions in Greek and Roman towns and from private gatherings, at which sacrifices might be made (in however perfunctory a fashion) to heathen deities, and this exclusiveness aroused unfriendly suspicions.[1] Under the early Roman emperors clashes between the more unruly elements of the Jewish and Gentile populations in the towns of the Levant were not unusual, and in Palestine itself these conflicts twice broadened out into a national rebellion (A.D. 66–70 and 131–134). The Roman emperors nevertheless persisted in their general policy of religious toleration in regard to the Jews, but they set a ban on proselytizing; and the rigour with which they suppressed the rebellions so reduced the number of the Jews in Palestine

[1] The rude sketch found in the imperial quarters of the Palatine, in which a certain Alexamenos is satirized for worshipping an ass-headed figure on a cross, refers to the story that there was an ass in the Holy of Holies. So difficult did the Romans find it to conceive of a religion without images.

that henceforth they were virtually a homeless people, and more concerned to preserve their religion among themselves than to spread it among the Gentiles.

In any case, the Jewish religion was hindered by its narrowly national basis, and by certain features in its ritual, from gaining many converts among Gentiles. Despite the attempts of Jewish scholars such as Philo of Alexandria (c. A.D. 40) to explain and commend it to educated Greeks, it always remained a puzzle to the Greek and Roman world, and its essential worth was never appreciated.

The early Christian communities were exposed to the same accusations of 'atheism' as the Jews, and their abstention from the public activities of the towns in which they lived gave opportunities of malevolent gossip about them. Tacitus, who himself describes Christianity as a 'deadly superstition', remarks that its votaries were 'detested on account of their enormities'; their talk about a 'Kingdom' seemed to imply political intrigue, and their phrase about the Communion bread 'becoming flesh' seemed to indicate cannibalism. In various towns the mob made a scapegoat of the Christians for any untoward happening such as a scarcity of food-supplies, and the cry 'Christianos ad leones!' went up on any slight provocation. These popular outbursts, it is true, became less frequent after A.D. 200, as experience showed that the suspicions which had been fastened upon the new religion were quite unfounded, and by the time of Constantine it was not unusual for pagans and Christians to live together in amity.

But from the outset the Christians had also to contend with the hostility of emperors and their officials. The grounds on which they suffered persecution were various. The Founder of Christianity was crucified at the order of Pilate because He was accused of having proclaimed Himself king of the Jews. In A.D. 64, when a great conflagration (almost certainly due to accident) burnt out the centre of Rome, and the angry populace murmured that it was another of Nero's mad pranks, the terrified emperor sought to shift the blame on to the Christians resident in the capital, as though these were capable of any wanton crime 'out of hatred of the human race', and ordered their wholesale arrest and execution. Provincial governors punished Christians for being members of secret societies, or for refusing to recognize the divinity of the emperor. Unlike the Jews, the Christians did not enjoy exemption from emperor-worship, and in A.D. 112 Trajan laid down the rule, in answer to an inquiry from his governor in Bithynia (Pliny the Younger), that Christians who refused to pay homage when challenged in court were to be punished as traitors. For the next two hundred years the Christians remained virtual outlaws, and on several occasions, notably in the first decade of the fourth century, they were systematically sought out and punished.

Yet on the whole the persecutions were spasmodic and half-hearted. Pilate was not convinced of Jesus' guilt and had misgivings in passing sentence upon Him. Trajan, who had been assured by Pliny that as a matter of fact the Christians were quite innocuous, made this concession to them, that he forbade his officials to hunt them down, leaving it to private informers to being them to court; and most of the emperors of the second and third centuries had recourse to the same illogical but salutary compromise. The Emperor Diocletian, the author of the great persecution of the early fourth century, acted under pressure from some masterful subordinates; he was himself a tolerant man, and many of his officials were remiss in carrying out the order to extirpate the Christians. Finally, in A.D. 312 the future Emperor Constantine became a convert to Christianity; in the same year he became master of the western half of the empire; and in 313, by the Edict of Milan, he accorded complete toleration to the Christians in his dominions. Ten years later he obtained dominion over the whole empire and extended freedom of worship to all Christians.

In the meantime, in the face of popular and official hostility, the Christians had provided themselves with an efficient organization. They had instituted a clergy with disciplinary powers over the laity, and a bishop in each important city. From *c.* A.D. 200 the bishops in the several provinces met in periodical congresses, in which the general principles of Christian policy and articles of faith were laid down. It was therefore but a final step when Constantine in A.D. 325 convened an 'ecumenical' or world-wide congress of all bishops of the empire at Nicaea in Bithynia, where the Christian faith was definitely codified in the Nicene Creed. Furthermore, as we have seen (p. 256), the Christians had by A.D. 200 completed the canon of their Sacred Books, and from about that date they engaged in a continuous and successful controversy against the able and sincere apologists of paganism. Finally, Christianity satisfied all those demands which enlightened Greeks and Romans had learnt to make on religion, and had made in vain on the traditional cults.

At the death of Constantine in A.D. 337 the Christians were still in all probability a mere minority of the population of the empire. But, to say nothing of the fact that all emperors henceforth, with the single exception of Julian, belonged to their Church, they had a far superior organization to all other religious bodies, and they had captured a large proportion of the more thoughtful Greeks and Romans. Their future supremacy in Europe was therefore assured.[1]

[1] The passing away of the old order in religion was sorrowfully proclaimed by the oracle of Delphi in response to the Emperor Julian:

Tell ye the king: to the ground has fallen his glorious dwelling.
Phoebus no longer possesses his cauldron, his laurel prophetic,
No, nor his babbling spring; for quenched is the voice of his water.

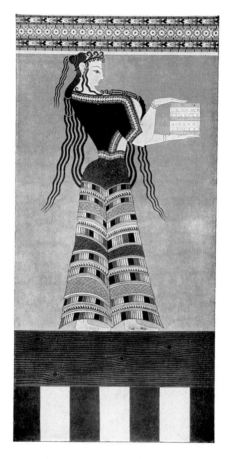

I   ELABORATELY DRESSED WOMAN

RECONSTRUCTION OF FRESCO FRAGMENTS FROM TIRYNS

2 (A) HUNTING THE BOAR
     (B) PART OF THE COMPANY SETTING OUT FOR THE HUNT
          (ATTENDANT WITH HOUND)
          BOTH RECONSTRUCTIONS OF FRESCO FRAGMENTS FROM TIRYNS

     (C) FRESCO FRAGMENT, FROM NORTH-WEST ANGLE OF PALACE
          OF CNOSSUS
                    CANDIA MUSEUM

3 SIXTH CENTURY VASE PAINTING

FLORENCE

4 TWO WHITE LEKYTHOI

MUNICH

5 STATUE OF HERACLES

FROM EAST PEDIMENT OF TEMPLE OF APHAIA AT AEGINA,
ABOUT 490–480 B.C.   MUNICH.

6 DEMETER OF CNIDUS

SCHOOL OF PRAXITELES

BRITISH MUSEUM

7 PONT DU GARD, AQUEDUCT OF NÎMES

8a POMPEIUS MAGNUS

THIRD QUARTER OF FIRST CENTURY B.C.,
GLYPTOTEK NY CARLSBERG, COPENHAGEN

8b PORTRAIT FIGURES, ON TERRACOTTA LID OF ASH-CHEST

VOLTERRA, MUSEO GUARNACCI IX, 811

9 ROMAN COPY OF POLYCLEITUS' SPEAR CARRIER

ROME

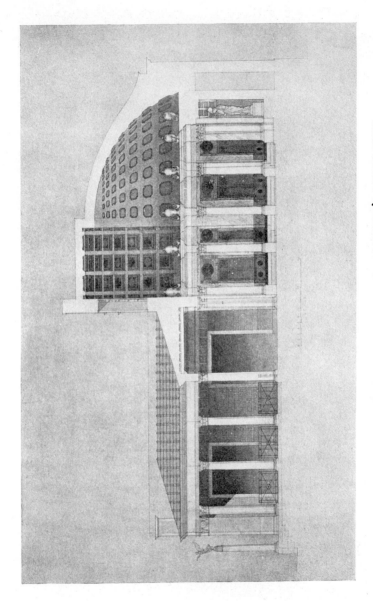

10 SECTION OF THE LIBRARY AT TIMGAD, PFEIFFER'S RESTORATION

SHOWING BOOKCASES AND FORECOURT

II LANDSCAPE FRESCO

VILLA OF LIVIA AT PRIMA PORTA

OPUS INCERTUM
POMPEII

OPUS MIXTUM
NEAR VIA APPIA

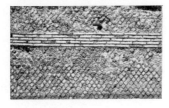

OPUS RETICULATUM
VILLA OF HADRIAN

TUFA
SERVIAN WALL

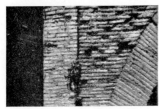

OPUS LATERICIUM
OSTIA

PEPERINO
FORUM OF TRAJAN

CONCRETE POURED INTO MOULD
PALATINE

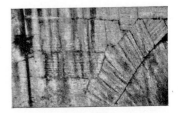

TRAVERTINE
PONS FABRICIUS

12 ROMAN BUILDING MATERIALS AND METHODS OF CONSTRUCTION

INDEX